Macmillan Bool

TEACHING READING SKILLS in a foreign language

Christine Nuttall

with a chapter on testing reading by J. Charles Alderson

MACMILLAN

Macmillan Education
Between Towns Road, Oxford OX4 3PP, UK
A division of Macmillan Publishers Limited
Companies and representatives throughout the world

ISBN 978-1-4050-8005-7

First edition 1982
Reprinted with corrections 2000
This edition 2005

Designed by eMC Design, Bromham, Bedford

Cover photo by © Wolfgang Kaehler/CORBIS

Illustrated by Kathy Baxendale, Roger Courthold and Clyde Pearson

THE AUTHOR and publishers wish to thank the following for permission to reproduce their materials and for providing illustrations: Werner Söderström Osakeyhtiö for the extract from *Ne Tulevat Takaisin* by Y. Kokko (1954); The Language Centre, University of Malaya Press/Thomas Nelson and Sons Ltd for the extracts from *Reading Projects: Science* (1979); and *Skills for Learning: Reading for Academic Study* (1979); Thomas Nelson and Sons Ltd for the extract from *Principles of Human Knowledge* by George Berkeley (1949); Andre Deutsch for the extract from *The Suffrage of Elvira* by V. S. Naipaul (1969); Collins Publishers for the extracts from *Life on Earth* by David Attenborough (Collins/BBC 1979); Oxford University Press for the extracts from *Reading and Thinking in English: Discovering Discourse* and *Reading and Thinking in English: Exploring Functions* © The British Council 1979, *English in Social Studies* by J. P. B. Allen and H. G. Widdowson © OUP 1978 and *English in Education* by E. Laird © OUP 1977; William Heinemann Ltd and Pantheon Books for the extract from *The Night Lords* by Nicolas Freeling (1978); A. D. Peters and Co for the extract from *The Data Bank Society* by M. Warner and M. Stone (George Allen and Unwin, 1978); The Holgate School, Nottingham for the photograph from the *Times Educational Supplement* (24 April 1981); Heinemann Educational Books Ltd for the extract from *Reasons for Reading* by E. Davies and N. Whitney (1980); Cambridge University Press for extracts from *Task Reading* by E. Davies et al. (1990) and *Authentic Reading* by C. Walter (1982).

Printed in Thailand

2014 2013 2012
12 11 10

Contents

Preface to the first edition

NO BOOK of this kind owes its existence to a single writer, and my debt to many others will be immediately obvious. First and foremost is the influence of the students and teachers with whom I have worked. To them, especially those at the Advanced Teacher Training College in Winneba, Ghana, I should like to dedicate the book, as a small return for all they have given to me.

It is impossible to mention here all those who deserve acknowledgement: the books I have read, the universities that have guided me, the colleagues who have shared their experience so generously. Their contribution has been so great that it seems impertinent that my own name should appear on the title page. I hope they will collectively accept this recognition that I am deeply aware of all I owe them and profoundly grateful.

I must, however, specifically mention certain materials produced as a result of the current renewal of interest in foreign language reading. For many insights and ideas for types of reading task, I have drawn freely on *English in Focus* (OUP), *Foundation Reading* (Chulalongkorn University Language Institute), *Reading and Thinking in English* (OUP) and *Skills for Learning* (University of Malaya/Nelson). Without the stimulus of these materials, this book would have been very different and much the poorer.

For help specifically with the text of this book, I should like to thank Alan Moore and John Moore for their time and trouble and their excellent suggestions; the publishers for their unfailing helpfulness; and finally, Gill Sturtridge and Marion Geddes for their support, without which the book would not have been written

Preface to the second edition

READERS familiar with the first edition of this book will find many changes in this one, the most obvious being the way the material is organized. It is now divided into three parts. The first presents the principles (about reading, texts and teaching) which underlie the way the book approaches its subject; the second part looks more closely at some of the theoretical issues and how they affect reading teaching; and the third, greatly strengthened by Charles Alderson's chapter on testing, focuses on the importance of extensive reading, the choice of materials and the way courses and lessons are planned, taught and assessed. The sequence of chapters has been altered to fit in with this new division; people used to the first edition may find this initially annoying, but I hope the result will ultimately prove easier to use.

Another obvious change is the addition of activities; they are intended to contribute to the exposition in the text, so I hope readers will make use of them. There is a key to some of them at the end of the book.

There are also changes in the substance of the book. Since the first edition, an enormous amount of relevant material has appeared, some of which I have managed to read. Most of it has strengthened rather than changed my views of reading, but in some instances has led to differences in emphasis in this edition.

I have, for instance, come to recognize that the schema (however much debated in cognitive psychology) offers a convenient framework for dealing with issues of presupposition, prediction, inference and so on; and that the notions of top-down and bottom-up processing are likewise useful in discussing the way we read. These, and other ideas drawn from discourse analysis and pragmatics, have influenced my thinking, especially since the mid-eighties, when I taught related courses in the University of Edinburgh and learned a great deal from both students and colleagues.

Some changes in this edition result from earlier miscalculations of emphasis; for instance, I had not intended the issues of reading speed and readability measures to figure so prominently in the first edition. The cautions included there were barely noticed; I hope in this edition that the emphases better reflect my thinking. It remains, however, a regret that despite the much enlarged extent of the book, there still seems to be no room for a proper treatment either of literature or of the teaching of literacy in a foreign language.

In spite of the currency of other opinions, I have seen no reason to alter my view that a good reader is one who can interpret the text as the writer intended. This is not to claim that meaning is unproblematic, and certainly not to hold that the reader must accede to the writer's intention. I am all for teaching critical reading (and I agree that I have not given it the prominence it deserves). However, reader response theory in its more extreme forms is not, in my view, a helpful influence in considering the sort of learners for whose teachers this book is intended: principally those whose language proficiency still hinders them from making plain sense of the text. Readers may interpret texts as they choose, but few will share their views if the interpretation is the result of ignorance or incompetence. Ellen Spolsky[1] says, 'understanding doesn't entail accepting'; I agree, and would like to turn the remark on its head, and claim that rejecting entails understanding.

Many reading text books have gone out of print since the first edition, and sadly this includes some excellent materials. I have kept some of them in Appendix B and in the bibliography, because I have found nothing comparable among current titles. Some very good new materials have become available, however, and many are listed and referred to. In response to requests, I have included some sample lesson plans, which I fervently hope will not be treated as 'models'; but this means that we have less room for extracts from published materials. As they are a major source of new ideas for teaching, I hope readers will seek out these materials for themselves.

There is now a section called *Further reading* at the end of each chapter and a much enlarged bibliography to support it. The chart comparing levels of graded readers has been omitted, because it rapidly becomes out of date and does not seem to have been much used. Finally, at last there is an index. I hope it will more than compensate for the much less detailed table of contents.

Many people have helped me with this second edition. I am most grateful for the comments of reviewers and others, and to Neville Grant, Brian Tomlinson and, above all, Norman Whitney for his very thorough comments. I am notably indebted to the colleagues and students who have influenced my thinking over the last twelve years, especially Charles Alderson, Joan Allwright, Liz Hamp-Lyons, Jeremy Henzell-Thomas, David Hill, John Holmes, the late Betty Morrish, Hugh Trappes-Lomax, Elizabeth White and – though they may not remember – Malcolm Coulthard and Michael McCarthy. Charmian Harrison, Joanna Rigg and Edward Ullendorff have patiently allowed me to try out ideas on them and many other friends and relations have been tolerant of my reclusiveness while the book was being re-written. I would like to thank them all.

[1] in 'I come to bury Caesar, not to praise him: teaching resisted reading,' **ELTJ** 43/3, July 1989: 173-9.

The revision could not have been undertaken without the library facilities made available to me by the Moray House College of Education, the University of Edinburgh (especially the Institute for Applied Language Studies and the Edinburgh Project on Extensive Reading) and the University of Lancaster (especially the Institute for English Language Education and the Charlotte Mason College of Education). Some of the library staff have been helpful far beyond the call of duty and I am very grateful to them.

Finally, I must acknowledge the excellent advice, hard work and moral support provided by the publishers, particularly Jill Florent of Heinemann and Louise Elkins and Damien Tunnacliffe of Phoenix Publishing Services; also designer Mike Cryer for his skill and patience. They have encouraged me over many a bad patch and, if the book proves to be useful, much of the credit should go to them. For the deficiencies that remain, of which I am probably more aware than anyone, I accept full responsibility.

CEN
September 1994

A note on gender

As it is tedious to repeat *he or she* and not always possible to use a neutral plural, I have adopted this policy: a writer or a teacher is referred to as *she*; a reader or a student is referred to as *he*. These are arbitrary decisions and carry no hidden messages.

A note to the reader

If you are daunted by the length of this book try reading Part 1 to introduce yourself to the basic principles and then move straight to Part 3 which is concerned with classroom application of these principles. Later you can return to Part 2 for further details if you wish.

A note about the activities

Answers/explanations for some of the activities are provided in the key (p262). This is signalled by a key symbol 🗝 at the head of the activity.

Abbreviations used in the text

EFL/ELT/ESL/ESP	English as a Foreign Language/English Language Teaching/English as a Second Language /English for Specific Purposes
EPER	Edinburgh Project on Extensive Reading (see p131 and Appendix D)
FL	foreign language
L1	first language (mother tongue, native language)
L2	second language
MCQ	multiple choice question
OHP	overhead projector
OHT	overhead projector transparency
SPQ	signpost question
SQ3R	study, question, read, recite, review (see p129)
T/F	true/false question
wpm	words per minute

Part One Introductory

Chapter 1
What is reading?

THIS BOOK is about reading a foreign language, and particularly about reading English as a foreign or second language (EFL/ESL). We shall be dealing mainly with the place of reading in a teaching programme; whether it is possible to teach people to read is a vexed question, but I believe we can at least help them to learn.

The book makes practical suggestions for the classroom, but it also reflects the view that, in the reading class, the most important thing is that both the teacher and the student should understand the reading process. It certainly seems to be true that some of the things that happen in classrooms may interfere with reading rather than promote it. So this first part outlines a view of reading which will be more thoroughly explored in Part Two and will underlie the practical suggestions in Part Three.

Defining reading

Different people use the term *reading* in different ways, which can cause much confusion. So we had better start by making sure that we are thinking about the same thing when we use the term. As a first step, it would be useful to find out what your own ideas are about reading, so please do Activity 1.1 before turning the page.

Activity 1.1 *What is reading?*

Take a piece of paper and write down a brief definition of the term *reading*.

Don't take more than five minutes over this.

Don't turn the page until you have written your definition of reading.

What sort of definition did you give? Did you use words from one of these groups?

a decode, decipher, identify, etc
b articulate, speak, pronounce, etc
c understand, respond, meaning, etc

Looking at the ideas reflected in these three groups will help to clarify the view of reading that is central to this book.

Teachers whose definition includes the ideas reflected in group **a** are focusing on the first thing of all about reading: unless we can recognize the written words, we cannot even begin to read. This is certainly important: we know that good readers are able to identify words very rapidly, and helping learners to do this is a key task for teachers of early reading. But it is debatable whether specific training can improve word recognition at later stages – which are our concern in this book – and no suggestions are offered. It is more likely that speed comes from massive amounts of practice, which we discuss in Chapter 8.

The words in group **b** reflect a common experience: in a great many classrooms, the reading lesson is used as an opportunity to teach pronunciation, practise fluent and expressive speaking, and so on. For early readers, again, reading aloud is important: they have to discover how writing is associated with the spoken words they already use. But this stage does not last long. What is the function of reading aloud after that? We shall return to this question later.

Before we deal with the words in group **c**, it would be helpful to do Activity 1.2.

Activity 1.2 *What have you been reading?*

Take five minutes to list all the different kinds of things you have read in the last few days, in any language. Remember to include things like these:

- telephone directory
- statistics
- label on medicine bottle
- engagement diary
- street map
- letter
- timetable
- instruction leaflet
- notice
- application form

Finally, categorize the items on your list according to the language they were written in. How many were written in English (or whatever foreign language you are interested in)? And how many of these were directly concerned with your teaching?

Reasons for reading

Reading in different ways for different purposes

Think about the things you listed in Activity 1.2. Why did you read each one? What did you want to get from it? Was it only information? What about the letter from home?

The detective novel? You will find that you had a variety of reasons for reading, and if you compared notes with other people, you would find different reasons again.

Now think about the way you read each item. How did the various reasons influence this? Do you read a telephone directory the same way as a poem? How about a street map or a diagram? Reading these is very unlike reading a book.

The way you tackled each text was strongly influenced by your purpose in reading. Quickly scanning a page to find someone's telephone number is very different from perusing a legal document. You probably noticed big differences in the speed you used. Did you also find that in some cases you read silently while in others you read aloud? What were the reasons that led you to articulate what you read? For most of us, reading aloud is uncommon outside the classroom.

Reading for meaning

Whatever your reasons for reading (excluding any reading for language learning), it is not very likely that you were interested in the pronunciation of what you read, and even less likely that you were interested in the grammatical structures used. You read because you wanted to get something from the writing. We will call this the ***message***: it might have been facts, but could just as well have been enjoyment, ideas, feelings (from a family letter, for instance).

Whatever it was, you probably wanted to get the message that the writer intended. You were interested in what the writing meant; hence the sort of words found in group **c** on p2 turn out to be the important ones if we are trying to make a definition that covers most authentic reasons for reading. (By *authentic* I mean reasons that are concerned not with language learning but with the uses of reading in our daily lives outside the classroom.)

The view of reading offered in this book is essentially concerned with meaning, specifically with the transfer of meaning from mind to mind: the transfer of a message from writer to reader. As we shall see, it is not quite as simple as that, but we exclude any interpretation of the word *reading* in which meaning is not central. We shall explore how we get meaning by reading, and how the reader, the writer and the text each contribute to the process.

Why do people read foreign languages?

Perhaps the advantages of knowing a foreign language are clear to your students – better jobs, access to literature or whatever. Reading is usually recognized as a necessary part of these activities. However, if the only foreign language items you have read recently (your list in Activity 1.2) were directly concerned with your teaching, it may be that you, and your students too, do not really need to read that language except for classroom purposes.

If this is the case, we must not be surprised if student motivation is low. This is a major problem for many language teachers: the motivation of *needing* to read is powerful. However, you can also motivate students by making their foreign language reading interesting in itself. The language is alive – its users have the same variety of purposes for reading as anybody has when reading their mother tongue – and this fact can be used by teachers to increase motivation.

I contend that by treating reading as a purposeful activity, we can make teaching more purposeful and classes livelier, even in the difficult circumstances just outlined. If you teach in such circumstances, please suspend your disbelief for the moment; we are going to discuss the way reading works when it is used for real life purposes, and this should give you a better understanding of it. Later (mainly in Part Three) we shall explore ways of using this understanding to help students read better, whether this is a matter of real necessity or just an examination requirement.

Getting a message from a text

We shall assume, therefore, that reading has one overriding purpose: to get meaning from a text. Other ways of looking at reading will not concern us. Our business is with the way a reader gets a message from a text. So we will begin by establishing what we mean by a message.

Reading and the communication process

Figure 1 gives a very simple model of the process of communication.

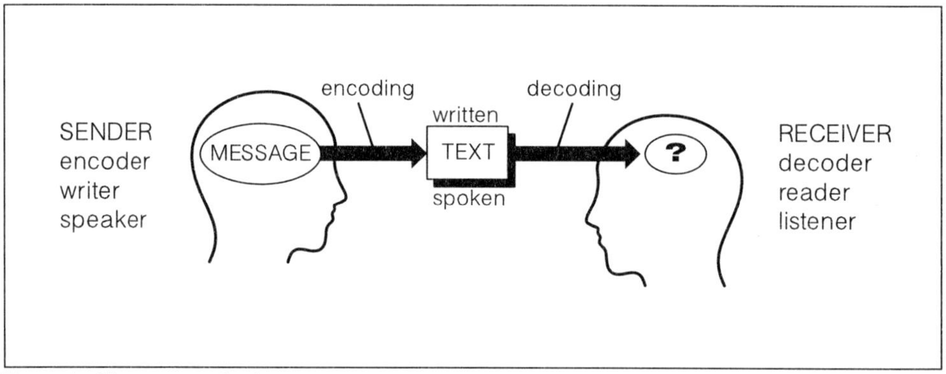

Figure 1 The communication process

On the left is the writer; but since she (we will make her a woman) could equally well speak her message, we will use the more general term *encoder* for her role. The encoder has a message in mind (it may be an idea, a fact, a feeling, etc) which she wants somebody else to share. To make this possible, she must first put it into words: that is, she must encode it. Once encoded, it is available outside her mind as a written or spoken text. The text is accessible to the mind of another person who reads or hears it, and who may then decode the message it contains. After being decoded, the message enters the mind of the decoder and communication is achieved.

Obviously this model is too simple, for things can go wrong at any stage. That is why there is a question mark in the decoder's mind, for we cannot be sure he (we will make him a man) has received the message intended. However, the process is clear enough for us to say that reading means getting out of the text as nearly as possible the message the writer put into it. (How we respond to this meaning – whether, for instance, we accept it, reject it or transform it by using our own imagination – is another matter.) We need to consider further the parts played by the writer, the reader and the text; and we will start with the reader.

Is the reader's role passive?

Figure 2 illustrates one fairly widely held view of reading.

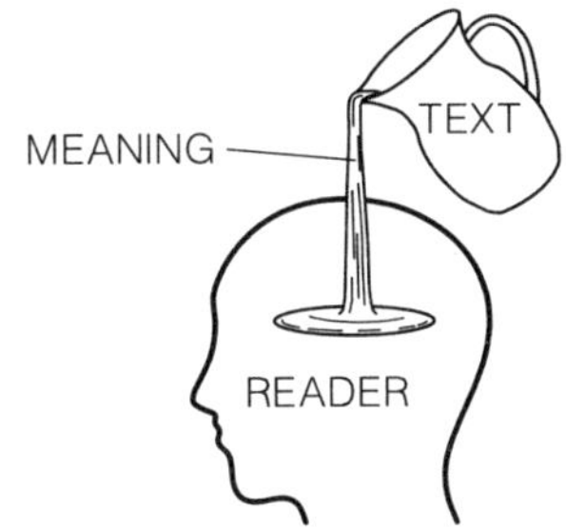

Figure 2 One view of reading

The text is full of meaning like a jug full of water; the reader's mind soaks it up like a sponge. In this view, the reader's role is passive; all the work has been done by the writer and the reader has only to open his mind and let the meaning pour in.

Why do we reject this? One reason is that it seldom happens like this. Not all the meaning in the text actually gets into the reader's mind. The figure should show at least some of the water trickling down the reader's face. The fact that the meaning is in the text is unfortunately no guarantee that the reader will get it out, for we know from experience that a text that seems easy to one person may seem difficult to another.

What makes a text difficult?

To throw some light on this question, we will examine in Activity 1.3 some texts that many people would find difficult. Do this before reading the comments that follow.

Activity 1.3 *Difficult texts*

Here are four texts that you may find difficult to read. They are difficult in different ways; study each in turn and decide in each case what makes the text difficult.

a Istuin eräänä tammikuun loppupäivänä Tiitin kanssa Kokkolasta Jyväskylään kulkevassa linja-autossa. Oli kirpeä pakkasilma, taivas oli kirkas, ja aurinko heitti lumihangille ja tien poikki puiden pitkeä sinisiä varjoja.

From Kokko, Y. 1954 *Ne Tulevat Takaisin* (Werner Söderström OY)

b In the first example, a carbon anion is formed that is stabilized by resonance (electrons delocalized over the carbonyl group and the α carbon atom). In the second case, a carbon anion is formed that is stabilized by the electron withdrawing inductive effect of the three chlorines.

From University of Malaya Language Centre 1979 *Reading Projects: Science* (University of Malaya Press/Nelson) c Ideas imprinted on the senses are real things, or do really exist, this we do not deny, but we deny that they can subsist without the minds which perceive them, or that they are resemblances of any archetypes existing without the mind: since the very being of a sensation or idea consists in being perceived, and an idea can be like nothing but an idea.

From Berkeley, G. 1949 *Principles of Human Knowledge* (Nelson)

d Cavorting in the vicinity of the residential area populated by those of piscatorial avocation, the miniscule crustacean was enmeshed in a reticulated object with interstices between the intersections.

This activity demonstrates some of the ways in which texts can be difficult.

If you found text **a** difficult, it is probably because you are not familiar with Finnish, the code (ie language) in which it is written. So a prerequisite for satisfactory communication is that writer and reader should share the same code. The implications for foreign language teaching do not need pointing out.

Text **b** is difficult for someone who, like me, knows little about science. It would not help if I looked up some of the words in a dictionary, because I should not understand the definitions. The only thing that would help is a chemistry course. The difficulty here depends on the amount of previous knowledge the reader brings to the text.

The vocabulary used in text **c** is not particularly difficult, but many people find that its message eludes them. Even if you have a vague idea what it is about, you probably cannot explain it clearly unless you have read a good deal more by Bishop Berkeley (who wrote it) and thought carefully about his arguments. For the difficulty lies not in the language, and not in the knowledge the reader requires, but in the complexity of the concepts expressed.

On the other hand, vocabulary is the only source of difficulty in text **d**, since you can 'translate' it into extremely simple English and the message is not challenging intellectually. For readers whose vocabulary is limited, this is more like the problem of text **a** than **b** or **c**: the writer's code is only partly the same as the reader's.

Shared assumptions

From these examples of textual difficulty, we can see how important it is that the reader and the writer should have certain things in common if communication is to take place. The minimum requirement is that they share a code: that they write and understand the same language. Text **d** also shows that they should have in common a similar command of the language: for example, if the reader's vocabulary is far smaller than the writer's, the text will be hard to understand. In foreign language reading, this problem is basic and familiar.

A more interesting requirement is that reader and writer should share certain assumptions about the world and the way it works: if the writer expects the reader to have a basic understanding of chemistry, the text will not be readily understood by anyone who lacks this. More insidiously, the writer may expect, or even intend, the reader to share her views (moral, political or whatever). So problems arise when there is a mismatch between the presuppositions of the writer and those of the reader.

Naturally there always is a mismatch of some kind. No two people have identical experiences, so the writer is always likely to leave unsaid something that she takes for granted, but the reader does not.

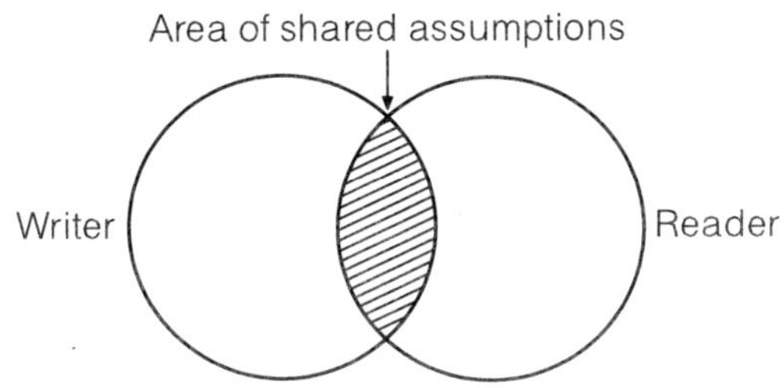

Figure 3 Presupposition and communication

Figure 3 is a simple way of showing how, for any two people, some kinds of experience are shared while others are not. The shaded area where the circles overlap represents what the two people have in common. In this area is all the knowledge – including knowledge of language – that they share. It also includes more intangible things like attitudes, beliefs, values and all the unspoken assumptions shared by people brought up in the same society. In the unshaded areas are the things not shared: the experiences and knowledge that are unique to each individual.

The role of the schema

The kinds of assumption we make about the world depend on what we have experienced and how our minds have organized the knowledge we have got from our experiences. A useful way of thinking about this is provided by schema theory. A ***schema*** (plural ***schemata***) is a mental structure. It is abstract because it does not relate to any particular experience, although it derives from all the particular experiences we have had. It is a structure because it is organized; it includes the relationships between its component parts. There is much debate about the precise nature of schemata, but this need not concern us. For our purposes, it is enough to recognize the schema as a useful concept in understanding how we are able to interpret texts.

The way we interpret depends on the schemata activated by the text; and whether we interpret successfully depends on whether our schemata are sufficiently similar to the writer's. We will illustrate this by an example. How do we make sense of this text?

> The bus careered along and ended up in the hedge. Several passengers were hurt. The driver was questioned by the police.

We make connections between the three sentences because we have a schema about buses; this includes the fact that buses carry passengers, and that a bus has a driver. Hence we take it that the passengers mentioned were in the bus (and not in a car that happened to be there) and that the driver was the bus driver, not from another vehicle. Yet the sentences do not actually tell us these things: we are making assumptions based on experience.

Another component of our bus schema is that buses run on roads; thus we assume that the bus was careering along a road, even though no road is mentioned. This means that our road schema is hovering at the back of our minds in case of need; and the road schema for some readers will include components such as walls, hedges, fences, which mark the limit of a road. These readers will easily visualize the bus going too fast, leaving the road and crashing into the hedge that bordered it. Readers whose experience (and therefore whose road schema) does not include hedges along roads will perhaps have difficulty here.

Finally, we will look at our driver schema; this will for most of us include the idea that the driver is responsible for the safety of the vehicle driven. Hence we are not surprised to hear that the police questioned him (probably our schema sees a bus driver as male!). Nor would we be surprised if the next sentence told us the driver was arrested, because we probably have a schema associating police questioning with guilt. How nice, therefore, to confound our expectations with this final sentence:

> She was later congratulated on her quick thinking and skilful handling of the bus when the brakes failed.

Yes, the driver was a woman. For readers who had not considered this possibility, their bus driver schema will change to accommodate it. This is another way of saying that they have learnt something from their reading. Schemata are built up from experiences; new experiences, including those derived from reading, change existing schemata. So a schema grows and changes throughout our lives, for as long as we retain the capacity to learn.

Thus reading at the same time makes use of existing schemata and modifies them. In a responsive reader – one who is alert and actively processing the ideas in the text – the relevant schemata are activated. That means they are ready to be called on to explain unstated relationships (eg that the brakes are the bus brakes) and also liable to be modified by new ideas.

Presupposition

The idea that past experience gives rise to knowledge organized into schemata makes it easy to see that many connections between facts can be left unstated in texts. We did not need to be told that the driver was the bus driver, that the hedge ran alongside the road; such connections are conventional, automatic, for ***target readers*** (that is, the readers for whom the writer intends the text).

It is equally easy to see that there may be problems for readers who do not share the relevant schema. The writer will not waste time spelling out facts and relationships that she assumes are already in the reader's mind. So the reader may be left with too little information to make sense of the text. Either he does not have the schema at all (eg he has no idea what a hedge is), or his schema is significantly different from the writer's (eg his road schema does not include the idea of hedges).

Because presuppositions are unstated, readers are often unaware of them. This makes them difficult to deal with; perhaps the reader has an uneasy impression that he does not fully understand the text but he cannot locate the cause. Readers who are aware of the potential problem are halfway to solving it; they can scrutinize the text for unstated assumptions and try to identify the mismatch that has produced their difficulty. Activity 1.4 is intended to help you to recognize the kinds of presupposition that can underlie texts so that you can help your students to do the same.

Activity 1.4 *Identifying presuppositions*

Study the following short texts and try to identify, for each one, the presuppositions that underlie the text and the assumptions the writer makes about the reader.

a **Red-wattled Lapwing:** In general shape not unlike the European Lapwing and found in similar types of country. (From a handbook of bird identification)

b The biggest problem in getting animation accepted has been the idea that 'animation' means Walt Disney. (From an article about animation in films)

c Rubber futures closed the morning easier at the lows and mostly from 0.70 to 0.80 pence per kilo down on yesterday. Turnover was 188 lots of 15 tonnes, including 26 kerb trades and two options. (From a newspaper business page)

d Total movement of the belt should be approximately 10 mm midway between the pump and jockey pulleys when checked with normal wrist effort. (From a car user's handbook)

e It was a puppy. A tiny rickety puppy, mangy, starved; a loose ribby bundle on the ground. It made no noise. It tried to lift itself up. It only collapsed again, without complaint, without shame. (From Naipaul, V. S. 1969 *The Suffrage of Elvira* (André Deutsch))

We will consider in turn each text in Activity 1.4. Remember that my own experience and culture make it difficult for me to see the texts through the eyes of a foreign student: you may have found difficulties in the texts that I have not noticed.

In Text **a** the difficulty is straightforward: the text is no use to readers who have no European Lapwing schema, ie who do not know what this bird looks like, nor in what sort of country it is found.

To understand Text **b**, the reader needs a Walt Disney schema that includes the fact that he is the best known producer of animated films; but in order to see that this contributes to a 'problem', the reader must also share – or at least recognize – the implied view that Disney films are in some way undesirable.

Text **c** relies heavily on the reader's knowing the code – having the schemata associated with the technical jargon (*futures*, *easier*, *lows*, *down*, *kerb trades*, *options*) and also a wider schema relating to the way rubber and other commodities are dealt with. For instance, is 188 lots a big turnover or not? Are lots always of 15 tonnes? (Presumably not, since it is specifically mentioned; in that case, what is the significance?) And so on.

The advice in Text **d** does not help me to check my fan belt, though that was its purpose. Why not? This writer too expects me to understand the code, including the abbreviation and the technical terms (*belt*, etc). I am also expected to know what wrist effort is 'normal', and what sort of movement of the belt is involved. (Where do I put a ruler to measure 10 mm?) Regrettably, my car engine schema includes none of these.

Finally, Text **e**. This is more complicated, because it is attitudes that are presupposed. Culturally determined schemata often differ not merely in the facts associated with the central concept (eg whether roads are bordered by hedges or not), but also in the way different societies view these facts. An example is the schema for 'sunshine' in the mind of a native of the northern countries (something to be sought) and in the mind of someone from the tropics (something to be shunned).

The writer of Text **e** expects us to share his attitude to the puppy; readers from some cultural backgrounds have interpreted it as disgust (misled by words like *mangy*), failing to tune in to the sympathy signalled by *tiny*, *starved*, and the half-admiring description of the puppy's stoicism and determination. No doubt the British tendency to be sentimental about animals influences my own view; but the puppy does become the hero of the book, so I suspect the author shares it. In this example the assumptions are so deep that they receive only the slightest linguistic expression.

Total understanding?

The final example in Activity 1.4 indicates the importance of background in understanding. People of similar background tend to have similar schemata; for them, the shaded area in Figure 3 – the common ground – is much bigger than for people coming from different backgrounds.

The greater the size of the shaded area, the easier communication is; readers whose language and background differ from the writer's can expect a more difficult task. On the other hand, if they are similar, the reader is likely to interpret the text without conscious effort. There are still dangers of misinterpretation, however: a careless reader may read into the text meanings that are not there, simply because his sense of having much in common with the writer is so strong. Such a reader assumes that the extent of the common ground is greater than it actually is.

When writers make similar false assumptions about the extent to which readers are likely to share their knowledge, beliefs, etc, readers may be conscious of having to struggle to understand, and sometimes they may fail. In fact, the widely different backgrounds make more obvious a fact that we sometimes forget: that we can never understand one another completely. Except in the most severely scientific writing, this seems inevitable, because all of us – however much we have in common – have different experiences which make us see things differently. But of course one reason for reading is that we want to understand other people's ideas; if we were all identical there would be no point in most communication. Fortunately, for most purposes, the understanding need not be complete; but the fact that we cannot get inside the writer's mind is no excuse for not doing our best to understand what she wants to say.

If we are having a conversation, we can stop the other person and ask for explanations and examples whenever we need them. The writer, however, is seldom available for consultation, so when we have difficulties in reading, the only way we can ask questions is to interrogate the text itself. This is exactly what good readers do; the way they read has indeed been described as 'active interrogation of a text'.

Active involvement of the reader

We can now begin to see why the model of reading shown in Figure 2 was unsatisfactory. The meaning is not lying in the text waiting to be passively absorbed. On the contrary, the reader is actively involved and often has to work to get the meaning out.

A model like Figure 4 is nearer the truth: it shows a view of reading in which the reader can be seen approaching meaning actively. The reader on the left is finding little difficulty in interpreting the text – the meaning is fairly clear to him all along, he has much in common with the writer and few problems with the language. To the reader on the right, however, the same text appears very difficult. To get at the meaning involves an uphill struggle and he is not at all sure of the route. He brings to the task so little of what the writer takes for granted that his way forward is continually blocked by problems of unfamiliar vocabulary, ignorance of facts and so on.

However, the reader on the right is not sitting down in despair. First of all, he is aware that he is having problems. This is important: poor readers often do not even realize that they do not understand. Recognizing that you have problems is the first step to solving them. Secondly, this reader knows roughly where he is going; he has a clear purpose in reading and knows what he expects to get from the text. This means that he will not waste much time going the wrong way or dealing with difficulties that

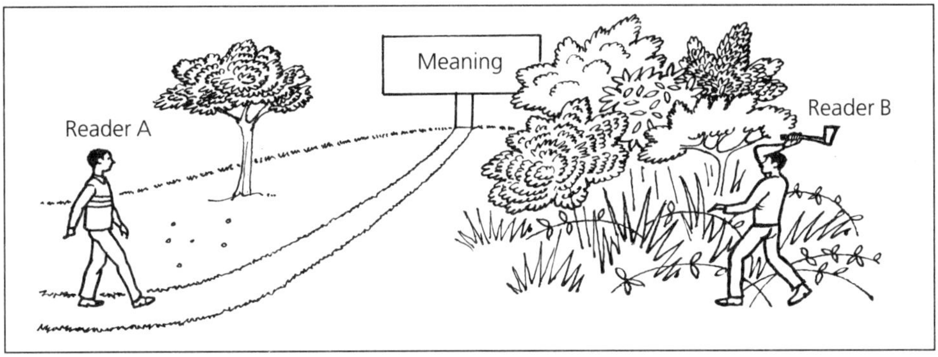

Figure 4 Another view of reading

do not really impede him. Thirdly, he has equipped himself for the journey and is tackling his problems with vigour and with all the tools at his disposal. He has realized that to reach the message involves his own efforts as well as the writer's; it is a co-operative task.

Reading as interaction

When we converse with people, it is obvious that we depend on one another; each participant relies on certain unspoken rules that the others will follow. These rules have been formulated as the so-called ***co-operative principle***. As it applies to reading, this principle might be extended along these lines:

The reader assumes

- **that he and the writer are using the same code (the same language);**
- **that the writer has a message;**
- **that the writer wants the reader to understand the message.**

This applies so strongly that you may even find yourself trying to make sense of writing that turns out to be nonsense. Generally, we assume that people are telling the truth and have something sensible to say, until contrary evidence is too strong to resist.

The writer makes similar assumptions; one of these is that the reader is willing to make some effort to get at the meaning. If either lets the other down, communication fails. If the writer is careless, the message may be impossible to recover. If she makes demands that the reader cannot fulfil, the message may be distorted, even though to another reader it is clear.

If the reader, on his side, is careless or idle, the result is similar: an incomplete interpretation or a distorted one. On both sides, lack of shared assumptions is likely to be the trickiest problem, because it is not always recognized. The reader tries to make sense of the text in terms of his own schemata, and it may be a long time before he is forced to recognize that they differ from those of the writer.

Reading, according to this view, is an *interactive* process – as conversation is – because both reader and writer depend on one another. The interaction is complicated by the fact that the writer is absent at the time of reading; so she gets no feedback and cannot know what parts of her text will cause misunderstanding. She has to guess and shape the text accordingly, but as she never knows who the readers will be, she will never completely succeed.

Making sense of the text

However, the writer has an advantage over the speaker: she has time to help the reader by making the text as straightforward as possible. The reader also has time at his disposal: he can stop and think, go back to check an earlier passage, reread the difficult parts. Unless the text takes for granted a body of knowledge that he simply does not have, a careful reader should be able to reconstruct most of the assumptions on which it is based. To do this he must assess the evidence – choice of words, selection of facts and so on – and draw appropriate inferences, so that he gets the message intended rather than the message he perhaps expected.

All this suggests that reading may be more like the process shown in Figure 5.

Figure 5 The text as a do-it-yourself kit

The text functions like a do-it-yourself construction kit. The message in the writer's mind is the perfect piece of furniture. The process of separating this into its component parts and packing them in a box with instructions for reassembly is a little like the process of putting thoughts into words and organizing them into a coherent text. A reader tackling a text resembles the amateur furniture maker unpacking his do-it-yourself kit and trying to work out how the pieces fit together.

It would not be wise to press this analogy far, but it does demonstrate the force of the metaphor *making sense*. The writer has to make sense (like a designer envisaging a perfect table and then shaping each part to be right for its purpose and to fit with all the others). The text itself has to make sense (like a kit containing all the pieces and clear instructions).

Finally, the reader has to make sense, like the amateur making the table; whether it turns out as planned depends not only on the kit, but on whether he understands the basic principles, follows the instructions properly and does not lose any of the pieces. Sometimes, moreover, he may supply pieces of his own and make a table better suited to his purpose – or even a different piece of furniture altogether; but he needs to be a skilled carpenter to risk doing this. We shall take up this issue of the meaning the reader constructs, and its relationship to the writer's meaning, later on (e.g. pp18, 225-6).

Prediction

A person who knows a bit about carpentry will make the table more quickly than one who does not. If the instructions are not very clear, or the shape of a piece is baffling, experience helps to sort it out. A really experienced carpenter can probably assemble the table without any instructions. And sometimes, experience can mislead – the table produced may not be what the designer intended, and may prove deficient.

Similarly, the reader's sense and experience help him to predict that the writer is likely to say this rather than that. A reader who shares many of the writer's presuppositions will be able to think along with the writer and use his own experience to resolve difficulties. He may even find the text so predictable that he hardly needs to read it at all. And occasionally, his presuppositions may lead him astray, to force an interpretation that is not in the text.

Prediction is important because it activates schemata: that is, it calls into mind any experiences and associated knowledge that we already have about the topic of the text. As we saw (p7), we make use of schemata to interpret the text. If the relevant schemata are activated, ready for use, we can understand the text more easily. Activated schemata are also more readily available to be modified by new ideas from the text: in other words, we shall learn better.

Prediction can begin with the title. You can, for instance, often determine the ***genre*** (the type of text): if you saw the title *The Scope of Ecology*, you would expect a chapter from a textbook or a popular educational article, not a newspaper story or an article from a children's magazine. (All these are examples of different genres.) Your schema of, say, a textbook chapter includes expectations about the way the text will be organized, likely and unlikely topics, and so on. These expectations focus your reading by limiting the range of things to look out for, and so you read more efficiently.

You can also often make a good guess about the topic of the text; which of the following is most likely as the central topic of a text with the above title?

a A description of how certain plants rely on animals for the distribution of their seeds. (*No – too narrow.*)
b A discussion about threats to the environment and the need to preserve it for future generations. (*No suggestion of this angle in the title.*)
c An account of the many different ways in which living things interact with one another and with their environment. (*Probably.*)

Again, having an idea of what the text is likely to be about helps a reader to make sense of it.

Prediction also helps us to make sense of sentences; even the first word sets up expectancies of what the next word will be, and as the sentence develops, our ability to predict what comes next often increases. Try Activity 1.5 (p14) to illustrate the point. Take a piece of card or paper before you start and use it to cover the activity: the point will be lost if you read the text first. When you are ready to begin, move the card down the page until the instructions are revealed. Do the activity now, before reading on.

Comment on Activity 1.5
Activity 1.5 demonstrates how grammatical features and meaning both influence what we expect to come next in a sentence. As the text grew, you became able to use meaning to choose between grammatically suitable options, because you had a growing understanding of what the sentence was about.

Similarly in longer texts both structure and meaning help us to predict; meaning assumes more importance as we become familiar with the topic and the writer's way of treating it. If we can predict that the writer is likely to present opposing arguments, we shall not be confused by them; if we can see that she is describing a farmer's work only to illustrate an economic theory, we shall not be surprised when she next turns to the work of a miner. This kind of longer term prediction is one of the attractions of stories: speculation about what will happen urges us to read to the end.

Activity 1.5 *Prediction within the sentence*

Keep the text below covered. Move the card down the page until you reach the line marked *. The sentence we are studying is presented one word at a time, printed in bold type on the left-hand side of the page. When you have answered the questions, move the card down until you get to the next *, and so on.

1 **An** What sort of word will follow? (Noun? Verb? etc). Which of the following words is most probable?
a large **b** animal **c** eat *

That was fairly easy, wasn't it? Now the text continues:

2 **An animal** What sort of word will follow? Which word is most probable?
a is **b** existence **c** live *

Why did you exclude *existence* and *live*? Now continue; decide what sort of word will follow and then choose the most likely in each case:

3 **An animal is bound** **a** must **b** for **c** to *

4 **An animal is bound to** **a** locate **b** depend **c** activity *

5 **An animal is bound to depend** **a** on **b** whether **c** although *

6 **An animal is bound to depend on** **a** similarly **b** other **c** supply *

7 **An animal is bound to depend on other** **a** plants **b** environment **c** living *

8 **An animal is bound to depend on other living**
a creatures **b** animals **c** plants *

9 **An animal is bound to depend on other living creatures,**
a ultimately **b** for **c** eg *

Did you notice the comma after *creatures*? Do you want to change your choice? *

10 **An animal is bound to depend on other living creatures, ultimately**
a these **b** animals **c** plants *

11 **An animal is bound to depend on other living creatures, ultimately plants,**
a for **b** because **c** to *

12 **An animal is bound to depend on other living creatures, ultimately plants, for** **a** food **b** its **c** influence *

13 **An animal is bound to depend on other living creatures, ultimately plants, for its** **a** activity **b** food **c** concealment *

14 **An animal is bound to depend on other living creatures, ultimately plants, for its food** **a** shelter **b** amount **c** supply *

FULL SENTENCE:

An animal is bound to depend on other living creatures, ultimately plants, for its food supply.

END OF ACTIVITY. RETURN TO TEXT ON p13.

I am not suggesting that readers are conscious of predicting in normal circumstances. Usually they are not; attention is only drawn to it when an expectation is contradicted (as in the example of the bus driver on p8). But it does seem to be the case that as we read we make hypotheses about what the writer intends to say. They are not made consciously; the process is not at all like the ponderous business of doing Activity 1.5.

The hypotheses we make are immediately modified by what the writer actually does say, and replaced by new hypotheses (perhaps involving different schemata) about what will follow. We have all had the experience of believing we understood a text until suddenly brought to a halt by some word or phrase that would not fit into the schema we had in mind; then we had to reread and readjust our thoughts to accommodate a different schema. Such occurrences support the notion of reading as a constant making and remaking of hypotheses – a 'psycholinguistic guessing game'.

If you are interested in finding out how far this idea accords with your own practice, try Activity 1.6. As with Activity 1.5, cover the activity before you begin and move the card down the page until you find the instructions.

Activity 1.6 *Prediction within the paragraph*

Below is a short text. You are going to use it to see how far it is possible to predict what the writer will say next.

Take a piece of card and use it to mask the text. Move the card down the text to the first*. One of the alternatives **a**, **b** or **c** is the next sentence in the text; choose the one you think fits and then move the card down to the next *. Check your prediction (ie the sentence you chose) against what the text actually says and use the new knowledge to improve your next prediction. To increase the accuracy of your predictions, look back to earlier parts of the text and keep in mind the overall development of the story as well as the detail in each sentence.

A Son to be Proud of

Last week, Rahman's wife had an accident. Rahman's youngest child, Yusof, was at home when it happened. He was playing with his new toy car.

a It was a plastic one which had not cost much money.
b Rahman had given it to him the week before, for his third birthday.
c His grandmother lived in a different town. *

Rahman had given it to him the week before, for his third birthday. Suddenly, Yusof heard his mother calling 'Help! Help!'

a He ran to the kitchen.
b He went on playing with his car.
c He started to cry. *

He ran to the kitchen. His mother had burned herself with some hot cooking oil.

a She was very foolish and Rahman was angry with her.
b She was crying with pain and the pan was on fire.
c Yusof ran back to fetch his car. *

END OF ACTIVITY

When you tried Activity 1.6, you were probably interested to find how much you could predict, though naturally we should not expect to be right every time – otherwise there would be no need to read. In 'real life' reading, it is not necessary (nor usually possible) to predict the actual words of the writer; you can be satisfied if you are right about the general topic or direction of the next sentence or paragraph (eg is it going to give an example? a definition?).

If some of your predictions do not agree with the text, this does not mean you are an incompetent reader. The writer always has various options; sometimes the one you predicted would have been equally good. However, it may be that you did not pay enough attention to the clues in each sentence or to accumulating evidence about the overall structure of the story or argument. Try predicting your way through other texts; but choose texts that are likely to have a predictable structure, such as exposition or description.

Conscious use of prediction is a strategy that can be helpful with a text that we find difficult; however prediction itself is not a strategy but a major element in the way we process text. This processing is what we shall now consider.

Top-down and bottom-up processing

These are complementary ways of processing a text. They are both used whenever we read; sometimes one predominates, sometimes the other, but both are needed. And, though normally unconscious processes, both can be adopted as conscious strategies by a reader approaching a difficult text.

The top-down approach

In ***top-down processing***, we draw on our own intelligence and experience – the predictions we can make, based on the schemata we have acquired – to understand the text. As we saw, this kind of processing is used when we interpret assumptions and draw inferences. We make conscious use of it when we try to see the overall purpose of the text, or get a rough idea of the pattern of the writer's argument, in order to make a reasoned guess at the next step (on the grounds that having an idea of what something *might* mean can be a great help in interpreting it).

We might compare this approach to an eagle's eye view of the landscape. From a great height, the eagle can see a wide area spread out below; it understands the nature of the whole terrain, its general pattern and the relationships between various parts of it, far better than an observer on the ground.

Figure 6 Top-down processing

A reader adopts an eagle's eye view of the text when he considers it as a whole and relates it to his own knowledge and experience. This enables him to predict the writer's purpose, the likely trend of the argument and so on, and then use this framework to interpret difficult parts of the text. The top-down approach gives a sense of perspective and makes use of all that the reader brings to the text: prior knowledge, common sense, etc, which have sometimes been undervalued in the reading class.

The bottom-up approach

In ***bottom-up processing***, the reader builds up a meaning from the black marks on the page: recognizing letters and words, working out sentence structure. We can make conscious use of it when an initial reading leaves us confused. Perhaps we cannot believe that the apparent message was really what the writer intended; this can happen if our world knowledge is inadequate, or if the writer's point of view is very different from our own. In that case, we must scrutinize the vocabulary and syntax to make sure we have grasped the plain sense correctly. Thus bottom-up processing can be used as a corrective to 'tunnel vision' (seeing things only from our own limited point of view).

Our image of bottom-up processing might be a scientist with a magnifying glass examining the ecology of a transect – a tiny part of the landscape the eagle surveys.

Figure 7 Bottom-up processing

The scientist develops a detailed understanding of that one little area (which might represent a sentence in the text); but full understanding only comes if this is combined with knowledge of adjacent areas and the wider terrain, so that their effects on one another can be recognized. In other words, bottom-up and top-down approaches are used to complement each other.

The interaction of top-down and bottom-up processing

Although logically we might expect that we ought to understand the plain sense if we are to understand anything else, in practice a reader continually shifts from one focus to another, now adopting a top-down approach to predict the probable meaning, then moving to the bottom-up approach to check whether that is really what the writer says. This has become known as ***interactive reading*** (confusingly: the meaning is quite different from interaction in the sense discussed on p11). Both approaches can be mobilized by conscious choice, and both are important strategies for readers.

Reading and meaning

The reader's purpose and the writer's purpose

Most of us are accustomed to thinking that meaning is somehow located in the text, waiting for us to uncover it; and, for convenience, this is how I shall often write in this book. Yet it is only partly true. As we have seen, the readers themselves contribute to the meaning they derive from text.

We all have different purposes in reading, different opinions, backgrounds and experiences, and thus different schemata. Inevitably we all get something different from a text. The differences may be slight: most of us would not interpret a train timetable or a recipe very differently, though some might do so more accurately than others. But they may be acute; for instance, readers of various political opinions might react very differently to a polemical tract; and you might hate a poem I love.

There is a lot of interest currently in this issue: if different readers understand a text differently, whose meaning is the 'real' meaning? Do we have to ask the writer what she meant? What if she has forgotten? In the end, our only resource is active interrogation of the text. Fortunately, the meaning of many texts is not in dispute; most readers agree what the recipe or the train timetable mean. With more controversial texts, we may have to accept the views of readers with the best specialist knowledge, or the greatest ability to provide evidence for their interpretation. Later in the book, when I write of 'the' meaning of the text, as if there could be no doubt about it, this consensus view of the meaning is what I have in mind. Where there is widespread disagreement, we must accept that various interpretations are possible and even (typically with poetry, for instance) enriching, and we can use the opportunity to explore them all.

Many texts used in class belong to the uncontroversial group, but there is always the possibility that a student will see things differently from the teacher. When that happens, it is only reasonable to pause and find out why. Occasionally students notice things that teachers have overlooked. Some different interpretations arise from ignorance or carelessness, others from the reader's reasons for reading. The teacher's task is to eliminate the former, but not the latter: to help students see what the writer intended (as far as that can be established), but not to expect everyone to agree with it, since good readers do not allow themselves to be manipulated by writers. We might indeed define a good reader as one who always interprets a text as the writer intended – except when he chooses not to.

Writers generally have fairly clear purposes when they write, and have in mind (consciously or not) certain target readers: the writer of a carpentry manual does not try to make it accessible to young children. If we are not among the target readers, we must not complain if the book does not suit us. On the other hand, we are entitled to oppose the assumptions the writer makes, or reject the position she tries to make us adopt. (This is often referred to as 'resisting reading'.) In this book, however, our primary aim is to consider the skills a reader needs to make sense of a text more or less as the writer intended. This is not to deny the importance of personal response, but to assert that to be entitled to disagree with a text, we must first understand it.

Meaning is central

To sum up: the view of reading offered here sees it as essentially concerned with meaning. This view of reading is valid at any level. A concern with meaning, and the reader's responsibility for getting meaning out of text, is appropriate even in the earliest lessons from a primer. Equally, the skills of interpretation needed by every reader are, when fully developed, precisely the skills needed for a sensitive appreciation of literature.

However, this book does not deal specifically with either the earliest reading lessons or the reading of literature. We shall concentrate on ways of developing the reading skills of students at an intermediate level.

Further reading

Williams and Moran 1989 surveys recent thinking on reading, with full bibliography. Williams 1984 is a concise introduction to many topics covered in this chapter. Davies 1995 surveys reading, text analysis and programme planning from a more research-based viewpoint.

Two important collections of papers cover more theoretical issues: Alderson and Urquhart 1984 is strong on the relationship between language proficiency and reading, the nature of comprehension, readability; it remains very relevant. Carrell et al 1988 discusses interactive reading (in the sense defined on p17), schema theory and top-down/bottom-up processing. Brown et al 1994 includes discussion of these and similar issues from a variety of viewpoints.

Widdowson (eg 1979, 1984) deals with reading as interaction in the other sense: that between reader and writer/text. Like Wallace 1992 and Cairney 1990 (both good introductory texts), he sees reading as a social process and stresses the reader's role in the creation of meaning.

Psycholinguistic accounts of reading include Oakhill and Garnham 1988 (very clear) and Rayner and Pollatsek 1989 (standard but more difficult).

Levinson 1983, Brown and Yule 1983 discuss schemata, presupposition, shared assumptions. An easier account is Cook 1989.

On text difficulty, see Brown 1989.

On predictability see Stubbs 1983. On reading as a 'psycholinguistic guessing game' see Goodman 1967; Smith (eg 1983, 1985).

The question of whether meaning is 'in' the text or not originates in reader response theory (see eg Hayhoe and Parker 1990). For various perspectives (including 'resisting reading') see Fairclough 1992; Cairney 1990; Wallace 1992; Williams 1983.

On genre, see Swales 1990; Littlefair 1991; also Wallace 1992; Cairney 1992. Lunzer et al 1984 shows the usefulness of this for teaching.

Beard 1990 gives an overview of initial literacy, with useful bibliography and list of addresses. Harrison and Coles 1992 covers similar ground and Weaver 1988 is a compendious account from a US viewpoint. All deal well with theory, especially as it relates to children learning to read their mother tongue, and cover issues such as record keeping and remedial work. Wallace 1986 relates mainly to second language learners in Britain.

People interested in literature in the language classroom might start with Collie and Slater 1987 or Hill 1986.

Chapter 2
Text and discourse

So far, we have considered mainly the reader's part in the reading process. It is time now to look more closely at the contributions made by the writer and by the text itself.

When she begins her text, the writer has in mind something – a body of facts, an emotion, an argument – which she wants to communicate. She has to shape the raw material to suit the people she hopes will read the text – the target readers – and the effect she wants it to have. To do this requires many decisions about the best way of organizing the text. Some decisions relate to the overall shape of the text – for example, should the story begin with the earliest possible incident? Or should it begin with a later episode and then go back in time to show what led to it? Other decisions relate to the way a paragraph or sentence is structured: is it better to begin with examples and draw a generalization from them, or to start with the generalization and then offer examples to illustrate it? Will the reader understand that this is a contrast, or shall I signal it with *however*? Can I continue to use *he* to refer to the king, or had I better remind readers who I am talking about?

The whole time she is writing, the writer constantly has to choose the best words, the most effective structure, for her purpose; many writers return to the text again and again, changing earlier decisions to make things easier for the reader, or more accurate, or more elegant. These choices – the way the meanings in the text are organized to convey the message – are what we mean by *discourse*.

Discourse analysis and pragmatics

The study of how discourse is produced and organized, ***discourse analysis***, has received a great deal of attention since the first edition of this book was published. A closely associated discipline, ***pragmatics***, studies how we use language in particular contexts to achieve particular purposes. Discourse analysis is more interested in how the sentences in a text are organized, how they relate to one another, while pragmatics is more concerned with how the reader is able to interpret the writer's intention. The borderline between the two disciplines is not important for us: we can make use of the insights of both. The most important for our purposes will be surveyed in this chapter and discussed further in Chapters 6 and 7.

Four kinds of meaning

In order to investigate how sentences combine to produce discourse, we will look at the kinds of meaning a single sentence may have. There are at least four, which sometimes we must distinguish. Let us use a very short text to clarify this.

> You should not expel my son just because he has failed. Examination results can be misleading.

We will examine how this text embodies each kind of meaning: ***conceptual***, ***propositional***, ***contextual*** and ***pragmatic***.

Conceptual meaning: the meaning a word can have on its own

Concepts can be found at any level, from a whole text down to a single morpheme. Every lexical item embodies a concept, sometimes simple (eg *son*), sometimes complex (eg *should).* Whole books are written on complex concepts such as probability or truth. Others can be expressed by the smallest meaning units, such as the concept of plurality, commonly expressed in English by the suffix *-s* (eg *results*).

All other kinds of linguistic meaning rest on conceptual meaning. Making a text normally involves putting concepts together to form propositions, which are then put together into larger units which in turn combine to constitute the whole text.

Propositional meaning: the meaning a sentence can have on its own

This is also known as ***signification*** or ***plain sense***. It is the meaning a clause or sentence can have even if it is not being used in a context. A word on its own, eg *misleading*, carries no propositional meaning; we cannot affirm it, deny it, question it. But as soon as the word is put into a proposition, these operations become possible:

Examination results are misleading.

We can now deny the proposition (*Examination results are not misleading*), doubt it, question it and so on.

This is the meaning that is common to every occurrence of a sentence, irrespective of context, and (with rare exceptions) the only kind of meaning a sentence can have when it is cited without a context (as we have just cited the sentence about examination results). (But, as we shall see, even to understand the plain sense, we usually need to understand the context.)

Contextual meaning: the meaning a sentence can have only when in context

This is also known as ***force***, or ***functional value***. As soon as a sentence is used in a context, it takes on a value derived from the writer's reason for using it, and from the relationship between it and the other sentences in the same text. For instance, in our example text (p20), the proposition *Examination results can be misleading* has the force of an explanation or justification of the claim that expulsion would be wrong.

Explaining, justifying and so on are often called ***rhetorical acts*** (or ***speech acts***). In a text, they are sequenced and organized into patterns conveying the writer's thoughts. We shall return to this rhetorical organization later.

Interpreting contextual meaning is crucial to effective reading; it is no use understanding the plain sense of a sentence if we cannot work out why the writer said it and how it connects with the rest of the text. I shall say more about this later in the chapter, and especially in Chapter 7.

Pragmatic meaning: the meaning a sentence has only as part of the interaction between writer and reader

This last kind of meaning is not always easily distinguished from contextual meaning. It is the meaning that reflects the writer's feelings, attitudes and so on, and her intention in setting these down to be read. It therefore includes the intended effect of the utterance on the reader.

Let us return to the sample text on p20. Suppose a mother utters this to the headteacher who is proposing to expel her son. If the head responded only to the propositional meaning of the second sentence (*Examination results can be misleading*), he might reply *How true!* But the mother clearly intends the remark as a plea or protest, to which the head has not replied at all. In any normal conversation, his reply would be construed as a sarcastic way of refusing to discuss the matter. If the head did not mean to be offensive, he has got the pragmatics badly wrong.

Pragmatic meaning involves interaction and can be seen most clearly in conversation. But it can also be found in texts, in the writer's interaction with the reader. We shall look at some examples later on.

The meanings in the text and the reader's understanding

Every sentence has these four kinds of meaning when it is used in a text, though sometimes one is more important than another. If we wanted to understand a text as fully as possible, we would need to understand every sentence in these four ways. In practice, we seldom need to understand with such complete thoroughness. Sometimes it is possible to get the message when we understand only bits of the text – only some of these kinds of meaning, for example. Using a top-down approach, we can make imaginative leaps from one bit to another, and if we find nothing to contradict our interpretation, we read on. We stop and go back to read more carefully, using a bottom-up approach, only if we discover inconsistencies. This is a sensible and effective way of reading provided it is not necessary to understand the text with absolute accuracy. (It is also a good way to approach the initial reading of a text we have to read with care.)

Signification and value

For the reader, the most significant distinction is between the propositional meaning of a sentence – which we will refer to as its ***signification*** – and its contextual meaning, which we will call its ***value***. Activity 2.1 is intended to clarify the distinction, an understanding of which is necessary to understanding discourse.

Activity 2.1 *Signification and value*

Think of as many situations as you can in which this sentence might be uttered:

Aren't you cold?

Note down the context (ie what is happening, when and where), the interlocutors (who is saying it to whom) and the speaker's purpose (why it is said). How many different purposes can be served by this one sentence?

Note: The word *cold* must have the same meaning in all your situations; exclude examples where its meaning is different (eg 'not loving').

The question *Aren't you cold?* may have the same signification in many situations. But its value may be quite different; the difference is in the distinction between what we say and why we say it. Said by a mother to her son, the question may express concern for his wellbeing. In a different context, it may express surprise at meeting someone unsuitably dressed. If it is said by someone feeling chilly to someone who has just opened a window, it may be a complaint. And so on.

The concept of value is important, because it is quite possible to understand the signification of a sentence, and yet fail to interpret its value correctly. The distinction is often used for comic effect:

'Waiter, waiter, there's a fly in my soup!'
'Hush, madam, not so loud, they'll all be wanting one.'

The customer intended to make a complaint; how has the waiter chosen to misinterpret her utterance?

Our concern, however, is the distinction between signification and value in writing, so a further example, this time more likely to be from a written text, may be helpful. Suppose we take the sentence *Warm air rises.* It is easy to think of contexts in which this sentence can occur with a variety of values:

- as a *reason*, eg in a description of how to position a heater;
- as an *illustration* or *example*, eg in a simple account of scientific laws;
- as an *objection*, eg to refute the suggestion that a heater should be positioned high up;
- as a *conclusion*, eg the culmination of an experiment to prove this fact;
- as an *assumption*, eg a given fact in an experiment to prove something else;
- as an *explanation*, eg of why one part of a room is at a different temperature from another.

Until a sentence is used in a certain context, it does not make sense to ask a question such as: *Is 'Warm air rises' a reason or an example?* We cannot reply except by looking at the work it is doing in its context. Occasionally the form alone gives the sentence a kind of value; for instance, *Warm air rises* is making a general comment about any or all warm air; its form (present tense, lack of specificity) entitles us to classify it as a *generalization*. However, the amount of information we can get from inspecting the form of a sentence is severely limited; its form offers very little guide to its value.

The target reader will understand both the signification and the value of every sentence in the text: not just what the writer says, but why she says it. For instance, if you interpret as a conclusion something that the writer intends as a hypothesis, you are not likely to follow the argument. In cases of doubt, the four kinds of meaning are helpful, as each supports the others. Sometimes, by using top-down processing, you can interpret the value of an utterance without being sure of its signification: if you had listened to the mother talking to the headteacher (example on p20), you would have recognized that she was protesting, even if you did not know the meaning of *misleading*; and you would realize that the word meant an undesirable quality, even though you did not know exactly what. At other times, using bottom-up approaches, you might try to ascertain the plain sense (signification) of a sentence whose apparent value seems implausible. The different approaches are possible because of the different kinds of meaning involved.

Moreover, even the plain sense often cannot be established by looking at the sentence in isolation. We all know that to determine the exact meaning of a word often requires reference to its context. But there are some words that cannot be interpreted at all without reference outside the clause in which they occur:

> However, she naturally did so.

Obviously we cannot assign a meaning to *she* and *did so* by inspecting this sentence alone; but the force of *however* and *naturally* is equally obscure, since we know nothing of the circumstances and assumptions involved. In fact, every word in that sentence shows that it has been taken from a text; it is not meant to stand alone. Every word ties the meaning of this sentence with the meaning of other parts of the text. These ties are the ties of cohesion; they contribute to the signification of the sentence and at the same time relate it to other sentences in the text. It is time to examine the nature of text in more detail.

Text and non-text

We can loosely define a ***text*** as a piece of language, complete in itself and written (or spoken) for a purpose. It could consist of a single sentence or even a single word, such as a sign saying *DANGER!* Brief texts like this have their uses for teaching reading, but we are usually more interested in texts composed of a number of sentences organized to carry a coherently structured message. We need to study the characteristics of text in order to discover what makes writing easy or difficult to follow. We have already noted (p5) several features that may cause difficulty. How can text structure influence the reader's task?

Let us start by examining this sample:

> There was no possibility of a walk that day. Income tax rates for next year have been announced. What is the defining characteristic of the ungulates? Surely you did not tell her how it happened?

This looks like a text, but the lack of relationship between the sentences is obvious. They go together only in the sense of being on the same page, misleadingly laid out like a text. It is difficult to imagine any context for them or to work out what their value, relative to one another, might be. In short, they do not constitute a text at all.

However, a common context is not by itself enough to define a text, as the following example shows:

> A man put some perfume into a drawer.
> James Brown forgot about some perfume.
> A man bought some perfume for Mrs Brown.

We can detect that these sentences might all relate to the same situation, but if so, it is not clearly described. For one thing the sequencing is unclear. A rearrangement may help; at the same time we will set out the sentences to show another feature that makes them unlike a text:

A man	bought	some perfume	for Mrs Brown.
A man	put	some perfume	into a drawer.
James Brown	forgot about	some perfume.	

Now the sentences are ordered in a way that suggests they are telling a story; but no reader would accept this as a normally coherent text. What is lacking? One way to find out is to rewrite the sentences to produce an acceptable text, noting the modifications you have to make to achieve the result you want. Try this before you read on.

Coherence and cohesion

You will have realized that the sentences can be interpreted as a story if we assume that 'James Brown' and 'a man' refer to the same individual in each case, and that the perfume is also the same each time. You have probably changed the sentences to show this, but you may have made other changes too. Perhaps you have produced something along these lines:

One day,	James Brown	bought	some perfume	for his wife.
However,	he	put	the present	into a drawer
and		forgot about	it.	

This now reads like a normal text (apart from the columnar layout). In order to show that the story is ***coherent***, various ***cohesive devices*** are used to make connections and signal relationships. Activity 2.2 is intended to remind you of the devices available.

Activity 2.2 *Cohesive devices*

Compare the text you produced (about James Brown and the perfume), and/or the version offered above, with the incoherent sentences on which it is based (on p24). By noting the changes made, make a list of the cohesive devices used, which show that the sentences tell a coherent story.

Check the key to this activity if you are unsure what cohesion involves. The activity illustrates only a few of the cohesive devices available, but it should be enough for the moment to demonstrate the difference between coherent discourse and a mere collection of sentences.

Coherence without cohesion

Coherence depends on the *value* (not just the signification) of the sentences that compose the discourse, not on the use of cohesive devices. In theory, therefore, it is possible to have a coherent discourse expressed by a text without cohesion; and in fact examples can readily be found:

John I'd love a cup of tea.
Mary It's half past two already.

On the face of it these sentences are totally disjointed; there are certainly no linguistic connections between them. Yet such exchanges are common, and readily understood in the situation in which they are uttered. Moreover, knowledge of the world frequently enables us to work out what that situation must have been; for instance, we can infer that Mary is anxious not to be late, or has some similar reason for discouraging John from having tea.

Examples of coherence without cohesion are quite common in written discourse:

> Suddenly from the dark road ahead came a terrible screaming. Gerard's hand tightened on his dagger.

We find this coherent because we share the writer's assumption that screams are associated with danger; so our danger schema is activated, and this includes the possible need for a man to defend himself, and so on. This is not made explicit in the text, but because the two sentences are in sequence, we assume there is a relationship and seek it. We should be surprised (and we should not know what new schema to activate) if Gerard took out his dagger and carved his name on a tree (though such counter-expectations are used for special effects such as humour).

Try Activity 2.3 to see if you can interpret coherence without the help of cohesive devices.

Activity 2.3 *Interpreting coherence without cohesion*

In each of the following examples, some elements of coherence are unexpressed and must be supplied by the reader in order to make sense of the text. In each case, identify the problem and if possible supply the missing links and rewrite the text so that the message is fully explicit.

a It is possible to walk across the sea bed of 400 million years ago. In the flat desert land of a cattle station in northwestern Australia, close to a place called Gogo by the aborigines, rises a line of strange steep-sided rocky bluffs, 300 metres high.

b When the male meets the female in the mating season, the two intertwine. The process looks rather laborious but at least it is not dangerous. Millipedes are entirely vegetarian.

c An external skeleton is an unexpandable prison. The insect's solution is moulting.

All extracts from Attenborough, D. 1979 *Life on Earth* (Collins/BBC)

Perhaps at first sight you did not notice the absence of cohesion in the examples in Activity 2.3. We assume (because of the co-operative principle, see p11) that sentences written as text are connected; as you are an experienced reader, your mind probably supplied the connections that are not made explicitly.

We know that a sea bed is (flat?) land, so we can identify the desert land and the sea bed in **a**. Example **b** is more complex: we assume the male and female are millipedes, but what has being vegetarian got to do with it? To see the connection, we need to know that, in some species, after mating one mate eats the other; so mating can be dangerous in a non-vegetarian species. In **c**, having grasped that a solution implies a problem, we need to identify the problem: describing something as *unexpandable* implies that expansion would be desirable; while *prison* speaks for itself.

Your rewritten versions, making these connections explicit, are probably longer and clumsier than the originals. A writer can produce a more economical text if the reader can be expected to supply some of the coherence by using top-down processing based on his own knowledge and experience. Cohesive devices explicitly instruct you to do this; without them, your own input is even more necessary.

But an unskilled reader (or one without the right schemata – about millipedes, for instance) may find such texts incoherent. Apparent incoherence, therefore, is a danger signal; perhaps the text has not activated the relevant schema in the reader's mind; perhaps he does not in fact possess such a schema, or it is deficient (eg he does not know that some species eat their mates). Or perhaps he has misinterpreted the value of some of the sentences; in that case, even if the signification has been correctly understood, the message will be incomplete or obscure.

Coherence depends on many things, including obviously the sequence in which sentences are arranged. In addition to other cohesive devices, a writer uses explicit ***discourse markers*** such as *thus, and, however, although*, which help to point out the intended value of the sentence in which they occur. If we read the word *thus* we expect to find a result; if *however* occurs, we look for a contrast to follow, and so on. Markers like this are often not needed if the text is straightforward; the reader can be trusted to identify the value of the sentences without their help. But where the text is complicated or deals with an unfamiliar field, markers are likely to be frequent. How far a writer uses them depends on the readers she has in mind.

Rhetorical structure

So coherence depends partly on how sentences are sequenced, and on the value that each has; each sentence takes its value from the others and in turn helps to give value to them. This complex network of relationships and the way the underlying ideas are organized within a text is its ***rhetorical structure***. It is built with the ***rhetorical acts*** (= values: explaining, describing, defining, etc) performed by the sentences in the text: not the words and grammar, but the way the sentences are used.

To understand more clearly what is meant by rhetorical structure, we need to think about the ***topic*** of the text, the writer's ***purpose*** in writing it and the ***audience*** she had in mind. If we ask what the topic is, we expect answers like 'Cancer research' or

'The threat to privacy created by computers'. If we ask about the writer's purpose, we may be told 'She's telling a story', or 'They are trying to convince us that their views are correct'. If we ask about the intended audience (target readers), we shall learn that the text is aimed at schoolchildren, or intelligent laymen, or academics, and so on.

Once you know the topic, purpose and target readers, you can go on to ask how the writer approaches her objective. Answering that question involves tracing the rhetorical development of the text. You would not expect a children's story to have the same sort of structure as a university physics textbook. Equally, two physics textbooks are quite likely to be similar in structure. Readers need to know that choice is possible, and to be able to recognize how a text is organized, since this can help them (through top-down processing) to reach an interpretation.

Organization within the sentence

At every level, from the clause to the whole book, the writer selects, weights and arranges her ideas and the words that express them. Try Activity 2.4 to help you to see the effect of this at sentence level.

Activity 2.4 *Matching sentence sequences*

Consider these two sentences:

1 The sports followed the arrival of the guests.
2 The arrival of the guests preceded the sports.

Which of the following continuations is likely to follow sentence 1, and which is likely to follow sentence 2? Can you say why?

3 Now, he felt, his weeks of strict diet and patient practice would be rewarded. He would win. He must win!
4 Now at last he would see her. Surely she had come? He searched anxiously among the crowds, but she was nowhere to be found.

You probably matched the sentences as I shall suggest (though different interpretations are possible); could you work out why? In **1**, the topic of the sentence is the sports, so we expect the writer to tell us more about them; hence **3** is a suitable continuation. In **2**, the topic is the arrival of the guests, so we expect to hear more about them, as in **4**.

Generally, a sentence begins by stating its ***topic*** or ***theme*** and then goes on to offer further information about it – called the ***comment***, or ***rheme***. A topic that both writer and reader already have in mind is treated as ***given*** – the least noteworthy part of the sentence. The comment, on the other hand, contains ***new*** information and thus requires most of the reader's attention. If the text is read aloud, these differences are reflected in the intonation. It is suggested that even when we read silently, we assign intonation to the text and sometimes reassign it if our interpretation proves faulty.

The organization of a sentence reflects the writer's view of her topic and the comments to be made on it. This in turn influences the progression of the reader's thoughts. A considerate writer structures every sentence so that its connection with the previous and following sentences is clear. The way she organizes the information can also indicate her attitude:

Mary is kind. Mary is not pretty.

We can join these sentences with *although* in two different ways:

> Although Mary is kind, she is not pretty.
> Although Mary is not pretty, she is kind.

Which of these would be written by a friend of Mary's? Why? And which of the following indicates disapproval?

> He stood up when I asked him to.
> He did not stand up until I asked him to.

Organizing sequences of sentences

Sequences of sentences are generally organized into paragraphs. These are sometimes just a way of breaking up a long text visually; but there is usually some unity of thought and often (not always) this is given focus in a ***topic sentence*** (one that sums up the main idea of the paragraph).

Recognizing the organization of a paragraph means identifying the topic, the main point, the minor or supporting points, and so on. It also involves recognizing that, for example, the first sentence makes an assertion, the second and third support it with examples, the fourth modifies it by a reservation, and so on.

Clearly this builds on other skills, particularly the skill of recognizing functional value. In fact, the two are interdependent: you need to identify the value of each sentence in order to plot the structure of the paragraph. Equally, if you recognize the paragraph structure, this will help you to assign the value of each sentence.

Many paragraphs conform to patterns which can be found in a wide variety of text types. For instance, the paragraph may be organized according to the sequence of events described, or according to a logical progression from general to specific, or from specific to general. Other commonly occurring structures are *problem – solution*; *evidence – hypothesis*; *classification – examples*; *cause – result*; and so on. Some patterns are particularly frequent in certain types of text. For example, *assertion – substantiation* (examples, explication, etc) is a common pattern in textbooks. (The present paragraph is of this pattern.)

Activity 2.5 reminds you of some common patterns of paragraph organization. It is useful to be familiar with them, but be careful: not all paragraphs have a clear pattern, though this need not mean that they are difficult to understand.

Activity 2.5 *Identifying patterns of paragraph organization*

Identify the patterns of organization employed in the following paragraphs (all from texts in Appendix A). In order to do this, first establish the functional value of each sentence in the paragraph.

Text 3 *Survival of the Fittest* paragraph 5: *This is natural ...*
Text 6 *Shin-pyu* paragraph 6: *Traditionally, a shin-pyu ...*
Text 8 *The Mountain People* paragraph 2: *It was that ...*
Text 9 *Good Neighbours* Gloria Hunniford, paragraph 1: *I used to live ...*
Text 10 *Adrian Mole* paragraph 4: *The emergency doctor ...*

Organization above paragraph level

The organization of a text is usually in some sense hierarchical: the largest unit is the whole text; this is composed of sections, each with some kind of internal organization and cohesiveness: the chapters of a book, for example. These in turn are composed of smaller units and so on, down to the level of the clause and even the word.

Different genres (types of text) tend to be organized differently. What principle is used to organize the text as a whole? Is it organized chronologically? Does it begin by outlining a problem; then offer a hypothesis; next, report experiments to test it; and finally sum up the findings and what they imply? And so on. This book, for example, roughly reflects the pattern: *general principles* (Part One); *elaboration* (*explication and exemplification*) (Part Two); *application* (Part Three).

If the writer has done her job well, understanding the organization of the whole text contributes to an understanding of individual parts of it. More importantly, recognizing the organization of the text usually leads to a clearer understanding of its overall message.

Footnote: text, discourse and the reader

However much help the writer provides – by adopting clear patterns of organization, signalling her intentions by discourse markers, and so on – the reader always has to draw on his interpretive skills to reconstruct the writer's presuppositions, draw appropriate inferences and generally make sense of the text. He cannot expect to absorb meaning effortlessly unless he restricts himself to the most undemanding material, and to subjects over which he already has total command. But we have assumed that people wish to read in order to find out things that they do not already know, to discover new ways of looking at things, etc. That always involves some effort.

Further reading

Excellent introductions to discourse analysis are Cook 1989 and McCarthy 1991; see also the suggestions following Chapters 6 and 7. The titles listed below relate only to topics not covered there.

On the distinction between signification and value see Widdowson 1978. Widdowson 1984 includes (pp54–67) a fascinating account of the writer's task in conveying meaning.

On the nature of text see Davies 1995, Brown and Yule 1983. Textual (rhetorical) structure is discussed in McCarthy 1991 and splendidly analysed for classroom use in Lunzer et al 1984; Davies and Green 1984.

Classic discussion of theme/rheme and given/new is Halliday 1985. See also Cook 1989; McCarthy 1991; Brown and Yule 1983. For a grammatical view see Quirk et al 1985 and Sinclair 1990.

Chapter 3
Approaching reading in the foreign language classroom

Reasons for using texts in the foreign language classroom

READING widely is a highly effective means of extending our command of language, so it has an important place in classrooms where language learning is the central purpose. However, students also need to learn how to read for meaning, and it is not always possible to teach for both purposes at the same time or with the same text.

Many foreign language learners have a specific need – dealing with overseas customers, keeping up to date with research in nuclear physics, and so on – which has nothing to do with language. They need to read for meaning. Language is simply the vehicle conveying the ***message*** which is important to them, whereas in language classrooms the message is too often the vehicle conveying the ***language***.

In this book we focus on the use of texts to convey meaning, partly because this is often neglected in the language classroom, partly because treating texts as if they meant something is more effective in motivating students and promoting learning.

Language lessons and reading lessons

Language improvement is a natural by-product of reading, and a highly desirable one, but it is not our focus in this book. We have discussed it only because text-based lessons are often lessons on pronunciation, vocabulary or structure, not reading lessons. You need lessons like this, of course, but you need reading lessons too, if your students want to be able to read in the foreign language.

It is necessary to stress the difference, because reading lessons are so often overlooked, especially for elementary students. Giving a lesson based on a text is not the same thing as giving a reading lesson: most of the skills practised are probably not reading skills at all. In what way is a reading lesson different?

First, the type of text used is likely to be different. In a reading lesson we use texts that have been written to inform, to entertain, and so on: not to teach language. Even if the language has been modified to suit the level of the learners, the purpose of the text is first and foremost to convey a message (in the widest sense of this term, explained in Chapter 1). Second, the teacher's aims, and therefore also the procedures, are very different. In a language development lesson, we focus on the vocabulary or structure, because this is what we want the student to acquire; the meaning of the text is subordinate. In a reading lesson, on the other hand, we want the student to use the language to derive messages from texts. The meaning is central, and any new language item learnt is an incidental benefit.

There can, however, be no fixed recipe for a reading lesson. Different kinds of texts make different demands on the reader, so the procedures used in reading lessons will also have to vary. Moreover, since views and interests vary, different readers respond in different ways to the same text. The reading lesson needs to make allowances for both the variety of texts and the variety of readers.

Aims of a reading programme

But if every text and every reader require different treatment, can we state any general aim for a reading development programme? We might try something along these lines:

> **To enable students to enjoy (or at least feel comfortable with) reading in the foreign language, and to read without help unfamiliar authentic texts, at appropriate speed, silently and with adequate understanding.**

Inevitably this seems too general to be helpful, but if we examine each part of it, we shall discover that it carries some fairly specific implications for teaching.

to enable students: The teacher can only try to promote an ability in the student; she cannot pass on the ability itself. This applies particularly to comprehension, which is a private process. Even the reader himself has no real control over it, although he can certainly improve it by well-directed effort. In a reading lesson, it is what the student does, not what the teacher does, that counts.

to enjoy (or at least feel comfortable with): A great deal of this book is about the hard work of reading, which can rarely be avoided by people who need to read for study or professional purposes. But the best teaching does not neglect the delight and interest that can be derived from reading. That is one reason why a good deal of space is devoted later in the book to the importance of an enjoyable extensive reading programme, and why we also emphasize the need to choose interesting material for classroom use.

to read without help: We can seldom expect help with the reading tasks we undertake in real life outside the classroom; the teacher does not stay at our side. Therefore students have to develop the ability to read on their own. Your responsibility as a teacher is to make your support unnecessary.

unfamiliar texts: Being able to read the texts studied in class is not enough; part of the work of extracting the message was done by the teacher or fellow students. You have to equip students to tackle texts they have never seen before. This implies that it is more useful to read two texts once than one text twice (though frequent rereading may be needed in the process of studying a text). It also implies that if you want to test reading ability (as opposed to memory), you should use a text that is not familiar to the students.

authentic texts: The reading skill is of no practical use unless it enables us to read texts we actually require for some real-life purpose. At least some of the practice should be with ***target texts***, ie the sort of texts the students will want to read after they have completed their course. If the needs of a single class are very varied, the practice material ought to be varied too. However, the stage at which target texts are introduced has to be decided according to the students' command of the language. Where this is seriously below the level demanded by the target texts, problems are predictable.

appropriate speed: A flexible reading style is the sign of a competent reader. Instead of plodding through everything at the same careful speed, or always trying to read as fast as possible, students must learn to use different rates for different materials and different purposes, and must have practice in assessing what type of reading is appropriate in various circumstances. Unless you encourage them to skim and scan and treat some texts with a degree of irreverence, they may never learn to take these risks, which are a necessary step towards becoming a more effective reader.

silently: We have already noted that people seldom need to read aloud except in the classroom. Reading aloud is useful in the early stages, but it commonly persists far longer than is desirable. This usually means that too little time is given to silent reading; yet all readers need this skill, and most would benefit from help in developing it. (For teachers and others who do need to be able to read aloud well, specific training is necessary; but it should not be equated with the teaching of reading nor the teaching of pronunciation: it is a distinct skill and not an easy one.)

with adequate understanding: It may cause surprise that I do not say 'with total understanding'. As in the case of reading speed, however, flexibility is required. We need to understand enough to suit our purpose, and this means that we frequently do not need to read or understand every word. Sometimes complete understanding is necessary, but it is wasteful to read with the same amount of care for every purpose. This implies that various kinds of reading task must be given, not all of which require the precision of careful study reading.

But I must not give the wrong impression: understanding is central to reading and is the focus of this book. If we settle for less than complete understanding in certain reading tasks, the reasons must be clear (to us and to our students). It must result from a conscious decision, not from incapacity to understand.

Implications for the classroom

Accepting the general aim explained above carries implications about what should be done in the classroom. These will be explored in more detail in later chapters, but here we will set the scene by discussing the roles of teachers and students, and outlining some of the issues which influence the thinking in this book.

The role of the teacher

Some people would go so far as to say that reading cannot be taught, only learnt. Certainly the measure of the teacher's success is how far the student learns to do without her help. Does this mean that there is nothing for the teacher to do? On the contrary: there is a great deal.

The teacher's responsibilities include these:

- enjoying and valuing reading ourselves, and showing that we do so by reading a lot at times when the students can see us (Chapter 14);
- helping students to enjoy and value reading, including making sure there is an attractive extensive reading programme (Chapter 8);
- understanding what reading involves, how language conveys meanings and how texts are put together (Chapters 4–7);
- finding out what the students can and cannot do, and working out a programme to develop the skills they lack (Chapters 9, 13);
- choosing suitable texts to work on (Chapter 10);
- choosing or devising effective tasks and activities (Chapters 11, 12);

- preparing the students to undertake the tasks (Chapter 9);
- making sure that everyone works productively and to their full potential by encouraging students, promoting text-focused discussion and providing 'scaffolding' to enable them to interpret the text themselves, rather than having to rely on the teacher (Chapter 9);
- monitoring progress to make sure that everyone in the class improves steadily according to their own capabilities (Chapter 13).

The rest of the book explores these responsibilities, but we will discuss some related issues in this chapter.

The role of the student

The role we have assigned to the teacher implies a reciprocal role for the student.

Taking an active part in learning
First and foremost, we have said that reading is learnt rather than taught, and only the learners can do the learning. So their first responsibility is to be active and take charge of what they do.

Monitoring comprehension
Like teachers, though to a lesser degree, students need to understand how texts work and what we do when we read. And they must be able to monitor their own comprehension – able, for instance, to recognize that they do not understand a text, find out why and adopt a strategy that will improve matters. This ability to think about what is going on in your own mind is often termed ***metacognition*** and is recognized as a key factor in people's capacity to develop as readers. We shall frequently use words like *aware, conscious, alert* to describe a good reader; students can learn to develop these qualities and teachers can help them to do so.

Learning text talk
We have seen that a good reader carries on a dialogue with the text. Students have to learn how to do this. An effective way to promote the skill is to talk about texts in class; teachers can plan activities for this purpose, and model the text talk, but it is the students who have to make the most of the opportunities by joining in.

Taking risks
Joining in means that they have got to take the risk of making mistakes. They won't learn much if they don't do this. The sooner students realize that a mistake is an opportunity to learn, the better. Similarly, they need to be prepared to admit when they do not understand. Of course they will only do this if the classroom atmosphere encourages it: it is up to the teacher to see that it does.

Learning not to cheat oneself
Learning to read is learning to give yourself an enormous advantage in life. It may lead to better jobs; it certainly leads to personal development, interest and enjoyment. Students who don't want to learn to read can easily cheat on many of the activities suggested in this book. But they are only cheating themselves. Nobody else will suffer, but they are wasting their opportunities.

So students have responsibilities which teachers must help them to understand and accept. Teachers also have to examine what they themselves do in the classroom, as we indicated above; it is time to consider classroom procedures for the reading lesson.

The wrong kind of help

No teacher tries to hinder students from learning, but there are some widespread misconceptions about what procedures are helpful. In many reading lessons, the teacher does too much of the work, or at least the kind of work she does is misguided. This may be easier to appreciate if we examine some commonly used activities.

Testing instead of teaching

A lot of the activities that go on in classrooms are better labelled 'testing' than teaching. For instance, the teacher asks questions and the students get some right and some wrong. What has this taught them? Not very much, if the teacher does no more than that; the activity is primarily intended to find out what the students can do. This has its place, but it is not the teacher's main task; she is there first of all to bring about learning, and only later to check that the learning has taken place. But probably she does do more than that: what kind of help does she try to give?

Doing what the reader must do for himself

The reader's most basic task is to associate the printed marks on the page with the spoken language he knows. A teacher who reads the text aloud before starting work on it has already done this for the students.

The reader next has to make sense of the text. So if the teacher begins by explaining or summarizing it, she is defeating the object of the lesson: she is telling the student something a reader ought to find out for himself. If, as the lesson proceeds, the student encounters problems and the teacher at once explains or translates, again this is the wrong kind of help: the student has to understand only the teacher, not the text.

All these activities are valid in some circumstances, but they do not promote the independent skills of silent reading. They lead students to see the reader's role as a passive one, for most of the work has been done for them. The teacher's well-meant help has undermined the purpose for which she is teaching.

Help of this kind also devalues the text itself. When the meaning is obtained largely through the intervention of the teacher (especially if she translates it into the mother tongue), the printed text becomes almost redundant. This may reinforce the problems produced by some of the texts found in foreign language coursebooks, which (being designed to present language rather than convey a message) can be very different from the reading materials we meet outside the classroom.

You may argue that without help of this kind, your students could not possibly understand the assigned texts. To this argument there are several responses. First, you may be wrong. Research shows that we commonly underestimate students. They may be capable of understanding far more than they at present have a chance to attempt. You can only find out by trying.

Reasons why students fail

If you do try, and the students are not successful, again there may be more than one reason for their failure.

Negative expectations
Perhaps you expected them not to succeed; negative expectations are easily detected and are known to influence student performance adversely.

Unsuitable tasks
Perhaps the tasks were at fault: too difficult, off the point or boring. Study them again and discuss them with colleagues. (See Chapters 11, 12.)

The wrong procedures
Did you use the tasks to promote learning (not just to test), by providing 'scaffolding' (see below, p36) to help students to develop their capacity to interpret?

Expecting them to run before they can walk
Were you expecting too much too soon? Students accustomed to a passive role must be gently eased into active participation, and required only gradually to take responsibility for their reading.

The wrong texts
If, in spite of every effort, you still cannot make progress without summarizing, explaining or translating most of the text, then the texts themselves are probably beyond the 'next step' level of the class (see below). You will have to consider changing them.

Of course there are other reasons why students do not learn, over which teachers have no influence. But the factors listed above are within our powers to change, so we clearly have to consider the question: what alternatives do we have?

Procedures that promote learning

We said that a teacher needs to know about reading and discourse to do her job properly, and we took a first look at these topics in the first two chapters. She also needs to know what material to use, and how to use it. These issues will be discussed at length in later chapters. However, there are some fundamental points about classroom procedures that need making now.

Most important is the difference between helping students to learn and testing. It lies first of all in the intention: in testing, we may expect some people to fail, but when we teach, it is in the hope that everyone will succeed. The difference in intention is communicated to students by the teacher's whole attitude, and by the way an activity is done: whether the teacher gives the students support, how she reacts when someone doesn't understand or gives the wrong answer.

The 'next step' level

It is helpful to think of the learner as being at a certain initial level when he enters the course; that is where you have to begin, and of course it is different for each student. If you don't push him to move ahead, he may stay where he is. If you push him too far, he will fail, become discouraged and perhaps stop trying. But beyond his initial level, there is a level which he can reach, not by himself but with your help. We can call it his 'next step' level. This is the level you should be aiming at: one step ahead of his initial level, and when he has reached it, one step ahead of that, and so on.

Scaffolding

So the teacher's task is to push the learner that one step at a time beyond where he is now. To do this, she provides ***scaffolding*** to support him until he can stand on his own feet. I must try to make clear how this differs from the kinds of help I have called 'misguided'. Think of a baby learning to walk. If babies are carried, they reach their destination, but without in any way developing. They will not succeed any better next time they try. So parents do not carry them, but urge them on, offer a hand to steady them, cuddle them if they fall, get them to try again. Gradually they become able to stand on their own feet and walk alone.

Scaffolding is a similar process. It is focused on enabling students to develop, move to the 'next step' level; never doing for them anything they are capable of doing for themselves with a little support. Some teachers, like parents, provide scaffolding intuitively, learning from experience what each learner is capable of and how to give the last little push each needs. Other teachers have to learn how to do it. There are hints throughout this book; some of the steps you can take – in roughly the sequence in which you would use them in class – are the following:

- ***encouraging:*** urging students to have a try, praising them for what they get right, not blaming them for what they get wrong but using it to help them improve;
- ***prompting:*** helping students complete the original task by giving cues, asking easier questions, setting supplementary tasks;
- ***probing:*** finding out why a student has given a particular answer, so that if need be you can help him to see where he went wrong;
- ***modelling:*** demonstrating appropriate ways of doing things so that the students will understand what is wanted;
- ***clarifying:*** giving examples, explaining and so on;

and other similar behaviours, including giving ***explicit instruction*** when that seems necessary.

This implies that teachers have to provide for the needs of individual learners; but in a class, each will only receive a fraction of our time. So in addition to the above, teachers have to use each individual's steps forward as opportunities for everyone else to learn as well. Hence, easier questions are directed to weaker learners, since everyone needs to feel some success; even the brightest student is made to show why he produced a satisfactory answer (and he only gets a fair share of the questions); and everyone learns to see why somebody has misunderstood, and what can be done to help. Learning as a class has to be seen as a co-operative effort, and provision made in other ways for the brightest and the weakest.

Oral classroom interaction

Most of this is best done through oral interaction in the classroom – first of all between teacher and class, because to begin with the modelling (including modelling scaffolding itself) must largely be done by the teacher. But as soon as some students begin to see how it is done, they can begin to provide scaffolding for one another. It is desirable to organize the class to work in groups or pairs so that they can interact without your intervention. (Groupwork is discussed in Chapter 9.)

Text talk

One of the main things students have to learn is how to interrogate texts: how to continually stop and ask yourself questions like 'Now, what does the writer mean by saying that?' or 'I don't understand this word: does it matter?' or 'When she refers to "the previous meeting", what meeting is she talking about?' In the early days, you may like to talk through some texts in this way with the class, thinking aloud about the questions the text raises. (There are examples of this later in the book.) Many students will have had no experience of reading as an active process, so it is helpful for them to see what interrogating a text looks like.

In addition, you will want to devise plenty of activities that focus attention on the text, especially on bits of the text that are important and possibly problematic. (I urge you not to focus on problems that don't matter, but teach students to ignore them.) We shall be giving a lot of attention (especially in Part Two) to the kinds of things that can give rise to misunderstanding in texts – the kinds of things a reader should treat as warning signals. I hope this will help you to recognize potential problems, so that you in turn can alert students to them, until they are able to do it for themselves.

Classroom atmosphere

One habit you may have to break is asking 'Do you understand?' and believing people when they reply 'Yes'. Try to think of other ways to check understanding, such as asking a question which they cannot answer unless they do understand. Or at least ask for an explanation.

However, the students will soon learn to admit that they don't understand, when they see that you don't consider this anything to be ashamed of (in fact, to admit it is positively admirable), especially if you succeed in creating a supportive, non-judgemental and constructive atmosphere. This is done by expecting people to have a go, not criticizing them if they do not fully succeed, and accepting frequent not-fully-successful attempts as the normal price to be paid for learning.

Your attitude to students who are unsuccessful needs to reflect a spirit of common endeavour, not assessment. Matter-of-fact and gentle recognition of error achieves more than criticism or condemnation, and the sooner the students follow your example in their attitude to one another, the sooner real learning will begin. We all learn from one another's attempts, and we learn more from those which are imperfect, because that is where you can use scaffolding to push the students towards their 'next step' level.

Learner training

Much of what I have suggested you do in the classroom can be summed up as learner training: a conscious attempt on your part to equip the students to make a conscious attempt on their part to find out what helps them to read better, so that they can adopt successful strategies for tackling texts. Obviously this should start as soon as possible. It takes time (patience and tenacity are useful qualities for a teacher), but it works, provided you adopt the kinds of classroom procedure described above and elsewhere in the book, and provided you make sure that the students always understand the point of what they are doing. Many students have never taken charge of their own learning, nor experienced critical thinking before. They find it difficult at first, but liberating and powerful once they have learnt how to do it; and you may be rewarded by seeing them develop remarkably.

Equipping students for the future

Conscious development of reading skills is important because we are trying to equip students for the future. It is impossible to familiarize them with every text they will ever want to read; but what we can do is give them techniques for approaching texts of various kinds, to be used for various purposes. That is the essence of teaching reading.

Teaching students just how to read Text A is not teaching them how to read. However, the generalized skills of reading can only be acquired through practising the specific skills required for reading Text A, Text B and so on. One of our responsibilities is to make sure that the bridge is built between the specific and the general. And one way of helping the student to generalize his skills is to make sure that he reads a lot and has a lot of practice in using the skills with varied materials.

Intensive and extensive reading

Most of the reading skills are trained by studying shortish texts in detail. But others require the use of longer texts, including complete books. These two approaches are described traditionally as ***intensive*** and ***extensive*** reading. Of course there are not just two contrasting ways of reading but an infinite variety of interrelated and overlapping strategies. Intensive and extensive reading are complementary and both are necessary, as well as other approaches which fit into neither category.

Intensive reading

The labels indicate a difference in classroom procedures as well as a difference in purpose. Intensive reading involves approaching the text under the guidance of a teacher (the right kind of guidance, as defined earlier) or a task which forces the student to focus on the text. The aim is to arrive at an understanding, not only of what the text means, but of how the meaning is produced. The 'how' is as important as the 'what', for the intensive lesson is intended primarily to train strategies which the student can go on to use with other texts.

Skills-based and text-based teaching

Within intensive reading, a further distinction can be made between skills-based and text-based teaching. In a ***skills-based*** lesson, the intention is to focus on a particular skill, eg inference from context. In order to develop this, a number of texts may be used, each offering opportunities to practise the skill. Other aspects of the texts will not be dealt with unless they contribute to the specific objective of the lesson. A ***text-based*** lesson, on the other hand, is what we usually have in mind when referring to an intensive reading lesson: the text itself is the lesson focus, and students try to understand it as fully as necessary, using all the skills they have acquired. We need both approaches, and others. Skills-based and text-based teaching are complementary, as intensive and extensive reading are.

Extensive reading and dealing with longer texts

It is often assumed that in order to understand the whole (eg a book), we must first understand the parts (sentences, paragraphs, chapters) of which it is made up. However, we can in fact often understand a text adequately without grasping every part of it; students have to be encouraged to develop this facility. This suggests we ought to pay attention to extensive as well as intensive reading.

Moreover, longer texts are liable to get forgotten in the classroom, since it is easier to handle short texts which can be studied in a lesson or two. But the whole is not just the sum of its parts, and there are reading strategies which can be trained only by practice on longer texts. Scanning and skimming, the use of a contents list, an index and similar apparatus, are obvious ones. More complex and arguably more important are the ability to discern relationships between the various parts of a longer text, the contribution made by each to the plot or argument, the accumulating evidence of a writer's point of view, and so on.

These are matters which seldom get much attention except in the literature class, but they apply to reading any kind of book. They cannot be ignored if students are to become competent readers.

But class time is always in short supply and the amount of reading needed to achieve fluency and efficiency is very great – much greater than most students will undertake if left to themselves. So we need to promote reading out of class. Some suggestions about how such a programme might be organized are made in Chapter 8.

Further reading

On the use of reading to promote language development, see Chapter 8 *Further Reading*. Johns and Davies 1983 makes the distinction between texts as vehicles for information and as linguistic objects.

On the teacher's role, see Richards 1990 Chapter 5. On the principles of teaching reading, see Smith 1983 Chapter 2; Williams 1986. Wood 1988 explains the concepts of scaffolding and the 'zone of proximal development' (cf my 'next step' level, Krashen's 'i + 1' (Krashen 1985, 1989), Prabhu's 'reasonable challenge' (Prabhu 1987). Cairney 1990 and Mallett 1992 also discuss these, and the related importance of 'text talk'. These concepts derive from Vygotsky 1978.

Practical applications include the 'apprenticeship' approach (Harrison and Coles 1992; Waterland 1988) and 'text talk' approaches, eg Lunzer et al 1984, which includes illuminating transcripts of reading lessons.

On learner training see Ellis and Sinclair 1989. Transcripts and think-aloud protocols such as Aslanian 1985, Block 1986, 1992 show the need to develop the metacognitive skills. On metacognition see also Davies 1995; Wray 1994; Carrell et al 1988; Casanave 1988; Spires 1990; Henshaw 1991.

On the treatment of longer texts see Collie and Slater 1987.

Part Two Reading skills and strategies

Introduction

In Part Two we examine in more detail the various skills and strategies a reader needs, and suggest ways of developing them.

Reading skills?

A great deal of research effort has tried to identify a catalogue of reading skills and establish their relationships with one another, but the issues remain controversial and this book does not address them. In any case, it is generally agreed that, if individual skills exist, they work together and are inextricably linked. Can instruction aimed at developing individual reading skills be justified?

Most people accept that we can at least identify certain ***strategies*** which readers can make conscious use of when reading difficult texts. Probably the best way to acquire these is simply to read and read. However, there is evidence that strategy training (or skills teaching – the terms are often used interchangeably) helps. (See eg Kern 1989, Pressley et al 1989, Moran and Williams 1993.) What we can safely claim is that certain kinds of practice are intuitively plausible and seem to help students to read more effectively.

Strategies of practice

Whether it is one skill or many, reading is improved through practice; so strategies of practice occupy much of our attention in this book. We also look at some of the underlying theory because teachers (and to some extent students) need to understand it in order to make proper use of strategies and see the point of practising them.

The strategies to be covered are diverse. To read efficiently involves both the partly physical strategies of reading flexibly and the study strategies of making the most of all the information the text offers – titles, diagrams, index and so on (Chapter 4). The most challenging part of this book, however, deals with the strategies needed for tackling texts that are difficult in one way or another.

Problems in understanding texts

We need to know what students are likely to find difficult, so that we can help them tackle texts independently. Chapters 5, 6 and 7 deal with the sort of difficulties that occur and with the kinds of tasks that may be useful. For practical reasons, the examples are limited to English, though similar principles apply in any language.

As we have seen, it is possible to have a pretty good idea of a writer's message without understanding the plain sense of every sentence, but it is not possible to be sure of it, nor to respond fully. We discuss difficulties of establishing the plain sense in Chapter

5, dealing with vocabulary, and Chapter 6, dealing with syntax, including cohesion. Even when the plain sense of every sentence is understood, the reader may still be unable to make sense of the text as a whole. Even L1 readers have this problem, which concerns the interpretation of value (not so much what the writer says as why she says it) and the relationships between different parts of a text, or between reader, writer and text. We deal with these in Chapter 7. Students naturally often have difficulties with the conceptual content of texts, particularly if the topic is unfamiliar or if writer and reader are from different cultures, but these are mostly outside the scope of this book. Aspects of the cultural background may well need explaining, and many teachers (especially those teaching languages for specific purposes – ESP and so on) find themselves willy-nilly teaching concepts as well. However, concept formation is arguably not the job of the language teacher and we shall give it very little attention.

Teaching text attack skills

Students need a range of strategies to deal with texts. As we want them to confront problems, instead of running away from them, we refer to these as ***attack skills***, borrowing a term from mother tongue teaching.

The first step is to identify the sources of potential trouble. Most students are well aware when they have problems with vocabulary (though not always, as we shall see), so they usually appreciate the need for **word attack skills**. Other sources of difficulty tend to be less familiar; training in **text attack skills** therefore involves making students aware of things they normally do not notice at all. This awareness is crucial; readers who understand what can go wrong can take steps to sort out their difficulty.

The problem of credibility

It is difficult to convince people that problems can arise from bits of the text they are hardly aware of. Some of the strategies required (eg working out what reference words like *it* and *this* refer to) may be dismissed unless the practice material offers genuine difficulties. It is important not to work on a skill unless you can demonstrate that problems occur.

The time to raise an issue is when the students have been brought face to face with a problem, and can therefore see the point of practising a strategy to deal with it. If you can manage without training on some of the duller aspects of text attack (dealing with complex syntax, for instance), so much the better – but not at the expense of leaving students helpless. My view is that a certain amount of specific strategy training is helpful, but that most of it should be ongoing, as problems are encountered in texts.

If you are not clear about the purpose of an exercise, or not convinced of its value, it is better not to use it, because it is easy to make training seem pointless.

An integrated process

It is convenient to assume that readers use different skills to make sense of different features of a text (cohesion, rhetorical organization and so on). This enables us to describe each aspect separately and to focus and simplify our approach.

The various text features are not however fully separable, but tightly bound up with one another, and it is important not to overlook the integrative skills required to make sense of the text as a whole. The reader must be able to respond to its overall message, evaluate the writer's success, and if appropriate appreciate the text as literature. These skills are briefly dealt with in Chapter 7 and discussed further in Part Three, although – because they are fairly familiar to teachers – they get less attention in this book than they deserve.

Sources of exercises

Throughout this book, I have taken advantage of the inventiveness of textbook compilers, both by using their tasks as examples and by analysing their tasks to offer you recipes for devising your own. Many more ideas can be found in the reading skills textbooks listed in the bibliography. The simplest exercises are often the most effective: start with these if you are hesitant. After further experience, you will be able to develop similar material of your own.

Displaying the text

For teaching text attack skills, it is often useful for the class to see not only the text but your handling of it; you may wish to underline, circle or draw lines from one word to another, use colour to indicate differences in function or structure, block off certain sections, annotate in the margins, and so on. You cannot do this if you only have individual copies; everyone must be able to see the copy you are marking, displayed as a ***central visual*** (ie one that the whole class can see).

The most effective solution is to use an ***overhead projector (OHP)***. You can write the text with a permanent (ie indelible) pen and annotate it with non-permanent ones in various colours, or better still use a separate transparent sheet as an overlay. This means the text can be prepared beforehand, stored easily and used again and again for different purposes. You can even use a photocopier to transfer texts, including illustrations, onto special kinds of transparency. Many photocopiers can also enlarge the text first, which is often necessary to make it visible from the back of the class. (See Wright & Haleem 1991 for further guidance.)

If you cannot get an OHP, you can of course write the text on the blackboard; the students can write their own copies at the same time. However, this takes up valuable class time. A portable blackboard or whiteboard (for use with special felt pens) is a better solution; or you can experiment with a roll-up board made from white plastic material (using non-permanent whiteboard pens) or black (using chalk).

Another method is to write the text with a thick felt pen on a large sheet of paper, to be stored flat or rolled. Get a sheet of strong transparent plastic and display the text by suspending it from bulldog clips with the plastic covering it. You can then annotate the text by writing on the plastic using non-permanent OHP pens. Thus the text is not marked and the plastic can be cleaned and used again with other texts.

Computer programs

The advent of personal computers in schools means that some teachers have a new and powerful aid at their disposal. Anyone who still thinks that a computer has to teach in a strictly mechanical manner should look at the many imaginative programs now available. The computer's ability to display text and then delete words, jumble texts, move bits of text about on the screen, etc, and above all the way it can offer the student choices about what action to take, make it ideal for practising some of the text attack strategies. Authoring programs are available which enable teachers to use their own choice of texts – all that is needed is simple keyboard skills to type them.

We shall not say much about computers in the chapters that follow, mainly because most teachers still do not have access to them, and because the programs available are changing all the time. But they are to be welcomed if you have the opportunity to use them. A good introduction to computers in language learning (CALL) is Jones and Fortescue 1987; those with some experience of computers will find many ideas in Hardisty and Windeatt 1989. UK publishers currently offering CALL programs include Cambridge University Press and Longman (addresses in Appendix D).

Instructional language: a warning

Tasks for training the text attack skills often sound quite complicated if you try to describe them, as you will find particularly in Chapters 6 and 7. Some of them are actually complicated; others are not, but are difficult to describe in simple language.

It is not helpful if the task offers more problems than the text. The students must at least be clear about what they have to do. The best solution is usually to demonstrate first; working through a similar task with the class should ensure that everyone understands it. If you yourself are unsure about the way a task works, try it out with colleagues before attempting it with students.

Occasionally, with a monolingual class, instructions in the L1 are the most efficient solution, provided you do not allow the L1 to take over. If neither demonstration nor instructions in the L1 serve the purpose, have another look at the task to see whether it is worth the effort. It is better to reject a task than spend most of your class time explaining how to do it.

Chapter 4
Efficient reading

EFFICIENCY means using the least effort to obtain satisfactory results; we want students to use their time and energy to best effect. Most of Part Two is about helping students to understand texts. But understanding is not the only criterion for efficient reading; another is the time taken to read. These two criteria often conflict: who has read more efficiently – someone who has understood more, or someone who has read faster? To answer the question, you need to know the reader's purpose.

Knowing what you want from reading

If you are in a hurry to find out how to use a fire extinguisher, speed is at a premium; but there is no advantage in reading the instructions quickly if you still can't operate the extinguisher at the end. So the demands of speed and understanding have to be balanced according to the purpose. The first requirement for efficient reading is to know what you want: then you can judge your success according to how well and how fast you achieve it.

The criterion of efficiency is of course not always appropriate. If you are reading for pleasure, there is not much point in defining your purpose (although it is difficult to enjoy a book if it takes ages to finish it). However, if you are reading to learn, or for many practical purposes (finding a train time, checking how to operate a tool and so on), the more closely you can specify what you want from your reading, the easier you make your job. This chapter applies chiefly to this kind of purposeful reading.

So the first thing for the student to do is to decide exactly what he wants to get out of his reading. It saves time in the end. Teachers can help by setting clear purposes for reading in class (see p154), and by helping people who are reading for assignments or professional purposes to define what they need to find out and then decide what and how to read. Try to set tasks that reflect the real needs of the class, or think of reasons why they may need to read in the not-too-distant future and base practice on these.

Choosing the right material

Once a reader has defined his objective, he must next decide what sources to consult. Here efficiency pays big dividends; it is so easy to waste time on books or articles that do not help. If students are able to use skimming and scanning (described below), they can shorten the time taken to choose material and also make their selection more reliable.

Using external resources

Advice and a bibliography from a knowledgeable person (eg the tutor who set your zoology assignment, the friend with long experience of your new hobby) are the first resources for choosing material. After that, you must rely on bibliographies from other sources, and on library catalogues and so on. Being able to use these is an essential study skill but does not fall within the scope of this book. Then when you find a possible title, you need to check that the material really is suitable and decide which parts of it to read. Let us consider what you can find out about a text without actually reading it.

Using resources within the text

Linear and non-linear text

When we use the word *text*, we normally have in mind the expression of ideas in sequences of sentences and paragraphs as discussed in Chapter 2. This is often called ***linear text***. Other parts of a text are ***non-linear***, in the sense that they do not enter into the organization of sentences, paragraphs and so on; yet they contribute to our understanding of linear text. Non-linear elements include:

- *reference apparatus*: all the parts of a text that help the reader to locate information or predict what the text contains (titles, index, blurb and so on);
- *figures*: we include under this heading all information such as diagrams, tables, maps, graphs and illustrations (including any words they contain);
- *graphic conventions*: layout, punctuation, type face, use of symbols and so on.

The first two categories are valuable for people trying to choose suitable material. (We deal with the third in a later section.) A skilled reader takes much of this non-linear information for granted, but even L1 readers benefit from learning how to use it. Exploiting non-linear information can make reading easier and more efficient, and is fairly straightforward, so it is worth spending time on.

Titles and headings

Titles are not always reliable indicators of content, but they are a reasonable starting point in choosing relevant texts; and titles of chapters or sections can be a great help in finding the relevant parts of a text. You can tackle them from several angles:

1 Get students to predict from the title the likely content of the book, article, etc. Include a few misleading titles to encourage wariness.
2 Get students to choose, from titles alone, the book/article they would consult first on a given topic. Include some highly relevant sources with uninformative titles to remind students to look also at other sources of information dealt with below.
3 Present students with an article or chapter that has headings at various levels (perhaps signalled by the use of different sizes or styles of type, or by a number system, eg main sections: 1, 2, 3, etc; sub-sections: 1.1, 1.2, 1.3, etc; sub-sub-sections: 1.2.1, 1.2.2, etc. Ask them to make a diagram showing the hierarchical organization of the chapter: this brings out the way the writer has structured the information presented. Figure 8 on the next page shows part of the structure of the present chapter; you might like to complete it.

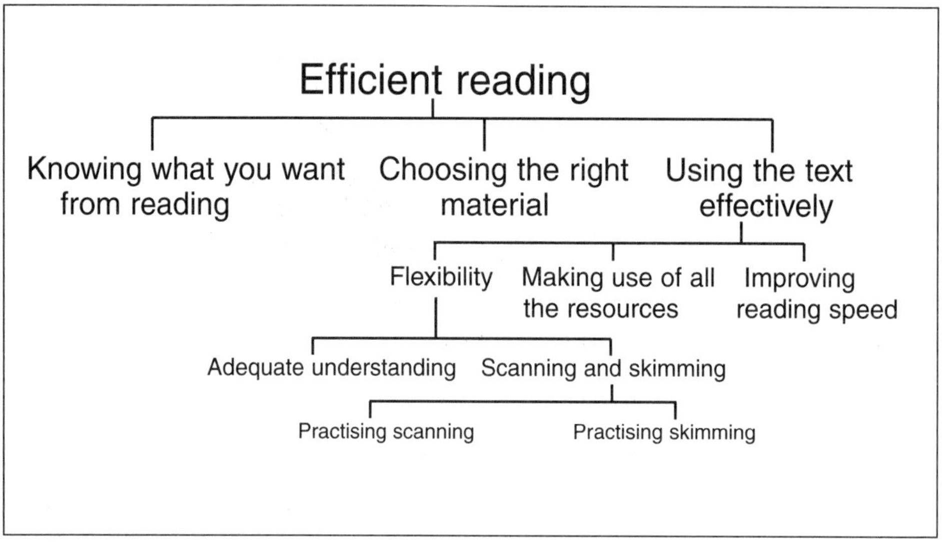

Figure 8 Diagram showing part of the organization of Chapter 4

The blurb

There is usually a blurb on the back cover of a book, or on the inside fold of the dust jacket.

Blurbs may include press comment (selective, of course), but normally consist mainly of the writer's own estimation of the book's purpose, principal features and strong points. Despite the probability of bias, blurbs are useful for selecting the right books; yet students often seem unaware of them. Use some of these activities to draw attention to them.

1 Supply a list of titles, or extracts from texts, and a selection of blurbs.
Task: Match the blurbs with the right titles/extracts.

2 Supply a selection of blurbs.
Task: Select the most likely books for a particular purpose; eg *Which book would be of most use if you wanted to find out how to repair your car yourself?*

3 Supply a selection of blurbs + titles, dealing with similar fields at different levels.
Task: Match prospective readers with books, eg *Which book would be suitable for a ten-year-old schoolboy? A university student? A housewife?*

4 Supply some blurbs.
Task: Study them in detail, extracting from them
a matters of fact, eg *There is a 200-item bibliography. Each chapter includes several exercises. The writer is Professor of History at Oxford University.*
b matters of intention (which may or may not be achieved), eg *Written for those with no previous experience in the field. Aims to give a readable version of recent research in this area.*
c matters of opinion, eg *There is a comprehensive bibliography of current research. Each chapter contains a wealth of stimulating exercises.*

Biographical information about the writer

Like the blurb, this often appears on book jackets or, in paperbacks, on the page preceding the title page. In journals, it may precede or follow the article, or be found in a separate section of notes on contributors. It can be valuable in indicating the writer's background and position, and thus her qualifications for writing the work. Draw attention to it by using a few activities similar to those suggested for blurbs.

The summary, running titles, table of contents, list of figures

All these are aids to estimating the suitability of a text and locating content within it. In scholarly journals, articles are often preceded by a summary. In books, summaries occasionally precede chapters, or are found in the first or last paragraphs. A similar purpose is served by a list of sub-headings below the chapter title or in the table of contents, or by sub-headings appearing as running titles at the top of each page. All these forms of summary are exceedingly useful for busy students, so draw attention to them through tasks, eg

1 Supply several books that provide summaries in different forms.
Task: Where/how does each book provide summaries of its contents?

2 Supply a table of contents and a set of questions.
Task: In which chapter would you expect to find the answer to each of the following questions?

3 Supply a table of contents of a book where topic X is likely to be mentioned in several chapters.
Task: You want to find out about topic X. Which chapters are likely to contain relevant information?

Point out to students that if the book includes diagrams and illustrations, a list of these, or a glance at the figures themselves, may also give some idea of the contents.

Preliminary material: foreword, preface, introduction

The usefulness of these sections depends on what use the writer makes of them; they often include statements of purpose and sometimes outline the writer's qualifications for writing the book. An ***introduction*** is typically longer and often used to relate the book to other work, or to estimate its contribution to the field; sometimes it is so substantial that it has to be considered part of the main text.

This kind of material can be used for purposeful practice in skimming (see p48–9). For example, supply preliminary materials from different books, some useful for evaluating the book from which they are taken, some not. Suggested tasks:

1 Which of these materials would not be useful for assessing the relevance of the book for any purpose?

2 For those which are useful, what does each tell you about the relevance of the book for ... (a purpose that suits the material, or the interests of the students)?

Index

Skimming through an index is another short cut in deciding whether a book suits your purpose; some of the exercises on using a dictionary (p76) can be adapted, and races between teams are enjoyed (eg How soon can you find the page on which topic X is dealt with? How many times does topic Y appear in the book? Is topic Z dealt with?).

Make sure students know that some books have several indexes (proper names, botanical names, etc) and practise locating terms in the appropriate index.

Bibliography

The bibliography in a text is a good indicator of its scope, especially for readers familiar with the field. It also gives some idea of how up-to-date the contents are.

1 Supply a carefully chosen page of a bibliography.
Task: Predict what the text is about and what approach the writer adopts.

2 Supply pages from several different bibliographies and brief descriptions of different readers/purposes (eg a doctor who wants to know more about Chinese medicine).
Task: Estimate the usefulness for each reader of the text from which the bibliographies come.

Using the text effectively

When you know what you want and have located suitable material, the next task is to use it efficiently. This does not necessarily mean reading as fast as possible, nor need it entail understanding every detail. Speed is not always appropriate: who wants to finish a good novel in ten minutes? Similarly, total mastery of the text is pointless if you only need to understand a single chapter. The important thing is to determine what is appropriate for your purpose.

Flexibility

One of the principal characteristics of a good reader is ***flexibility***. He varies his speed, and his whole manner of reading, according to the text and his purpose in reading it. For students who have read little except in the lock-step of reading aloud in the classroom, the concepts of both speed and flexibility need careful explanation and plenty of practice.

Adequate understanding

People who read flexibly are skilled at judging what they need to get out of a text to accomplish their purpose. With an urgent need to put out a fire, such a person skips the technical details about the fire extinguisher and goes straight to the section that tells him how to operate it. But when deciding which extinguisher to buy, he might read the technical details carefully and only skim the operating instructions.

Reading flexibly means always keeping in mind how much you need to read in order to satisfy your purpose. This helps you to decide which parts of the text to ignore, which to skim to get the gist, and then which parts (if any) to study closely.

Scanning and skimming

The idea that some parts of a text may be ignored or skipped is strange to some students, but efficient reading, and specifically the techniques of scanning and skimming, require it.

By ***scanning*** we mean glancing rapidly through a text either to search for a specific piece of information (eg a name, a date) or to get an initial impression of whether the text is suitable for a given purpose (eg whether a book on gardening deals with a particular plant disease).

By ***skimming*** we mean glancing rapidly through a text to determine its gist, for example in order to decide whether a research paper is relevant to our own work (not just to determine its field, which we can find out by scanning) or to keep ourselves superficially informed about matters that are not of great importance to us; much newspaper reading is skimming.

The distinction between the two is not particularly important. In both, the reader forces his eye over print at a rate which permits him to take in only, perhaps, the beginnings and ends of paragraphs (where information is often summarized), chapter headings and so on.

Scanning and skimming are important techniques; they do not remove the need for careful reading, but they enable the reader to select texts, or parts of texts, that are worth spending time on. And skimming to get a top-down view is valuable as a way of approaching difficult texts.

Students need plenty of practice in these techniques; it is a good idea to devise races to practise them, to ensure the necessary pace. Many tasks can be done in groups, which makes the supply of materials more feasible.

Practising scanning

Tasks for scanning must be delivered orally, so that you can force the pace. It is not scanning unless it is done fast. Exercises are easy to devise; the easiest ask students to scan for a single word or a fact in a book that all possess. For instance:

1 Look at p5 and find out when Shakespeare died.

2 How many times does the word *this* occur on p27?

3 (Using the index) On what page is topic X mentioned?

More complex activities can be used if you can get several copies of the same newspaper, magazine or book – enough for each group to have one. The suggestions below should spark off other ideas for similar practice.

4 Supply a copy of the same newspaper for each group. (Each group member could take one or two pages.)
Task: Locate the page and column where various headlines (which you read aloud or display) can be found. Variations include locating regular features – editorial, letters, etc; locating pictures you describe/give the captions of; locating news items (which you outline without giving headlines – this involves skimming as well as scanning).

5 Supply a page of advertisements, eg from a newspaper.
Task: Answer a series of quiz questions asked orally (eg *What tour agent offers holidays in China? Where can you get a holiday for £180? What ship will take you to Crete? How many agents have holidays for young people?*).

Practising skimming

Skimming requires closer attention to the text than scanning does; it is difficult to skim if a text has to be shared by more than two people. Some of the activities below can be done in groups, each member skimming one or two items. Have time limits and emphasize the need for speed, but be cautious about races. The tasks must not ask for subtle comprehension, otherwise they cannot be answered by skimming. Tailor the task to make sure it can be completed by skimming rather than careful reading.

You can simply ask students to say what a text is about, or you can give specific questions. For example:

1 Supply a text and several titles.
Task: Which title fits the text best? (The titles must not differ in subtle ways, or careful reading would be needed.)

2 Supply a text and a list of topics.
Task: Which topics are dealt with in this text?

3 Supply a text and several figures (photographs, diagrams, etc).
Task: Which figure(s) illustrate the text?

4 Supply a dozen or so letters (you might collect suitable items from newspapers or magazines).
Task: Categorize the letters in some way, eg Which letters are complaining about something? asking for help? praising? offering an opinion on an issue?
Note: One category only, initially. Make sure there are several letters in the category, and several not.

5 Supply copies of news items from different papers about the same incident.
Task: Categorize the stories in some way, eg Which imply that X is guilty? Which include opinion/conjecture? Which explain the background to the events? Note as for 4.

6 Supply several texts, some dealing with topic X, some not.
Task: Which of these texts deals with topic X?

Making use of all the resources in the text

Texts – especially books – contain a variety of resources which help readers to understand and find their way about in the linear text itself. We looked at many of the important ones, in connection with choosing the right text for our purpose. Once the text is chosen, sub-titles, summaries, tables of contents, are aids to efficient reading. They enable you to read selectively (omitting irrelevant sections) and offer some clue to meaning by signalling what you can expect to find in which part of the text. Use practice activities similar to the ones on pp45–47, relating not to different texts, but to different parts of the same text.

Other reference apparatus

Other reference apparatus which students need to be able to use if they are to get the most out of their reading includes:

- appendixes
- notes (footnotes, notes at the end of the chapter or book)
- bibliographical references in the text
- lists of symbols, abbreviations, etc
- lists of special terms, glossaries

For practising the use of reference apparatus (including tables of contents, sub-headings and so on) you need a class set of books to refer to; perhaps textbooks in other subjects can be used. Otherwise, base exercises on books in a library accessible to all students, or borrow a collection of books for use in class. Students should be able to:

- explain the kind of material likely to be found in an appendix;
- locate notes indicated (by superscript numerals, etc) in the text;
- give the full details of an abbreviated bibliographical reference (eg *Potter 1990*) by referring to the bibliography, and identify the author, title, publisher, etc;
- use a bibliography to choose potentially suitable texts for further reading for a given purpose;
- look up the meaning of any symbol, abbreviation, or technical term and interpret accurately the passage of text in which it occurs.

Graphic conventions

Writers and printers use a variety of conventions to help readers find their way through a text: print size and style, layout, even punctuation. You have probably come across the difficulties that unfamiliar writing conventions cause, particularly if the students' mother tongue and the target language have different writing systems. These conventions are often neglected, because experienced readers take most of them for granted; but it cannot be taken for granted that students will interpret them without help. For instance, do your students realize that different type faces are used for different levels of heading and therefore signal the way the text is structured? Do they know they should give special attention to words in bold or italic type? These matters are easy to teach, so it is worth checking to see if you need to deal with them.

In English, the conventions that are useful but likely to be unrecognized by some learners include the following.

Layout, spacing, indentation

Layout in general is used to indicate which parts of the text go together, to signal the start of a new topic, show which parts are subordinate to others, and so on. This makes it a valuable aid to comprehension, because it indicates the way the text is organized.

Spacing between letters and words is seldom significant, but spacing between lines is; it shows which parts of the text go together. For instance, paragraphs are often separated by wider spaces, and sections by wider ones still. Other uses are to indicate a shift of topic or (in fiction) the passage of time.

Indentation (ie variation in width of the left-hand margin) often signals the start of a new paragraph or section. It may also indicate a different kind of material; for instance, sub-sections may have different margins, and quoted material is often distinguished by wider margins at both sides.

Type face

It is safe to say that a change in type is usually significant, but less easy to say how, since publishing houses have different styles. Type can vary in four ways:

1 *Type design:*
This is printed in Times Roman.
This is printed in Garamond.
This is printed in Gill Sans.

2 *Standard, italic or bold:*
This is printed in standard (roman).
This is printed in italic.
This is printed in bold.

3 *Type size* (measured in units of *points*):
This is printed in 6 point.
This is printed in 8 point.
This is printed in 12 point.

4 *Upper or lower case* (capital or small letters):
this is printed in lower case.
THIS IS PRINTED IN UPPER CASE.

Newspapers and magazines use differences in typeface simply to provide visual variety and make the text look easier to read by breaking it up. But a more important function is to distinguish different kinds of text, or different parts of a text (look for example at Appendix A Text 9). For instance, to differentiate several short items that might otherwise look like a continuous text; or the words of different speakers in an interview; or parts of a text with different functions (eg stage directions and dialogue in a play; ingredients and method in a recipe).

The functions just outlined are not difficult to interpret, once you are aware of them; more tricky – and often more closely associated with meaning – are variations occurring within the linear text. Typically these involve the use of italics or bold type in an otherwise standard/roman text; but size, case and style can also be used to distinguish words from those that surround them.

The main functions are as follows:

1 *To make words easy to locate:*

a Proper names in some styles of journalism:
In Paris recently, **Professor John Smith** voiced his views.

b Technical terms at the point where they are defined:
Sounds may be classified by this *point of articulation*.

c Phrases of linear text that serve as summaries or sub-titles:
Clearly, *the age of the students* is another factor that must be taken into account.

2 *To mark the use of a foreign word or phrase:*
A species of viola, *viola calaminaria*, is a useful indicator of zinc.

3 *To cite the title of a book, film, etc:*
One of the most successful films ever is *Gone with the Wind*.

4 *To distinguish a cited word/phrase (ie one that is being referred to):*
What is erroneous about the use of *exact* in this text?

5 *To indicate emphasis:*
This is a tricky function, because it depends on spoken style; it may signal contrast, or simply that the writer considers something important:
We don't *know* this is so, we only believe it.
There is no cause for alarm *provided the temperature remains normal.*

It is worth pointing out that many of these uses are catered for by the use of underlining in handwritten texts. But it is usually inappropriate to try to reproduce other variations when writing by hand.

Punctuation

This is another area often neglected in the reading classroom. Yet punctuation reflects meaning; students who know that commas and semi-colons function differently, and that quotation marks have uses other than indicating speech, have more clues to help them make sense.

There is no space here to discuss punctuation adequately, and formal instruction may not be needed; but you should look out for opportunities to check that students have noticed and understood usages that may help them.

Symbols

Apart from punctuation symbols, a variety of others are regularly used with a variety of functions. These include:

- symbols referring to notes such as asterisk*, dagger†, superscript numbers^3 and so on;
- symbols relating to text continuity such as the arrow or similar pointing symbol in a magazine that tells you to turn to another page to continue the article; the row of asterisks (****) indicating a switch of topic; the blocking symbol (□ or similar) indicating the end of the article.

Make sure they are noticed and understood when they occur in class texts.

Figures

The figures accompanying text are the final resource to be discussed; again, they are often under-used, yet can be of enormous help to the reader. Included in the term are illustrations (pictures, photographs), diagrams, maps and plans, graphs, pie charts, Venn diagrams, tables, flow charts, and similar methods of representing information.

We described these earlier as not part of the linear text, but this is often inaccurate. In many kinds of text, such as instructions for operating machines or descriptions of biological structure, the figures are so fully integrated with the linear text that it cannot be understood without them.

Even when the relationship is less integral, figures are often a great help in interpreting the text. Used together, they support each other: an obscure section of text may be clarified by a diagram, or the significance of a graph may become clear from the text. This can be exploited even in the early stages of reading: a learner stumbling over a word (*John is holding a ...*) is urged to look at the picture and work out what the word must be. In more advanced reading, the relationships are more complex, but the usefulness is similar.

The ability to interpret figures is largely independent of language, so it transfers readily. This is a case where a skill derived from the L1 can contribute positively to the interpretation of foreign language texts: students should learn to turn to the figures for help, and to distinguish figures that will be useful from those that will not. However, it is risky to assume that all students are able to interpret figures. Check their competence and give specific instruction to those who need it.

When you are showing students how to exploit figures, find texts which are quite difficult (even impossible) to follow on their own, but reasonably accessible read in conjunction with the figures. First present the linear text only, with questions to check comprehension. Then add the figures and let students attempt the questions again. If the text and questions are well chosen, this should prove the usefulness of figures in interpreting text. (Chapter 12 covers the kinds of practice that can be used to show the value of figures in interpreting text.)

Improving reading speed

This topic comes last because, as we have seen, speed is not the only factor to consider when judging someone's reading efficiency. But if two readers understand a text equally well, of course the one who performs more quickly is judged more efficient. We saw that readers can speed up their work by finding the relevant texts/sections and focusing on these; now it is time to consider the speed with which they process the linear text itself.

Speed and comprehension

Reading crucially involves the mind, and most of this book focuses on the mental aspects of reading. However, it is a physical activity too: it involves vision and the movement of the eyes. Poor vision makes for slow reading; small or unclear print has the same effect. In discussing reading speed, we are dealing with the physical as well as the mental aspects of the skill.

The relationship between reading speed and comprehension is complex, but they are certainly closely linked. A slow reader is likely to read with poor understanding, if only because his memory is taxed: the beginning of a paragraph may be forgotten by the time he has struggled to the end of it. But it is not clear which is cause and which effect: do people read quickly because they understand easily, or do they understand easily because of the speed at which they read? Each influences the other, a major consideration in extensive reading as we see in Chapter 8. Similarly, there is a strong relationship between speed and interest or enjoyment, presumably because motivation spurs us on to get to the end of the story as quickly as we can. Again, the causal relationship is not clear, but these facts suggest that students will more easily improve their speed on material that is readily comprehensible and of interest to them. And again, this provides justification for an extensive reading programme.

Eye movement and sense groups

A great deal of work has been done on the improvement of reading speeds, stemming at least in part from the discovery that good readers do not read word by word. As we read, our eyes follow the text, moving from left to right (in English) and then jumping left again to begin the next line. If you watch a reader's eyes, you will see that they do not move continuously along the line but cover the distance in several jumps, called ***fixations.***

A good reader makes fewer fixations than a poor one; his eye takes in several words at a time. Moreover, they are not just random sequences of words: an efficient reader chunks a text into ***sense groups***, units of meaning each consisting of several words. Each chunk is taken in by one fixation of the eyes. So a good reader may chunk:

The good old man / raised his hand / in blessing.

Or he might manage with only two fixations for this short sentence. He would certainly not chunk like this:

The good / old man / raised his / hand in / blessing.

Nor would he read word by word.

The words of a text are like jigsaw puzzle pieces. Often you can see that several pieces fit together, so you can build up various parts – chunks – of the picture separately. After that you can fit together whole chunks without paying attention to the small pieces that compose them. Clearly it needs less effort to fit together a few larger chunks than a lot of small pieces.

In the same way, a good reader takes in the sense of a whole chunk without pausing to consider the individual words. It is quicker to fit together the sense of two or three chunks than to do the same with all the separate words that compose them. So the larger the sense groups the reader can take in, the more easily he will turn them into coherent messages.

The student's problem is often that he does not know the target language well enough to chunk effectively. Many students read word by word, especially if the text is difficult, so to encourage good reading habits, a lot of practice with easy texts is needed. There is never enough time for this in the classroom, so this is yet another important purpose for an extensive reading programme (Chapter 8).

Training students to take in longer chunks

Opinions differ about how far it is possible to train students to recognize sense groups and take in longer chunks at each fixation. Getting them to skim through the text before beginning to read it properly may help by giving a rough idea of what it is about; this may reduce the need for a word by word approach. There are also exercises that some claim are helpful, for example:

1 Texts are set out in narrow columns with one sense group on each line. The student tries to force himself to make one fixation for each line, for example by moving his finger down the centre of the column and making his eye follow it.

In this way
it is hoped
he will accustom himself
to taking in
increasingly long chunks of text
at a single eye fixation.

2 You can prepare similar material (using the column layout) for use on OHP, covering the text with a mask that you then move down the text to reveal each consecutive line at the speed you consider appropriate.

3 Practice material is available on film and computer with one sense group displayed at a time, the rate of presentation being steadily speeded up as the student's skill increases. In the case of computers, the student can often control the speed himself.

However, the physical act of taking in the sense group is not the same as assimilating its meaning. We shall return to this point later.

Choosing texts for speed practice

The time needed to read a text depends on its linguistic difficulty and on the density of the information it carries. A text is ***dense*** when the minimum number of words expresses the maximum amount of information. A dense text is usually more difficult to follow than one which presents information in a more extended way.

Students need the security of familiar language and concepts when they begin work on skimming, scanning and faster reading. Dense texts are unsuitable. The material used needs to be well below the level of the current language textbook; to begin with, it should contain no language difficulties at all.

When students accept that they really can get the gist without reading every word, you can move to similar exercises using slightly more difficult material. The next thing is to prove that unfamiliar vocabulary is often no bar to comprehension. You may have to deal with guilt feelings about skipping unknown words instead of looking them up in the dictionary; this is dealt with at greater length in Chapter 5.

If the text contains more than a few new words, or is difficult in other ways, it is dangerous to make students try to read it fast. It is simply not possible to read fast, and also with understanding, if the text is beyond their language proficiency or contains complex ideas. If they are obliged to study it for professional purposes, they will have to learn how to use skimming and scanning, and the other short cuts outlined earlier in this chapter, to identify the parts they need to read with care.

What speeds should be expected?

Since it is obviously more difficult for a student to improve his reading speed in a foreign language than in the L1, and much riskier, you may wonder if it should be attempted.

It used to be claimed that people could read at several thousand words a minute, but today we recognize that this is an extreme form of scanning, not reading proper. Such exaggerated claims are unhelpful, but students can usually make and maintain significant improvements in speed once they realize that this is possible and useful. Progress may be particularly striking where initial speeds are very low.

Secondary school pupils in countries where English is a second language may read at 120–150 words per minute (wpm) before training. University students in similar areas may read at about 200 wpm, but have been found to study at rates as slow as 60 wpm; presumably the texts were difficult and had to be understood thoroughly. University students in countries with little tradition of reading may read as slowly as 40 wpm even in their L1. All these students can make significant advances in speed after training; doubling the rate is not uncommon. An average increase is about 50 per cent.

Comparisons are meaningless unless you know exactly what is being measured. But it may be useful to know that an L1 speaker of English, of about average education and intelligence, reads at about 300 wpm. The range among L1 speakers is wide: rates of up to 800 wpm and down to 140 wpm are not uncommon.

Finding out students' reading speed

First get the students' co-operation by explaining the programme; this is important. Most people are keen to find out about their reading speed, and motivation plays an important part in improving speeds. Honesty is essential if you are to get reliable results, so individual results need not be made public and must not count towards assessment; hence cheating is pointless.

Begin by finding out how fast your students read now. This will show the size of the problem and later their improvement can be measured. Choose a shortish unfamiliar text that is not difficult for the students (preferably with no new words). Count the number of words in it. Devise straightforward questions on it – preferably five or ten, so that the percentage answered correctly is easy to calculate. Multiple choice or true/false are the simplest to handle (see Chapter 11).

Explain how the activity will be organized (see below) and emphasize that nobody must start reading until you are ready. Then give each student a clearly legible copy of the text with the number of words stated, and finally give the signal to start.

While the students read, your job is to indicate the time that elapses. Prepare a chart on the blackboard or OHP, as shown below, to cover the time you consider the slowest students will need to read the text. The figures represent ten-second intervals.

1	2	3	4	5	6	(1 minute)	
7	8	9	10	11	12	(2 minutes)	and so on.

Stand beside the chart where every student can see it and keep count of the time (you need a timepiece that indicates seconds). Move a pointer along the rows of figures as each ten-second interval elapses.

When the student finishes reading, he immediately looks at your pointer and notes the time it shows. For instance, if it is pointing at 8, he has taken 1 minute 20 seconds (ie 80 seconds) to read. He can then calculate his reading speed in words per minute by means of a simple equation:

$$x \div y \times 6 = z$$

Here, **x** is the number of words in the text
y is the number of ten-second intervals he needed to read the text
6 is the number of ten-second intervals in a minute
z is the reading speed in words per minute (wpm).

For example, if the text contains 250 words and the time taken to read it is 80 seconds (eight ten-second intervals) the equation will read:

$$250 \div 8 \times 6 = 187.5$$

The reading speed is 187.5 wpm.

The procedure is more complicated to explain than to do! I recommend a trial run with a short text before the first real test, so that everyone understands what to do. You do not want the results to be compromised by people not doing it properly. One likely hitch is that some students will not know how to set about reading quickly; earlier practice with texts on the blackboard or OHP, with you moving a pointer down the lines at a reasonable reading speed, may help them to realize what is needed.

After the first test, give regular reading speed tests during the course so that each student can observe his own steady improvement and you can monitor the effects of your teaching. Remember though that improved speed cannot be measured if you give increasingly difficult texts, so *for progress tests use a similar level of text throughout.*

Balancing speed and comprehension

After noting the time taken, the student answers the questions. When everyone has finished, you can discuss the answers; students mark their own (since they can cheat only themselves) and weigh the score against their reading speed.

As reading is partly a physical skill, to some extent speed can be improved without reference to comprehension. However, speed is worthless unless the reader understands what he reads. That is why we measure comprehension. But interpreting the results is problematic. Which is the better reader: one with a score of 100 per cent and a reading speed of 140 wpm, or one with a score of 70 per cent and a speed of 200 wpm? And what score is to be considered adequate? The general view seems to be that about 70 per cent is enough.

We need not be too concerned with such problems; as we saw, they depend partly on the reader's purpose and the nature of the questions. An apparent target of less than 100 per cent worries some people, but it would be misleading to think that the aim is a comprehension score of 70 per cent. The purpose is quite different: it is to increase speed, and to achieve this we are prepared – temporarily, and only in speed-training exercises – to accept some reduction in comprehension. The expectation is that eventually both speed and comprehension will increase. In the reading programme as a whole, comprehension remains the overriding consideration.

Reading habits in the L1

We noted that some students do not read efficiently even in their L1. This hinders the development of efficient reading in the foreign language, for there is a strong transfer of reading habits from one language to another.

Few readers manage to bring their foreign language speeds up to anything like their L1 speeds. But if the L1 is not much read, and if bad L1 reading habits have developed, attention to Ll reading is a useful preliminary, especially where the writing system is similar to that of the target language. Improved L1 reading habits can then transfer to foreign language reading.

Faulty reading habits

The books listed in *Further reading* include techniques that can be adapted to speed training in any language. Some were written with learners of English as a foreign language in mind, but others are for L1 readers, so we need to treat cautiously some of the suggestions made about faults in reading technique – some of which are not accepted by L1 teachers either.

For instance, several early reading habits are alleged to slow down the reader when they persist into later stages of reading. One of these is ***subvocalizing***, that is, forming the sounds of the words you are reading, and even murmuring them aloud. This gives elementary L1 readers the support of the spoken language, with which they are more familiar. Understandably, foreign language readers also value this support.

Like reading aloud, subvocalization is much slower than silent reading (the eyes move faster than the tongue), so efficient readers do not subvocalize. But we should be cautious in urging students to break the habit; is it just a pointless defect left over from early reading days, or is it a symptom of insecure command of the language, a prop that they still need?

Similar criticism is made of ***finger-pointing*** such as children use to fix their concentration on the word they are deciphering. Again, this slows down the reading if the finger points word by word. A better idea is to use a cardboard guide (as described below), but fingers can also be made to move swiftly if the student realizes this can help him.

The habit is particularly common when the L1 and foreign language writing systems differ. Choosing texts with large type may help to eradicate it. Perhaps you can use a large typeface for materials you prepare yourself, or an enlarging photocopier. You may be surprised how much more confidently students tackle texts in oversize type (books prepared for visually handicapped L1 readers are popular).

Another often-criticized habit is the occurrence of ***regressive eye movements***, that is, the eye moving back to check previous words instead of sweeping steadily forwards. Naturally this makes reading slower. However, as we saw in Chapter 1, a skilled reader continually modifies his interpretation as he reads. To do this he may have to return to earlier parts of the text and reinterpret them. In this case, regression is the sign of an active and responsive reader, not an incompetent or insecure one.

Thus, urging students to move their eyes continually forward is a technique to be applied with caution. It may be helpful, but pointless regressions can probably be best eliminated by practice with easy material. In any case, students need to know that difficult material may positively require regressions, so they should not be afraid to regress when the aim is comprehension rather than speed.

Caution

All these habits can slow down a reader, so students need to be aware that efficient readers seldom use them. But any reader faced with difficult material makes use of them occasionally. So insecure students should not be harassed. With improved reading skills and increased confidence, these habits will eventually disappear naturally.

Some approaches to improving reading speed

Using a card guide

Most of us do not have access to the specialized equipment that exists to force students to read at a given rate, without regressions, by exposing text briefly, a bit at a time. However, a similar effect can be obtained by using a cardboard mask which the student moves down the page as he reads.

This can be simply a piece of card about the same width as the page; you hold it just above the first line and then, as you read, move it down the page at the desired speed. This focuses the eyes on the line immediately below it and discourages regressions. (Many students place the card below the line, but this interrupts the sweep of the eye from one line to the next.)

Slightly more sophisticated is a cut-out mask (see Figure 9 on p60) designed to reveal the whole of one line and the first few words of the next. The eye passes without a break from one line to the next, as the hand moves the mask down the page.

Using a mask means that students control their own speed, but they do in fact usually move the mask quickly enough to force up their reading rate, and the control they exert may itself be motivating.

Figure 9 Mask to promote reading speed

Projected texts

Slides and particularly overhead projector (OHP) transparencies offer advantages; the projected text holds readers' attention and improves concentration. It is impossible for them to use finger-pointing, and you may be able to spot those with problems such as subvocalizing or using head movements (slower than eye movements and therefore more inefficient and quite needless). Use of the dictionary is also made impossible.

The major advantage is that you have complete control. First, speed: you can use a mask (on the OHP or, less conveniently, on the screen), as just described, to expose as much or as little of the text for as long as you wish. Second, the sequence: for instance, you can expose questions before, during or after the reading of the text. The same text can be briefly exposed for a scanning task and later projected again for other purposes.

Computers and other machines

Sophisticated machines (such as tachistoscopes) are now rather out of favour; but computers can play a valuable part in helping students to read more quickly. Programs are available which allow you to type in texts (and questions) of your choice for students to use for speed practice; so you can ensure that the practice material is suitable.

The text is displayed at a speed selected by you or by the student (which may motivate him). Two modes of controlling speed are possible: the whole text (or as much as fits on the screen) may be offered, and then scrolled off the screen at a steady rate. Alternatively, the text may be presented chunk by chunk, each in turn flashed onto the screen for a given length of time. Another variation is to present the text in a narrow column (as shown on p55) to encourage the student to use just one fixation per line.

The challenge of the moving text is reportedly motivating, and the reader's progress is charted without the need for tedious calculations, since the computer takes care of those. The computer is a very worthwhile adjunct to a speed reading programme for those who can afford it.

A speed reading programme

In speed exercises of all kinds, students should be urged to beat their own records, not to compete with one another. There is no sense trying to read faster than someone else. But there is much sense in trying to improve your own performance, and almost everyone is capable of this.

Students should keep a record of their progress, especially if you set up a regular programme of speed training. You must be prepared for plateaus which normally occur now and again, when no progress is made. In general, speed steadily improves, despite occasional falls because of difficult material or an off-day, and it is this general tendency that counts and gives satisfaction and continual motivation.

Remember that all the texts used should be of similar difficulty, otherwise speeds will vary with the text and the results of the training will not be identifiable.

A reminder

If you cannot organize a regular programme, at least talk to students about reading efficiently and give them practice in some of the strategies we have considered: clarifying their reading purpose, choosing the right materials, adjusting their reading style to the purpose (skimming, scanning and so on), increasing their speed and making use of all the resources the text provides. Above all, make sure they realize that *flexibility* is the sign of effective reading, and that there is no merit in reading something carefully if they can get the result they want in half the time.

Further reading

On different types of reading see Davies 1995. On study skills training see eg Glendinning and Holmström 1992; Smith and Smith 1990; Fairbairn and Winch 1991; Northedge 1990. Williams 1989 gives guidance on how to use a library. Mallett 1992 discusses similar training in the junior school.

Quirk et al 1985 Appendix III gives a full account of English punctuation.

On reading speed training see de Leeuw 1990 and, for foreign learners, Mosback 1976; Fry 1963. For a critical survey, Banton-Smith 1972 is still as good as any: the absence of recent titles indicates diminished interest in the topic. On eye movements see eg Oakhill and Garnham 1988.

Chapter 5
Word attack skills

The vocabulary problem

YOUR students probably consider not having a big enough vocabulary their main problem in reading. It has been suggested that moderate L1 readers can recognize about fifty thousand words; yet foreign language syllabuses present only a few hundred words a year. Even granted different interpretations of 'a word', 'knowing a word' and so on, the difference is enormous. How can students cope with a learning problem of this size?

Dictionaries and informants

Students who meet a word they cannot interpret are likely first to ask what it means, which is fine as long as an informant is available, but not practical as the basis for independent study. So most students turn to the dictionary. This is perfectly natural and in some circumstances advisable. Nevertheless, one of the first things to be said about a dictionary is *don't use it* when you are reading. The reason is simple: many students use it far too much. Sometimes they are urged to look up every new word. This chapter explains why this might be undesirable. It would be idiotic to ban the use of dictionaries, but like many useful tools, they can be dangerous. Learning how to use them properly is an important part of any vocabulary development programme. We shall return to this later (p76).

A great many words are learnt from reading. However, students who keep looking up new words read much less effectively. Every time you break off to consult a dictionary, you slow down your reading and interrupt your thinking, which should be following the development of thought in the text. A competent reader can cope with occasional interruptions, but constantly referring to a dictionary makes effective reading impossible.

Freeing students from the dictionary

How can you free students from dependence on a dictionary or an informant? First, and most important, you can make sure that they read a great deal more. The L1 reader did not learn his fifty thousand words by being taught them; most were learnt by meeting them in context. Usually this involved assimilating the meaning gradually, after frequent encounters. In the classroom, students simply do not get enough exposure for this natural assimilation to be possible. Therefore solutions outside the classroom must be found. *An extensive reading programme is the single most effective way of improving vocabulary*. It is relatively easy to organize, enjoyable for the students and extremely cost-effective. (See Chapter 8.)

Second, you can provide a programme of organized vocabulary development: showing students how the vocabulary of the language is structured, how words relate to one another, how to make proper use of a dictionary, and so on. Some publications which do this for English are listed in *Further reading*.

Third, you can follow the suggestions in this chapter, which focuses on the place of vocabulary in a reading programme. It will not help much if your students' vocabulary is really weak; for that purpose, the two earlier strategies are more appropriate.

When we discuss reading skills, we often assume that the reader's vocabulary is 'adequate', a slippery concept to which we shall return; it has been suggested that a vocabulary of about five thousand words is needed to start independent reading. This is beyond the reach of most students; we might settle for about two thousand words as an acceptable threshold for the sort of work we want to do – not independent reading, but preparation for it, using carefully chosen texts. If even this is beyond your students, you may have to emphasize language development initially, because you cannot develop reading skills with texts that are loaded with unfamiliar words.

But naturally we do not expect students to know every word in the text. How should they deal with the unknown ones? Which can be skipped without losing the message? It is such questions that we consider in this chapter.

Lexical items

This chapter will often refer to 'words', for brevity, but most of what is said applies to any ***lexical item***. This can be loosely defined as a word or group of words with a meaning that needs to be learnt as a unitary whole – that would, for example, need a separate entry in a dictionary. It is useful to think of new lexical items, rather than new words, as the things the student must learn.

There are two reasons for this. First, some lexical items consist of more than one word: for instance, a phrasal verb is a single lexical item, although it can consist of several words: *take in, put up with*, etc. Second, some superficially identical words represent more than one lexical item: for instance, the spelling *saw* represents several lexical items, among them the past tense of *see* and the word that means a tool for cutting wood.

Discussing what is and is not a lexical item would take us too far from our purpose. It is enough to stress that what readers have to deal with are units of meaning. Students need to be aware that these may be packaged as one word or several, and that some words that look alike have different meanings.

Active, receptive and throwaway vocabulary

Not all words are equally important. A primary attack skill is identifying the words that can be ignored, so that the other words that really stand in the way of comprehension can be tackled by some of the strategies described below.

If you examine your own L1 vocabulary, you will find two categories of known words: an ***active*** vocabulary of words you know well enough to use yourself, and a ***receptive*** vocabulary of words you recognize and can respond to, but cannot confidently use. This is equally true of a foreign language. It is important for students to become aware of this – perhaps through considering their own L1 vocabulary – and to recognize that receptive vocabulary becomes available for active use naturally, if it is important, by being frequently encountered in context. This may make their attitude to new words more relaxed.

You can further reduce tension by not asking students to 'make sentences' with newly learnt words. (You are likely to get a sentence that is either trivial or wrong.) Immediate active use of words encountered when reading is seldom necessary. If the word is important enough, students will meet it again and again (this is where the extensive reading programme is so important) until they are confident enough to use it themselves. By that time, with luck, they will know how to use it properly. Continued exposure to the language is far the best way to transform receptive words into active ones.

But there is also a third category of words that students will meet once they move on to unsimplified material; these I label ***throwaway*** vocabulary. Not all the words we meet are worth learning, even to the receptive level. Students with a vocabulary of, say, three thousand words cannot afford to clutter up their minds trying to learn words like *boost* or *epicene*. Instead, they must learn to ignore what is not important for their immediate purpose.

Of course no word is throwaway of itself; it all depends on the context, the student's level and reasons for reading. Perhaps an electrical engineer would find *boost* an essential item; perhaps for a specific text *epicene* would have to be understood, but that does not make it worth learning for recall.

Teachers make the problem worse by paying attention to every detail of a text. Intensive reading is likely to strengthen students' belief that they ought to pay this sort of attention when they read on their own. Certainly they must be able to do so when their purpose demands it. But they must also acquire strategies for dealing with texts that need not be mastered so completely.

Learning when to ignore difficult words

One mark of a skilled reader is the ability to decide what may be safely ignored. This is something many students have never contemplated; it may seem wrong, because it is not done in class. Therefore it needs to be done in class to make it respectable. It may also seem dangerous, and it is, which is why it needs to be practised under your guidance.

When tackling a difficult text, readers should have these questions in mind:

Before reading:	Why am I going to read this? What do I want to get from it?
While reading:	Do I need to stop and look up the meaning of this word, or can I get the gist without it?
After reading:	Have I got what I wanted? If not, where in the text is it hidden? Can I get at it by looking up any words? If so, which?

This procedure is of course not so simple to put into practice. It takes a competent reader to be aware that he is not understanding and it sometimes takes a very skilled one to be aware *why* he is not. So our responsibility includes helping students to:

- recognize that they do not understand;
- locate the sources of difficulty;
- develop strategies for coping with the difficulty (including strategies for not wasting time on words they don't need to know).

If you doubt the possibility of ignoring words, try Activity 5.1, intended to demonstrate that we can often get the gist of a text without understanding every word.

Activity 5.1 *Understanding gapped text: eye movements*

Read the text. Do not worry about the gaps in it but get what sense you can from it. Then answer the question below.

Eye-movement: Studies of readers and text

The question of speed reading is _ in detail _ (Pugh 1978) and it is not the _ _ in the present paper. The history of eye-movement research in _ , and with _ to reading in particular, is fairly _ _ , as are _ details of various apparatus; therefore a brief _ and guide to _ is all that is _ here. What is not so easily _ is a _ of the _ of eye-movement studies as they _ to reading of the type _ in LSP (Language for Specific Purposes). Nor is there full _ of the possibilities, resulting from _ in eye-movement _ apparatus and from _ interest in text structure by _ and _ _ , for _ studies of _ _ related to text structure.

From Pugh and Ulijn 1984

Which two or three of the following do you expect to be dealt with in the article from which this introductory paragraph is taken?

a A full account of the history of eye-movement research.
b Details of the results of eye-movement research relating to LSP reading.
c A discussion of the possibilities for studies of eye-movements in relation to the structure of text.
d Discussion of opportunities opened up by developments in apparatus used in eye-movement research.
e A discussion of speed reading.

Did you find it possible to answer the question in Activity 5.1? If so, you understood 'enough', despite the gaps in your understanding. (The gaps in the text represent words the reader does not know.) There are no hard and fast rules about which words can be ignored, but we can do two things to help students. The first is to convince them that ignoring new words is both acceptable and necessary. Next, having crossed this biggest hurdle, we can go on to give practice in identifying the sources of difficulty and judging whether a word is worth attending to or not. Here are some suggested activities.

1 To prove that it is possible to get the gist without understanding every word, supply a gapped text (lexical items omitted here and there, with omissions indicated, as in Activity 5.1). Ask some simple top-down questions that can be answered from the incomplete text.

2 The same sort of exercise as in **1**, but using complete texts with difficult words which are not essential to the gist. Holmes 1987 makes a convincing case for even using texts in unfamiliar languages for initial confidence-building.

3 To help students to identify the words they really need to look up, supply a short text containing a few new words, and simple questions requiring understanding of some of them. The task is to see how many questions can be answered without looking up any words, and to make students think very carefully before choosing which to look up. This can be done competitively, the winner having correct answers and fewest words looked up.

4 As an extension of **3**, supply a text in which you consider a certain number of words must be looked up in order to answer the questions. The task is then:

> You are allowed to look up the meaning of only (five) words. Decide which (five) you most need to understand in order to answer the questions. List them, then look them up and prepare your answers.

This is best done in small groups. Afterwards discuss the words chosen and the effect the choices had on the answers.

In exercises of this kind, student discussion (both during the task and as a class afterwards) plays an essential part. It is then that learning occurs; without discussion, such tasks are more like tests than teaching activities.

What makes words difficult?

Not all words are difficult, and many are difficult only in some contexts or for some readers. However, we can identify some kinds of lexical item, and some ways in which words are used, that frequently present difficulty to a foreign language reader.

Idioms

An ***idiom*** is a lexical item consisting of several words, with a meaning that cannot be deduced from the individual words. Students may know that phrases like *seeing red* are idiomatic, yet fail to recognize the problem in sentences like these:

> He was beside himself.
> I can't go through with it.
> They solved it once and for all.

The problem idioms are the ones composed of simple words, each of which the student understands. Without your help, he may not realize that he does not understand the whole sentence: so ask a question which cannot be answered unless the idiom is understood. Once students are aware of the deceptively simple ones, you can keep them on the lookout for idioms and deal with them individually as they occur.

Words with several meanings

Any word with more than one meaning is potentially troublesome. Some of the most dangerous misunderstandings arise when everyday words are used in specialized fields. The mathematician's use of *argument*, the statistician's *random*, the communications engineer's *noise*, are all very different from the layman's. Once again, the difficulty arises partly because it is not immediately apparent.

To tackle these unexpected misunderstandings, we must first be aware that they may occur and then use common sense in deciding whether to accept a familiar meaning or check whether another is possible. You can give specific practice by supplying sentences containing words used with unfamiliar meanings; students choose the appropriate one from several definitions. Or supply a technical text; students find all the familiar words used in unfamiliar ways. Training in using a dictionary (see p76) will also help, because it involves selecting the meaning appropriate to the context.

Sub-technical vocabulary

If you teach language for specific purposes, English for technologists for example, you know that students often have difficulty not with the technical jargon (which usually has a unique L1 equivalent, familiar to students from their specialized studies), but with the common core of semi-technical words that occur in most disciplines.

Troublemakers are words like *average, approximate, effect, combination, determine.* They are needed in most fields of study and are therefore worth attention even if you are not teaching a homogeneous class. The problem, however, is conceptual rather than linguistic. To make sure the concept has been grasped, ask students to give concrete examples; or offer examples yourself, getting the students to distinguish one that illustrates the concept from one that does not.

Superordinates

These are words of more general meaning viewed in relation to other words of more specific meaning which could also be referred to by the general term. For example:

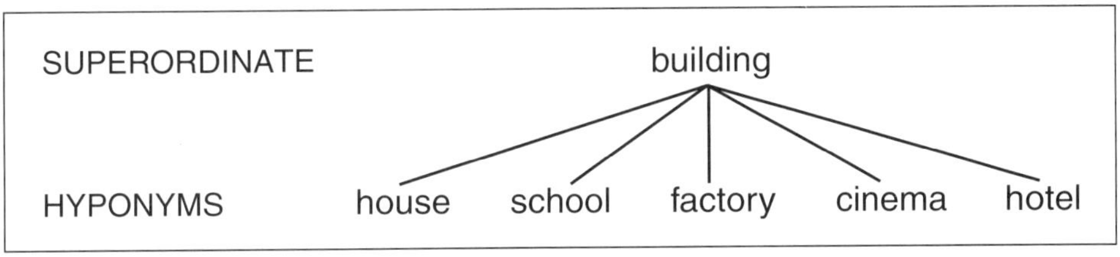

You can see that the superordinate, *building*, could replace any of the hyponyms in many contexts. Difficulties arise if the reader fails to realize that the two terms have the same referent:

> **Mrs Hill** came in slowly. **The woman** looked tired, I thought.

Here, to make sense of the text entails recognizing that the general word *woman* refers to Mrs Hill.

The example is trivial, but interpreting superordinates is not always so simple. Sometimes the superordinate and its hyponym are different parts of speech:

> The **diseased** limb was cruelly deformed; **leprosy** has no mercy.

Sometimes the hyponym is expressed by a sentence or an even longer stretch of text:

> A six-year-old boy recently gave a performance of the Beethoven violin concerto. **This feat** was reported in the press.

The feat, of course, is not just playing the concerto, but playing it at the age of six.

The last example illustrates another difficulty with superordinates: some of them embody judgements. You may not think it remarkable for a child of six to play the concerto, but the writer evidently does. Students have to learn to watch out for such evidence of the writer's attitude.

Transfer of meaning

Metaphor and similar kinds of transferred meaning are always potential problems. Like idioms, they do not mean what at first glance they seem to mean. The difficulty is not faced only by students of literature; when he reads of a tapeworm budding off sections from its tail end, a student may wonder if he is reading zoology or botany. A student of accountancy may be puzzled by *galloping inflation, profits wiped out, fringe benefits*, and so on.

Metaphor may lie in a single word or be far more extensive (and so not really a lexical problem at all). It always involves an implicit comparison between A and B, so one way of handling it is to analyse what A and B have in common that is relevant to the context. For instance, *galloping inflation* suggests comparison between inflation (A) and a horse (B). What characteristics of the horse are relevant? Even the first step – identifying A and B – can be tricky: for instance, what are they in *profits wiped out*?

This is a systematic but not necessarily pedestrian approach that students can apply for themselves:

1 Identify the two terms of the comparison, A and B.
2 Identify the characteristics of A and B that are relevant.
3 Check that your interpretation makes sense in the context.

Irony

Irony is chiefly a problem of pragmatics rather than lexis. The words may be simple, but the way the writer uses them is not. The difficulty is the mismatch between the apparent meaning and the writer's underlying intention.

Word attack is involved when irony hangs upon a single word. Colin Turnbull (Appendix A Text 8), writing about the death of a child, is expressing despair, not admiration, when he says the parents 'even' pulled stones over the child's body. The reader who does not pick up this mood might mistakenly believe that the writer approves of what was done.

Irony is one of the most difficult uses of language. The only way to handle it seems to be at the level of a whole text, since interpretation depends on assessment of the writer's attitude from other evidence in the text. It is probably best dealt with as examples arise in texts used for other purposes.

Other kinds of difficulty

Two other categories, ***text-structuring words*** and ***pin-down words***, are dealt with in Chapter 6 (p92) because they are involved in textual cohesion. Pin-down words, often abstract in meaning, also offer difficulties that are lexical in nature.

A note about synonyms and antonyms

Fondness for lists of these seems to be a characteristic of students. The problem here is not the words themselves (almost any word can fall into one or other category in some context), but the attitude to them, which is encouraged by rubrics like *Choose the word that means the same ...*

The point is that two words rarely do mean exactly the same (*I am determined, you are stubborn, he is pig-headed*). The writer probably selected with care the alternative she thought most appropriate. So a sophisticated reader looks for distinctions between words rather than – or at least as well as – similarities.

Students, especially if they hope to appreciate works of literature, need to understand what difference it makes if we say A rather than B, and therefore, why the writer chose the alternative she did.

Word attack skills

Now we must turn to some ways of dealing with these difficulties. Reducing the scale of the problem by ignoring inessential words (as described above) is a first step. Next, the students must acquire strategies for dealing with the lexical items that really block comprehension. We shall discuss three: the interpretation of structural clues (both syntactical and morphological); inference from context; and the use of the dictionary.

Structural clues

One of the most useful word attack skills is the ability to use structural information to assign meaning to a word. Two kinds of information are relevant:

1 The grammatical function of the word: its place in the sentence.
2 The morphology of the word: its internal structure.

Structural clues: grammatical function

By looking at the position of a word in a sentence, we can establish at least its grammatical category (whether it is a noun, verb, etc). This tells us the kind of meaning to look for and is thus a first step on the road to understanding. Try Activity 5.2, working with colleagues if possible, before reading the discussion below.

Activity 5.2 *Establishing grammatical function: sploony urdles*

Consider this sentence: *The sploony urdle departed.*

1 How many questions can you devise to check 'understanding' of this sentence?
2 Think of three real words that might replace *urdle* in this context. Think of three words that could NOT replace *urdle* without violating the grammaticality of the sentence.
3 For each suggested substitute for *urdle*, think of two possible meanings for *sploony* that would fit the context.

How did you start to make sense of this? Perhaps – even if you did not express it in grammatical terms – you worked it out like this:

1 Either *sploony* or *urdle* must be a noun, because the gap between *the* and a verb is always filled with a noun.
2 *Sploony* looks like an adjective, because *-y* is a common adjective suffix; in that case, *urdle* is the noun.
3 If *sploony* were the noun, *urdle* would also be a noun, because
a only a noun or an adverb could occur in that position (experiment with other sentences to prove that to yourself);
b it is unlikely to be an adverb, as those which could occur in that position either end in *-ly* or belong to a familiar restricted set (*soon, then*, etc).

Explaining this process is laborious, but you probably did not find it particularly difficult to do. Most students beyond the elementary level can identify grammatical categories in this way, even if they cannot explain how they do it. Having done it, they can ask and answer questions like 'What sort of an urdle was it?' 'What did the urdle do?' 'Who/what departed?' and so on. They do not know what an urdle is, but they have identified *urdle* as a noun and are a little nearer to understanding the sentence.

But we know more about the urdle than this. People tend to offer words like *man, train, cow*, as replacements; they do not offer words like *wall, tree, theory*, because these rarely, if ever, collocate with *depart*. The point is that the choice is not completely random; the options are constrained by the meaning of *depart*. And other grammatical categories (adjective, article, conjunction, etc) are ruled out because they cannot be used in this position.

When you moved on to suggest replacements for *sploony*, you were even more constrained, now more by semantics than by grammar; the choice of adjectives for this slot was by no means random and may have been very narrow, depending on the meaning you proposed for *urdle*.

This activity shows that, although we may not be able to fix the exact meaning of an unknown word, the structure constrains the possible meanings, which may, when we consider the context, turn out to be quite limited. It is easy to demonstrate this to students, by preparing exercises similar to Activity 5.2 or by making use of the opportunities offered by new words in class. Using structural clues then becomes another strategy for dealing with difficult text.

It is useful for students to be able to label the grammatical categories (*verb, noun*, etc). What is essential is that they should be able to disentangle the structure. Getting them to devise and answer questions – like the questions you asked about the urdle – is a good way of checking that they have grasped the structure. This should be done before establishing the meaning of the new item: the purpose at this stage is to demonstrate its part in the structural pattern – its structural meaning, not its lexical meaning.

Identifying the grammatical function of a lexical item is an important preliminary, which sometimes enables the reader to understand the text sufficiently for his purpose. In any case, it ensures that inappropriate meanings can be dismissed and, when an appropriate meaning is established, it can be slotted straight into its place.

Structural clues: morphology

The morphology or internal structure of a word may offer valuable clues to its meaning, so it is well worth learning something about it. In English, this involves the study of affixation, and of the ways in which compound words are built; maybe also of the way phrasal verbs are put together.

You can start making students aware of affixes as soon as they meet the simple ones such as *UNhappy, teachER, DISagree, examinATION*. However, unless you approve of learning uncontextualized lists, organized study must be postponed until they have a reasonable vocabulary.

Serious work can begin when students have a big enough vocabulary to provide other examples of the same affix (*UNwilling, UNkind, UNwrap*, etc) and of bases (ie the words or parts of words to which affixes are attached: *willing, kind, wrap*, etc). Students need to know which affixes can combine with what bases, which affixes can co-occur (*UNwillingNESS, DISagreeMENT*, etc), what changes in spelling or pronunciation occur when affixes are added, and so on. An analytical approach to morphology pays big dividends in enabling students to work out the meaning of new words.

Some recipes for exercises follow; others can be found in some of the books listed in the *Further reading* section at the end of the chapter.

1 Supply an affix (eg *UN-*) and a number of bases (eg *happy, slow, tidy*).
Task: Indicate or find out from a dictionary which of the bases can take the affix.

2 Supply a base (eg *sharp*) and several affixes (eg *UN-, -LY, -EN, -MENT, -NESS*).
Task: Indicate/find out which of the affixes the base can take.

3 Supply a list of affixes of similar function (eg the adjective-forming suffixes *-FUL, -OUS, -Y, -ISH*) and a list of bases.
Task: Indicate/find out which basewords take which affixes, and if more than one is possible, what variations in meaning are involved (eg *manful, mannish, manly*).

4 Supply an incomplete table of forms consisting of basewords with various affixes.
Task: Complete the table by filling the gaps. Here is an example.

1	2	3	4
educate	education	educable	ineducable
....	variation	....	....
....	....	observable	....
define	....	....	....
....	....	....	unpronounceable
....	....	recognizable	....

5 Supply sentences containing words of a particular form, eg verbs.
Task: Rewrite the sentences in a specified way entailing the use of a different form of the given word (eg nouns instead of verbs), for example:

Fill in each blank with a noun related to the verb in the preceding sentence.

a The enemy *attacked* at dawn.
The .... was completely unexpected. (*attack*)

b They *bombarded* the walls with cannons.
The .... finally gave them the chance to scale the wall. (*bombardment*)

c The city was *destroyed*.
The .... of the city caused the deaths of 15 000 inhabitants. (*destruction*)

There is a finite set of affixes and many of them are highly productive (ie a great many words can be produced by means of them). Hence they repay study. Studying affixes also requires the study of bases; but roots are a different matter. In English, many words (especially in academic terminology) contain roots which cannot stand alone, for example *educ-* (or *-duc-*) in the words *education, educator*, etc.

How far students need to know such roots depends on their field of study. For instance, a biology student might find it useful to understand the meaning of *cyt*, as in *cytoplasm, cytology, leucocyte*. But students who rarely encounter these words would do better to treat each as a whole.

Nevertheless, the relationship between words like *edible, edibility, inedible* can still be recognized, without troubling to identify the root: as long as *edible* is understood, the others can also be interpreted. Students can practice deducing the meaning of an affix (or a root, if worthwhile) by studying well-known words in which it occurs; what they find out for themselves will be better remembered.

As well as investigating the structure of ***complex*** words (ie those produced by affixation), students need to understand the patterns of ***compound*** words, those formed by combining two normally independent words, such as *software, gunsmith, painstaking, second-hand, spoon-feed, dry-clean*. It is worth drawing attention to compounds encountered in texts, because the meaning can often be worked out from the meanings of the component parts. It is also worth studying the ways they are formed, as patterns that are permissible in one language may be impossible in another: it is important to distinguish a *houseplant* from a *planthouse*, for instance.

Inference from context

A structural approach, while valuable, may not deliver enough meaning for the reader's purpose. In order to arrive at a more satisfactory interpretation of unfamiliar words, the reader needs to make use of the context. Inferring meaning is a skill we all have in our L1. We learnt most of our L1 vocabulary by using it: meeting the spoken words frequently and in situations that we understood, we gradually assimilated their meanings. Later, when we met in books words that we had not previously met in the spoken language, we sometimes used a dictionary. But as experienced L1 readers, we have learnt from reading a great many words that we never looked up in a dictionary and never had explained to us. We did this by getting a rough idea of a word's meaning from the context in which it occurred; and with every subsequent occurrence, the meaning became more precise. Activity 5.3 gives an example of how the process works. Have a piece of paper ready before you start.

Activity 5.3 *Accumulating meaning: tock*

Cover the numbered sentences below with a piece of paper. Now read them one at a time. After you have read the first one, make a note of what information you have about the meaning of the word *tock*. Then go on to find out how much more you know after reading sentence 2, and so on.

1 She poured the water into a tock.
2 Then, lifting the tock, she drank.
3 Unfortunately, as she was setting it down again, the tock slipped from her hand and broke.
4 Only the handle remained in one piece.

You no doubt completed this easily, partly because you are an experienced reader, partly because the word was a simple one, partly because the sentences were devised for the purpose. (The way you may have processed the information is demonstrated on p73.) In real-life reading, inference may not be so straightforward, and not all readers are good at it, even when reading their L1; but it can certainly be developed by training.

The best readers do not need to make much use of this strategy, because their vocabulary is sufficient for their purpose. But for less fluent students, conscious use of inference is invaluable: by using it, they can get a meaning – not necessarily completely accurate, but enough for their purpose. Many students are not aware that they can understand new words without being told what they mean. So the first thing is to demonstrate that it is possible. After that, you can encourage students to adopt a positive attitude ('I can work it out if I try') instead of the negative one ('Help! Where's the dictionary?') they instinctively adopt.

Learning to use inference

Students who can infer meaning from context have a powerful aid to comprehension and will ultimately read more quickly. Learning how to infer can, moreover, be enjoyable. Its problem-solving character appeals to most people and it challenges students to make use of their intelligence.

You could begin by using sentences with nonsense words, like the ones about the tock (p72). It is easy to show students that they can get a good deal of information from the sentence, even though they do not fully understand it.

A second step might be to get students to suggest what range of words could complete a sentence such as *In order to repair the car, I shall need* ... Ridiculous suggestions (a glass of milk, a camera, a comb) and borderline ones (a plastic bag, a piece of string) can be discussed. You can consider what difference it would make if you knew what was wrong with the car, and so on. The students will begin to recognize that the possibilities are not limitless; turned on its head, they can later use this recognition when they try to work out the meaning of a word from its context.

This kind of activity requires us to make use of schemata – in this case, schemata concerning cars and repair activities. Because we have certain expectations about repairing cars, we know that some things are more likely than others to be referred to in discussing car repairs. Our knowledge of the world helps us to narrow down the possibilities when we are looking for a concept to fill a gap in the sense.

The next step is to show that this fact (that possible fillers for a slot in a given sentence are limited) enables us to work out the sort of thing an unknown word must mean, by carefully considering its context. You could find suitable passages from real texts, or you can use nonsense word sentences again, for the initial stages. Write the sentences on the board one at a time, or mask them with a sheet of paper which can be gradually removed. An overhead projector would be ideal for this.

An example is the 'tock' sentences on p72. This extract illustrates how one teacher handled the activity; she asks a few leading questions and the students do most of the work.

Q: What can we learn from sentence 1?
A: That a tock can hold water? (Probably – but what about a sieve? Would you say *poured into a sieve*, or *through a sieve?* etc.)
Q: Suggestions?
A: A bucket – a bowl – a hole, etc.
Q: Do we know what she was pouring from? How would it affect our ideas about what a tock might be if she was pouring from a bucket? a kettle? a test tube? etc.

Q: How does sentence 2 narrow down the possibilities?
A: We know a tock can be lifted (so it isn't a hole, for instance) and that it can be drunk from.
Q: Do we know whether it is intended to be drunk from?
A: No. Perhaps she's drinking from a shell – a hat – some other makeshift container in an emergency.

Q: What new information do we get from sentence 3?
A: We know a tock is fragile – it broke when she dropped it.
Q: All tocks?
A: This tock, anyway.
Q: What might it have been made of?
A: Glass – china – perhaps very thin metal, but unlikely – it would dent rather than break. Clay? Stone? The shell again?

Q: And sentence 4?
A: If it has a handle, it's probably a cup.
Q: Can we exclude a jug? Other things with handles?
A: No, but in the absence of other evidence, we choose what seems the most likely.

The activity shows students how inference works and how the gradual accumulation of evidence enables us to infer the meaning of a word from its context, the way we learn much of our L1 vocabulary. They begin to see that they can consciously use their prior knowledge of the world when they are stuck over a word. However, a couple of words of caution are needed.

First, the slow progress from one sentence to the next is not intended to model an ideal way of reading; this needs to be pointed out. You can in fact use the experience of doing the activity to demonstrate the advantages of not spending too long puzzling over one sentence; a good reader reads on quickly, both to collect more clues and to make sure an inference is supported by all the evidence: 'Think of all the time we wasted on sentence 1 when there were so many valuable clues in later sentences!'

Second, it also needs to be said that inference is about probabilities, not certainties. It would be wrong to believe that sentence 4 'proves' that *tock* = *cup*. It is important for students to understand that for many purposes, a rough idea of the meaning is all we need; the demand for a hundred per cent certainty is what drives them to their dictionaries. It depends on our purpose, and on how crucial the word is to the text.

The more often we meet a word, the more exact our understanding of it becomes, so that probabilities gradually turn into certainties without our being aware of it. This is the reason why some people advocate using in the classroom longer texts, or texts on similar topics; the chances of vocabulary being repeated, and hence assimilated as a result of frequent encounters, are obviously greater than if you use short texts on a variety of topics. For ESP courses, this has much to recommend it; even for classes with greater divergence of interests, it is worth trying. But the quantity of repetition needed means that we must rely mostly on the extensive reading programme to provide such exposure.

Recipes for exercises

Convincing students that it is possible to infer meaning is an important first step. After that, activities similar to those already described can be used. The variations that follow use a multiple choice format, so that students do not have to rely completely on their own resources. However, this is intended only for the initial stages of training. Subsequently, similar exercises with no alternatives supplied will help students to move towards independent use of this strategy.

1 Supply one or more short texts in which a repeated key word is replaced by a nonsense word. The task is to choose the best real word to replace the nonsense word; any multiple choice alternatives must be words familiar to the students. For example:

Read the text and decide what the word *flet* means. Choose the best answer.

Flet means:

a shadow **b** reflection **c** colour **d** spectrum **e** rainbow

Flets are solar spectra formed as sunlight passes through drops of water. Flets may be seen when a hose is adjusted to a fine spray. The drops act like prisms, refracting sunlight to produce the spectrum. A single, or primary, flet has red on the outside, violet inside. Its arc, 40 degrees in radius, is always on a line with the observer and the sun. When you see a flet, the sun is behind you. Sometimes a secondary flet forms outside the primary. It is fainter, with colours reversed – red inside, violet outside. The secondary flet is formed from light reflected twice within drops.

(Answer: **e**)

---

2 Supply a text/texts including an unfamiliar key word. Offer a choice of explanations/definitions, adjusted to the students' level. The task is to eliminate the explanations not supported by the text. Example:

A coelacanth is a kind of living fossil, first discovered when one was caught off Madagascar in 1938.
A coelacanth is a kind of **a** rock; **b** plant; **c** fish; **d** animal. (Answer: **c**)
Clues: *living* (not a rock), *caught* (not a plant), *off Madagascar* (in the sea?), **d** is possible but less likely

3 Longer texts provide more evidence for inferences. This example (from University of Malaya *Reading for Academic Study*) advises students to read the whole text before attempting to choose the answers; they must learn to look beyond the immediate environment for evidence.

1 Some of the green plants we have mentioned live on the land and others *dwell* in the waters of the earth, but usually live fairly close to the surface where they are in contact with the all-important sunlight.
a live **b** fight **c** breathe
2 The purple sulphur bacteria and the chemosynthetic bacteria, on the other hand, *are inhabitants of* swampy and marshy areas.
a live in **b** cannot be found in **c** do not live in
3 All other organisms are directly or indirectly dependent upon them for their *sustenance*.
a homes **b** food **c** air
4 The bacteria paramecia, for instance, are eaten by tiny fish and crustaceans and the crustaceans, in turn, may be *devoured* by small fish.
a chased **b** protected **c** eaten

(Answers: **1a**, **2a**, **3b**, **4c**)

This type of exercise, if you use a multiple choice format, can be readily adapted for use on a computer.

Students (particularly if they are going to work on their own) must understand that 'succeeding' in these activities means learning how to think, not just choosing the correct answer. This becomes crucial when the multiple choice format is discarded. The key ingredient is discussion in the classroom, in which students cite evidence and compare plausible alternatives. This mirrors the kind of critical thinking they must do when working alone; it helps if they work with others outside the class, so that similar discussion can be maintained.

Clues and lexical density

In order to infer meaning from context, we must have clues. So lexical inference will not help readers with all the difficult words. If the context does not offer enough clues, inference is impossible. Students need to be aware of this, and teachers too; it is unproductive, as well as unfair, to give exercises where the clues are too few to make any but the most trivial inferences possible.

This becomes an important issue when, after training along the lines suggested, you move on to practise with any text you happen to be using in the reading class. When you prepare to deal with a new text, instead of assuming that all important new words must be taught in advance, set aside those which you can use for further practice in inference. For each selected item, check:

- that there are enough clues to make inference possible. Clues can be inserted, but most texts contain enough suitable items without this;
- that the other new words in the text will not interfere with the attempt to work out the meaning.

The second point relates to the ***lexical density*** of the text, that is, the proportion of new words it contains. If the sentence containing the item for inference also contains several other new words, or if the whole text is very difficult, the accumulation of uncertainty may be too great for inferences to be drawn.

Using a dictionary

I said earlier that students should be discouraged from using dictionaries. But this is only because the usual tendency is to use them far too often. It is essential for them to realize that they can cope without one, and that it is wasteful to look up every new word, but any students reading for a serious study purpose need to be able to look up key words. So they must learn to use a dictionary effectively and with discretion.

The first step towards using the dictionary as a tool instead of a crutch is to decide which words to look up – and to accept that they should be as few as possible. Having decided to look up a word, we want to do it quickly and to make the best use of the information in the dictionary. Both skills need training.

Some students take ages to find a word in the dictionary; this is particularly likely if their L1 does not use the same alphabet as the foreign language. Exercises on alphabetical order, and on using the guide words at the head of each page, will help. Even practice in opening the dictionary as nearly as possible at the right page is useful. Such exercises can often be done as races.

Dictionaries vary, so students need to be familiar with the kind of information offered by their own. As far as reading is concerned, by far the most important is the semantic information, together with examples if any. Practice is needed in selecting, from several meanings offered, the one that is relevant to the given text. It is easy to devise multiple choice exercises along these lines, either asking students to choose from several different definitions for a word in a short text, or to match definitions with several short texts each containing what looks like the same word.

Continual insistence on the use of this skill is needed. This means you should make frequent use of the dictionary in class (even though it is quicker to give the meaning yourself); and that it should be the students, not you, who select the appropriate definition.

A note on phonics for EFL readers

Phonics (not to be confused with phonetics) is the study of the relationship between sounds and spellings, particularly the regularities that help readers to identify words. For instance, a child can use phonics to work out that *b-a-t* means *bat*, because the letters represent their most common sounds; but phonics is no help in reading *eye*, where there is no correspondence between the letters and their usual sounds.

Even in English, despite its irregularities, there are many regular sound–spelling correspondences. They are described and exemplified in books for teachers of reading to English-speaking children, although some teachers consider that they are not useful, because the many rules and exceptions confuse children.

The question for us is whether phonic rules can help foreign language readers to identify unfamiliar words. The use of phonics assumes that once readers know how a word is pronounced, they will associate it with the spoken word and therefore understand it. But from the intermediate stage at least, the new words that students meet in texts are usually not words they have already heard spoken. So working out how a word might be pronounced is not going to result in understanding.

For these reasons, I do not think phonics can help EFL learners to identify new lexical items. No doubt many readers want to be able to pronounce the words they meet, but this is a different issue and (given the complexities of phonics) they would do better to use the phonetic symbols in their dictionary.

Phonics may be helpful in the initial stages of English reading, although people whose first language is written with great phonic regularity may find it difficult to adjust to the irregularity of English. In general, students will find it more useful to concentrate on meaning in context, rather than on pronunciation.

Further reading

On vocabulary in TEFL, see McCarthy 1990 for lucid and thorough coverage, including suggestions for teaching, and Nation 1990. Carter 1987a surveys work up to that date. Also useful are Carter 1987b; Carter and McCarthy 1988, and Nation and Carter 1989.

Tomlinson 1991 surveys some recent teaching materials; particularly worth looking at are Harmer and Rossner 1991 and McCarthy and O'Dell 1994. Gairns and Redman 1986 and Morgan and Rinvolucri 1986 are also very useful.

Several publishers of dictionaries offer workbooks to help learners to use them: see eg Fox and Kirkby 1987; McAlpin 1988; Owen 1989. Some publishers provide free worksheets and practice leaflets: it is worth enquiring.

On word formation in English, see Quirk et al 1985, Appendix 1; and Collins Cobuild 1993.

Chapter 6
Reading for plain sense

THIS chapter is about how we establish the *plain sense* of what we read, and will focus mainly on how to use bottom-up strategies – paying close attention to language, especially syntax and cohesion – to interpret difficult text. Chapter 7 is about how we establish the *value* of what we read – why the writer has said it – using mainly top-down strategies.

In some respects, the skills of reading for plain sense are the basic ones: we can't get far without them. But it does not follow that when we start reading, we use them first. In fact, it makes sense to start by using a top-down approach: first, activating all the prior knowledge you can about the topic and the type of text, and second, skimming to get a rough idea of the content and structure. This should give you an idea of the context and the general direction of the argument or narrative: an eagle's eye view of the text which will be invaluable if you later lose your way.

If the top-down approach does not throw enough light on the meaning, you use the bottom-up one. This involves getting to grips with the syntax and so on, making use of top-down insights to weigh up competing interpretations. Finally, arriving at a possible interpretation of the text, you assess its plausibility using top-down means.

The skills in this chapter are for the getting-to-grips stage of this sequence. They are sometimes complex and can seem tedious out of context. But approaching 'heavy text' in a spirit of problem-solving can be intellectually stimulating. In any case, many readers cannot choose their texts; however difficult, they have to cope.

It has to be faced that understanding texts is closely associated with understanding syntax. The reading lesson is not the place for extensive grammar teaching, but reading does require grammatical skills. When faced with a text whose meaning they cannot untangle, students must be able to identify the constituents of its sentences – the subject, verb and so on – and to analyse these if they are complex. How to label constituents is up to you; grammatical terminology is not essential but helps to clarify one's thinking.

Unless you are going to wash your hands of the problem, you will have to find ways of helping students to deal with heavy texts. The tasks suggested here may not suit everyone, but they work for many students, and there are no easy options.

Text attack skill 1: understanding syntax

Warning to readers
This section is DIFFICULT! It will make better sense if you first make a serious attempt to do Activity 6.1. If you do not wish to do this, skip it and move on to text attack skill 2 (p86).

Long sentences and difficult syntax can block comprehension even when vocabulary is familiar. To remind yourself of the problems, try Activity 6.1, to which we shall refer frequently in subsequent discussion. Attempt each step before moving on to the next and assess which steps helped you to understand the text. Note down any other means you used to improve your comprehension. The experience will be much more productive if you can work with colleagues.

Activity 6.1 *Dealing with heavy text*

The paragraph below (sentence numbers added) is from the introduction to a book on the role of intonation and how it should be taught. The authors have earlier explained that most manuals describe various intonation features and their effects on meaning in various contexts. Instead of this piecemeal and complex approach, they hope in this book to provide a more generalizable and coherent description of how intonation affects meaning, mainly by presenting pairs of utterances which are different in meaning but, except for their intonation, identical in form. The authors consider that a full understanding of the intonation meaning system is essential only for teachers.

Read the paragraph straight through, quickly, to get the gist. Then follow the instructions below. Work with colleagues if possible.

> **1** We hope that two features of our approach might make it especially acceptable to teachers. **2** One is that by describing the meaning system in terms that have general validity we provide the teacher with analytic tools to handle the authentic spoken material, however complex, which he judges suitable for a particular learner or group of learners. **3** By contrast, existing partial descriptions, and the highly specific values they tend to ascribe to intonation features, inevitably engender disappointment and frustration when they are applied to material other than the set of items the manual writers invent to exemplify them, while speech produced spontaneously and in real time almost always presents problems for which earlier systematic work has provided no preparation. **4** Earlier descriptions, and teaching materials based on them, have tended to oversimplify to the point of falsification. **5** While there are certainly good pedagogical reasons for beginning to give conscious attention to intonation in connection with utterances where there is a fairly predictable relationship between tidy syntactic forms on the one hand and phonological forms on the other, a teaching programme must surely visualise an eventual need to confront the far more interesting cases where the relationship between the two modes of linguistic organisation runs counter to what, on probabilistic grounds, we would expect. **6** It is in precisely such cases that existing accounts of intonation are lacking.
>
> From **Brazil D.**, **Coulthard M.** and **Johns C.** 1980 *Discourse Intonation and Language Teaching*. Harlow: Longman

Complete steps 1 and 2 below without rereading the text. If you cannot complete them, go on to question 3.

1 **Try to predict, in general terms, what the topic of the next paragraph is likely to be.** If you think you can, what clues did you use?
2 **Try to summarize the main message of the text.** Compare your attempt with those of others if possible. Then go on to step 3.
3 Most people find 1 and 2 difficult. Yet the vocabulary is probably familiar. To check this, **reread the text, underlining any unfamiliar words.** (I predict not more than five. The rest of the task will be more difficult for you if your total exceeds that, but attempt it anyway. Check the meaning of any unfamiliar items if you wish.)

If vocabulary is not the problem, what is? Steps **4–6** should help you to answer this. Even if you could do **1** and **2**, complete the rest of the steps to identify the kind of problems some readers have, and to check that your own interpretation was accurate.

4 Without returning to the text, **organize in your mind or on paper all the ideas you have formed about its overall message. Then formulate all the questions which you think the text is trying to answer** (eg *What are the authors hoping to achieve? How does this manual differ from previous ones?*).
5 **Now reread the text, to see if it provides answers to the questions you formulated and to check your general impression of its message and clarify it if necessary.** This may help you to complete steps **1** and **2** more satisfactorily. Repeat steps 4 and 5 as often as you like if this approach is helpful.
6 If you still feel unsure about the message, this step may help. **Reread the text, sentence by sentence, and check that you have grasped the plain sense of each sentence before going on to the next.** Refer to the text as often as you wish. Try using the 'Nation approach' (see pp82–6) for sentences that prove difficult. Return to earlier steps when you feel ready to do so.

What did you learn from Activity 6.1? It was intended to set you thinking about the difficulties readers encounter and to consider ways of solving them. The text is from a book written for teachers, but you may be cheered to know that English L1 teachers (including me) find it difficult. The tasks were designed to give you a learning experience about tackling difficult texts, not to test your reading (and certainly not to increase your knowledge of intonation teaching). What you learnt depends on your attitude (the task infuriates some people) and your previous knowledge of the topic, as well as your competence as a reader and your level of English.

Understanding the syntactic problems that can arise should help you to help the students, so before you read on, reflect on (and discuss if possible) what was difficult for you. The activity presented one possible sequence of steps for approaching difficult text; was it helpful? We will discuss what you did; as you read on, evaluate the usefulness of each step for your own reading; the aim for the reader is indicated by **R**. The activity also had aims for you as a teacher, indicated by **T**. The whole process was intended to give you experience to draw on when helping students to tackle equally difficult text.

Step 1: **Aims** ***R*** *To predict how this paragraph fits into the wider text*
T *To recognize that this can be difficult to do*

Trying to predict what comes next is a good way of seeing whether you have a clear top-down view of the text. You were asked to do this without rereading, specifically to see how clear a view of the argument you got after a single reading. It is often possible to make a good guess, but here you probably found it difficult. The task is a bit unfair, as the strongest clue is in the opening sentences (S1, S2): the next paragraph in fact goes on to discuss the second feature of the approach.

Step 2: **Aims** ***R*** *To get a top-down view of the text*
T *To show that it is difficult to get the gist of heavy text*

You were asked to do this, too, without rereading. Summarizing is an excellent way to clarify your top-down view of a text. The T aim is to find out how much it was possible to grasp after a single reading: in a reasonably accessible text, you should have got the gist. Did you manage to provide a summary without rereading? (If not, you are like most of the people who have attempted this.) If you did, how accurate did it prove to be, on further reading? If your summary was satisfactory, the further steps were redundant for you; but other readers may have found them useful. Discuss if possible.

Step 3: **Aims** ***R*** *To check whether there are any lexical barriers to comprehension*
T *To show that vocabulary is not the only source of difficulty*

At this point, you counted the new words. Probably you did not find many; in that case, if you found the text difficult, the reason must lie elsewhere. Part of the problem is lack of context, but not all paragraphs out of context are hard to read. The main difficulty is the complex syntax of the long sentences; there are many subordinate clauses and phrases and several 'nested' constructions (modifiers which are themselves modified, etc).

Step 4: **Aims** ***R*** *To identify gaps in the message received after one reading*
T *To show that this process makes a rereading more purposeful and effective*

In this step you organized your ideas about the text's message, and focused subsequent rereading by asking yourself questions which you thought the text might answer. Did this preparation help you to understand better? If not, what did help?

Step 5: **Aims** ***R*** *To fill in the gaps shown up at Step 4*
T *To show that a focused rereading improves overall understanding*

After completing this step, you should have had a clearer top-down view of the text. This may have enabled you to complete Steps 1 and 2, suggesting that the overall message has been understood. But if some parts of the text remained baffling, you needed either to repeat Steps 4 and 5, or to go on to Step 6.

Step 6: **Aims** ***R*** *To unravel the syntax of problem sentences*
T *To show one method of dealing with complex syntax*

Step 6 requires you to adopt an analytical approach to problem sentences. You would use it if earlier top-down approaches failed. The 'Nation approach' (see below, p82) is troublesome to describe because it looks so complex and long-winded (as the key demonstrates). But it is not really too difficult if you work steadily through the sentence, unravelling each difficulty as you get to it. Use it orally in class to familiarize students with the approach and train them to think analytically.

Treat these six steps as one possible approach to difficult text; as you have seen, satisfactory performance at Step 2 means that you need not follow the remaining steps; the same is true of Step 5. Hence Step 6 is often unnecessary.

If you found the text straightforward, the activity has probably not served to remind you of the difficulties for students; in that case, beware of underrating their problems, and take other steps to find out what these are. One way would be to work through the activity with one or two advanced students, getting them to 'think aloud' about the difficulties and discussing each step. Or set yourself a similar task with a text you do find difficult (but not for lexical reasons) and monitor your own procedures for understanding it.

By reflecting on your own performance, you can find out which steps are helpful to you. Perhaps you have found other ways of tackling the difficulties, which you can pass on to your students. Different readers prefer different strategies; your teaching needs to take account of this.

Simplifying sentences

The text in Activity 6.1 contains many examples of the structural complexity that can paralyse unconfident readers. If you found Step 6 necessary – that is, if earlier readings did not enable you to interpret the text plausibly – an analytic approach is unavoidable. The procedure suggested here derives from Nation 1979 and is more tedious to describe than to use, but it does require concentrated effort.

The principle is to remove all the optional parts of the sentence systematically until only the essentials remain and the bare structure of the sentence is clear. Then you can restore the optional elements one by one, fitting them into the structure so that you can make sense of them. After doing this with every problem sentence, you can combine the sentence meanings and work out the overall message of the text. This is real bottom-up work.

Each step in the procedure is described below, illustrated by reference to the text in Activity 6.1 when possible. For a fuller illustration turn to the answer key under Activity 6.1, where sentence 3 of the text on intonation teaching is analysed.

1 Identify the cohesive elements and find out what each refers to.

Cohesion, including reference, is explained below (text attack skill 2, p86); when you have identified the cohesive elements, ask questions such as 'Who/what?' 'What sort?' to establish what each refers to. For example, in S2 you would ask 'One what?' and find the answer 'One of the features of our approach'. In addition to predictable reference words (eg *they, one, the [manual writers], such*) it is important to look for other words which require you to go beyond the sentence in order to make sense of them. Examples are *by contrast* (S3) [What items are contrasted?], *descriptions* (S3, S4) [Descriptions of what?] *earlier* (S4) [What is earlier than what?]

2 Rewrite the sentence as two or more sentences by removing co-ordinating conjunctions such as *and, but, or*.

The co-ordinating conjunctions in the sample text join not clauses but noun groups (eg *a particular learner or group of learners*; *disappointment and frustration*) and are unlikely to offer difficulty. But in some texts, it is hard to determine which items are joined: single words, phrases or clauses, for example:

> He looked at the child with surprise that he should know such words at his age and indignation that he should be permitted to use them.

Here the item that parallels *indignation* is not *age* (as a careless reader might assume) nor *words*, but *surprise*. The parallel items are:

> A surprise that he should know such words at his age
> B indignation that he should be permitted to use them

Both items stand in the same relation to the first part of the sentence:

> He looked at the child with A.
> He looked at the child with B.

Rewriting may help to make this clear.

3 Find the nouns and remove any items following them which are part of the same noun group.

Nouns are important because they are often essential sentence constituents (eg subject, object). A noun group consists of a head noun modified by adjectives or other words which may precede (*two FEATURES, authentic spoken MATERIAL, a fairly predictable RELATIONSHIP*) or follow it. Generally the post-modifiers (those that follow) give most trouble. There are several examples in the sample text, eg *FEATURES of our approach; MATERIAL, however complex; VALUES they tend to ascribe to intonation features.*

This noun group from S5 demonstrates the potential problems:

> ... good pedagogical REASONS for beginning to give conscious attention to intonation in connection with utterances where there is a fairly predictable relationship between tidy syntactic forms on the one hand and phonological forms on the other ...

The head noun is *reasons*; the rest of the quotation consists of its modifiers. This example is particularly complex because the post-modifier includes various phrases/clauses nested inside each other, including noun groups (each modifying a noun in the preceding phrase/clause) with head nouns *beginning, attention, intonation, utterances, relationship.*

Students need to learn what kinds of post-modifiers occur (prepositional, infinitive or participial phrase, adjective clause, noun in apposition, adjective), eg by means of bracketing and labelling activities. Knowing what structures to expect equips readers to analyse those that occur in texts which give them trouble.

4 Search the text for nominalizations and if necessary establish what proposition each implies.

Nominalization is the process of making a noun group out of a clause. In addition to the problems common to all noun groups, nominalizations have some of their own, as this example demonstrates:

> The implementation of the recommendation that child allowances should be restricted to the first three children was delayed for several years.

Here a complex noun group is made more complex by nominalizations. There are two, with head nouns *implementation* and *recommendation*. To unravel the meaning of the sentence, it is helpful to realize that these words conceal unstated propositions:

A Someone recommended that child allowances should be restricted.
B Someone implemented (the recommendation in) A.

These propositions have been turned into noun groups and fitted into the frame *X was delayed*. Once you have worked out the propositions, it is fairly simple to see that B was delayed for several years. In the sample text, there are several nominalizations, for example:

> S2 *describing the meaning system ... validity*
> (relates to the proposition: *we describe the meaning system ... validity*)
> S4 (*to oversimplify to the point of*) *falsification*
> (relates to: *[to oversimplify to the point that] they have falsified [the description]*)
> S5 (*visualise*) *an eventual need to confront*
> (relates to: *[visualise that] eventually it/the students/the teacher will need to confront ...*)

You will notice that in working out the unstated proposition, the reader may have to supply some constituents, such as *we* in the first example, *the description* in the second and *it/the students/the teacher* in the third. The process of working out what these unstated elements are (not always clear, as the last example shows) is an important part of the struggle to understand.

Students must first learn to recognize nominalizations. This is often simple, as most have head nouns derived from verbs, mostly with one of a limited range of familiar suffixes (eg *-ation*, *-ment*, *-ure*), although others (such as *need*) are less obvious. Others may have head nouns related to adjectives, such as *the accuracy of his work* (relates to: *his work is accurate*) or occasionally other complements, eg *her headship* (relates to: *she is the head*).

Having identified them, the procedure for dealing with nominalizations is first, to treat them as other noun groups (as in **3** above) and then:

- work out the underlying proposition (and give it a label – eg A – to use as shorthand, when slotting it into the sentence);
- work out how the proposition fits into the rest of the sentence.

5 Identify the verbs and use the 'Who/what does what?' technique to find the subject/object, etc of each.

To reveal the bare bones of the sentence structure, you need to identify its main verb and any other finite verbs, find their subjects and any objects or complements, and establish the boundaries of each clause. One way to tackle verbs is to ask, about each in turn, 'Who (or what) is (or does) what?' For instance, in S1 there are two finite verbs, *hope* and *might make*. The student will ask 'Who hopes what?' and locate the answers:

> *Who hopes?* 'We', ie the authors.
> *What do they hope?* That two features might make their approach acceptable.

The verb *hope* needs something to complete its meaning; commonly, as here, a clause explaining the hoped-for situation. Having recognized this, the student must then establish the structure of this clause by asking 'Who or what might make what?' This exposes further complexity:

> *What might make (something)?* Two features (of the authors' approach).
> *Might make what?* Might make it (the approach) especially acceptable to teachers.

This verb *make* is not the plain transitive verb (*make a table/mistake*, etc); in addition to its object (*it*), it requires a complement (*especially acceptable to teachers*) to complete the sense. Students need some knowledge of verb patterns – which verbs can or must take an object; which can be followed by an infinitive, and so on – so that they can cope with all kinds of clauses.

All subordinate clauses contribute to sentence complexity; students need to be familiar with their structures and functions. The one in the example is doing the work of a noun: it is the object of *hope*. Noun clauses are particularly troublesome because they are often essential sentence constituents (subject, object, etc), not optional ones as adjective and adverb clauses usually are. This can make it difficult to establish the bare structure of the sentence. The 'What does what?' approach offers the best chance of clarification.

6 If any participle, infinitive or preposition clauses/phrases are still unaccounted for, use the 'Who/what does what?' technique to find out where they fit in.

Participles (*describing, produced*) and infinitives (*to handle, to ascribe*) can occur in non-finite clauses; these often function as modifiers (and are thus optional elements of sentence structure). For example:

tools to handle the authentic spoken material ... learners
invent to exemplify them
speech produced spontaneously and in real time
teaching materials based on them

But sometimes the clause is an obligatory element (*tended* ***to oversimplify to the point of falsification***). And of course non-finite clauses can function as nominal groups, and thus can be subjects, objects, etc:

Eating people is wrong.
I don't like having my hair washed.
To work part-time would suit her better.

In such cases, the clause is dealt with like other noun groups (see **3** above). Non-finite clauses do not have expressed subjects, though a subject may be understood and it may be important to identify it. For instance, in S2 the unexpressed subject of *describing* is clearly the sentence subject, namely (*we* = the authors); but in S5 the subject of *beginning* has to be inferred: *teachers* or *a teaching programme* or something similar. In other respects non-finite verbs operate like finite verbs, with their own objects, complements and adverbials. Thus non-finite clauses can be lengthy and can contribute to the complexity of the sentence in which they occur.

Phrases dependent on prepositions may also be lengthy, and it is sometimes difficult to know where to attach them. Those which are part of a noun group (eg *features* ***of our approach***; *relationship* ***between the two modes of linguistic organization***) will be taken care of by the procedures in **3** above. Others modify adjectives or verbs (*suitable* ***for a particular learner***; *oversimplify* ***to the point of falsification***).

The procedure to adopt for all unaccounted-for phrases/clauses includes:

a Check which instances of *to* are prepositions and which belong to infinitives. Then proceed to **b** or **e** below.

Preposition phrases

b Check if any words in the text regularly go with a preposition (eg *acceptable TO, provide WITH, suitable FOR, base ON*), or whether a fixed expression is involved (eg *BY contrast, TO the point of ..., IN connection WITH, ON the one hand*).

c For other prepositions, find out if they join two nouns (*group OF learners, attention TO intonation*) and if so link them.

d Deal with other preposition phrases ad hoc, seeking to find out what words they modify. A variation of the 'What does what?' approach seems useful: ask 'What *[PREPOSITION]* what?' and give the simplest answer possible, leaving out modifiers, etc. For example, in S2 ask 'What *BY* what?' and formulate an answer along the lines of 'We provide the teacher with [something] *BY* describing the meaning system [in a certain way].'

Non-finite clauses

e Work out the unstated subject of the non-finite verb, and identify any objects and complements by using the 'Who/what does what?' technique. Remove any optional modifiers which the clause contains.

f Find out whether the clause functions as a modifier, a noun group or another obligatory element (eg part of a verb pattern). Then:

- deal with those acting as modifiers by working out (i) what word(s) are modified; (ii) whether the modifier is optional; if it is, remove it to allow you to establish the bare bones of the sentence;
- deal with those which are noun groups as in **3** on p82–3;
- deal with those functioning in other ways by identifying which words they go with and reducing the clause to [*something*] (eg *tend to [something]*) until you have worked out the main structure.

Complex structures are not necessarily a sign of incompetent or inconsiderate writing. Try to paraphrase them: the result is almost always a much longer text, and its length may actually make it more difficult to process. Moreover, paraphrasing sometimes proves extremely difficult. When the ideas are complex, it is not always possible to avoid complex constructions. Readers have no alternative but to master enough syntax to cope with them.

Text attack skill 2: recognizing and interpreting cohesive devices

We now come to ***cohesion***, that part of grammar that reflects the coherence of the writer's thought and helps the reader to make the right connections between ideas. We shall look at the aspects of cohesion that seem likely to give trouble, or to be helpful, to the reader.

Some ***cohesive devices*** directly affect the signification of a sentence. A sentence that includes ***pro-forms*** (***reference, substitution***) or ***ellipsis*** does not itself offer all the information required to convey its plain sense:

> Pro-forms: He took one immediately. (Who is *he*? What is *one*?)
> Ellipsis: The second was more influential. (The second what? More influential than what?)

There are gaps in the sense (which I shall sometimes indicate by ▲ in the case of ellipsis) which readers must fill by referring to other parts of the text or to their knowledge of the context. When the missing information is identified, we use it to supplement the information actually expressed.

Other cohesive devices include ***lexical cohesion***, which is dealt with here because it often operates in a way similar to reference; and the ***discourse markers***, which are treated separately (text attack skill 3), since their function is very different.

Text attack skill 2 sub-skill 1: interpreting pro-forms

What are pro-forms and why are they used? This sub-skill involves identifying the meanings of words like *it, our, this, those, then, one* (as in *the wrong one*), *so/not* (as in *I think so, it appears not*) and comparatives (*smaller, same, additional, such, other*, etc). The writer uses such words to avoid needless repetition. They signal to the reader: 'You should be able to identify this person, object or idea, because (1) I have referred to it before, or (2) it is something we both take for granted in the context.' The reader retrieves the ***referent*** (the person, etc referred to) from the text, or from the context, including his prior knowledge of the subject.

Problems with interpreting pro-forms

Experienced readers often cannot believe that anyone has difficulty interpreting pro-forms, but a quick check is likely to convince you that many students do have problems. Of course most occurrences cause no difficulty; if the writer is considerate, the referent is easily identifiable. It is the occurrences where it is not easy that make it useful to draw attention to possible misinterpretations. Activity 6.2 illustrates some of the problems.

Activity 6.2 *Interpreting pro-forms*

Identify any sources of possible misinterpretation caused by pro-forms in this text.

> James glared at his brother, took the money from the box and threw it angrily into the fire, where it crackled swiftly into flame. This appeared to amuse him, for he burst out laughing and walked towards the door, which did not improve matters. Mary marvelled that he could be so nonchalant. Surely its loss could not leave him unmoved?

Problem one is that the references are ambiguous. What did James throw into the fire – the box or the money? Who was amused – James or his brother? The text does not say.

The second problem is with *this* and *which*: it is not clear how much of the text they refer to. Presumably 'he' was amused not because the object burst into flame, but because of the whole incident; only a closer knowledge of the context will tell us. Experience of the world suggests that it was not the door that 'did not improve matters', but does not help us decide whether *which* refers only to the second action (walking towards the door) or the whole of the preceding part of the sentence.

Thirdly, what about *its loss*? Presumably *it* refers to the money, or the box, but for some readers the referent is too distant to identify. Similarly, a referent in a complex sentence may be difficult to find because of general uncertainty about the sentence meaning. Finally, since reference may be ***anaphoric*** (looking backwards in the text) or ***cataphoric*** (looking forwards), readers may be unsure where to look for the referent. Usually it is found in the preceding part of the text, which makes it all the more disconcerting when occasionally it follows, as in the first sentence of the next section on this page (*he ... the reader*).

Dealing with pro-forms

Before he can tackle the problem, the reader must recognize that it is the reference word – the pro-form – which is causing it. Since words like *it* and *this* are so common and look so harmless, the first step is to make students take the problem seriously. They are unlikely to do so until confronted with cases – in texts read in class – where they cannot identify the referent.

Once students recognize the source of their trouble, they can take steps to deal with it. They can ask themselves questions along these lines:

> He handed her a letter. This gave her food for thought.
> Q What made her think: the letter, or the fact that he handed it to her?

> Such a contingency must be avoided.
> Q What event is referred to as a contingency? What kind of contingency is it? (ie what features make it one to be avoided?)

In other cases, different rules apply.

Q Other than what? (ie from what case(s) are these cases distinguished?) Different from what? (The text will have described, or at least referred to, these rules.)

The car got a puncture but the spare wheel was nowhere to be found.

Q What spare wheel? (Here a car schema is required – we need to know that cars generally carry a spare wheel.)

The answers to such questions have to be found by searching the text and/or using common sense and knowledge of the context, making use of relevant schemata. It is a good tactic, if you find yourself puzzled by part of a text, to look for pro-forms and ask the kind of questions exemplified above.

Training sub-skill 1

It is not worth preparing many exercises for training this sub-skill, since the point is lost unless each example is located in an extended text. The best way is to draw attention to these reference words whenever the referent is hard to identify. When you begin teaching a new class, part of the settling-in process will be to ask a lot of the kind of questions given above, thus discovering what they find difficult. Then you can analyse the reasons for the difficulty. As soon as possible, restrict questions to cases you predict will be difficult, otherwise the training will seem pointless.

This should be an ongoing activity, but some specific exercises may also be given:

1 Students enjoy making their own questions, searching the text for items to baffle their colleagues. This gives practice in identifying potential problems, a skill they need for tackling texts independently. (This needs to be preceded by studying pro-forms in class, to give some idea of the range of items involved.)

2 Supply a text containing varied pro-forms. Put boxes round suitable items, or number or colour them.
Task: Students find all other items with the same referent as the boxed or numbered item, and identify them by giving them all the same number or colour. (Demonstrate first by working through a text on the OHP or blackboard; see Figure 10 on p89 for an example.)

3 Supply a text with (some) reference items omitted and replaced by gaps. Supply also a list of the omitted items, in random order.
Task: To insert the items in the correct gaps. (More advanced students can manage without the list and supply the items themselves.)

4 Special practice is needed in the use of the words *this* and *which* to relate to an extended idea/event/occurrence, etc (as in Activity 6.2 on p87), which can be expressed only by using several sentences. Draw attention to examples and ask students to explain the reference, perhaps giving them several alternative answers to choose from.

A youthful hero

Last week, Rahman's wife Leila had an accident. Rahman's youngest child, Yusof was at home when it happened. He was playing with his new car. His father had given it to him for his third birthday the week before.

Suddenly the little boy heard his mother calling 'Help! Help'. He left his toy and ran to the kitchen. The poor woman had burned herself with some hot cooking oil. She was crying with pain and the pan was on fire.

Rahman had gone to his office. Both the other children were at school. The youngster was too small to help his mother and she was too frightened to speak sensibly to her son, but he ran to a neighbour's house and asked her to come and help his mother. Soon she put out the fire and took the victim to the clinic.

When her husband came home, Leila told him what had happened. Of course Rahman was very concerned about his wife, but was also very proud of his sensible son. 'When you are a man, you will be just like your father,' he said.

Instructions

1 Read the text.
2 Note the three boxed items (Rahman, Leila, Yusof).
3 Find all the other items in the text that refer to the same person as each of the boxed items.
4 Using a different colour for each of the three people, circle each item with the same reference.

Note: In the figure, the items with the same reference as Rahman have been circled.

Figure 10 Exercise to practise the use of reference

Text attack skill 2 sub-skill 2: interpreting elliptical expressions

It is a principle of efficient communication that the writer does not give the reader more information than necessary. To make the reader's task easier, there is normally a certain amount of redundancy; but to avoid needless repetition, we use pro-forms. For the same reason, we prefer to omit rather than repeat information that the reader's common sense can readily supply. The grammatical form of this omission is called ***ellipsis***.

Like the pro-forms, ellipsis directs the reader to supply information from elsewhere; something necessary to the sense (and often to the structure) is left unsaid. For example:

The days are hot and the nights ▲ cool. (= the nights are cool)
They came although they were asked not to ▲. (= not to come)
I looked everywhere for apples but I couldn't find any ▲. (= any apples)
The most expensive ▲ was selected. (The most expensive what? The previous text will tell us.)

In short simple sentences like these examples, there is little difficulty; but the dislocated syntax produced by ellipsis can be puzzling, as Activity 6.3 shows.

Activity 6.3 *Identifying ellipsis*

Read the two extracts. Complete tasks 1 and 2 for each extract.

a Man is seen in perspective as just another piece in this grand jigsaw, and his activities in terms of the effects, good or bad, that they are likely to produce on the communities and soils from which he derives his food.
Adapted from Ashby, M. 1963 *Plant Ecology* (Macmillan Co. of Canada, in Moore 1979–80)

b Our experience suggests that for many people some such programme of active listening and rehearsal is essential if our transcriptions are to be followed and the main lines of the exposition they are used to illustrate grasped.
From **Brazil D.**, **Coulthard M.** and **Johns C.** 1980 *Discourse Intonation and Language Teaching*. Harlow: Longman

1 Identify the location of the ellipsis.
2 Rewrite the sentence without ellipsis, changing as little as possible.

Will unskilled readers recognize how *and his activities* fits into the structure of the sentence? Will they be able to match *grasped* with its subject?

To deal with ellipsis, a reader must

a recognize that the information is incomplete;
b search the text and retrieve the required information.

The problem is that there is no signal to alert the reader. Rather, he has to identify the absence of something. This is harder than noticing the presence of a signal. These examples show why ellipsis offers problems:

> I carried the bag and my friend ▲ the suitcase.
> What will a weak student make of *my friend the suitcase*?
>
> We agreed that she should be taken to hospital and ▲ her house ▲ locked.
> How will the student interpret *her house locked*?
>
> He told us where it was hidden and despite the disapproving glances of the others ▲ promised to show us the way.
> Who promised to show the way? Some students will reply 'The others.'
>
> She said that her informant had revealed the name but ▲ would say nothing more.
> This demonstrates how ellipsis can produce ambiguity. Will the student perceive that it is not clear whether the informant or the woman refused to say anything more?

Of course common sense often comes to the rescue, but some students lack the confidence to use it. Most writers are considerate enough to avoid the more extreme forms of ellipsis, but students need to be aware of it and to know how to tackle it when they encounter problems.

Training sub-skill 2

You might begin by presenting examples similar to those above, and framing questions to draw attention to the ellipsis; for instance:

> I carried the bag and my friend the suitcase.
> 1 How many things did the writer carry?

or **2** Who carried the suitcase?
or **3** Tell me something about the writer's friend.

Use simple examples of the same pattern to begin with; for instance, sentences where all the omitted words are verbs, or all the subjects of verbs. Practice will be needed later with all parts of speech, including more complex expressions, as in the second example above, where we have to supply *(we agreed that) the house (should be) locked.*

The next stage is to supply texts in which elliptical sentences occur and signal the ellipsis by means of a caret (omission mark) ▲:

I carried the bag and my friend ▲ the suitcase.

The task is to expand the sentence by including the elided elements, noting how clumsy most of the resulting sentences are; this should help students to see why ellipsis is used.

Later still, supply a suitable text without carets and ask students to locate the elliptical expressions and then either expand them or prepare questions to draw attention to them. This is more difficult, but particularly useful because the ability to identify ellipsis is needed for effective reading. The task is suitable for groupwork.

You can also supply an expanded version of a text in which ellipsis occurs. The task is then for students to restore the original elisions by rewriting the text omitting redundant expressions. This exercise would not be suitable for all students; but for those able to cope with it, it will clarify the need for ellipsis and the way it works.

Text attack skill 2 sub-skill 3: interpreting lexical cohesion

The main lexical issues are dealt with in Chapter 5. Here, our concern is with the problems caused when a reader fails to interpret the relationship between a lexical item and other parts of the discourse.

The most obvious problem occurs when a writer uses different lexical items to refer to one and the same thing. This is common in English, where the preference is for 'elegant variation', that is, avoiding repetition by using a different expression with similar meaning. This can take several forms:

Synonymy

The house stood at the end of a quiet neat street. *The little dwelling*, however, looked neglected and cheerless.

Here, *house* and *dwelling* refer to the same building. Readers who fail to recognize this will not realize that *little, neglected* and *cheerless* all describe the house.

Hyponymy

The boy heard *his mother* calling: *the poor woman* was crying with pain.

This illustrates the special synonymous relationship explained on p67. The asymmetrical relationship (a mother is necessarily a woman, but a woman is not necessarily a mother) often gives more trouble than symmetrical synonymy.

Metaphor

Light dawned; for the first time, *he felt he understood what it was all about*.

Metaphor was discussed on p67–8, though not in relation to cohesion. The problem of interpretation is increased when the metaphorical term is used as a form of elegant variation. The reader must not only understand the metaphor as such, but also recognize that it has the same referent as other non-figurative terms. (Here, *light dawned* and *understood* refer to the same experience.)

The problem in all these cases is the same: to recognize that two or more different expressions ***co-refer*** (have the same referent). As the co-referring expressions may be separated by several sentences or even paragraphs, this is not always straightforward. We will now look at a further category of words which can present similar problems, though they are not exactly co-referential.

Text-structuring words

These are words which, though not as empty of meaning as the pro-forms, operate in a similar way: they are signals telling the reader to fill out their meaning, usually from information elsewhere in the text. For example:

> The *issue* will not be resolved by *such methods*.

The meaning is not clear unless the issue and the methods can be identified. Sometimes text-structuring words relate to background knowledge the reader is expected to share:

> Recent *events* suggest that *Brown's views* are correct.

We need to know what events are referred to and what Brown's views are. Like pro-forms, text-structuring words can refer forward as well as back:

> Various *explanations* of these *phenomena* can be offered.

While *phenomena* relates back to something just described, *explanations* signals what will probably follow. Being able to fill out the meaning of such words is a crucial skill for interpretation of text.

Pin-down words

We saw in Activity 6.1 that in nominalization (p83), certain words carry underlying propositional meaning; and that in order to understand the text fully, the reader has to ***pin down*** this meaning, ie work out the unstated subject of the proposition and so on. Apart from nominalizations, there are many other lexical items which need to be pinned down in similar ways. This is particularly the case with abstract words; it is dangerously easy to let the mind glide over these without pausing to work out exactly what is meant or thinking of concrete examples and relationships. Pinning down may involve reference to other parts of the text, or to external facts, common sense, etc.

We can illustrate this by referring again to the text in Activity 6.1 (p79). In the very first line, we find the word *(our) approach*. Unless the reader can explain that, in this context, the writers mean *(our) way of describing intonation and how it affects meaning (and perhaps how it should be taught)*, he cannot be said to understand the text adequately. In the same sentence, the word *teachers* might also need pinning down: here, it refers specifically to teachers of English as a foreign language – not to teachers in general.

Other examples from S2 of the same text are:

- *meaning system* (Meaning of what? In what way a system?)

- *terms that have general validity* (Paraphrase? What's the opposite of *general* here? Example of a description that has only limited validity?)
- *analytic tools* (Analysis of what? Example of a tool for this purpose?)

There are other examples in S2, and plenty elsewhere in the text. For instance, in S3, who feels disappointment and frustration – and why? In S4, what is oversimplified? And can you explain in what sense a teaching programme can be said to visualise, as it is in S5?

Pin-down words should make readers stop and ask themselves questions (as illustrated above) and would figure prominently in 'think-aloud' reading (see Chapter 3, p37). Look out for examples of pin-down words and phrases and help students to see that clarification is needed by asking them questions to elicit specific explanations. Later the students will formulate the questions, and eventually they should also identify the pin-down words themselves.

Training sub-skill 3

First and foremost, students must understand the way lexical cohesion works. Then they must develop the skill of identifying referents when these are not obvious, and specifying the references in text-structuring items and other pin-down words. Draw attention to such expressions; for example, by asking questions to demonstrate that two terms have the same referent:

eg Appendix A Text 3: Read the first four sentences of the text. Apart from the word *moth*, what other word is used to refer to the same creature? (*prey*)

These terms are often scattered throughout a text, making it difficult to devise specific activities, but you can build up a stock of examples over the years and use these to illustrate the problems. A few suggested activities follow.

1 Supply a suitable text, preferably several paragraphs long.
Task: To indicate terms with the same referent, using numbers or colours as in Figure 10 on p89. This is a good activity to start on, especially if you have an OHP.

2 Supply a text as in **1**.
Task: To collect related terms and show their relationship diagrammatically. For example (from the text in Figure 10):

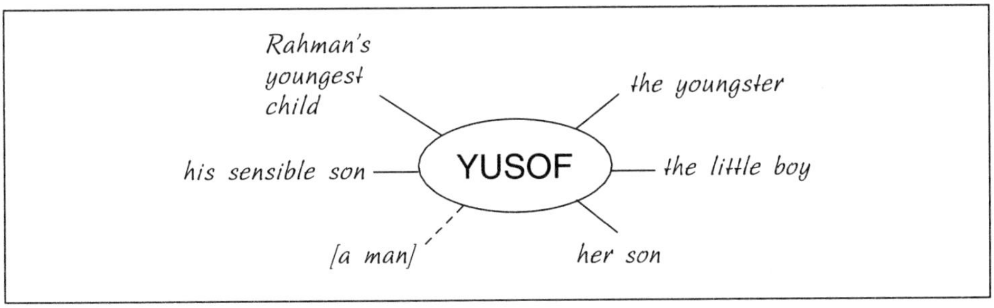

Texts dealing with classification often lend themselves to this; eg in a text discussing various kinds of aircraft:

Complete the diagram by writing the correct terms from the text in boxes A, B, C.

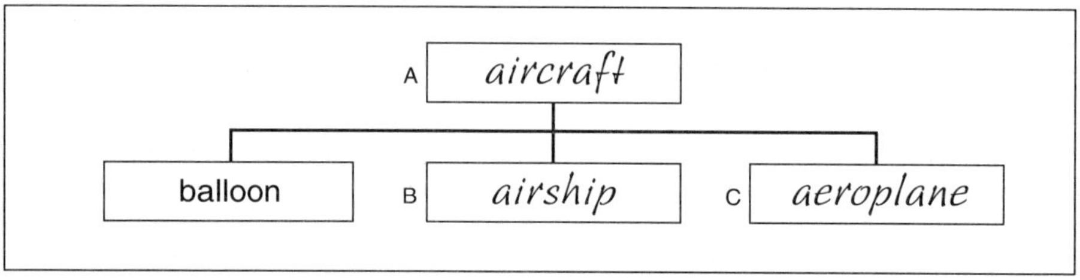

Only the word *balloon* will be supplied; the student has to search for the others. Naturally it will be necessary to do similar exercises in class first so that students become familiar with the conventions used in this kind of diagram.

3 Supply a suitable extended text.
Task: To locate and number text-structuring words, or other kinds of pin-down items; then for each to explain where the meanings needed to supplement it can be found (including outside the text if necessary).

Text attack skill 3: interpreting discourse markers

The cohesive devices dealt with in text attack skill 2 are all concerned with identifying references in order to understand the plain sense of the text. We now turn to other cohesive devices, the ***discourse markers***, most of which are not directly concerned with signification. Instead, they signal relationships: between different parts of the discourse, between the writer and his message. Often they indicate the functional value (p22) of the sentence in which they occur.

Most of these markers are not difficult in meaning, though it is important that students understand them. The main reason for studying them is their usefulness in helping the reader to work out the meaning of difficult text. They often show the relationship the writer intends between two parts of the text; so if you can understand one part, the discourse marker is a possible key to the other part. For example:

> Rain had been forecast for the morning; however, by noon no precipitation had occurred.

Readers who do not know the meaning of *precipitation* may reasonably guess that it is a synonym of *rain*, on the grounds that the second part of the sentence, being introduced by *however*, must counter in some way the expectation set up by the first part. We need to know how discourse markers work so that we can use them in this way.

From the reader's point of view, the markers fall into three main classes:

1 Markers which signal the sequence in which reported events occurred.
2 Markers which signal the writer's manner of organizing the discourse.
3 Markers which indicate the writer's view of the facts, etc written about.

The groups are very dissimilar in function, but the markers in each operate in similar ways. Some words operate as markers in more than one group, according to the way they are to be interpreted.

The main features of each group are as follows.

1 Markers that signal the sequence of events

Examples: *then, first, at once, next, the following day.*

Markers in this group (unlike the other two) contribute to the signification of the text: they answer the question 'When?', not explicitly (eg *on Monday*) but by reference to other events mentioned in the text. For example:

> The guests arrived. Then the sports took place.

We need to know the time the guests arrived if we want to establish the time the sports began. The marker enables us to work out the time relationship between the events. To that extent, these markers are search signals, like the cohesive devices discussed earlier.

2 Markers that signal discourse organization

Examples: *in conclusion, that is to say, for example, to resume, in short.*

Unlike those in group 1, these markers are in a sense outside the substance of the text. They tell us what the writer is doing in a particular clause or sentence by indicating its relationships with other parts of the discourse: this is a repetition of that, A is an example of B, here is the next point to be made, now I will summarize my argument, etc. They can be grouped according to the type of function performed:

Sequencing	*first of all, next, at this point, in conclusion*, etc
Re-expressing	*that is to say, or rather, to put it another way, ie*, etc
Specifying	*namely, that is to say, viz, to wit*, etc
Referring	*in this respect, in that connection, as we said, apart from this*, etc
Resuming	*to resume, to return to the previous point, getting back to the argument*, etc
Exemplifying	*to illustrate this, thus, for example, eg*, etc
Summarizing	*to sum up, in short, to recapitulate*, etc
Focusing	*let us consider, we must now turn to, I shall begin by*, etc

The writer may signal the text organization by using lexical items or ***meta-statements*** (ie statements about the discourse rather than part of the discourse), as well as markers proper. In fact it is hard to draw a line between them; the list above includes lexical items such as *conclusion, illustrate, resume*, etc; phrases like *to return to the previous point*, and the beginnings of sentences like *We must now turn to* ... Whether we call these 'markers' or not, we need to recognize that they all perform similar functions.

Most of the group 2 markers do not occur in either of the other groups, with one major exception: it is not surprising that the sequence of discourse itself can be signalled by many of the same markers that we use to signal a sequence of events, ie those in group 1. The difference is usually easy to see:

> First she cut up the chicken, then she fried it.
> (The first thing she did was ...)
> First, let us consider the legal aspect.
> (The first thing this discourse will do is ...)

3 *Markers that signal the writer's point of view*

Examples: *moreover, incidentally, similarly, however, as a matter of fact, in any case, therefore, in order to, if, certainly, more importantly.*

These markers are quite distinct. They show us the relationships the writer perceives between the facts or ideas about which she writes, eg the relation of cause and effect. They also show the relative importance the writer attaches to each, and other things about her attitude: whether she considers facts or ideas unexpected (or feels that her reader will do so), whether she sees similarities between them, whether she takes them to be hypothetical or factual.

This group too can be sub-divided:

Additive

These markers introduce further facts/ideas, seen by the writer as adding to or reinforcing those already dealt with. The basic marker of this group is *and*. Others have more specific functions:

Introducing (and emphasizing) further evidence	*moreover, furthermore*, etc
De-emphasizing a further point	*incidentally, in passing*, etc
Comparing a further point with a previous one	*likewise, similarly*, etc

Adversative

These markers introduce information that the writer sees as contrary to what is expected or hoped, or to what has been said. The basic marker may be seen as *but*, though it does not cover the sense of all the sub-groups.

Denying expectation	*yet, though, however, nevertheless*, etc
Admitting the unexpected	*actually, as a matter of fact*, etc
Correcting from expected to unexpected	*instead, on the contrary*, etc
Contrasting	*on the other hand, at the same time*, etc
Dismissing	*in any case, anyhow, at all events, either way*, etc

Causal

These markers indicate relationships of cause, intention, condition. These relationships may be between **a** external facts or **b** parts of the writer's argument. In the second case, the marker is used in a meta-statement. The difference can be seen in these examples:

a She felt extremely tired. For this reason, she did not leave her room.
b This matter is extremely complex. For this reason, we shall not go into it further at this point.

The relationships covered include these:

General	*so, hence, therefore, for, thus, consequently*, etc
Reason	*for this reason, on account of this, it follows, because*, etc
Result	*as a result, arising from this, so ... that*, etc
Purpose	*with this in mind, to this end, in order to, so that*, etc
Condition	*if, unless, otherwise, in that case, that being so*, etc

Disjuncts

It is convenient to mention here the category of adverbial variously called *disjuncts*, *sentence adjuncts* or *sentence adverbials*. These are markers that convey the writer's attitude either to what she is writing (*content*) or to the way in which she is writing it (*style*). They overlap to some extent with the three groups described above.

The ***content disjuncts*** express the writer's degree of commitment to the truth of what she says, or a more specific judgement about it. Examples are:

Degree of truth	*certainly, obviously, doubtless, presumably, admittedly*
Judgement:	*rightly, surprisingly, fortunately, more importantly*

The writer often uses markers of this kind to get support for her views; the reader needs to be alert to the covert persuasion being exercised:

She obviously cannot be expected to pay for it herself.
Inevitably, the increased work has led to additional expenditure.

The ***style disjuncts*** comment on the language used or the writer's way of using it: *strictly speaking, briefly, generally, put simply, to be precise.*

The viewpoint indicated by a disjunct can, of course, be expressed by a clause, sentence or even a longer stretch of language; in such cases, the intention is usually not open to doubt (as it may be with a disjunct).

Training text attack skill 3

As usual, the main purpose of training is to create awareness of these markers, and the main method is to use the opportunities that arise when you are studying texts in class. When there is a difficulty in a sentence containing a discourse marker, students should first see if the marker can throw light on the meaning. To do this successfully, they must understand how each marker operates. Some suggestions for specific training are given below. The ideas can be adapted for use with any of the groups of markers.

1 Supply a text with markers omitted and replaced by gaps. Offer two or three markers (multiple choice style) for each gap.
Task: To choose the alternative that suits the context.
Note: Like any multiple choice work, this can be deadly if treated as a test. Its value rests in the quality of discussion about the choice of alternative. First demonstrate a similar task in class, with the text on an OHP if possible. Get students to think closely about the relationships between the sentences, and to discuss the differences in meaning produced by choosing different markers.

2 Supply a text as above, but with the gaps left empty. Supply also a list of suitable markers in random order. (See Figure 11 on p98 for an interesting layout for this task.)
Task: To allocate markers to gaps.
Note: A good variation for groupwork: prepare a set of small cards, each with one of the markers on it (with extras if necessary to make up the number). Distribute cards to the group. Everyone first silently reads the text to see where his own marker(s) will fit. Then the group discusses the best allocation until agreement is reached. (If you include extra markers, make sure the group realize that not all will be needed.) Again, it is best to demonstrate first, the cards being distributed singly among the class.

EXERCISE D
Relationship between statements

This diagram contains sentences from paragraph 4 but they have been slightly altered. Read paragraph 4 again carefully, then look at the diagram, and decide where the linking expressions from the list below fit into it, so that the meaning stays the same as the meaning in paragraph 4. Now write out the completed diagram as a paragraph.

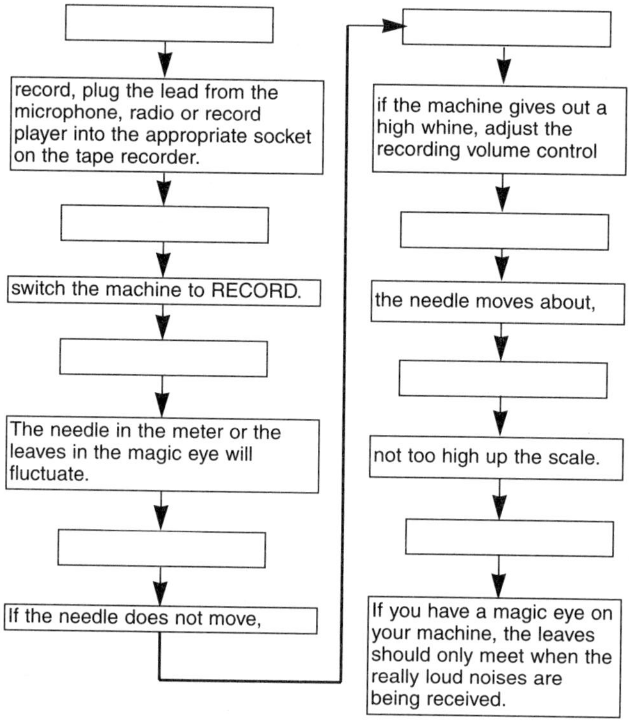

either/on the other hand/in order to/now/so that/or/though/next

Figure 11 Practising the use of discourse markers
From Laird, E. 1977 *English in Focus: English in Education* (OUP)

3 Supply a text as above, but do not list the omitted markers.
Task: To select suitable markers to fill the gaps.
Note: This should not be tried until students have shown that they can cope with the simpler tasks described above.

4 Supply a text in which the first few sentences are given in full, but after that suitable sentences are presented in a multiple choice format, the discourse markers being given, each followed by two alternative sentence completions. For example:
If the state is considered to be impartial, then
a we can accept that it will use the statistics it collects to benefit all its citizens.
b we must treat with suspicion its claim that statistics are needed.
Task: To choose the completion that suits the context and gradually reconstruct the entire text in this way.
Note: This is also good for group discussion. Students will find that in many cases, one of the alternatives is ruled out when the context and markers are considered together. In this way they should begin to see that markers can help to make sense of a difficult text.

5 Supply a text similar to that in **4**, but instead of giving alternative completions, leave gaps between the markers so that only a skeleton text remains. Supply the omitted completions, without markers, each on a separate slip of paper.

Task: To reconstruct the text by deciding which completion fits in which gap. This too is good for groupwork.

6 Supply a text containing discourse markers inserted at random; or with some original markers replaced by others which do not make sense.
Task: To identify which markers were not in the original.

Note: In all the tasks described, it is possible to restrict the type of marker being practised, though it may be difficult to find suitable texts. Even elementary students should be able to deal with sequencing markers (group 1) in some of these ways.

Further reading

On the role of language knowledge in reading see Carrell 1991 and papers in Widdowson 1990; Alderson and Urquhart 1984; Carrell et al 1988; Hulstijn and Matter 1991. Nation 1979 is a key text for exploring some of the specific language features that cause trouble for student readers.

For reference grammars of English, see Quirk et al 1985 (the standard work); Leech and Svartvik 1994 is practical and clear; Sinclair 1990 is user-friendly and particularly strong on examples. All three also deal clearly with cohesion. Crystal 1988 is popularized but reliable, managing to present the essentials of grammar clearly and succinctly.

Winter 1982 attempts the difficult task of accounting for contextual meaning; fascinating but not for the faint-hearted.

Halliday and Hasan 1976 is the most complete account of cohesion in English; more recent discussion includes Halliday 1985, Halliday and Hasan 1989. See also Cook 1989 for a clear introductory account, Brown and Yule 1983. McCarthy 1991 is particularly good on lexical cohesion, also treated in Carter 1987b and Hoey 1991 (a more academic study).

Note: Beware of confusing differences in terminology among grammarians; for instance, what I call discourse markers are called conjuncts/subjuncts by Quirk et al, conjunctive items by Halliday and Hasan, and so on.

Chapter 7
Understanding discourse

Beyond plain sense and into discourse

We saw in Chapter 6 that the discourse markers indicate the functional value of sentences. However, many sentences contain no discourse markers. How do we interpret functional values in such cases? And how do we understand what the writer means but has not explicitly stated – presuppositions, implications? Here we look at the skills needed for these purposes, and also those needed to trace and interpret the way the writer organizes the text so that it conveys the intended message.

In short, we are here concerned with ***discourse***: how the underlying patterns of meaning are expressed through the medium of text. Of the four kinds of meaning discussed in Chapter 2 (p20), contextual meaning and pragmatic meaning are now our main concern; and not only the meanings of individual sentences in a text, but also the way they combine with other sentences, and with unstated but implied meanings, to produce a coherent message.

Because understanding discourse depends on understanding the functional value of the text sentences, this is the first skill we shall discuss.

Text attack skill 4: recognizing functional value

Readers have to recognize value in two distinct circumstances:

a when it is signalled by a discourse marker or other means: *therefore, however, I conclude, let us define it as, it can be assumed*, etc.

b when there is no explicit signal and the value therefore has to be inferred. Readers have to work out for themselves whether the writer intended the sentence to be a hypothesis, an example, a definition, etc. This recognition – usually unconscious – needs to be brought to students' attention, so that when in difficulties they can check to see if they have misinterpreted.

Categories of functional value

It is perfectly possible to understand texts without understanding the terminology required to describe functional value and rhetorical organization. But you do need to understand functional value itself, and if you want to discuss these matters, terms such as *generalization, classification, prediction* are unavoidable. Students may be familiar with these concepts from L1 studies; if so, you may be able to build on this knowledge. If not, you will have to teach the concept along with the term.

There is no accepted taxonomy of functions, but we can identify three categories associated with three of the types of meaning discussed in Chapter 2. They are:

1 Independent functions (associated with propositional meaning).
2 Text-dependent functions (associated with contextual meaning).

3 Interaction-dependent functions (associated with pragmatic meaning).

It is important to understand that a single sentence can have all three kinds of meaning, and can therefore perform (at least) three separate functions at the same time. This will become clearer when we look at some examples. First we will look at each category in turn.

Type 1: Independent functions

In some cases, the form of the sentence and its signification are enough to signal the function, even out of a context. For example:

Defining	A thermometer is an instrument that measures temperature.
Classifying	There are two types of acid: organic and inorganic.
Generalizing	Women live longer than men.
Naming	The ridge behind the teeth is known as the alveolar ridge.
Describing	The north of Iran is mountainous and well watered.
Reporting	Several experiments were carried out successfully.
Speculating	It is possible that people from Peru colonized Easter Island.
Predicting	If water is added to Dettol, the liquid will become cloudy.

Even these few examples show that there are problems: for example, what is the distinction between a report and a description? In the absence of any accepted list of functions, we are all free to define our own categories.

Note that you cannot always identify, say, a definition from the form of the sentence; and conversely, sentences of varying form frequently perform similar functions. Often you only know from its context that a sentence is, for instance, defining something. It is important for students to understand this and concentrate on the work the sentence is doing, not its form.

Type 2: Text-dependent functions

These can be defined only in terms of the relationships between sentences of the same text.

In the examples below, the right-hand column contains the sentences of a continuous text. They are in the correct sequence, otherwise we could not interpret them in terms of the labels in the left-hand column. For instance, you can only see sentence 3 as an explanation because it follows sentence 2. There is nothing in the form of sentence 6 to indicate that it functions as a hypothesis here; and so on. It is true that the example and explication contain markers that tell us their value; but it is also true that you cannot have either unless you have had something to exemplify or explicate first.

Asserting	There is great danger to wildlife in the pollution of water.
Exemplifying	A good illustration of this is the oil released from tankers at sea.
Explaining	It kills all kinds of sea animals, including fish, plankton and other forms of marine life.
Reinforcing	Birds are also frequent victims, for they become oiled.
Explicating	That is to say, their feathers become covered with oil and they are unable to fly.
Hypothesizing	Certain tankers are believed to regularly flout the regulations governing the discharge of oil at sea.
Commenting	If this could be proved, we should be in a better position to take action.
Concluding	As it is, the authorities are almost powerless and the slaughter continues unchecked.

Type 3: Interaction-dependent functions

This is the most controversial category, but it is worth trying to distinguish it from the others. A writer makes various assumptions about her readers. Sometimes these are explicit, as for example when she directly addresses the reader and shows that she expects a reaction. But – explicitly or not – what she writes always has pragmatic meaning: that is, she expects the reader to feel, think or act as a result of having read. This is what concerns us here. Unlike types 1 and 2, these functions can only be interpreted if we assume that some kind of relationship exists between the writer and the reader. Some examples:

Conceding	Admittedly the facilities are not yet completely ready.
Evaluating	Not surprisingly, several of the clients have complained.
Inviting	Let us now consider some methods of classifying metals.
Instructing	Calculate the difference before proceeding to the next stage.
Apologizing	Unfortunately, I cannot at present offer any explanation for this.
Suggesting	If time permits, we could consider making the journey by boat.
Complaining	The authorities refused to issue the necessary permit, so we were obliged to cancel the show.
Complimenting	You will, of course, easily follow the reasons for this.
Warning	(Example discussed below, p103.)

Some of these can be classed as meta-statements – that is, they draw the reader's attention to the way the writer is organizing the text, rather than being part of the text content. Perhaps we should differentiate this from other reasons for addressing the reader; however, the area is still ill-defined.

The multi-functional sentence

The categorization above is a reminder that we need to look beyond the plain sense and establish what work the sentence is doing if we are to interpret effectively.

Any sentence in a text has a value from each of these three categories simultaneously; and may in fact have more than one value from each as they are not necessarily mutually exclusive. To make this clear, try Activity 7.1 before going on to the discussion that follows.

Activity 7.1 *The multi-functional sentence*

This text is from an account of a detective searching for a missing car. He is thinking about where it might be hidden. Try to assign functional values (of all three types if possible) to each sentence.

> **1** It is very difficult indeed to hide a car at all efficiently in the country. **2** The number of disused quarries, flooded gravel pits, deep pools in rivers, etc is strictly limited. **3** You have to know about them, meaning you must know the countryside really well, and you will almost always leave tracks. **4** It is much easier to hide a leaf in a forest. **5** In the city. **6** It won't stay hidden very long, but long enough for you to vanish.
> From Freeling, N. 1978 *The Night Lords* (Heinemann)

The whole of this short text repays study, but we will look particularly at sentence 4. The present tense verb and the use of the indefinite article (*a leaf*) suggest that this is a generalization. It is also a comparison, as the word *easier* shows. But what is the force of it? What is easier than what? Why is the writer talking about leaves in a forest? What is the connection between this and the elliptical sentence 5?

To interpret this sentence, we have to be able to think along with the writer (or the detective) until we can reconstruct his chain of reasoning, which seems to be along these lines:

> It is much easier to hide a leaf in a forest than in a place without trees, that is, it is easier to hide something in a place where there are many others of the same kind, so that it is not noticeable. So if you want to hide a car, the best place will be one where there are many cars, eg the city.

If this reconstruction is correct, sentence 4 is seen to be a metaphor, a generalization, a comparison, an inference (drawn from the detective's reasoning about what the criminal will probably do), a speculation (about what the criminal is likely to do), a hypothesis. And it leads to a more specific hypothesis in sentence 5, upon which the detective proceeds to act.

Which of these is the value of the sentence? The fact is that we have to recognize all of them in order to make coherent sense of the text. It is true that the laconic style of the example makes for difficulty; but similar difficulty can be found in many texts. The extreme instances occur in poetry.

There is nothing unusual about this; it is not a symptom of poor writing. But it does mean that we cannot always expect a simple answer to the question 'What is the functional value of this sentence?' Another example may make this clearer; try Activity 7.2 and then look at the comments that follow.

Activity 7.2 *Interpreting complex functional value*

This text comes from an account of the loss of privacy that results from widespread use of computers, especially their use by bureaucracy and the consequent availability to many different departments of a wide range of information about an individual.

Read the text and work out the functional value of the final sentence.

> In the past, the power of the bureaucracy was in effect limited by the enormous problem of processing enough information about a given subject, and then acting on it in relation to certain policy goals. In the near future, however, this inefficiency will be markedly diminished.
> Slightly adapted from Warner, M. and Stone, M. 1970 *The Data Bank Society* (Allen and Unwin)

The final sentence of the text is interesting. It is an assertion and, since it refers to the future, a prediction. The marker *however* shows that it is in some way counter to the previous sentence, which refers to a problem. So the last sentence perhaps suggests a solution (diminished inefficiency = increased efficiency = solution of problem).

So far so good. But the reader who gets no further than this has missed the message. Since inefficiency is usually undesirable, it is tempting to view the last sentence as an auspicious forecast or even a promise. But if the context has been understood, it is clear that the opposite is the case. Inefficiency in the past has protected the individual; now this protection is to be removed. The prediction is thus to be seen as a warning, and anyone who does not realize this will not make sense of the text.

Training text attack skill 4: recognizing functional value

The value of a sentence arises from its relationships with the other sentences in the text, and from the context. Hence most practice must be with texts. Exercises dealing with specific functions or based on single sentences are of very limited use.

Practice in class is necessary to begin with, since the concept of value is probably unfamiliar. To help students see that the value of a sentence depends on how it relates to other sentences, it may be helpful to prepare the text so that each sentence begins on a new line (as in the type 2 examples on p101). This gives you room to write comments or labels in the margin.

Choose short simple texts. They could involve classification, a sequence of actions, steps in a process, straightforward cause and effect, and so on. School textbooks (eg in science) are good sources.

The activities suggested below are intended to introduce the basic terms and above all the concepts. They are not exercises in mere labelling: none of them are worth doing unless they are used to investigate how the text works. Ideally, choose texts where there is room for doubt about the value of some sentences, in order to provoke discussion. Once the basic concepts are understood, the best approach is to discuss interesting examples when you meet them in a text.

1 Supply a simple text and a set of alternative function labels for each sentence, or for key sentences, eg:
Sentence 1 is ***a*** *an assertion* ***b*** *a hypothesis* ***c*** *a classification*
Task: Choose the most appropriate label. (Later you can give more than one appropriate label, to exploit the multi-valued nature of sentences.)

2 Supply a text, with alternative descriptions of it in terms of functions, or alternative text diagrams setting out its functional structure.
Task: Choose the description or diagram which best reveals the pattern of functions in the text. Activity 7.3 is a task of this kind.

Activity 7.3 *Matching diagrams to text structure*

Read Appendix A Text 5, *Airships*, paragraph 1. Then decide which of these diagrams fits the meaning of the paragraph best.

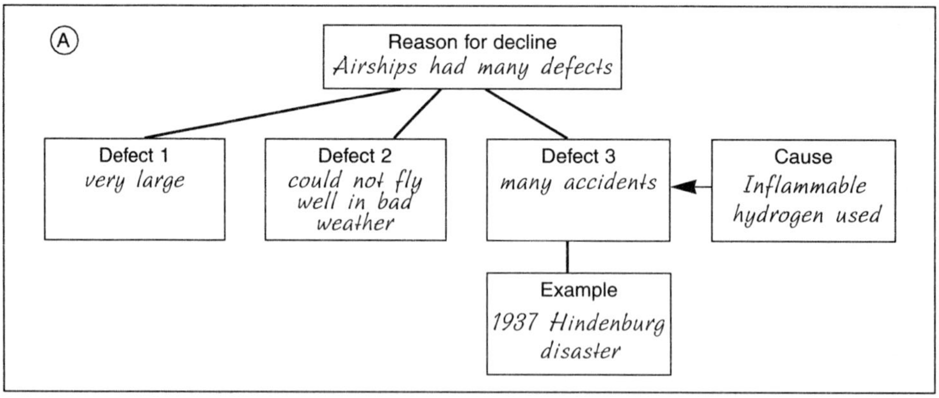

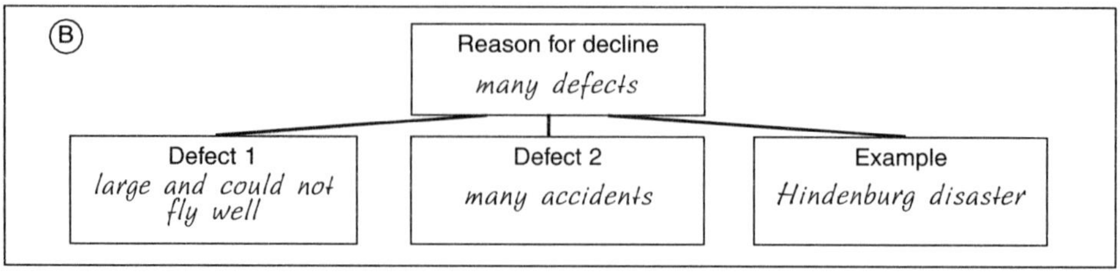

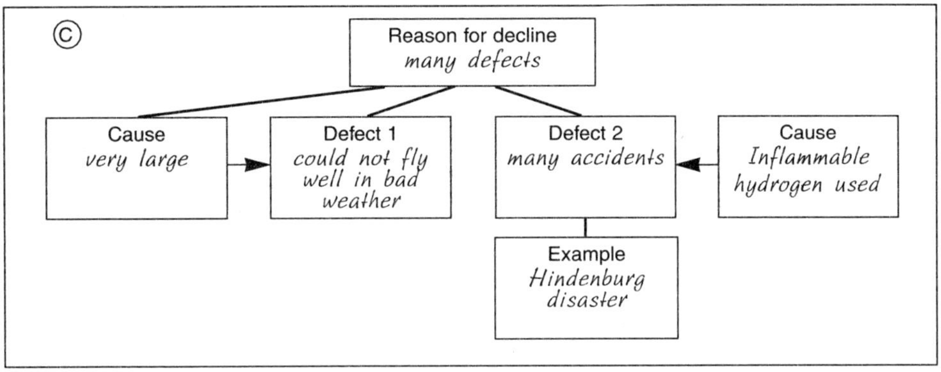

3 Supply a skeletal functional description of a short text a few sentences long. Supply all the sentences of the text, in random order. You may need to make small changes first, otherwise the form of the sentences would make the task so easy that students would not think about the work the sentences are doing.
Task: Arrange the sentences to match the functional skeleton, so that they make a coherent text in which each sentence has the intended value. Activity 7.4 is an example of this technique.

Activity 7.4 *Reconstructing rhetorical structure*

Arrange the sentences below so that they make a text with this structure:

assertion – example – explanation

Make minor changes (eg replace nouns with pronouns) needed to produce a coherent text. Use *for instance* in the example and *thus* in the explanation.

Sentences
1 Foxes will collect seagull eggs during the nesting season and bury them in scattered places.
2 Foxes often conceal the food items they obtain.
3 Seagull eggs can be eaten at times when food supplies are scarce.

Here is the original text on which Activity 7.4 was based:

Foxes often conceal the food items they obtain. For instance, they will collect seagull eggs during the nesting season and bury them in scattered places. These can thus be eaten at times when food supplies are scarce.

Your own version may differ slightly from this, yet still be a good text of the structure sought.

4 This is a variation of **3**, suitable for somewhat longer texts.
Supply **a** a functional skeleton of a text; **b** the sentences of the text, each written on a separate piece of paper.
Task: Students in groups arrange the strips so that they produce a text of the required structure.

Text attack skill 5: recognizing text organization

Rhetorical structure

Tracing the rhetorical development of a text means perceiving how, given the raw material, the writer has selected from it, organized it and given it coherence, until it suits her purpose. Although the reader does not pay attention to rhetorical organization in normal circumstances, it is useful to be able to analyse it. For instance, if you are evaluating the success of a writer, it makes sense to ask what the effect would have been if she had made different choices.

This is particularly helpful to readers who have to tackle involved and difficult texts. If you can identify the principle by which the text is organized and see how the ideas hang together, it is easier to interpret difficult sentences. Readers who cannot do this may find the text resembles a jigsaw puzzle in which the parts can be identified but the way they fit together is obscure, so that the complete picture (ie the overall meaning of the text) is never recognized.

Paragraph organization is certainly worth studying, as some patterns occur frequently. Recognizing the pattern may enable us to predict the likely values of sentences; and this in turn helps us to interpret difficult ones. If you teach students of a particular discipline (eg chemists, economists), it is worth examining typical textbooks or articles, to identify frequent paragraph patterns which can then be used for practice.

However, a word of caution: not all paragraphs display a clear pattern of organization; and within some paragraphs, it is possible to identify more than one organizing principle. The fourth paragraph of Appendix A Text 3 *Survival of the Fittest* is an example. It begins with a cause–effect pattern (see Figure 29 on p196), then moves on to pose a question, comment on it, introduce a new concept (natural selection), discuss and explain it (in eight sentences contributing in various ways which you might like to analyse). Many paragraphs are organized in such non-typical ways; but that does not necessarily make them difficult to understand.

Organization above paragraph level is also important, and is easier for students to grasp. Chapters and journal articles can be used in class, but there is seldom time to deal with longer texts unless you use books already familiar to the class. You could use a class reader (p145) or, if the students use target language textbooks in their other fields of study, you could use some of these to examine the organization of longer texts, by looking at chapter headings and skimming the contents. Knowing how the text is organized enables a student to follow the argument better, read more selectively and locate more readily information needed for a specific purpose.

Training text attack skill 5: rhetorical organization

Preparing practice material for this attack skill often involves little more than the ability to use scissors; see examples below. Admittedly, judgement is involved in deciding which bits to cut, and in leading discussion afterwards, but you do not need to be particularly creative. Moreover, tasks of this kind are popular with students and extremely effective. They have the advantage that they draw on many of the other reading skills that we have looked at, so that students learn how to integrate these.

Though simple to prepare, these tasks are challenging and take time to do properly. Most of them are excellent for groupwork; they demand critical thinking, which is easier and more stimulating if pursued through discussion.

Another possible advantage of groupwork is that groups can work with different materials. One copy of each task is enough; the groups can exchange materials after completing them. However, this means sacrificing the whole-class feedback session which normally concludes such tasks; this is quite a severe loss.

Organization of paragraphs into texts

To make students aware that rhetorical organization exists, and is useful, it is probably easier to begin with the organization of paragraphs into texts (rather than of sentences into paragraphs, which we will deal with later).

1 Supply a text several paragraphs long, with one paragraph omitted. Supply the omitted paragraph separately.
Task: To decide where in the text the omitted paragraph fits.
Note: This can be made easy or difficult by choosing a text with a very clear sequence or one with a looser structure.

2 Supply a text several paragraphs long with the opening or concluding paragraph omitted. Supply separately several possible opening or concluding paragraphs, including the original one.
Task: To decide which paragraph best fits the text.
Note: This entails working out the purpose of the text, in the case of the opening paragraph; and the conclusion it reaches, in the case of the concluding one. If you choose paragraphs that differ in style, the exercise will be easier, but for the wrong reasons: the idea is to get students to trace the sequence of thought.

3 Supply a text several paragraphs long with the key (topic) sentence of each paragraph replaced by a gap. Supply separately a set of sentences including the omitted topic sentences (with others as distractors for advanced students).
Task: To decide which sentence fits into which paragraph.
Note: The topic sentences, if they were arranged in the correct sequence, should provide a skeletal summary of the text organization. So to concentrate on them should make the student aware of the organization.

4 Supply a text several paragraphs long with one paragraph in the wrong place (eg original paragraph 2 is moved to a later position in the text).
Task: To decide which paragraph is out of place and where it ought to be.

5 Supply a text, several paragraphs long, with the paragraphs arranged in random order. Or cut up the text so that each paragraph is on a separate piece of paper or card: this method is more fun to use and is particularly suitable for groupwork. Keep each set of paragraphs in a labelled envelope.
Task: To arrange the paragraphs to make a coherent text.

6 This is a variation of **3** and **5** combined.
Supply the paragraphs of text, arranged in random order, with the topic sentences removed and replaced by gaps. Supply the topic sentences, arranged in the correct sequence, to provide a skeletal summary of the text.
Task: To match the paragraphs with the topic sentences and produce a coherent text.
Note: If you number the paragraphs and sentences (in random order of course), you can prepare an answer sheet giving the correct sequence of numbers. Alternatively you can supply the full original text, as for all these exercises.

Organization of sentences into paragraphs

Similar exercises can be used to investigate the organization of sentences within a paragraph. This is likely to be more difficult than working at paragraph level, although clues to sentence sequence are available in the shape of discourse markers, reference devices and so on. These tasks give useful practice in interpreting signals of this kind, as well as in thinking about the sequence of sentences.

7 Supply a paragraph with the key sentence omitted and replaced by a gap. Supply separately a number of possible key sentences.
Task: To choose the correct key sentence.

8 Supply a paragraph with one sentence omitted (but not indicated by a gap). Supply separately the omitted sentence.
Task: To decide where in the text the omitted sentence should go.

9 Supply a paragraph with one sentence out of place (cf **4** above).
Task: To decide which sentence is out of place, and where it should go.

10 Supply a paragraph with one sentence omitted. Supply separately the omitted sentence, plus several others.
Task: To decide where a sentence has been omitted, and which of the separate sentences is the omitted one.

Note: In 8, 9 and 10, by choosing carefully the sentence you omit, you can make the student focus on different aspects of rhetorical structure. Choose sentences where the sequence is clear, otherwise unprofitable discussion can result.

11 Supply a paragraph in which all the sentences are scrambled (ie arranged in random order). The most interesting way to do this is to type each sentence beginning on a new line, and then cut the paper into strips bearing one sentence each. Keep the sentences in a labelled envelope indicating how many there should be inside, as they are easily lost.
Task: To assemble the sentences into a coherent paragraph.
Note: The sentences can be typed in random order instead of being cut up. An interesting layout for this kind of task is given in Figure 12.

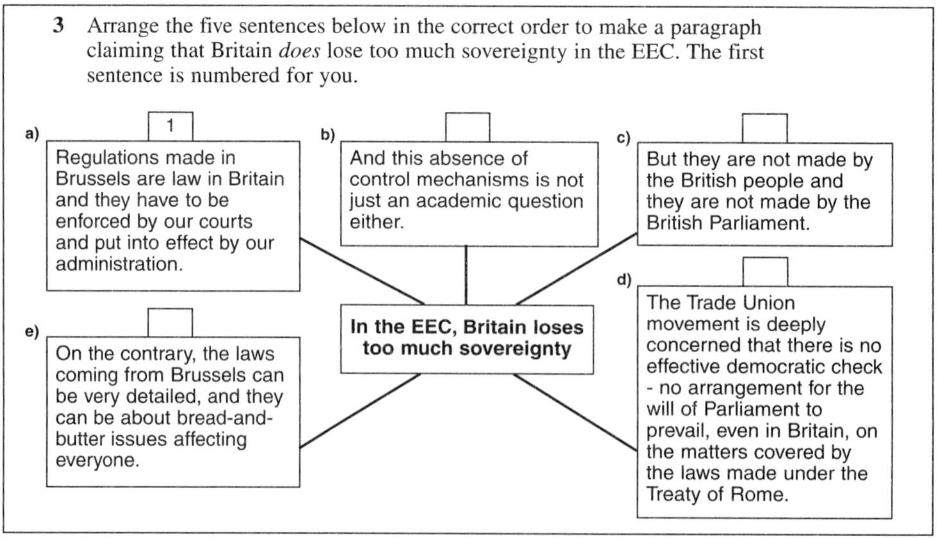

Figure 12 Task practising organizing sentences into a paragraph
Taken from Barr, Clegg and Wallace 1981 *Advanced Reading Skills* (Longman)

12 Supply two or three paragraphs, taken from different texts, prepared as in **11**. The sentences, on strips of paper, are all scrambled together.
Task: To assemble the sentences into two or three unrelated coherent paragraphs.
Note: The first time you use this task, number the sentences of each paragraph in the correct sequence. The students will thus have three sentences numbered 1; they must choose which sentence 2 goes with which number 1, and so on. The more similar the texts in style and content, the more challenging the exercise will be.

Text diagrams

Text diagrams are intended to display the structure of the text: the way the ideas and information are presented. Various equally useful kinds of diagram – chronological sequence, cause → effect, etc – which display the information in a text, but do not reveal how the text itself is organized, are dealt with later (p194-9).

True text diagrams aim to help the student by setting out the relationships between parts of the text (usually sentences or paragraphs) and showing what each part contributes to the whole. Their great advantage, which outweighs the disadvantages we shall discuss, is that they demand close study of the way the text is put together, and promote text-focused discussion. They are useful either to display common patterns of paragraph organization or to elucidate the structure of complex text.

Figure 13 shows the use of a simple text diagram to help students recognize the way the text (not included here) is organized. Notice that the pattern of organization is presented to them; all they have to do is identify the various parts of the text that correspond to the parts of the diagram.

6 Study this diagram which shows how the topic is organized in the first section of the passage.

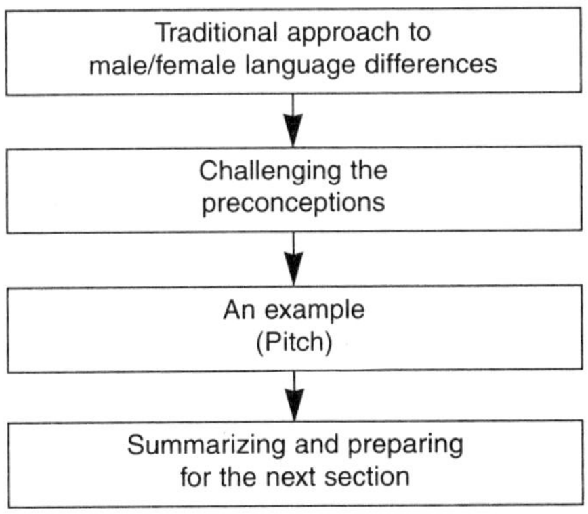

Read through the first section again, concentrating on how the topic is developed. Write down the line numbers where the different sub-topics shown in the diagram begin and end.

Figure 13 Identifying text organization with the help of a diagram
From Tomlinson and Ellis 1988

Activity 7.5 is a similar activity for you to try.

Activity 7.5 *Text diagram: archaeopteryx*

Study the text *Archaeopteryx* (Appendix A Text 1), and then do the tasks.

Task 1: These labels describe the functions of the paragraphs in the text. Arrange them in the correct order to match the paragraphs.

KEY EVENT	EXPLANATION 1	SUBSEQUENT EVENT	CONTEXT
	EXPLANATION 2		

Task 2: These boxes contain brief expansions of four of the labels, describing the content of the paragraphs. Match each one with the correct label and supply a suitable expansion for the missing one.

Geological processes underlying event	Description and assessment of significance	Sensational discovery of fossilized feather	Characteristics of limestone, effects of this and examples

Diagrams displaying the way a paragraph is organized are less straightforward, largely because of the terminology needed to describe the functional value of sentences. A fairly complex paragraph diagram is Figure 14 opposite, which represents the structure of paragraph 4 of Appendix A Text 1 *Archaeopteryx*. The handwritten portions might be supplied by students; or the complete diagram could be offered for discussion if the text seemed difficult for them. Before studying the diagram, study the paragraph and see if you find it easy to understand. If you do, try to devise a text diagram to show its structure; then compare it with Figure 14. If you find the paragraph difficult, refer to the diagram, discuss it with colleagues if possible, and decide whether it helps you to understand.

A few words of caution

1 A text diagram made by the teacher imposes the teacher's view of the text. Obviously this is the justification for using diagrams, and it can be helpful. (It is also a feature of most teaching.) But having to put the text into diagram form forces decisions and can thus obscure valid differences over the interpretation of ambiguous or otherwise doubtful parts. Advanced students can discuss these, but others may be confused.

2 In the effort to represent the text visually, a structure may be imposed that is not entirely present in the text. In this case, the diagram may lead to distortion rather than interpretation.

3 Labelling boxes involves the use of abstract terminology that may cause more problems than it solves. But this seems impossible to avoid in studying textual organization by whatever means, as we noted earlier.

4 It is sometimes difficult to get the students to understand what you mean by your diagram. Sometimes it is harder to understand a text diagram than to understand the text itself. (You can help the students to understand what you have in mind by filling in the key boxes for them.) If the task is so dominating that it seems more important than the text, it should be changed or scrapped. Familiarize yourself with the problem by trying some of the diagrams in the textbooks listed in the bibliography.

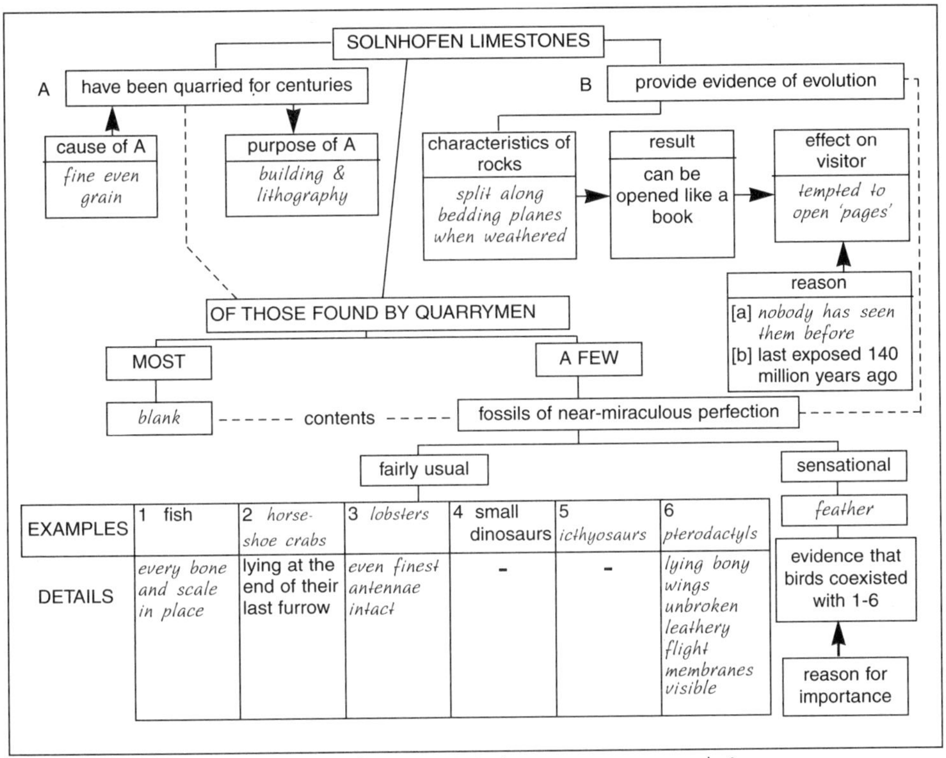

Figure 14 Text diagram for Appendix A Text 1 *Archaeopteryx*, paragraph 4

Despite these cautions, text diagrams used sensibly provide a helpful way of looking at text organization. Students usually find them interesting to work on, and able students will enjoy discussing alternative possibilities. All the same, the point of using a diagram is to illuminate the text; if it falsifies or obscures it, it is better to abandon the diagram and seek another approach.

Using text diagrams

Text diagrams can also relate to longer texts – the chapters of a book, for instance – provided you reduce the amount of detail represented. Some kinds of text lend themselves to diagrammatic representation; for others, there are better approaches.

The point about a text diagram is that the person who devises it must first understand the text and then find a way of representing this understanding so that it will help less skilful readers. This is quite a difficult task, not least because writers so often do not follow a simple paragraph structure. (And if the structure is simple, could students understand equally well without a diagram?)

You have to decide what to write in the text diagrams you prepare for your class. You can make them easier by filling in most of the boxes, leaving just a few for the students to do. If you want to draw attention to the relationships between ideas, you can give suitable labels to the boxes (as in the examples above).

Advanced students who have worked with text diagrams made by other people can devise diagrams themselves. This is particularly effective when done in groups, because it produces discussion strongly focused on the text. There is, of course, no right or wrong way of representing any text; only ways that are more justifiable or helpful than others. A good way to evaluate the resulting diagrams is to let others try them out and offer comments in a feedback session.

Work on text diagrams can be varied in these ways:

1 In whether or not metalinguistic labels are used. (See **3** under *A few words of caution* above.)
2 In the number of boxes that are completed for the student and hence the number he has to fill in himself.
3 In whether the labels or the contents of the boxes are supplied (in random order) or whether the student has to word them himself.
4 If they are supplied, in whether the student simply has to write the number of the correct sentence/phrase in the box (which is more suitable for testing than teaching) or whether the actual words are to be entered. (If the number is used, the diagram can be much smaller, but the text structure is more readily seen when the words are used.)
5 Boxes can be labelled with alternatives from which the student has to choose. For example:

Purposes/effects of hallucinogens	Explanation of/example of previous point

6 Two (or more) alternative text diagrams may be offered, from which the student must choose the one that best represents the text. Activity 7.3 (p104) is an example.
7 Text diagrams can be used as the basis for written work. While this is not a reading skill, it will add to students' understanding of text structure. For such an exercise, supply a completed text diagram; the task is to re-create the text it represents. This is more successful if the students first study a text of similar structure, with a diagram of it.

Text attack skill 6: recognizing the presuppositions underlying the text

Sometimes, when we follow a writer's train of thought from one sentence to the next, we cannot see the connection between them. Two possible explanations are of interest. First, the writer may expect us to bridge the gap by drawing *inferences* (see p114). Second, she may make mistaken *assumptions* about our knowledge or point of view – about how far our schemata coincide with hers (see p7). Inference is dealt with in text attack skill 7; here we concentrate on presupposition (assumptions); the two are closely related, as we shall see.

The presuppositions that concern us can be roughly divided into two groups:

1 The knowledge and experience that the writer expects the reader to have.
2 The opinions, attitudes, emotions that the writer expects the reader to share, or at least to understand.

Look again at the examples of presupposition in Chapter 1 (p8–9). Most of them belong to group **1**, although the second example also expects the reader to recognize the writer's view of Walt Disney. The last example, about the puppy, belongs to group **2**: it is the point of view or emotion that must be shared. However, the two groups are not completely separate, since our experience affects our views.

The second category is the more dangerous, because a strongly held point of view may so blind us to the existence of different views that we cannot interpret the words of someone expressing them. This is particularly likely if the writer does not set out her opinions, but simply assumes that we share them.

This example is from an article about drug smuggling:

> For ports such as Felixstowe, which handles more than 4000 containers a day, widespread manual searches would cause havoc. Consequently, the proportion of containers thoroughly searched in the UK is less than 1 per cent.
> (From Curtis, J. 'Containing Danger', *The Independent* 17 May 1993)

The writer assumes that readers will see these facts as problems: but what if the article is read by a drug smuggler? And what about this extract from a review of an opera production?

> Her stage is a grubby canvas, ever changing but always blank – Wozzeck's world: desolate. Hildegard Bechtler's designs are all soiled, distressed surfaces; a single black curtain swishes between scenes like a cinematic wipe.
> (From Seckerson, E. on Opera North's *Wozzeck*, *The Independent* 17 May 1993)

Someone who either does not know the opera *Wozzeck*, or dislikes its bleakness, may find it hard to recognize that this comment is favourable. Activity 7.6 demonstrates the kind of presupposition that is difficult to deal with if we are immersed in our own culture or attitudes.

Activity 7.6 *The Mountain People*

Read Appendix A Text 8 *The Mountain People* and decide what kind of book it comes from: a novel, a factual account, or what. Was it easy to do this? Why?

Then read more carefully and note any parts that you find difficult to interpret. Try to work out why. Are the words or grammar a problem, or is there some other reason? Do you detect any problems relating to the writer's presuppositions?

You probably did not find the language of *The Mountain People* a problem; but you may have felt confused by the moral assumptions that appear to underlie it. They are so foreign to the value systems most of us share that students often decide this is from a novel. In fact it is an account of an anthropologist's fieldwork among a tribe on the edge of starvation, whose acute deprivation had resulted in a reversal of normal moral values. The text is not dispassionate, however; it uses a kind of savage and understated irony – to some extent imposed by the situation (look again at the examples of food which delighted Adupa and at the final sentence) – which adds to the reader's disorientation. You would need to read the book to have a hope of even partial understanding.

The writer of *The Mountain People* was well aware of the disturbing effect his account would have. Other writers may be blind to the possibility that their readers hold different opinions; others again may know this very well but choose to write as if the possibility did not exist. This is the basis of the persuasive writing found in advertisements or in dishonest argument: they pretend to take it for granted that everyone agrees with them. For example:

> Made with the same care and attention to detail as our famous long sleeved shirts, these cool short sleeved shirts are now available at a 10% discount. They feature

> those little extras that set the *[trade name]* shirt apart, such as double stitching, long tails, removable collar bones and a breast pocket ...
> (Advertisement by James Meade Ltd, *Daily Telegraph Magazine* 15 May 1993)

Notice how this writer pretends to assume that you are familiar with the long-sleeved shirts and their quality. If you aren't, you may feel you should be (after all, they are 'famous'). Similarly, the word *those* implies that you will recognize (and admire) the *little extras* mentioned. It is implied that everyone familiar with the long-sleeved shirts will be impressed by the fact that the new shirts offer *the same care and attention*, and thus that you too – despite your regrettable ignorance – can be sure of the quality.

A similar kind of persuasion informs this holiday advertisement, where the writer pretends to assume that you have been familiar with the place for years and can thus recognize the force of the repeated comparisons:

> Many of our visitors return to our shores each year because on Guernsey the welcome you receive is as warm today as it's always been. ... The tapestry of colours – leafy green lanes and riotous flowers – is as rich as always; the air as fresh and the sea as clear.
> (Advertisement by the Guernsey Tourist Board, *Daily Telegraph Magazine* 15 May 1993)

A particular difficulty involving presupposition is recognizing irony; correct interpretation rests entirely on the reader's sharing the writer's views. A famous example in English is Swift's *Modest Proposal* (1729), which recommended that an Irish famine should be alleviated by eating the children, thus cutting down the mouths to be fed and increasing the food supply. It is remarkable how convincingly his arguments read. (His real intention, of course, was to provoke action to remedy the horrific conditions.)

You cannot tackle a problem if you are not aware of it. It is difficult to be unaware of an unfamiliar word but easy to overlook unstated assumptions – especially those insidious ones intended to cheat the reader into accepting the writer's views unquestioningly. Students need to be alerted to the potential for problems when the writer's assumptions and schemata do not coincide with the reader's.

Even if we do not share the writer's views, clear thinking and use of inference usually lead to the correct interpretation. So presupposition is bound up with inference, the skill we shall discuss next, and it is convenient to deal with them together for practice. However, not all presuppositions can be inferred from the context; there are real problems here, which your students should be aware of. We shall examine further examples in Activity 7.7 below.

Text attack skill 7: recognizing implications and making inferences

We have seen that inference can often be used to reconstruct the writer's unstated presuppositions. It can also be used for a different purpose: when the writer expects the reader to draw certain unstated conclusions from facts, points in an argument, etc. In this case, the reader has all the evidence required, but is expected to take the final steps himself. In practice the division between these uses of inference is not always clear.

As an example of the way a text can require a reader to infer, look again at the text on p102 about the detective looking for a car. The logical steps of the detective's main line of reasoning go something like this:

1 It is difficult to hide a car in the country. (We will omit the reasons for this assertion, though they too involve inference.)
2 Therefore it would not be sensible to hide one there.
3 Therefore it is likely to be hidden somewhere else.
4 Where could that be? We need to consider what would make a good hiding place.
5 A good hiding place might be one where it is easy to hide something.
6 It is easier to hide something in a place where it will not be noticed.
7 If there are a lot of things of the same kind in a place, you don't notice any particular one.
8 Therefore such a place is a good hiding place.
9 If you are hiding a car, you might choose a place where there are a lot of other cars, for that reason.
10 Where do you find a lot of cars?
11 In the city.
12 Therefore the city would be a good hiding place for a car.

Of these steps, only **1**, **6** and **11** are made explicit; and **6** is expressed figuratively. The others must be inferred; unless they are, the reader will find the text incomprehensible. In order to infer, we make use of common sense, powers of reasoning, knowledge of the world and schemata; our schema of what constitutes a good hiding place, for instance, or our schema of the concept 'city', which surely includes the presence of many cars.

Text attack skills 6 and 7 are closely connected with text attack skill 4 (recognizing functional value): the presuppositions the writer makes, and the inferences she expects us to draw, affect our interpretation of the value of a sentence. For instance, if we have not followed the reasoning outlined, how can we interpret the sentence *In the city* as a hypothesis which the detective is putting forward as a suggestion to himself?

Inference is therefore an essential skill, but a tricky one, because often it is not clear how much the writer expects us to infer. Consider this example:

> The second of these statements is demonstrably untrue.

Are we to infer that the first statement is true? Or just that the writer cannot disprove it? We need to be alert to the ambiguity so that we can go back and correct the inference if necessary. Similarly:

> The treatment was later withdrawn. Next day the patient died.

The sequence of sentences suggests, but does not assert, that the withdrawal of treatment caused the death. This kind of doubt is of use to writers who wish to equivocate – to imply something they know to be untrue, without actually lying. (This is a form of innuendo; the political context springs to mind.)

To explore the way presupposition and inference are involved in the interpretation of apparently straightforward texts, let us examine in Activity 7.7 a text that offers several relevant difficulties to students.

Activity 7.7 *Tits*

Read the text, taken from a book intended for the general public in Britain, and predict the difficulties it might contain – other than vocabulary difficulties – for your own EFL students. After you have done this, attempt the specific questions below and see if they lead you to modify your predictions.

> The acrobatics of tits are matched by a mental agility in solving problems and tackling unusual situations. If a great tit, largest of the family, wants to get a nut dangling from a string it will pull up the string with its beak, and hold down loop after loop with one foot until the nut is reached.
>
> But the liveliness which makes tits amusing to watch also turns them into clever nuisances at times. Great tits and blue tits are the chief culprits in sporadic outbreaks of milk-stealing. A few individuals find they can prise off or peck through the tops of milk bottles to get at the cream, and the rest imitate them. Some years ago 57 out of 300 bottles left at a school in Merstham, Surrey, were opened in a single morning.
>
> However, this is more than offset by their value to the gardener. The young are brought up largely on the caterpillars of moths, especially the winter moth, and it has been estimated that in three weeks of feeding their brood a pair can destroy 7000–8000 caterpillars and other insects. So wise gardeners put up nest-boxes.
>
> (From *Book of British Birds* 1969 (Drive Publications for Readers' Digest Association Ltd and Automobile Association))

1 Assuming the reader has never heard of tits before, what evidence is available in the text to enable him to infer what kind of creatures they are?

2 In paragraph 1, sentence 2 (*If a great tit* ...), can you explain what details of the writer's presupposed schema of the great tit might puzzle a foreign reader, even if the plain sense was clear?

3 What background knowledge is needed, or what inferences must be made, to make sense of the account of milk-stealing in paragraph 2?

4 Trace the logical chain of inferences/presuppositions that lead to the conclusion in paragraph 3: *So wise gardeners put up nest-boxes.* (Set them out in sequence as was done with the detective's reasoning on p115.)

If you have attempted Activity 7.7, and checked the key, you will realize that this text is not as straightforward as a British reader might think. Working out that tits are birds is simple, but interpreting the milk-stealing incident, and the reason for putting up nest-boxes, demands considerable inferencing; while in the case of the nut on the string, there is no possibility of a correct inference from the text alone, as the evidence is not supplied. Thus in this one text someone lacking the schemata assumed by the writer has to use inferencing at four points in order to interpret it adequately.

Because inference requires readers to use their intelligence, it is often considered an advanced skill and tends to be neglected. This is a pity, because it is easy to improve it by training. The best way to develop it is to make the students work out the inferences needed, setting them out step by step if they are complex, when you deal with texts that lend themselves to this. Similarly, the underlying presuppositions should be identified when you feel students may fail to recognize or share them. This often entails (as the above text shows) activating or establishing facts about the world, the cultural background and so on (getting students to do this by means of inference whenever possible).

Some specific training of text attack skills 6 and 7 may be helpful; since they are so closely related, we will consider them together.

Training text attack skills 6 and 7: recognizing presuppositions and making inferences

1 Supply sentences involving presuppositions (such as those in Activity 1.4, p8-9), and several related statements of fact for each.
Task: Read the sentence/text and then read the facts stated below. Tick the fact if you think it is true that you have to know the fact to understand the sentence/text.
Example:
The pintailed pigeon is not unlike the orange breasted pigeon, though slightly larger. Coloration is similar, though in the pintailed the green of the back extends to the head and the orange breast band is absent. The slender tail is considerably longer.

a The orange breasted pigeon is mostly green. ✓
b The orange breasted pigeon has a grey head.
c The orange breasted pigeon measures 29 cm. ✓
d The orange breasted pigeon has an orange breast band.
e The tail of the orange breasted pigeon measures about 10 cm. ✓

You could follow this up by discussing what facts about the orange breasted pigeon can be inferred from the text: that it has not got a green head, that it has an orange breast band.

2 Supply sentences or very short texts in which certain facts are implicit.
Task: Read the text and then read the facts stated below. Tick all the facts that you think are implied by the text.
Example:
One of the Archaeopteryx specimens was at first wrongly catalogued as a small pterodactyl, because its feathers were very difficult to discern. This shows how even the experts considered it a reptile.

This implies that:

a Archaeopteryx is a reptile.
b Pterodactyls do not have feathers. ✓
c Pterodactyls are reptiles. ✓
d Pterodactyls are typically larger than Archaeopteryx. ✓
e Archaeopteryx has feathers. ✓

3 Supply a longer text, followed by a set of statements and a rubric similar to the rubric in **2**. Practice with a longer text is needed because some inferences can only be made by putting together facts taken from various parts of the text.

Example: Appendix A Text 2
Read the text and then read the facts stated below. Say which facts can be inferred from the text.

a Rahman had three children. *(Yes)*
b Yusof was three years old. *(Yes)*
c Yusof was playing in the kitchen. *(No)*
d Leila was frying something. *(Probably – not sure)*
e Rahman was a clerk. *(No)*
f Yusof had a brother and sister. *(No – sex not indicated)*
g Rahman's house was not isolated. *(Yes)*

h The neighbour was a nurse. *(No)*
i Leila needed medical treatment. *(Yes)*

4 Supply a longer text and a set of statements, as before. This time students must judge whether the statements are presupposed, implied or neither.
Example: Appendix A Text 1
Read the text and the statements below. Mark each statement A, I or O according to this system:
A = assumed (ie you cannot understand the text unless you know this)
I = implied (ie you can infer this from information contained in the text)
O = not assumed and not implied

You need to know/you can infer:

a that Bavaria is in Europe. (O)
b that a centimetre is this length: ├────┤ (A?)
c that limestone is a sedimentary rock. (O)
d that birds have feathers. (A)
e who the Red Indians are. (O)
f that Red Indians use signs to convey messages. (I)
g that dinosaurs lived over 63 million years ago. (O)
h what lithographic printing is. (O)
i what evidence exists for evolution. (A? I?)
j what a bedding plane is. (I, partly)
k how a book opens. (A)
l that pterodactyls have wings. (I)
m how big a pigeon is. (A)
n that birds do not have claws on their wings. (I)
o that Darwin wrote *The Origin of Species*. (I)
p that Huxley was alive at the time Archaeopteryx was discovered. (O)

Note: Clearly exercises like these provoke a lot of discussion. Often it is a matter of interpretation which answer you consider to be correct. They are therefore ideal for groupwork followed by guided discussion.

Text attack skill 8: prediction

Each of the preceding text attack skills has related to some specific feature of the text. This one does not, except that it relates to the text as a sequenced development of thought. Prediction is possible because writers organize their ideas, because people tend to think in similar ways, and because certain kinds of text (eg fairy tales, recipes) have predictable structures with which experienced readers become familiar.

The ability to predict is both an aid to understanding and a sign of it. If you understand a text, you can say with a fair chance of success what is likely to come next and what is not: you can predict *because* you understand. How far it is possible to use prediction *in order* to understand is less clear, but it is a principle of learning that new information is more easily assimilated if it can be fitted into an existing framework of ideas. Thus if you can frame the kind of thoughts the writer is likely to put forward next, it will often help you to understand the text, even if you predicted wrongly. The questions in Appendix B Text 2 *Survival of the Fittest*, steps 1–6, make use of this fact.

Some kinds of text lend themselves more to prediction than others. Fiction is often difficult at the micro level (ie guessing what the next sentence or paragraph will contain) but enjoyable at the macro level, because a good writer purposely foreshadows the story in the way she writes it. For example, my students predicted amazingly accurately how a story by Somerset Maugham would develop, because the first paragraphs prepared the ground so skilfully. And it is not very difficult to imagine the next day's entry in *The Secret Diary of Adrian Mole* (Appendix A Text 10)!

Other kinds of text, particularly those with easily identifiable patterns of organization, lend themselves more readily to prediction at the micro level. In a discursive text, for instance, it is often possible to recognize the point at which the writer will introduce an opposing argument. Again, if a paragraph opens with a generalization, you can predict that an example or explication is likely to follow. If you have discovered that sentences beginning *It is true that* ... tend to be followed by sentences beginning with *But* ... , you have a helpful expectation. Similarly, if a student learns the way standard scientific articles in his field are organized, he will be able to predict the pattern of a new article, which should help him to interpret it.

Prediction begins from the moment we read the title and form expectations of what the book is likely to contain. The first part of the lesson on the text *Shin-pyu* (Appendix C Lesson 1) is intended to make students aware of this. Even false expectations start us thinking about the topic and make us actively involved. Prediction need not be 'successful' to be useful.

Predictions can be formulated as questions which you think the text may answer (as in the SQ3R technique, p129). This gives an added purpose for reading: to see which of your questions are in fact dealt with, and what answers are offered. The clearer your purpose, the more likely you are to understand.

Naturally predictions are often incorrect, but this need not mean you are a poor reader: a writer has many options, often equally valid. What is important is to recognize when your predictions are not fulfilled and to improve them as you read on. It helps if you can work out why you expected the wrong thing: did you notice all the available clues? Were you misled by something? Have you been working on false assumptions? This is part of the 'active interrogation of the text' that we said long ago (Chapter 1) was the mark of an effective reader.

Working on prediction involves using schemata about the way stories work, the way texts are constructed, the way people tend to think. It also involves looking for clues – sometimes small ones like the use of *It is true that* ..., sometimes large-scale ones like the way a discussion is organized or, in a novel, the way the characters behave. Because it involves such a variety of input, prediction is a good activity for integrating many of the reading skills we have discussed. And it ensures the reader's active engagement with the text.

Training text attack skill 8: prediction

You could start by getting students to predict the content of books, articles and so on from their titles, as suggested in Chapter 4. The exercises that follow are all concerned with textual prediction.

1 For this and other exercises below, you will need a text for use as a central visual if possible (on OHP, for example).
Method: Expose the first paragraph and allow time for the students to read it. Make sure it is understood. Discuss what the paragraph is doing: for instance,

perhaps it is making a generalization. Or it may be the beginning of a story.

Next ask what the next paragraph is likely to do: will it give specific examples to support the generalization? Or will it qualify the generalization in some way? If it is a story, what will happen next? The students should look for clues as to the line the writer is likely to follow, and should be encouraged to propose questions they think the writer will have to deal with either now or later.

When it has been discussed enough, expose the second paragraph and discuss how far it agrees with the predictions, and the reasons for choosing this rather than another way of developing the text. Then repeat the above process with this paragraph, and so on.

2 Use the same approach as in **1**, but hand out copies of the text to group leaders and do it as a group activity. Hand out the text a paragraph at a time; the group signals when it is ready for the next one, and you can discuss briefly what they have predicted before handing the next to them.

Note: For Exercises 1 and 2, a story text is particularly enjoyable and enables the technique to be used with less advanced students. It also promotes creative thinking.

3 Prepare a text for use as a central visual. Arrange to cover the text so that you can reveal only one line at a time.
Method: Expose the first few sentences of the text, allow time for students to read them, discuss if necessary. Then:
either show two or three possible continuations (ie the actual sentence that follows, plus one or two possible alternatives, in random order); the students are to choose the most suitable.
or show two or three questions that a reader might ask at this point. The students are to choose which question they think is likely to be answered.

When the students have discussed their responses and agreed on the most likely, expose the next sentence to confirm what the writer actually said and then repeat the process either with the next sentence or after reading a few more sentences, according to suitability.
Note: The text may be written continuously, but be careful to begin on a new line at points where you wish to pause for prediction. The possible continuations or questions could be written separately; they could indeed be printed on individual worksheets. However, it is probably more effective to interrupt the text, provided you don't want to use it for other purposes, and embed the questions in it, as shown in Appendix B Text 2 *Survival of the Fittest*, and in Activity 1.6 (p15).

4 Prepare to read a text for which a reasonably informative title is given.
Task: **a** Write a list of questions that (judging from the title) may be answered in the text.
b Read the text and find out which questions are actually dealt with.
c Discuss why the others were not dealt with and whether they should have been. (This promotes discussion about the difference between the writer's purpose and the reader's.)

This is a good way of focusing reading for study purposes.

5 For advanced students, two further techniques may be tried:
a Supply a suitable text and get the students to work through it, individually or in groups, sentence by sentence. (Sometimes even clause by clause may be better; or you can vary the amount covered by inserting two obliques // at every point where you want them to stop.)

Task: To write a question to which each sentence, etc supplies the answer. This is not in itself prediction, since the student already has the answer in front of him and has to work backwards, so to speak, to make the question. But it does help to show how the text grows.
Note: Do this in class first before asking for individual or groupwork, so that students understand what to do.
b Supply a text and ask students to read it, covering the unread part with a card. It should be read sentence by sentence or clause by clause, as appropriate. Advanced students may be able to decide for themselves how much to read at a time.
Task: After reading the first sentence, frame a question that you think the writer will answer in the next. Then uncover the next and check how accurate your prediction was; repeat with the next sentence, and so on.

Integration and application

I do not call these attack skills, since they presuppose that the reader has finished the work for which attack skills are needed; they are included here for want of a better place. All the other skills lead the reader to this point: understanding the text as a whole. This includes recognizing its relationship with external facts (has it added to accepted knowledge? introduced a new way of looking at things? distorted the truth?) and with the knowledge, views, etc in the reader's mind (has it taught me something? annoyed me? tried to make me share a view I wish to reject?).

This important stage includes activities such as *evaluation* (how far has the writer succeeded?), *appreciation* (what effects has the writer achieved?) and *application* (what use can be made of this information?). There is no room to give this stage, which involves a whole range of reading and thinking skills, the treatment it deserves, but the ground is familiar to most teachers and you will be able to add ideas of your own.

To understand a text, a reader must be able to distinguish between

- important and unimportant points and supporting details;
- fact and opinion;
- relevance and irrelevance;
- sound and unsound conclusions; adequate and inadequate evidence; valid and invalid inference;
- hypothesis, evidence, inference and conclusion;
- general (*all*), restricted (*some*), particular (reference to specific case);
- certainty, probability, possibility, necessity and their absence;
- causes, effects, purposes, conditions.

This list is not intended to be exhaustive, but to remind you of the many kinds of feature that students have to be able to deal with.

Different texts require different combinations of skills; literary texts in particular require skills that are not even mentioned in this book. Some of the skills required to deal with the list above were discussed in earlier chapters, though not in relation to whole texts. They are important, but will not be dealt with further, because they can only be illustrated by working through extensive texts for which we have no space.

Many activities for practising integrative skills are suggested in Part Three. Here we shall suggest mainly activities requiring students to apply what they have got from a text. We often read and think we have understood, without having really considered or registered the practical implications. It is important to push students to this final stage if you can, using activities such as the following.

Applying what we have got from the text

1 Supply a text explaining a set of principles, rules, laws, etc; and the description of a situation, case, etc to which the principles apply.
Task: To apply the principles to the case and explain what the effect would be. Figure 15 below provides an example of this; others are Appendix B Text 2 *Survival of the Fittest*, Activity D, steps 8, 9, 10; and Text 3 *Notices*, tasks D, E, F.

The task in Figure 15 follows a detailed description of the rules of the game *ayo*, accompanied by diagrams similar to those in the task.

Task 5

Below are some diagrams showing 'the state of play' during a game of ayo.

With a partner discuss what the next move should be in each case.
Be prepared to justify your choice. Write down how many seeds would be gained by each of your chosen moves.

1 It's player **A**'s move

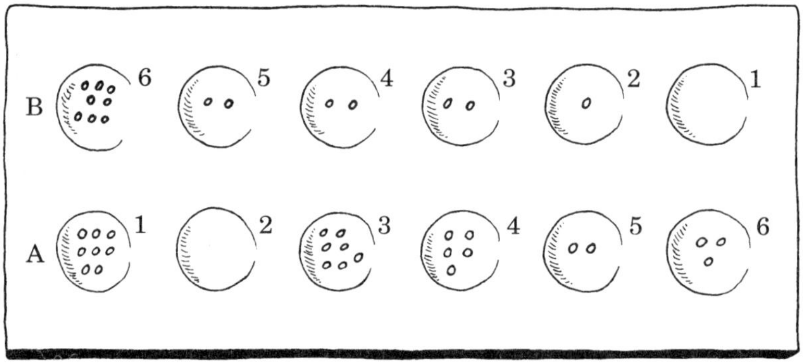

2 It's player **B**'s move

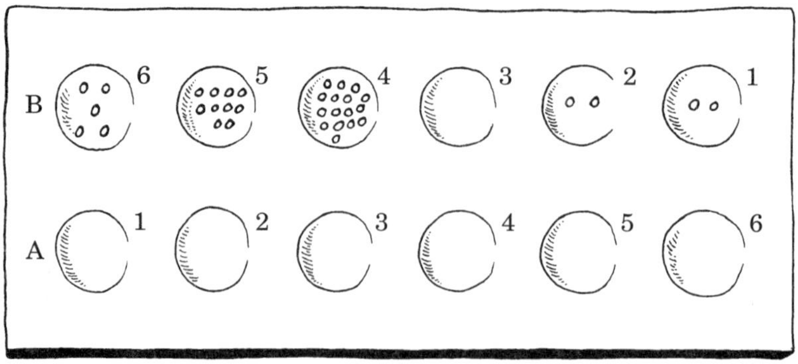

Figure 15 Applying what has been learnt from the text
Taken from Tomlinson and Ellis 1987

2 Supply a text and several statements of fact or opinion, or several examples.
Task: To assess whether each one follows from the text, supports it, contradicts it, or is assumed (presupposed) by it.

3 Supply a text and a series of specific examples relevant to theories discussed in the text or general statements made there.
Task: To categorize the examples in terms of the theories, etc. For instance, suppose the text has talked about various types of motivation. The examples might describe various people doing things for various reasons; the task would be to say which type of motivation each was demonstrating. Or the text may have discussed the climate and soil conditions needed for cultivation of various types of crops: the exercise might describe a region and ask the student to suggest which crops succeed there.

4 Supply a text and a description of conditions, or an experiment, relating to theories discussed or conclusions reached in the text.
Task: to predict what will happen in the given conditions, or what will be the outcome of the experiment. For instance, suppose the text has described investigations into the effectiveness of certain types of advertising in influencing certain types of prospective customer; the examples might describe a new product and intended customers, and might then offer sample advertisements for the product and ask the student to predict which one would be most successful.

5 Supply a text and a problem which can be solved by making use of principles or other information in the text.
Task: To solve the problem.

6 Supply a text and a set of questions, some of which are answered in the text.
Task: To distinguish those that are answered from those that are not. (This task can be made simple by including obviously irrelevant questions, or difficult by including questions which a careless reader might assume are answered. It can be extended to include questions to which the answers can be inferred from the text, though they are not directly given.)

Caution
Throughout this chapter, there is the underlying assumption that texts are organized in recognizable ways and that writers communicate effectively. Some writers make their own rules and structure their texts in unusual ways; when such a text is studied, the reader's job is to ask what the writer is doing and why, not to apply stereotypes and complain that the writer does not keep to them.

However, some writers – being human – are not very good at their job. If they fail to communicate their message effectively, the reader must be capable of recognizing this. It is worth exposing students to a few imperfect texts on purpose, so that they can learn to deal with them and be reassured that it is not always their fault if they do not understand.

Further reading

In addition to Cook 1989 and McCarthy 1991, introductory works on discourse analysis include Stubbs 1983, Coulthard 1985 and Nunan 1993. Brown and Yule 1983 is a full account, academic but accessible.

On pragmatics, see the above titles and particularly Levinson 1983 (full and scholarly) and Blakemore 1992 (a university textbook, particularly clear, though limited in scope). Leech 1983 is intentionally more controversial.

On functional value (illocutionary force, speech acts), see the above titles, particularly the works on pragmatics, and Halliday and Hasan 1989.

See Chapter 1 for some titles on genre/rhetorical structure. Urquhart 1984; Carrell 1984, 1985; Jonz 1989 and Roller 1990 all argue that knowledge of text structures facilitates reading. Williams 1984 includes an excellent brief survey of text structure and ways of introducing it to students. Davies 1995 discusses the issues in more depth.

On presupposition and shared assumptions (implicatures) see Levinson 1983, Brown and Yule 1983; and several papers in Brown et al 1994, especially that by Wilson. On prediction see Smith 1983; also McCarthy 1991, Stubbs 1983.

Introduction

We have discussed separately various aspects of reading that are really parts of an integrated process; in this last part of the book we shall try to put everything together. Here we are concerned with developing and monitoring a reading programme: the role of reading outside the classroom, the patterns of lesson you can use, the choice of materials, the kinds of things you can do with them, and the place of assessment.

The decisions you make on these issues depend partly on the general principles outlined in this book, and partly on your own teaching circumstances. Start by analysing these circumstances: What sort of students are you teaching? What is their real level of competence in the target language? Why do they want or need to read it? What would be an ideal programme for them? And so on. (On the design of reading programmes, see Davies 1995. For more general discussion, see Rowntree 1982, 1985; Marland and Hill 1981; Hutchinson and Waters 1987; Richards 1990; Bloor 1985; Nelson 1984.)

These are the preliminaries. Next you have to take account of the constraints: amount of teaching time, class size, examinations, and so on. Many teachers have little freedom, but there are always choices to be made. A clear idea of your goals will help you to choose effectively, so we will outline possible objectives suggested by the earlier parts of the book.

Objectives of a reading programme

In Chapter 3 an overall aim for the reading programme was proposed:

> ***To enable students to enjoy (or at least feel comfortable with) reading in the foreign language, and to read without help unfamiliar authentic texts, at appropriate speed, silently and with adequate understanding.***

You may well want to improve on this; if so, now is the time to think about alternative formulations to suit your own circumstances.

Having established your overall aims, it is useful to prepare a set of objectives, making them as explicit as possible. This is not very fashionable at present, but it is a splendid way to sharpen your thinking, and to throw up any doubts or misunderstandings. The main points made in this book can be outlined as a very general set of objectives as follows:

> ***After completing the reading programme, the student will read in the foreign language for his own purposes, and in doing so will:***

- recognize the importance of defining his purpose when he reads;
- read in different ways according to his purpose and the type of text;
- respond to the text as fully and accurately as his purpose demands;
- recognize that both top-down and bottom-up approaches to text are valuable, and use each as appropriate;

- be aware, when necessary, that he has not understood the text and be able to locate the source of misunderstanding and tackle it;
- not worry if he does not understand every word, except where accuracy is important;
- use skimming when necessary to ensure he reads only what is relevant, and to assist subsequent comprehension;
- make use of non-linear information (figures, titles, layout, etc) to supplement the text and increase understanding;
- make use of word attack skills and the skills of interpreting syntax and cohesion, in order to establish the plain sense of the text,
- be aware that a sentence may have a different functional value in different contexts, and be able to identify the value;
- make use of rhetorical organization to help interpret a complex text;
- be aware that his own expectations influence his interpretation and recognize those occasions when the writer's assumptions differ from his own;
- be aware that a writer does not express everything she means, and be able to make inferences as required to fill out the meaning;
- recognize that a good writer chooses her words carefully and would have meant something different if she had chosen A rather than B (advanced students will also be able to explain the difference);
- use library catalogues, titles, contents pages, etc to identify relevant material.

This list is simply a reminder of the many things a reading programme might seek to achieve. You may need to omit some and add others. If you want to use any of them in preparing your own programme, you will need to integrate them with objectives for the other language skills (writing, etc), and then break them down into sets of more specific ones for teaching purposes. A rough sequence of objectives must also be considered, but as reading does not lend itself to a rigid framework of teaching, their best use may be as a checklist to ensure nothing is neglected.

If you prefer not to use objectives, you will need to devise some other means of describing the reading programme and explaining its rationale (to the principal, colleagues and so on – and to clarify your own thoughts). Only you can do this (preferably with colleagues), because the programme must be specific to your teaching circumstances.

Priorities and possibilities

You next need to prioritize your objectives and decide where to start. Be realistic: your goal may be that the students read articles in target language scientific journals; but if they come to you with a low level of proficiency, your objectives for the early part of the course may not look much like the list above.

Critical, reflective or responsive reading cannot be developed in a hurry, so if there is little time to reach the ultimate objectives, you will have to help students to develop coping strategies – ways of tackling texts which enable them to understand enough for their purposes. This is a stop-gap measure; the students will have to continue to improve their reading on their own, and equipping them for this then becomes one of your objectives. Once you have established your objectives and decided in what order to approach them, it is time to plan the programme, look for suitable texts and decide what activities you will use with them. This is what we shall discuss in Part Three.

Chapter 8
An extensive reading programme

BEFORE discussing the teaching part of a reading programme, we will move away from the classroom for a little, into the private world of reading for our own interest. There are two reasons for this. First, getting students to read extensively is the easiest and most effective way of improving their reading skills. Second, it is much easier to teach people to read better if they are learning in a favourable climate, where reading is valued not only as an educational tool, but as a source of enjoyment.

Most of this book is occupied with the help teachers can give to inexpert or reluctant readers; here we are mainly concerned with what the students can do for themselves. But teachers have to create the right conditions for reading to become a valued part of every student's life. They have first to ensure that attractive books are available and second to use every trick they know to persuade students to 'get hooked on books'.

The cycle of frustration and the cycle of growth

We will take it for granted that you are convinced of the importance of reading. Why is it that many people fail to make progress in such a valuable skill?

Many of us teach students who are trapped in the vicious circle shown in Figure 16.

It doesn't matter where you enter the circle, because any of the factors will produce any of the others. Slow readers seldom develop much interest in what they read, let alone pleasure. Since they do not enjoy it, they read as little as possible. Deprived of practice, they continue to find it hard to understand what they read, so their reading rate does not increase. They remain slow readers.

Somehow or other we must help them to get out of this cycle of frustration and enter instead the cycle of growth represented in Figure 17.

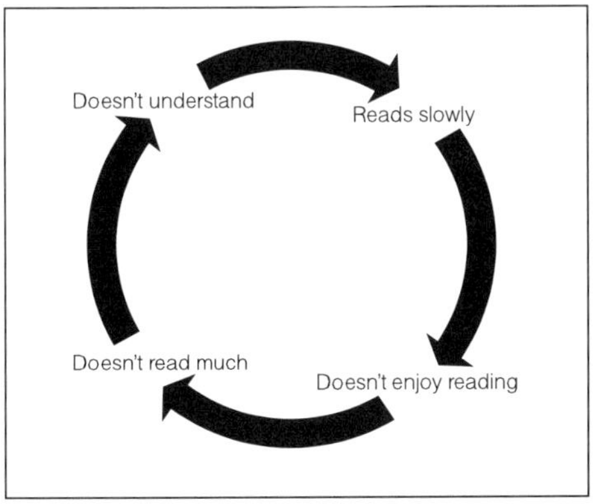

Figure 16 The vicious circle of the weak reader

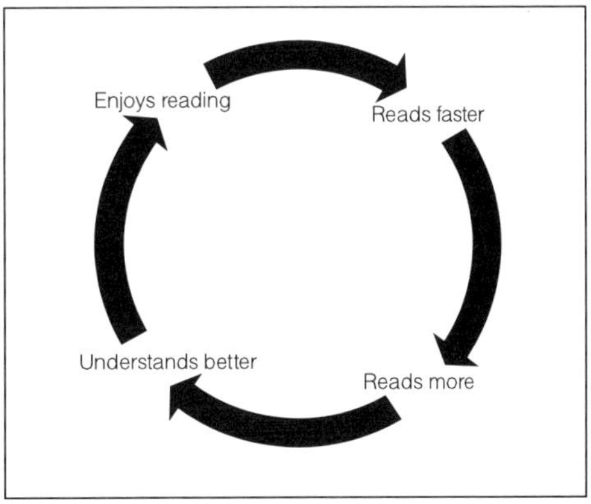

Figure 17 The virtuous circle of the good reader

We saw earlier that speed, enjoyment and comprehension are closely linked with one another, and with the amount of practice a reader gets. Any of these factors can provide the key to get us out of the vicious circle and into the virtuous one. The most readily attainable is *enjoyment*, closely followed by *quantity*. It is these factors that this chapter focuses on.

Extensive reading and language learning

At the heart of this chapter is Frank Smith's slogan:

> ***We learn to read by reading.***

This has been quoted by countless people precisely because it is true. However, we learn something else by reading too, and this provides another slogan:

> ***The best way to improve your knowledge of a foreign language is to go and live among its speakers. The next best way is to read extensively in it.***

Experienced teachers know this, and there is research evidence to justify it (see *Further reading*). This is useful when persuading head teachers to give you funds to buy books, or convincing parents that reading is not a waste of time. Students who read a lot will not become fluent overnight, and it may take a year or two before you notice an improvement in their speaking and writing; but then it often comes as a breakthrough. They will progress at increasing speed and far outstrip classmates who have not developed the reading habit.

Reading more and reading better

We want students to read *better*: fast and with full understanding. To do this they need to read *more*, and there seem to be two ways to achieve this: requiring them to do so and tempting them to do so. The latter leads us straight back to the enjoyment factor, which we shall later consider at length; but first let us consider the former.

Requiring students to read

Reading in the classroom

A 1979 study (Lunzer and Gardner 1979) showed that in British classrooms surprisingly little reading is done, right across the curriculum. Reading occupied no more than 15 per cent of lesson time overall and was often fragmentary rather than sustained. Even reading comprehension work involved more writing than reading. Ten years later, the education inspectorate reported that the situation had not improved (Department of Education and Science 1989). Probability and observation suggest that the position is not very different in many other countries. Of course this is unintentional and it has taken people a long time to realize what is happening, but since so little use is made of reading, students may be starting to consider it redundant.

Perhaps teachers feel that reading is better programmed for out-of-school work, so that class time can be used for things that cannot be done elsewhere. This is fine as long as out-of-school assignments that require reading are in fact given. If they are not, some students never feel the need to read at all and thus never develop the habit or the skill. No wonder reading standards are low.

Second language reading across the curriculum

You cannot provide enough reading assignments on your own. Find out from colleagues the amount of reading they require students to do. Even if assignments are in the L1, the reading habit created will help. And if the target language is a medium of instruction in other subjects, or a library language, then reading assigned by other teachers contributes directly to your own efforts. It is important to get them on your side. If other teachers are ready to co-operate, you can help them in these ways:

Selecting texts for study in other subjects

Examine the target language textbooks students are expected to read in other subjects. They may be beyond their language level. Explain the problems; maybe the subject teacher can alleviate them. If it is impossible to choose a different book, she may be able to give guidance as described in the next paragraph.

Guiding study reading

A textbook in any language is studied more effectively if students are given a specific purpose, not merely told to read and make notes. They can be asked to find certain information, trace an argument, explain the evidence for the writer's conclusions, and so on. Many of the ideas in Chapter 12 can be applied to study reading; interested subject teachers might read the chapter themselves.

The SQ3R technique

Work in any language, in any subject, benefits from this strategy for private study reading. It consists of five steps: Survey (S), Question (Q), Read (R), Recite (R), Review (R). Some of these labels are a little misleading, so read the notes below or refer to the source (Robinson 1964).

Survey: Skim the text to make sure it is relevant and to get an overview of the main points.

Question: Pause to ask yourself questions you want the text to answer; beginners should write them down. Note that *it is the reader who asks the questions*; this is intended to make you think about your purpose – what you want to get out of the text. It also involves prediction: what help do you expect the text to supply?

Read: Now read carefully, looking for the answers to your questions and noting anything else that is relevant.

Recite: This is not reading the text aloud, but speaking aloud the answers to your questions, to fix them in your mind; alternatively, write them down. The essential thing is to reprocess in some way the salient points gained from the text.

Review: Think about what you have learnt, and organize the information in your mind, consider its implications for other things you know, assess its importance and so on. The aim is to integrate it into your previous knowledge and experience. This stage may usefully take place later, to provide reinforcement and revision.

This study technique is for use particularly when the teacher has provided no guidance; the second step in effect makes the student responsible for guiding himself. With able students, this promotes purposeful and active involvement, but even weaker and younger readers have improved by using this approach.

Using other subject texts for intensive reading

Use texts from target language textbooks in other subjects for some of your reading lessons; this helps everyone and deepens your understanding of the problems students face.

The above are just suggestions; but colleagues may be more willing to set reading assignments if you offer help of this kind, thus supporting your efforts by increasing the amount of reading students are required to do.

Reading in the target language and the L1

If you are not teaching a second language, much of the last section is less readily applicable, but it is a pity to work in isolation from the reading work done by L1 teachers. If you can agree on common approaches, each teacher's work will complement the others'. Most of the suggestions in this book apply to reading in any language, including the mother tongue, and reading skills can be transferred from one language to another. So work done in either language will benefit the other if similar approaches are used.

You may not get much support from the L1 teachers if reading is not encouraged in the social culture, or if L1 reading materials are few or unattractive. But there is a compensation; if students are starved of food for their minds and imaginations in the L1, it is easier to promote target language reading by offering attractive material, particularly fiction.

However, reading skills are better developed first in the L1, so it is in everybody's best interests to have a strong L1 programme on which your target language programme can build.

Making students want to read

Increasing the number of reading assignments gives one prong of a two-pronged approach to increasing the amount of reading done. The second is to make students *want* to read. *Needing to read*, for study or other purposes, is an incentive for some people, but *wanting to read* is an incentive for everyone. Enjoyment is the key.

Promoting the reading habit

It is not as difficult as you might think to establish the reading habit. In any class, some people respond slowly or not at all to the attractions of reading, but many more develop a real appetite for it. It may even be difficult to provide enough books, but this is a problem to be proud of – it shows you have succeeded.

Where reading is actively promoted, and plenty of enjoyable books are available, it is common to find students reading a book a week, or more. A great deal depends on the difficulty of the books; to become an effective reader, it is far more useful to read a lot of easy books than a few difficult ones. The class library therefore should have at least twice as many books as there are students; four times the number is better. 'Books' here means different titles: think twice before buying two copies of the same book rather than two different ones.

Active promotion of reading is needed if you want good results. One school had uniforms with pockets big enough to hold a book, and it was an offence to be caught without one: extreme, perhaps, but it worked. We shall consider other devices later, so if at present you find it hard to push students through even one book a term, do not despair but read on.

Choosing books

There is one major condition if students are to develop the reading habit: *the books offered must be enjoyable.* This is more powerful than any other motivation. We shall consider how to organize a programme focused principally on making reading enjoyable.

The criteria for selecting texts are discussed at length in Chapter 10. For extensive reading, the criteria of ***readability*** (ie suiting the linguistic level of the reader) and ***suitability of content*** are even more important than for use in class, because we expect the students to read the books on their own.

SAVE to promote extensive reading

We can use the acronym SAVE to summarize the main criteria for choosing extensive reading materials:

S *Short* The length of the book must not be intimidating. Elementary students, and anyone undertaking extensive reading for the first time, need short books that they can finish quickly, to avoid becoming bored or discouraged.

A *Appealing* The books must genuinely appeal to the intended readers. It helps if they look attractive, are well printed and have (coloured) illustrations – more pictures and bigger print for elementary students. They should look like the books we buy from choice, not smell of the classroom – notes and questions unobtrusive or excluded.

V *Varied* There must be a wide choice suiting the various needs of the readers in terms of content, language and intellectual maturity.

E *Easy* The level must be easier than that of the current target language coursebook. We cannot expect people to read from choice, or to read fluently, if the language is a struggle. Improvement comes from reading a lot of easy material.

EFL readers

Anyone teaching English as a second or foreign language is fortunate; they can easily select a varied and plentiful collection of books. The major EFL publishers have a good range of supplementary readers and the quality is getting better every year. Many are now very well written and presented, with stories that would appeal to anyone. A list of the major British publishers in this field is given in Appendix D.

Survey reviews of graded reader series in the *English Language Teaching Journal* have been prepared by staff of the Edinburgh Project on Extensive Reading (EPER). EPER provides a comprehensive supply and advisory service on the setting up of extensive reading programmes; brief details in Appendix D.

Acquiring books

If you teach English outside the UK your problem is more likely to be how to obtain books than how to choose them. Ordering problems can be solved through EPER or the publishers. Getting enough money may be more difficult, but teachers have found some ingenious solutions.

Securing institutional funds

If you do your homework first, the principal may agree to allocate funds. Find out the cost of the books and anything else you need (bookshelves, transparent plastic for covering books, labels, etc). The target should be a collection of three or four books per student; to start with, at least one per head, with ten or twenty extra per class to provide minimally for choice and varying competence. Work out procedures for safeguarding and lending books, so that you can answer all the questions the principal will ask. The *EPER Guide* (Hill 1992) would be a help here. And be ready with a convincing explanation of the expected advantages (outlined earlier in this chapter).

Getting students to contribute

If each students buys or, better, provides the money for one book, a class of thirty students will have thirty different books to read (provided you do not duplicate titles). A good foundation, but you will need additional titles from other resources to provide the range needed.

Organizing fundraising events

The class can help in this; they will appreciate the books more if they make some effort to raise the money. Sponsorship is one possibility: a student's family and friends promise a certain sum of money if the student succeeds in some activity (eg a cent for every mile run or word correctly spelled). Figure 18 shows how one class increased the size of its library by means of a sponsored spelling test!

Figure 18 Results of a sponsored spelling test

Appealing to local donors

Individuals, firms and organizations are all possible sources of funds. Ask for money rather than books, since donations of books from people who do not know your students are likely to include unsuitable titles. (It is not true that any books are better than none: see below, p138.) Try to offer inducements: a label in the books saying *Donated by ...*, or a publicity story in the local newspaper – anything which will appeal to the potential donor and cost you little or nothing.

Multiple loans from a public library

Some libraries are prepared to organize book boxes, on loan for about a term and then replaced by a new selection. Try to help to select the books to ensure they are suitable.

Help from booksellers

Sometimes booksellers are prepared to co-operate; help them to select suitable titles, which they can bring along to display and sell during the lunch hour, at the Language Club, at a parent/teacher meeting when students are also present, and so on. A display of colourful new books is a persuasive means of getting people to buy. Encourage students to donate the books to the class library after reading them, or to organize a book exchange scheme by means of which they swap books regularly.

Schemes involving money sometimes provoke distrust, but a cautious and tactful approach, and meticulous accounts and organization, may win the day. The principal's approval is essential and securing the co-operation of fellow teachers is a priority; other teachers of the same language should be fully involved from the start, building up collections for their own classes, so that planning and fund raising are done jointly, and so that an integrated scheme results. Seek the support of the parent/teacher organization, or the Old Students' association, by making sure they understand the aims and details of the programme. Involve them as far as you can, to make them feel proud of the scheme instead of mistrusting it.

Once the books have been prepared for borrowing, invite parents, teachers, donors and other supporters to inspect them, handle them and admire your organization. In this way everyone will see that the funds have been used to good effect. Keep up the momentum by organizing termly or yearly book events, with displays of student work and other evidence that the programme continues to deserve support.

Organizing a library

The first decision is whether to house an extensive reading collection in the school library, or whether to build up class libraries.

A class library

There is a lot to be said for a class library. You can choose books that are particularly suited to the age, proficiency and interests of the students; this means they do not waste time and get discouraged by looking through inappropriate books.

If students help to buy the books, they naturally prefer them to be kept in their own room. There they become an essential part of classroom life, picked up in spare moments, referred to for information, easily available without making a special trip to the library or waiting for it to open. And you can keep a closer eye on the books, and who reads what.

The school library

If funds are very limited, putting all books in a common collection avoids duplication, since several classes are likely to want copies of the same book. A central library can manage with fewer copies and can afford to cater for minority interests: there may be a dozen railway enthusiasts in the whole school, but only one in any one class. So a good central collection has to have priority, but class libraries should be set up if you can possibly afford them.

If the extensive reading material is stored in the main library, make sure that it opens at least once a day, at a time when all students are able to go, for both browsing and borrowing. And be there frequently, to help students choose books and find their way round the collection.

Running the library

It is important to keep the library tidy and attractive, and to have an efficient control system to minimize losses. Much of the work can be delegated to students, even young children. I remember a library full of old papers and dusty books piled in dark cupboards and populated by frogs. Not surprisingly, nobody went there. A year later the frogs had decamped, shelves had replaced the cupboards, it had been redecorated and new books bought. It was thereafter kept that way as long as I knew it by a student librarian and his assistants, who ran it so well that, while many books were borrowed, hardly any were lost.

There should be no question of not allowing borrowing. The great strength of an extensive reading scheme is that it operates mostly out of class time. For one thing, there is nothing like enough time in class for the amount of reading needed; and for another, we want to stop students associating books only with the classroom. The system must allow students to borrow at least one book and keep it long enough to read it. A card in the book can be removed when it is borrowed and filed until it is returned. A card with spaces to record names of borrowers can give you information about each student's tastes, and about the popularity of the book.

Storing supplementary readers

You may have to keep the class library in a lockable container such as a cupboard or box. This is not an attractive way of storing books, so avoid it if possible (for instance, if the room itself can be locked). In any case the library monitor should take out the books and put them on display each day while the room is in use. Given the right classroom atmosphere, it is surprising how few books are lost from such collections.

One of the problems with short books, such as many EFL readers, is that they have no spine, so the title is not visible when the book is placed on the shelf in the usual way. A shelf of readers stored like this looks untempting, and it is difficult to find the book you want. Try to display at least some books so that the front cover (often attractively illustrated) shows. Below are some ways of doing this:

- A sloping shelf running round the classroom – under the windows, for example, unless rain would be a problem (Figure 19).
- A freestanding book rack, similar to ones sometimes found holding paperbacks in bookshops (Figure 20). This is ideal if you have space.
- A folding lockable library corner (Figure 21). This is very practical but heavy and takes up a good deal of space.

- Hanging wall pockets (Figure 22). Several will be needed, as they do not hold many books. They are easy to store when empty – leave them on the wall or roll them up in a cupboard.

You need not display all the readers at once, but get the library monitor to choose different ones every day or week.

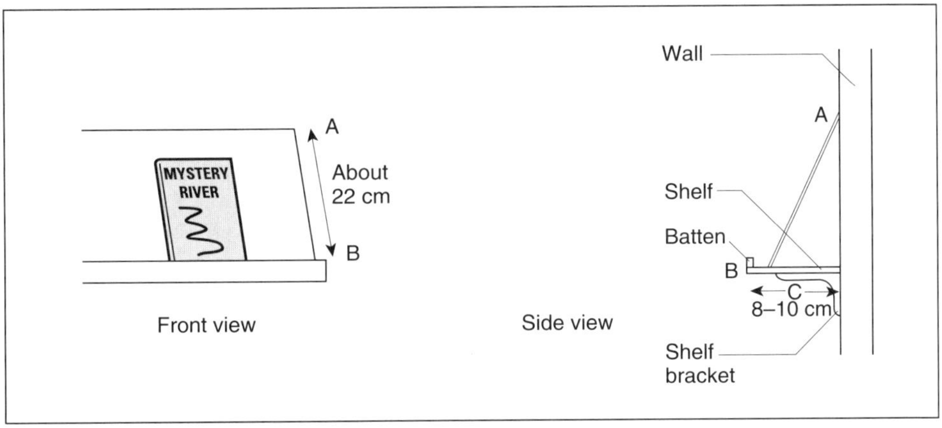

Figure 19 Sloping shelf round classroom wall
The sloping shelf should be made of light stiff material such as plywood or hardboard. It is supported by a little shelf attached to the wall by a bracket; the shelf need only be 8–10 cm deep. Along the front of the shelf and at the foot of the slope runs a short vertical batten preventing books from sliding off.

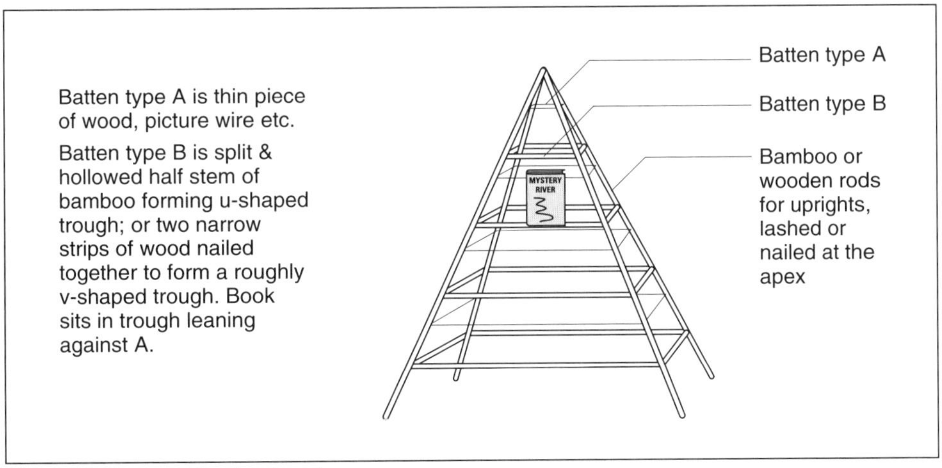

Figure 20 Freestanding book rack
This can have either three or four legs and be from about 1–1½ metres in height, depending on the space available. Check the sizes of your books before finalizing your design: the distances between the battens can be adjusted to take varying heights. The B type battens (in which the books stand) will need to be on average about 22 cm apart from one another, while an A type batten, against which the books rest, will be about 10–15 cm above each B type.

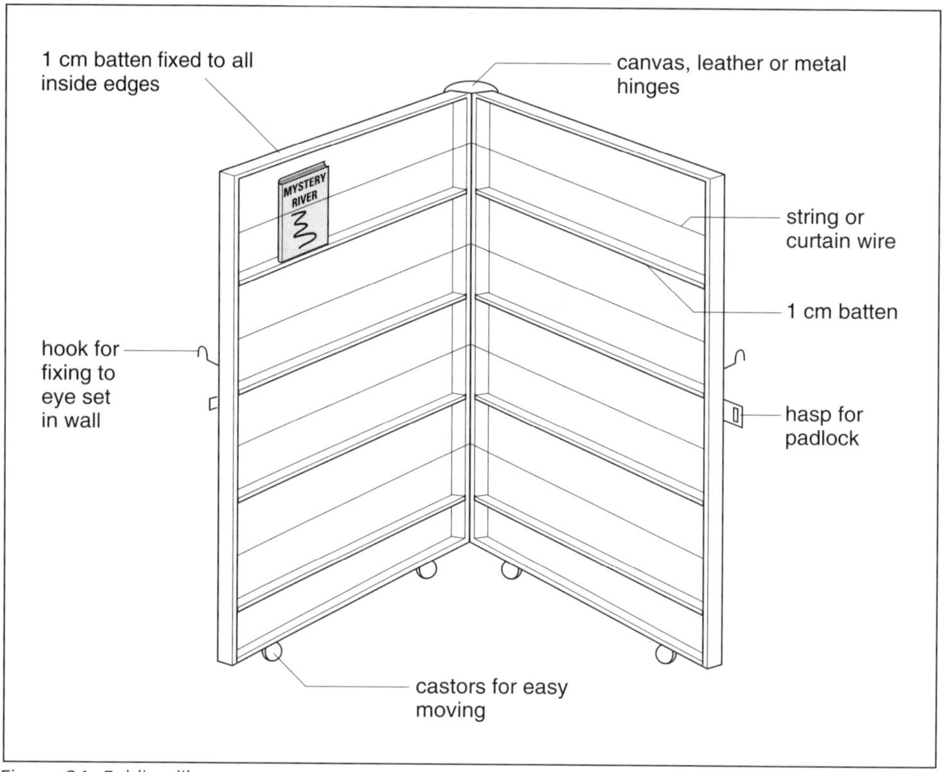

Figure 21 Folding library corner
The two screens are of hardboard, plywood etc, each 1–1½ metres high and 60–77 cm wide. Join down one side by means of hinges. Fit a hasp which can be secured by a padlock when the two open sides are brought together so that the library is closed. The books can remain in position, standing on narrow battens and kept upright by tight curtain wires stretched across in front of them, about 10–15 cm above each batten. If the screen can be placed in the corner of the room, it can be kept steady while open by fixing two hooks into eyes set in the walls.

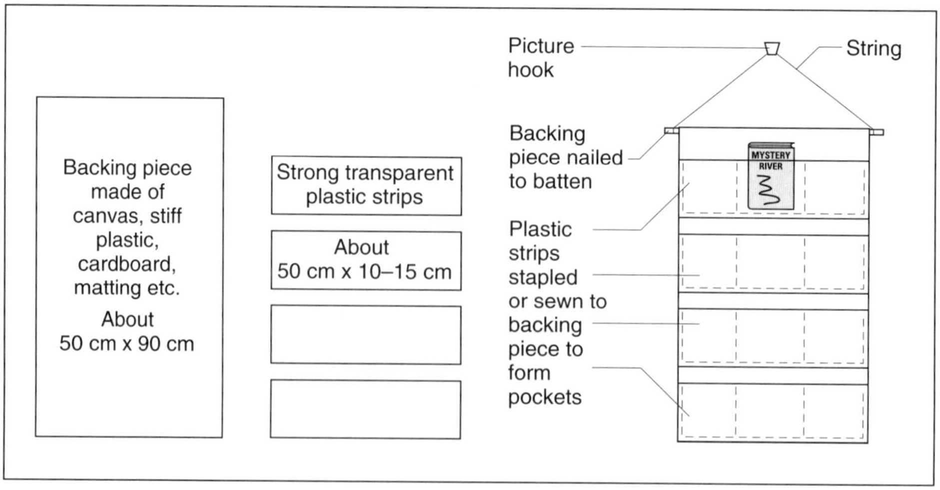

Figure 22 Hanging wall pockets for storing readers
The plastic strips need to be divided into three or four pockets, about 18–20 cm wide, according to the size of the books and the width of the backing piece.

Classifying the class library

Ordinary libraries are classified according to subject (fiction/non-fiction, with sub-classification into different subjects, different kinds of story, etc). Books for language learners are often classified according to linguistic level. Which is more useful?

Sometimes a student reads a book because it enthrals him, even though the language is difficult; sometimes because, though not particularly interesting, it is written in language he can understand. So either may be the decisive factor. Ideally, for reading to become a pleasurable habit, both content and language must suit the reader.

If the class library does not need to cater for widely differing proficiency levels, classify it according to content, because once the language level is left out of account, it is the content that determines the student's choice. Otherwise, it is more helpful for the primary classification to be in terms of linguistic level, so that students do not get discouraged trying to find a suitable book.

Coding linguistic levels

It is helpful to have a coding system for linguistic levels that can operate throughout the school, so that when students move from one class to another they do not have to learn a new system each time. You could base it on a readability index (see p175) or on the publisher's grading. But your own intuition may be the best criterion of all, and once the programme has been operating for a while you can also make use of students' opinions to fine-tune the gradings.

For a full range of learners (beginners to advanced), you will require quite a lot of levels. The EPER system has nine levels; EFL publishers' series seldom have more than six, but as they overlap the total range is greater. For more homogeneous students (eg all roughly intermediate), you will need fewer levels, or you may prefer to make the grading more sensitive, by defining each level more narrowly. Hence, in one school, level 3 might include books of 1000–1500 words, while in another, level 3 might be 1000–1250 and level 4 1250–1500.

These decisions depend on your own circumstances. If you are not very experienced, set up a system that you can modify later if it does not work very well. In any case there will always be a need for modifications, eg to re-code a book which has proved too easy or difficult for its initial level. Get the students to tell you when a grading seems mistaken.

EFL teachers are particularly well served, with carefully worked out grading schemes ready made. Some EFL publishers (Appendix D) supply free leaflets about their grading systems, which are worth asking for. However, different publishers grade according to different criteria, so it is not possible to match exactly the books produced by any two of them. An approximate match is enough, since students are not at exactly matched levels either. Even publishers' grading systems are not foolproof, so be prepared to change the level of a book that turns out to be misgraded.

Simple information books in the target language are worth including, especially if you use project work in language teaching. You can find excellent ones prepared for mother tongue speakers. Assess their language level by one of the methods outlined in Chapter 10; use the same method to assess a few samples from each of your graded levels so that the ungraded books can be slotted in appropriately. Or grade them according to intuition and adjust the grading on the basis of experience.

Colour-coding the levels

When you have worked out the best system for the collection, you may find yourself with, say, twelve levels, for instance:

Level 1	Up to 500 words vocabulary	red
Level 2	500–750	yellow
Level 3	750–1000	dark green

And so on. The colour-coding shown on the right makes shelving and choosing books easier. Stick coloured paper spots or strips on the spines of the books so that the level can be identified at a glance. If you cannot find enough colours, differentiate levels by using shapes (circle, square, etc) or numbers of spots as well. If books are shelved according to level, the shelf labels can carry the same code.

Classifying supplementary readers in the main library

If graded readers are classified according to subject (eg by the Dewey system), they are dispersed all over the library and you lose a major advantage of grading, namely that students can choose suitable books easily because they are shelved by level.

If the librarian agrees to shelve them separately, foreign language books can be classified by the same system as class library books. For library users from a wide age range, you can sub-divide according to whether the books are for children or adults. Use extra colours or a special symbol, eg a red star, for children's titles and shelve them separately if possible.

Try at least to get the graded fiction readers shelved separately – at the end of the main fiction section, for instance, instead of scattered throughout according to the author's name. Since most graded readers are fiction, this would be a very helpful concession.

The librarian will very likely agree to use a colour-coding system for the language levels, provided she does not have to do the coding herself. This is better done by a professional language teacher anyway, so you and your colleagues should be prepared to undertake it. Colour-coding works well with the normal system of classifying by subject; the reader looks for books on the desired subject and then uses the colour code to find those suitable for his own level.

Discarding books

If you inherit a library, skim through each book to see whether it should be there at all. A surprising amount of junk is found in libraries that are not regularly weeded. This is particularly likely if the medium of instruction has changed; many of the books may no longer match the proficiency of the students. Throw them out, unless they are so attractive that students enjoy them despite their linguistic level.

Be equally ruthless with graded readers that are tattered, dirty or too old-fashioned or foreign in content to attract the students. Interpret this with common sense: a popular book may be shabby, but must not be discarded if it is still readable, unless it can be replaced. Let the students decide which books are appealing. The best guidance comes from noting which books are often borrowed; they are not always the ones we predict.

Many people have been put off reading for life by being faced with shelves full of unsuitable books, among which the suitable ones are hardly visible. Don't let this happen in your library. Shelves of suitable books, cared for and attractively displayed, are hard to resist. It is better to have a few that are suitable than a lot that are mostly not.

Losses and damage

Some librarians lock up their books rather than run the risk of anyone borrowing them. But then why buy them at all? The more people read them, the more justified the expenditure.

Book losses are certainly a problem, but it is important to get agreement that they can be borrowed. Use all your patience, logic and good humour! The first step is to establish the principle that library books cannot survive as long as tables and chairs. A paperback in frequent use lasts only four or five years – and even furniture gets written off eventually.

Books may need to be written off for several reasons: they may be lost, too damaged to read, or unsuitable. Obviously we must minimize all of these, and be seen to do so, but a reasonable principal will agree that each year a proportion of your books may be written off. About ten per cent is considered acceptable by public libraries; you should be able to do better. If you write off fewer than seven per cent a year, your principal should congratulate you.

The best way to reduce loss and damage is to educate students in valuing and caring for books. Your own attitude is more important than anything else, especially if students come from homes where books are little used. In your class, books are handed to the student, not thrown. You never read to the class from a book that is folded back on itself, nor have you ever been seen to turn down the corner of a page to mark your place. You set the example, and also draw attention to good reading manners. Gradually the students see that, if we are privileged to read new, clean, attractive books, we are under an obligation to keep them that way.

It helps if students have a lot of the responsibility for caring for the books, as described earlier. From this comes pride in a well-run library and consequent reduction of losses and damage. (Students often know who has borrowed a 'missing' book and can recover it more easily than you.)

In addition, take sensible precautions to protect books from both loss and damage. Cover them with transparent plastic; check them regularly for damage that can be repaired, and get students to report damage or repair it themselves. Set up proper systems and make sure they are kept to. But take every step you can think of not to discourage borrowing, otherwise there is no point in having a library.

Recurrent budget

Recurrent expenditure is always needed, even if your library is about the right size (for the main library, about eight times as many books as users; for a class library, about four times). This is sometimes overlooked by those who control the funds, so it is important to get the principle accepted. Books have to be written off and new ones must be added to keep the library attractive and up to date.

Find the average cost of a supplementary reader at the time when you have to submit a budget. Add, say, 10 per cent for inflation (according to local conditions) and budget for replacement or purchase of a number of books equivalent to about 15 per cent of your collection. Add whatever is needed for other materials (labels, plastic covers, etc). The calculations might look like Figure 23.

Class Library budget calculation

			£
a	Average cost of a reader at time of calculation		1.50
	Add 10% for inflation		.15
	∴ Price used for calculation		1.65
b	Total book stock this year	=	200 books
	Expected losses/discards: 12%	=	24 books
	Hoped-for expansion 4%	=	8 books
			£
c	To replace losses/discards: 24 x £1.65		39.60
	To expand collection: 8 x £1.65		13.20
	Materials, stationery etc.		10.00
		total	62.80

Round up total to nearest £1:
Budget requested next year: £63.00

Figure 23 Sample class library budget calculation

Training library skills

Having assembled a good collection of books, classified them helpfully and shelved them attractively, you cannot just sit down and expect them to be well used. Most students have to be motivated to read; we shall return to this shortly. Another task is to train them to use the library.

Effective use of a library is not really a reading skill, so it is not discussed fully here; but since it gives access to books, it is important in a reading programme. The main librarian is the best person to do the training, and both she and the students should have provision for it in their timetables.

Library skills cannot be acquired in a single lesson; they need continual development. Ideally this begins with some intensive training for new students, and continues at intervals, becoming more sophisticated as students' needs change and they take more responsibility for their work.

The best library training is practical. Students learn most from tasks that make them use the catalogue, locate books and so on. A team race to answer, say, 50 questions testing basic library skills is fun as well as instructive for first-year students. (I mean the sort of questions that require them to run round the library and use the catalogue, such as: How many books by J. Anderson does the library hold? How many of them are on the shelf at present? What does the classification 401 mean? Where are the cassette recordings kept?)

Later, subject specialists should collaborate by setting assignments requiring the use of references, so that students can be shown how to find information on a specific topic, and how to select suitable sources and reject unsuitable ones for a given purpose. This involves using the reference skills described in Chapter 4.

The L1 will be used for this training, if that is the medium of instruction; but you must take some responsibility for helping students to find their way round the foreign language collection. To do this, you need to be familiar with the collection, and to have some knowledge of the contents of many of the books.

When students are choosing books, try to be available to suggest, describe, check that a chosen book is not too far beyond them linguistically. When students are at a loss, choose several books that might suit them and let them make the final selection. Find out about their preferences so that you can order books to satisfy them. Chat about books they have just finished, so that you can assess without formal testing how far they have been understood. Make sure the books are treated with respect and the borrowing system works. Notice the students who read little and give them special encouragement. In short, be a help and show an interest.

Organizing an extensive reading programme

Co-operation

If possible, get together with other teachers and plan a programme for the school. If this doesn't work, you can still plan for your own classes, but an integrated programme is much more effective. By the time you have succeeded in making your students want to read, they may be about to leave you to join someone else's class. This doesn't matter if all teachers are working in a similar way; but if they are not, your efforts may have less success than they deserve.

Creating interest in reading

The first thing to do, when introducing a reading programme, is to get the students interested in the books. Here are some suggestions. For such activities, have the class sitting round you in a group – on the floor, perhaps – and keep the atmosphere friendly and informal.

- Read aloud, stopping the story at a tantalizing point. Help the class to speculate about what happens next and encourage them to read on by themselves.
- Get a student who has enjoyed a book to talk about it or write a brief note for display (without giving away the end of the story!).
- Show the class new books and talk a little about each one – enough to whet the appetite but not to give away the plot.
- Buy cassette recordings of some graded readers for loan with the books. Play parts of them in class. Or play a whole cassette in instalments of about five minutes at the end of each lesson. (If you or a friend read well, make your own recording if the commercial ones are beyond your pocket.)
- Encourage students to make or do things arising from their reading; they might prepare pictures for display or tape a dramatized version of the story. Students may enjoy preparing materials of this kind to interest their friends in lower classes, with benefit to both.
- Promote discussion of the practical or ethical problems faced by people in the books. This can take place after a fair number of the class have read the book, or follow an outline of the problem given by a student who has read it; either way, others may be tempted to do the same.

Incentives to read

Some students are more willing to read if they have visible signs of their own progress. The long-term results of a reading programme become apparent too late to be an incentive, so something more immediate is needed.

Moving from one reading level to the next is the most obvious sign of progress, but it happens infrequently, since learners may need to read as many as twenty books at one level before moving to the next (it depends on the way the levels are structured). Finishing a book is one of the best incentives; for this reason, it is important to start students off with short, easy books. The achievement will motivate them to start another book (make sure that a choice is available) and success will build on success, provided they don't move to more difficult books until they are ready.

Some teachers like to display a chart showing the number of books each student has read; for children, this can be in the form of a ladder, each step representing a book, with students' name cards moving up the ladder as they read. It's nice to see your name climbing steadily upwards, but depressing to stay on the bottom step for weeks, so charts of this kind may be counterproductive for weak students. A less competitive form of display may be better; for example, a graph showing how many books the whole class finishes each week.

However, it is really the individual's progress that matters, so it is more useful for each student to keep a personal chart or graph showing how much he reads each week (eg in terms of number of pages), or how many books he has finished. He might also record the titles and a few comments about each book, but this must not become another dull chore or it will take away the pleasure of the achievement.

Your own interest and encouragement are an incentive to read, particularly for your weaker students, so give as much individual attention as you can.

Monitoring extensive reading

Should you check how well a student has understood an extensive reading book? This is a controversial issue. Some people believe that a student should always answer a few questions to show that he has really read the book, and claim that students get satisfaction from being able to do this. Others point out that since extensive reading is essentially a private activity and intended to be above all enjoyable, any attempt to make it seem like school work is likely to be a deterrent.

In fact, it is likely that different people respond to each approach. As a student, I hated having my leisure reading interfered with by teachers' questions (but I liked them to take a friendly interest – very different) and I would not want to inhibit anybody who felt the same way. Equally, I would happily offer questions to those who wanted them.

Partly this issue depends on whether you have to assign marks for extensive reading. As explained in the next section, I very much hope you don't, because as soon as marks come in, reading for pleasure becomes reading for credit.

If you decide to supply questions, make them quick to do, write them on a card and keep the card either in a pocket stuck inside the book cover, or in a file in your desk. In the second case, the student comes to you for the card when he is ready: you can make this optional or obligatory. However, you can find out by chatting to him at least as much as you can from written answers, and it is a less intrusive way of checking progress and finding out what help is needed.

Reading records

For your own information, keep a record of what each student reads and any problems he has. The easiest way is to have a book with a page for every student; loose-leaf is best, in case some students need extra pages. You can get the information from the system for recording loans, or ask students to see you each time they finish a book. The record helps you keep an eye on students who are not progressing, provides information about students' tastes (to help with book ordering) and is of great value to the students' next teacher, who should have access to it.

If a student has kept a book for several weeks, or if you can see that he is struggling with it, find out what is wrong and, unless there are good reasons why he should continue, encourage him to return the book without finishing it and pick something else. The whole point about extensive reading is that students are free to choose; they can be encouraged and even urged to read, but there is no virtue in finishing a book if you are getting nothing out of it.

Assessment in the reading programme

Placement tests

When you get a new class, you will need to discover their level of reading ability so that you can choose suitable books. You may be able to get information from the previous teacher (*Homer reads mainly at level 4 but has enjoyed a few titles from level 5. Keen on war stories and travel books.*) This is more informative than test results, so organize reading records that are passed from one class to the next; a loose-leaf form allows for students transferring to other classes. If this is not possible, you can find out their reading ability from a ***placement test*** (provided they are not complete beginners). Suitable tests are described in Chapter 13.

Other kinds of testing

Regular formal testing of extensive reading is not recommended. It is difficult to organize because everyone reads different books and also because progress is only measurable over an extensive period. No doubt you will measure progress from time to time in connection with classroom lessons, and the results will incorporate the benefits the student has gained from extensive reading.

Testing extensive reading can even be damaging, if it makes students read less freely or pleasurably; and they may try to cheat, which is not difficult in a programme of this kind. It is best to make cheating pointless by not including extensive reading in the end-of-year assessments; in an ideal programme of personal reading development, a student is in a position to cheat nobody but himself.

Finally, formal testing is pointless, because the records described in the previous section give all the evidence of progress you need. The student's developing ability is shown by his moving up from one level to the next, and the time it takes tells you whether to be pleased or worried.

Remedial reading

If you administer a reading placement test, you must be prepared for some surprises. Some of them may be pleasant: if students turn out to read unexpectedly well, your only problem will be to keep them supplied with suitable books. The main problem will be the students who turn out to read very badly. For those who simply read too slowly, it may be enough to provide a lot of very easy material on which they can improve their speed with little help. But for those with more severe problems, special attention will be needed.

In some school systems, there are remedial classes for those who need help, but in many there are none. In that case it is your responsibility. If the foreign language is also the medium of instruction, remedial work is crucial to the student's future, whether the school officially recognizes the need or not.

It is not possible here to go into the question of remedial work adequately, though you will find in other chapters many ideas that can be adapted for the purpose. Even though the goal is silent reading, for very weak readers the initial approach must be oral.

A ***language experience approach*** (eg Mackay et al 1979, Rigg 1990, Walker et al 1992) is often a good way to begin because students and teachers together prepare the materials, based on the individual's interests and experience; it can thus be adapted to any age and type of learner.

For a group of learners, explore the ***shared book approach*** (Holdaway 1979), where the teacher uses a big version of the text so that all can see and read it together; the content need not be childish, though you will have to make your own large copies.

Recent work with weak mother tongue readers has laid emphasis on the importance of help from the home. If this is practicable – if a parent or sibling is competent in the language – then invoke their help in hearing the student read. They need only listen and offer the correct word if the student stumbles.

Similar devices for supporting weak readers have been developed for use in the classroom. One is ***paired reading*** (see eg Martin 1989), where students work in pairs on a variety of tasks, one having a text, the other having a task for which he needs information from the text. Another is ***reciprocal reading*** (see eg Moore 1988), where the student gradually takes over the teacher's role (which has been carefully modelled for him) and questions, summarizes, predicts, etc for other students, being rewarded by praise and encouragement. Peer tutors (ie fellow students who are good readers) have been successfully used for this technique.

The most important ingredients for a remedial programme, however, seem to be time and genuine concern for the learners' progress. It helps if weak students read some of the easiest books together with the teacher, but this takes time that may be hard to find. You can gain some time by using groupwork as suggested in Chapter 9, or by using very easy worksheets or reading cards (see next section) that the student can work through on his own, though they are difficult to devise for the lowest levels. (Suitable cards are available from EPER; see Appendix D.) Other activities that can be done without a teacher include listening to taped readings while following the text in the book (described in Chapter 12); this is helpful and is enjoyed.

Reading cards and reading laboratories

Useful additions to an extensive reading programme are reading cards and their more elaborate relatives, reading laboratories, even though they tend to be directed more to skills development than to reading for pleasure. A ***reading card*** consists of a text with questions or other tasks, printed or pasted on a card which can be stored with others in a box file, filing cabinet, etc. A ***reading laboratory*** is a collection of reading cards, graded in level and intended to be used systematically to improve reading skills.

Reading cards are used independently of the teacher and can be borrowed like graded readers. They are popular with students, especially those for whom even a short and easy book seems out of reach. Successfully reading a short and easy card encourages them to progress to other cards; a good supply of simple cards often produces rapid progress and high motivation. The student can gradually progress to longer cards until he develops enough confidence to try reading a short book, which should be at an easier level than the last card.

If you make your own cards, they can be tied in with the collection of supplementary readers. Extracts from readers can be used as texts on cards; some students will move on to read the book. Plan a series of cards at the lower reading levels and colour-code them by the system used for library books. Students should achieve consistently high scores at one level before moving to the next.

Texts for cards can come from many other sources too. Sometimes old books (even old textbooks) contain suitable material: you can cut up the book and throw away unwanted parts. However, the material must be new to the students: it must not come from books they have used in class. If you enjoy writing your own material, you can find stories in newspapers or magazines like *Reader's Digest* which you can simplify to the level required. Even quite dull texts have been successful when made into a set of cards, but they must be simple enough for the students, and kept very short: ten lines is ample to begin with. Include pictures if possible (eg cut from magazines).

The questions or other tasks on the card can follow the patterns suggested in Chapters 11 and 12. For weak readers, keep them few and simple so that they experience success and gain confidence in working independently. If you supply answer cards students can check their own work; the results will not (I hope) need to be recorded except by themselves, and by you to monitor their progress.

The main snag about reading cards is that you need a great many, since you must cater for students at various levels. Co-operating with other teachers helps; one set of cards can be used with several classes, especially if copies are made (eg by photocopying – but take care to check the copyright position before doing this). Provide plenty of cards at the lowest levels so that they can be used for remedial work. Since cards are intended to be used independently of the teacher, they are ideal for any student who is far below or above the level of the others.

Using a class reader

Using a reader in class is a way of requiring students to read; but the aim is to make reading enjoyable, and the stress is more on appreciation than on skills development. If work on a class reader does not increase interest in reading, it is best avoided, because it is easy for lessons on a set book to be dreary and not at all likely to tempt people to read more. But they do not have to be like that; properly handled, they can become favourite lessons. So a few suggestions may be useful.

First, as usual, is the choice of book. If it doesn't appeal to most of the class, your efforts will be in vain. Use the criteria in Chapter 10 to find something that everyone will enjoy. Reading level may be a problem; pitch it lower rather than higher, because students are going to do most of the reading on their own. If it has to be so low that you can't find any books of interest, do not use class readers.

The second crucial element is the way you deal with the book. A common practice with set books is to read them aloud round the class for perhaps one lesson a week. This makes it difficult to create and maintain enthusiasm for any book because it takes such a long time to finish. Moreover, any students who are interested tend to continue reading ahead out of class and are consequently bored during subsequent lessons. It is more satisfactory to assign most of the reading to be done out of class. In this way you can get through a book quite quickly; the aim should be to take only four or five weeks over an average reader (about 80 pages).

You will see the importance of choosing a book that is not difficult; it should be a good deal easier than the current textbook, so that you can reasonably push students to read it quickly. It is possible to read six or seven books a year, if enough suitable class sets are available, and the extra practice pays dividends at examination time.

However, supplying enough class sets, even if each set is used by several classes each year, is expensive. Thirty books in a class set means only one title to be read by any individual student, whereas thirty titles in a class library means that he can read all of them. If you cannot afford enough class sets to meet your needs for a whole year, just use what you can. But do not spin out the reading to cover a longer time; get through each title quickly to maintain motivation.

Approaching work on a class reader

This approach assumes that class periods are used mainly not for reading but for discussion, so choose books that are worth thinking about. You will not be asking typical 'comprehension' questions, but questions that require students to respond to the book and think about what is important in it.

A typical programme for a book might look like this:

Lesson 1
Introductory (setting the scene, creating anticipation, etc). Teacher reads aloud part of the opening chapter or plays a tape of it or sets silent guided reading. Follow up with discussion and speculation: What sort of story is it going to be? Who seem to be the main characters? What sort of people are they? What might happen to them? And so on. Set the first reading task to be done outside class: Chapters 1–5, with signpost questions (SPQs – described on p160) which focus on the development of plot or characters, especially aspects that may not be well understood.

Lesson 2
Discuss answers to SPQs and go on to wider discussion of Chapters 1–5. (What do we now know about the characters? Why did X do that? Was it right/sensible? What does Y think about it? How do you know?) Deal with any problems, discuss the predictions made in lesson 1 and make others in the light of new evidence. Set reading task with SPQs: Chapters 6–10.

Lesson 3
As for lesson 2 but dealing with Chapters 6–10. Set reading task with SPQs: Chapters 11–17 (last chapter).

Lesson 4
As for lesson 3, but dealing with Chapters 11–17. Set final task: overall response (eg a letter from character X to Y written after the story ends; a summing up of the story

seen from the viewpoint of a minor character; a letter to the author saying what you thought of the book).

Lesson 5
Discuss overall response to/evaluation of the book. Follow-up activity (eg dramatization, picture, project).

Obviously the details must vary; the only essential features are that almost all the reading is done outside school hours, and that the book is dealt with fairly rapidly. And of course that the emphasis throughout is on enjoying the story and getting the most out of it. The suggestions made in Chapter 9 about introducing a text, making reading tasks purposeful and asking signpost questions (SPQs) can all be applied without destroying motivation. But the SPQs will focus on understanding the characters and the plot. There is no detailed work on the text unless it contributes directly to appreciation and does not interfere with enjoyment.

Key passages

There is one technique which combines the methods of intensive reading with the broader approach needed when studying a whole book. A passage is chosen which illuminates some aspect of the book that you consider important: perhaps someone's character, or a critical point in the plot, or some central problem. The passage may be as short as ten lines or so, or as long as two or three pages.

Set the passage for homework, with questions to draw attention to the features that make it significant in the book. Or study it in the classroom as part of an intensive reading lesson; this enables you to relate the passage to its wider context in a way that is impossible with texts that are divorced from the books from which they are taken.

After the class have attempted the questions on their own, discussion can focus on the significance of the passage and its place in the book. (It follows that this work is often best done after the book has been finished.) It should be possible to make the students themselves draw most of the conclusions, since the questions you set ensure that a lot of thinking along the right lines has already been done. More advanced students can choose key passages and set the questions themselves.

Overall response and follow-up activity

The last piece of work on a class reader should help the class to see the book as a whole. Some of the activities suggested in Chapter 12 may be appropriate, or questions of personal response (see Chapter 11) can be discussed. The aim is to help students to understand and evaluate the events and people in the book, not just to check whether they can recall them.

This approach brings us to the edge of literature and is an excellent preparation for students who go on to study it. It encourages them to explore the motives of characters, the way one event in the plot leads to another, whether an action is right in the writer's view and in the view of the class, and so on. Here are a few suggestions for discussion to give some ideas about how to exploit a class reader:

Was X responsible for (a key event)?
Why did X ...? (Not worth asking unless the motives or causes are complex.)
Was X wise to ... ? What would you have done?
Did X deserve what happened to him?
Was X a good (friend/mother/boss, etc)?

Who was more (unlucky), X or Y?
Why was (key event) so important?
What would have happened if ...?
What will happen to the characters after the end of the story?

I have assumed that the class reader will be a narrative, rather than a non-fiction book, because stories are more commonly enjoyed by the whole class, and the aim is for everyone to enjoy the experience so that they are encouraged to read more on their own.

Further reading

For evidence of the value of extensive reading for language learning, see Elley and Mangubhai 1983; Elley 1991; Tudor and Hafiz 1989; Hafiz and Tudor 1989, 1990; Brusch 1991; Krashen 1989, 1993; Wodinsky and Nation 1988. Robb and Susser 1989 report its value for improving reading skills.

On reading across the curriculum see Marland 1977; Gillham 1986.

On the relationship between L1 and foreign language reading see Hulstijn and Matter 1991.

For ideas on the selection, use and management of supplementary readers, see Bamford 1984; Hedge 1985; Hill 1992; Chambers 1991; Davis 1995. For general advice on running a library, see publications of the School Library Association and the Library Association (addresses in Appendix D).

For reviews of graded reader series see Hill and Reid Thomas 1988a,b; 1989; Reid Thomas and Hill 1993. Bamford 1984 also includes student ratings for over 500 titles. Rönnqvist and Sell 1994 report successful titles for teenagers.

On remedial reading (mainly in schools, but similar principles apply at other levels) see eg Beard 1990; Harrison and Coles 1992; Pumfrey 1991; Weaver 1988. Meek 1983 and Martin 1989 contain illuminating transcripts of failing readers talking about reading.

On reading laboratories see Lunzer and Gardner 1979; Pumfrey 1991.

On the use of class readers see Hedge 1985; Ellis and McCrae 1991; Greenwood 1988. On literature teaching see Hill 1986; Collie and Slater 1987; Maley and Duff 1989; Duff and Maley 1990; Carter and Long 1991; English Language Teaching Journal vol 44/3 (July 1990); all include many ideas of wider application.

Chapter 9
Planning reading lessons

CREATING a climate in which reading is valued, and getting students to read more, are indispensable if they are to read better. Now we consider more teacher-controlled activities which contribute to the same aim.

Some preliminary issues

Separate reading lessons?

Teaching reading does not mean excluding speaking, listening and writing. It is a question of focus: some lessons concentrate on reading, others do not. The other skills are always needed, to provide variety (eg sometimes listening to a text read aloud), to enable the students to learn effectively (eg discussing the text) or to give you feedback (eg preparing written work based on the text).

Whether the work on a text is done in a period labelled 'Reading' on the timetable, or forms part of one labelled 'Foreign language', is not important. But we do not keep language skills in separate boxes, so activities that integrate them reflect our use of language in real life, as well as being interesting. In any case, the text will surely be used as a starting point for work on the other skills, just as it always has been.

So the activities discussed in this chapter might take place in a separate lesson or in part of a lesson during which reading is the focus of attention. Separate reading materials may be desirable, but you can also apply the ideas to texts in the coursebook. The important thing is not to leave reading to take care of itself, even if the textbook does not make specific provision for it. For many students, it is the most vital skill, and the one that provides the most spin-off for general language learning.

What teachers can do to help students learn: a reminder

First of all, you might like to look again at Chapter 3, where we discussed some popular ways to stop students from learning how to read. In the same chapter, we summarized what teachers can do to help readers to make sense of texts for themselves. Most of those responsibilities are dealt with in other chapters. Here we look at planning lessons so that all the students will participate and learn: at procedures that direct attention to the text, foster text-focused talk, and provide scaffolding when it is needed. First we will consider the general pattern of a reading lesson.

The need for a flexible programme

It is not my intention to offer a blueprint for reading lessons. Different texts need different treatment and cannot all be handled within a single framework. Moreover, to explore a specific strategy, such as detecting presuppositions, we might use several texts, none of them studied very thoroughly. Some skills may be practised by referring to whole books, a few even by studying sentences.

The reading programme therefore must be flexible, so that it can include different kinds of text and skill, and so that you can respond to unforeseen needs and move quickly over areas that give no trouble. This chapter simply offers suggested components for reading lessons. We shall discuss how these components (eg an introduction, a signpost question) can help, and how to make them effective. You will decide whether to include them, bearing in mind the nature of the text and the purpose of the lesson.

Skills-based and text-based lessons

We distinguished between skills-based and text-based lessons in Chapter 3, and in Part Two we identified a number of skills or strategies which can to some extent be dealt with separately. But many lessons need to focus on the texts themselves, to practise integrating the skills in order to make sense of the whole. As the course progresses, text-based work is increasingly likely to predominate. We dealt with specific skills in earlier chapters, so we shall be looking here mainly at text-based lessons.

Planning a text-based lesson

Studying the text

We will assume you have a text (or texts; for convenience I will usually write as if only one were involved) that satisfies the criteria set out in Chapter 10 – at the right level, interesting and so on.

The first step is to find out what potential the text offers; we shall return to this shortly (p153). Next decide what aspects of the text to focus on. It is not possible to cover every aspect, so decide which are most helpful to the class. Apportion the time available and decide if you want to use a whole lesson period, part of a period or a series of periods for the work.

Activities for a text-based lesson

In a text-based lesson (or series of lessons), you will normally want the students to do some of the following – perhaps all of them, occasionally:

- practice general reading efficiency: skimming, scanning, rapid reading, use of reference apparatus (Chapter 4)
- tackle the interpretation of the text by using non-linear information (Chapter 4), word attack skills (Chapter 5) and text attack skills (Chapters 6, 7) through the intervention of various kinds of question or other task (Chapters 11, 12)
- produce some kind of outcome based on response to the text as a whole (see p166 and Chapter 7 p121; Chapter 12)

Whatever else you include, interpretation and response are the core of a text-based lesson. We want students to be capable of interpreting the text fully and accurately and responding to it as the writer intended. However, we also want them to read flexibly: to use the text for their own purposes, not the writer's, if they wish; to read critically; to skip difficulties when accuracy is not essential; and to respond according to their own personality. We shall look at ways of promoting these aims.

Global or detailed study?

Usually the ultimate objective is for the students to achieve ***global understanding***: that is, to understand the text as a whole and relate it to personal experience, other sources of knowledge, other texts and so on. Which is to come first in our teaching – the top-down approach, leading more directly to global understanding, or the bottom-up study, leading to mastery of detail?

It is logical to suppose that we must understand the parts before we can understand the whole, but we know that comprehension does not work so tidily. Sometimes we can interpret difficult parts of the text because we have already grasped the overall message: we use a top-down approach to predict 'This part must mean something like X', and then use the prediction to disentangle it. Similarly, the top-down approach enables us to dismiss misinterpretations because they flout common sense or do not fit in with the global meaning of the text. Then we go back to the words of the text and try to work out a more sensible interpretation.

All this implies that we should begin by using a top-down approach and later switch between the two approaches, as each kind of interpretation supports the other according to the needs of the moment. It is helpful to students bogged down in a complex paragraph to stand back and consider the wider view. It is helpful for those confronting unfamiliar or implausible ideas to check that they have correctly interpreted the plain sense. Figure 24 illustrates one practical route to studying longer texts which shows the interplay of top-down and bottom-up approaches.

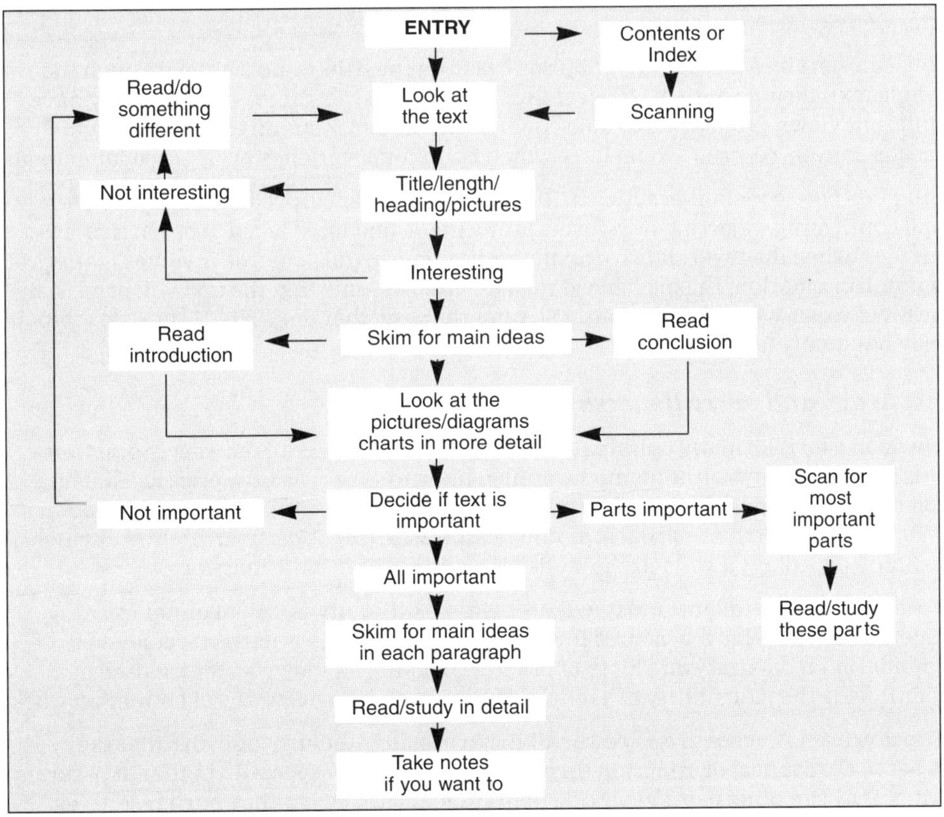

Figure 24 A basic method for reading long texts
From Revell and Sweeney1993

Reading as making hypotheses

The chief danger of the top-down approach is that the reader may try to read into the text what he thinks ought to be there, rather than what the writer intended.

To counteract this, students should learn to support their first impressions with detailed evidence from the text. They should learn to treat interpretation as making a series of hypotheses, rather as scientists do. If the first hypothesis ('I think this text means so-and-so') is correct, all the evidence in the text will support it. If it is incorrect, it will prove increasingly difficult to justify as you read on and encounter contradictory evidence.

Less able readers may persist in their original hypothesis, devising ingenious explanations for conflicting evidence. This ***perseverative reading*** (see eg Kimmel and MacGinitie 1984; Pressley et al 1990) is not the sort of perseverance we want. Competent readers notice contradictions and take the trouble to sort them out, even if it involves going back to reinterpret the text in the light of new evidence. With very difficult texts, this process may have to be repeated several times. It is not a sign of incompetence, but the reverse.

Readers can often produce a reasonable hypothesis about a text after skimming it, by using a top-down approach. This means that a lesson can start on a positive note: 'What do we know about this text? So what do you think its message is likely to be?' instead of starting with negative factors such as unfamiliar vocabulary. It is also good strategy, for students must learn to utilize their resources of common sense, general knowledge and experience.

You can start by asking for hypotheses based on the title, or on a skim through the whole text. Do not confirm or reject the students' answers at this stage. If they have different views, point out that subsequent reading can focus on establishing which is most accurate; return to them later, when bottom-up work has progressed far enough.

Students need constant practice in forming hypotheses (ie predictions about a text), and confirming, rejecting or reformulating them, and must learn to be particularly vigilant when the text relates to an unfamiliar culture or topic, or involves matters of opinion or emotion. Inexperienced readers often assume that the text will echo their own views; or, where this is manifestly not the case, that the writer is hostile – which may be equally false.

Accuracy and overall message

Work on a text normally culminates in response to the overall message. Sometimes this should be done without much detailed interpretation, to give practice in using top-down strategies and ignoring trivial difficulties. Appendix C Lesson 2, *Good Neighbours,* uses this approach; and in Lesson 3, *Adrian Mole,* you might go straight to Step 9 (roleplay) if you felt the students could cope with the language.

To do this safely students must judge whether a difficulty is trivial or not by determining how far it obscures the overall message. This is not as circular as it sounds, but it does rely on plenty of practice in using top-down strategies and monitoring the plausibility of a top-down interpretation by means of bottom-up work.

Top-down approaches are so powerful in harnessing students' abilities that they deserve a great deal of attention throughout the course, especially in the early stages when they can build confidence and help students to see that they have resources which can be brought to bear on the text.

Nevertheless, it is probably right to devote more class time to bottom-up work. First, it is what learners find most difficult. Second, learners who can read with complete accuracy, if they need to, may be more willing to read for the main idea and ignore the details. And third, the reader's response to a text is worth little unless it is based on accurate understanding. For all these reasons, in this chapter we shall give a good deal of attention to ways of developing bottom-up approaches.

Assessing the learning potential of a text

At this point it seems a good idea to look at a text and work out how you might use it in class. Activity 9.1 asks you to do this. You will get the greatest benefit from this if you do not look at Appendix B or C until after you have really worked on the text yourself.

Activity 9.1 *Planning what to do with a text*

Do this activity with a group of colleagues if possible. Work on the same text and start by doing so individually; this will produce more variety of insights and approaches than if you work together from the beginning. In subsequent discussion you will all benefit from this variety.

1. Skim the texts in Appendix A (except 1 and 2). Choose one that you would like to use, preferably with your own class.
2. Study the chosen text until you are satisfied that you understand what the writer expected you to get out of it.
3. Consider how you could help your students to understand it equally well. What sort of tasks would you set? What questions would you ask? How would you help them to cope with the difficult parts (not by explaining or translating, please!)? How would you deal with global understanding? What specific reading skills can you practise?
4. Prepare a lesson plan outlining the work you want to do and including as many actual questions, tasks, etc as possible. Do this jointly if you are working with colleagues.

Sometimes, when you are deciding what to do with a text, ideas come quickly; if there is a lot of physical description, you might get the students to produce a map or diagram; if there are statistics, a chart or graph might be a suitable outcome; if the text is from a persuasive advertisement, a list of the actual facts given about the product might be salutary. But not all texts offer simple solutions. Usually it is necessary to devise a number of tasks in order to explore the text thoroughly.

Most texts offer opportunities for practising some of the reading skills we have discussed. This of course contributes to an understanding of each particular text; but when you ask students to scan for a piece of information, or infer the meaning of an unknown word, or work out what evidence there is of biased reporting, they should be made aware of the skills involved, so that they can apply them to other texts. Both aspects need to be kept in mind.

When you have decided what you want to get out of the text in Activity 9.1, and how you might do it, refer to Appendix B or C. There you will find the same texts exploited by other teachers. By studying the notes, tasks and so on, decide what they want their students to get out of the text. If their objectives differ from yours, are they equally valid and useful? What means do they use to achieve them? How do they differ from yours? Advantages and disadvantages?

If you do this with several of the texts, you will begin to get a feel for the learning potential of a text (further discussed in Chapter 10 as ***exploitability***).

After completing this activity, turn to the texts you are actually going to use in class and treat some of them in the same way. If they come from a textbook, ignore for the moment any questions provided; they may be excellent, but look first at the text itself. What do you want your students to get from this text, for reading, not for language practice? How will you do it? Again, work with colleagues if possible. Plan how you will use the text and what tasks you will set, eventually incorporating any suitable ones supplied in the textbook and arranging them all in the best sequence. Reject textbook questions if you have good reasons to do so, but bear in mind the textbook writers' purposes, which it may be important to retain, even if you want to introduce others.

Repeat this process with several texts, preferably of very different kinds, until you feel confident that there is little danger of overlooking any significant learning potential in any kind of text.

Guiding your students

Having worked out broadly what you want the students to get out of the text, how are you going to tackle it in class? You can, of course, simply ask the students to read it and then answer the questions; with the right class, and the right tasks, this can work. But most students need more support than this. In Chapter 3 we discussed the kind of support that emphasizes the value of the text and of the students' role as readers. Remind yourself if necessary of the issues discussed, as they underlie all the suggestions made in this chapter.

We will consider the kinds of guidance that can be given at each of three stages: before reading, while the reading is under way, and after the reading is completed.

Guidance before reading

Before the students begin to read the text, we can do quite a lot to make their task more explicit and their way of tackling it more effective. We will consider these points:

1 Providing a reason for reading
2 Introducing the text
3 Setting a top-down task
4 Breaking up the text
5 Dealing with new language
6 Asking signpost questions

Providing a reason for reading

In most classrooms, it is not practicable for the students to choose their own texts. Having to read texts chosen by somebody else raises the issue: why should the students want to read this?

In real life, we read for a purpose that influences the way we read. Consider for example Text 7 in Appendix A, *Danger from Fire*. You would read this in one way if your aim was to find out what to do in a fire emergency, but in a very different way if you wanted to work out the best way to present the information, so that you could prepare an improved version.

In the absence of a real reason for reading, it is helpful to give students an imaginary one, so that they can judge what to skim over and what to attend to in detail, otherwise the reading lesson may simply strengthen their belief that if they do not understand the text completely, they cannot read it at all.

There are many purposes (understanding a legal document, for example) that do require us to understand every detail of a text, so this must be practised. But other ways of reading are valid in certain circumstances, and they too need practice. Students usually need a lot of practice in adjusting their way of reading to their purpose – what we might loosely call 'reading for relevance'.

Consider Appendix A Text 9, *Good Neighbours*. What difference would each of these purposes make to the way you read?

1 You want to enter the competition yourself.
2 Your sister knows Lucy Brown; you want to tell her about Lucy's nomination.
3 You want to write an article on contemporary views of what makes a good neighbour.

By devising similar sets of purposes relating to a single text, you can make students aware of the effect of purpose on the way we read.

Let the students sometimes focus their reading for a specific purpose and ignore the rest of the text. You can always follow this with more detailed work if you wish. Reading the same text first for one purpose, then for another, generates interest as well as flexibility of approach. The reason for reading does not have to be a simulated 'real life' reason: it can also be the completion of a task, and if the task is mind-engaging, this can be just as motivating.

Introducing the text

It is often helpful to introduce a text before starting work on it, but the wrong kind of introduction is worse than none at all. The commonest faults in an introduction are these:

- It is too long.
- It gives away too much of the content of the text.
- It is irrelevant (and thus confusing rather than helpful, since it sets up misleading expectations).
- It is a monologue by the teacher with no student involvement.

First ask yourself why you want to introduce the text. Usually the intention is to point the students in the right direction (eg by activating relevant schemata in their minds), get them into the right mood for this particular text and, if possible, make them feel interested in reading it. It is seldom useful to give a potted biography of the writer, even if it has direct bearing on the content. (If curiosity is aroused, it can be satisfied later.) Nor are extensive background details often necessary; for example, you may not need to know much about Switzerland in order to understand a text on Alpine mountaineering. Indeed, you may be able to find out a good deal about Switzerland by reading carefully.

A lengthy introduction takes up valuable time and is also likely (if it is not irrelevant) to give away too much of the content of the text. Have a look at the tasks you want to set. Will the students be able to attempt any of them on the basis of the introduction alone? If so, change the introduction. It should not include anything the students can find out from the text, either directly or by inference. If it does, you are doing their work for them.

On the other hand, some texts are difficult to understand if you do not know the background. If it is not possible to deduce enough information from the text itself, it may be sensible to give the students some facts. However, this should not be done without careful thought.

Why? Compare the *Tits* text (Activity 7.7, p116) and *The Mountain People* (Appendix A Text 8): in the former case, most of the background information can be inferred; in the latter, you could not expect most students to work out what the context is. However, it does not follow that you ought to tell them all about it before reading; motivation to read is stronger if there are mysteries to solve and clues to look for.

Moreover, it is surprising how often a student can give you the facts if you ask the right questions. A good rule is: **Never say anything yourself if a student could say it for you**. Most things that need saying can be elicited from the class, and the best introductions are the ones that the teacher mostly draws out from the students. Like most good things, elicitation can be overdone (to the point where it frustrates and annoys students), but a monologue from you is less likely to kindle curiosity than a discussion involving everyone: some teachers use debate and roleplay as ways of getting the class into a receptive frame of mind.

It is often easy to incorporate a signpost question (see below, p160) into the introduction, and you can often introduce new language naturally at this point (see p159). This is convenient, but the principal goal is to arouse interest in the text and show its relevance for the class by discussing questions like 'Have you ever ...?' or 'What would you do if ...?' or 'What's your opinion of ...?'

To give some practice in evaluating introductions, attempt Activity 9.2 before reading the next section.

Activity 9.2 *Assessing an introduction*

Suppose you wanted to use Text 1, *Archaeopteryx*, from Appendix A. Read the text and decide which of the following introductions you would choose and why. Then work out why you would reject each of the others. Finally, devise your own introduction if you can think of a better one.

a I suppose you have all studied the geography of Europe and know where Bavaria is. It is a region of southwest Germany, bordering on Austria, over 27 000 square miles in size and with a population of over 10 million people. It is particularly well known for its beautiful mountains ... (continue with further description of the region).

b How many of you have heard of David Attenborough? I expect some of you have seen films with his brother Richard Attenborough in them. Well, David is interested in films, too; but he doesn't act in them, he makes them. If you have a TV, you've probably seen some of them. Can anyone tell me what kind of films they are? He made a famous series called 'Zoo Quest'. He studied zoology at Cambridge ... (continue with information about David Attenborough).

c This text comes from a book called *Life on Earth*. Have any of you read it or seen the TV series? What's it about, if you have? Well, what do you think it's likely to be about? Do these chapter titles give you any clues? 'The Infinite Variety' – 'Building Bodies' – 'The First Forests' – 'The Conquest of the Waters' – 'The Invasion of the Land'. Who has heard of Darwin? What theory did he put forward? Now, skim through the text and see who can be the first to tell me what this text has to do with the theory of evolution.

d Have you ever heard of dinosaurs? Pterodactyls? When did they live? We are going to read about a creature that lived at about the same time, a sort of half bird, half reptile, called archaeopteryx. We know about it because its skeleton has been found embedded in limestone. I want you to read the text quickly and tell me where the limestone was found. I'll give you one minute.

e What sort of rock is sedimentary rock? Can you tell me the names of any sedimentary rocks? ... Yes, limestone is one. Do you know what kind of sediment limestone is formed of? It was mainly calcareous, the remains of living organisms. What's the meaning of calcareous? The same sort of substance as chalk for instance. .. Yes, it produces quicklime. Do you know what that is used for?

What has Activity 9.2 suggested about the qualities of a good introduction? We will discuss each example in turn.

a This introduction is off the point. Knowledge about Bavaria is not important to an understanding of the text.

b This starts off promisingly but gives too much biographical detail, much of it off the point and none of it very helpful.

c I don't think this is ideal, but it is the one I would choose if I couldn't think of something better, because it tries to help the student to see the significance of the text in relation to the overall theme of Attenborough's book.

d The initial questions might have led to an interesting introduction, but there is too much information here which the student ought to extract from the text. And the skimming question focuses on a fact of no importance to the theme of the text.

e Understanding how limestone is formed may help the student interpret the text, but the concentration on geological fact gives quite the wrong emphasis: the text is not about geology. This introduction also includes information that should be extracted from the text and the last bit is completely irrelevant.

If you prepared your own introduction, discuss it with colleagues, along similar lines.

Several of the introductions in Activity 9.2 include questions; these are a good way of preparing to read, since the stimulus of trying to find the answers gets students actively involved and (provided they are the right questions) thinking along helpful lines.

To sum up, a good introduction has these qualities:

- It makes the students want to read the text.
- It helps the students to relate the text to their own experience, aims, interests.
- It involves the students actively, for example by means of questions or discussion.
- It does not tell the students anything they can find out by reading the text.
- It is usually short.

Setting a top-down task

Detailed work on a text is more rewarding if students first get a global impression of the kind of text it is, and a rough idea of the way it is organized. This provides a contextual framework that facilitates the more detailed work that follows. So instead of, or as well as, an introduction, it is a good strategy to set a task requiring the reader to look at the text in a top-down way. As an initial task, choose something fairly straightforward; it is not the intention that students read with close attention at this stage.

You might for example start by asking for predictions about the text based on the title or an illustration (eg Appendix C Lesson 1), or get the class to skim the text for the answers to simple global questions (eg Appendix C Lesson 4). Checking how far the responses are correct then becomes one purpose for reading.

Many of the tasks outlined in Chapter 7 can be used at this stage. For instance, students might assign simple labels to paragraphs (as in Activity 7.5), sequence jumbled paragraphs (see p107) or predict the content of a paragraph you have removed from the text. Such tasks give students an overview of the text's structure. Again, subsequent work can focus on finding out which responses agree with the original text.

If you don't think your students are ready to embark on work related to the whole text (but try it!), you can still start work on each section of the text (see below) by giving a global activity relating to that section.

Breaking up the text

A long text is daunting to readers who are not very skilled or speedy. When you ask the class to read it silently, the slower students feel inadequate while the faster ones finish long before the time allowed, becoming bored and restless.

You cannot change the fact that some people read better than others, but you can reduce the effects of the differences by dealing with the text in several short sections instead of all at once. In this way, the quicker students are kept waiting only a couple of minutes for each section (not long enough for much mischief), instead of a much longer time if the slower ones have to finish the whole text.

Advantages of breaking up the text

If you are using the text for intensive work, breaking it up has other advantages. It is easier to work thoroughly on a short section than on a complete text. Locating words and sentences for comment is quicker. The new language can be dealt with section by section, in digestible portions. And it gives you a simple way of dividing the work if you need several periods for it.

Moreover, it is easier to hold students' interest if you deal with one section fully and then move on to a fresh one. This is particularly true if the students read aloud (despite my disapproval! p201). And it is easy to vary the approach, using silent reading for some sections, practising skimming with others, reading aloud a difficult section yourself, and so on.

Finally, it leads to more effective learning. Thorough understanding of the first section helps students to interpret the second; interpretation becomes steadily easier as it builds on the understanding of earlier sections. This is particularly helpful to slower students. You can also encourage prediction by asking what the writer is likely to say in the next section, what will happen next, etc.

How to break up the text

You can divide the text arbitrarily if there are no natural boundaries (eg paragraphs) in it. Any break is better than none for the first work on the text. You can combine sections for later work if you have to split a part that ought to be read as a whole.

For elementary students, sections of four or five lines are long enough (50 words or so). Aim at sections of up to 20 lines (about 250 words) with fairly advanced students.

Identifying learning points in the text

Having decided where to break the text, you must decide three more things:

1 *What is important in this part of the text?*
The answer depends on your view of the text as a whole, and the reason for reading. How does this part contribute to the whole? What must be emphasized, what can be ignored without affecting the purpose?
2 *What problems are the students likely to have in understanding this part well enough to see what it contributes to the whole?*
This involves predicting stumbling blocks and assessing their importance. Persuade students at least sometimes to ignore problems that do not interfere with adequate global interpretation. When you do not want to do this, the next point comes into play.
3 *How am I going to help the students tackle the predicted problems, and any others that emerge in the course of the lesson?*
This is the most difficult of the questions. We have discussed many suggestions already (especially in Chapters 5, 6 and 7). Further ideas are given later in this chapter.

Working with the whole text

For some kinds of work, the text cannot be handled in sections. For example, skimming or scanning related to the whole text has to be done at the beginning, before the section-by-section work. On the other hand, work requiring a thorough understanding of the whole (eg studying the development of the plot or argument, analysing relationships between paragraphs, evaluating the overall success of the writer) is best tackled at the end, after all the sections have been dealt with.

Two words of caution. First, it is not always necessary to study every section closely. But even if you want to push students to read fast, just for the gist, it is still easier to work with short sections to begin with.

Second, time must be allotted for working with the whole, even if some sections are dealt with less thoroughly than you would like. You can turn this necessity to advantage by showing that some parts are more important than others. It is easy to forget that the objective is understanding the whole text, especially if it is difficult and needs a lot of time.

Dealing with new language

This is a controversial issue. Some teachers like to teach all the new words and structures in the text before reading begins. I am not going to say that this should never be done, but this is often the dullest part of reading classes, and the new language would often be more easily and effectively learnt during the process of reading.

Frequently a new structure hardly needs explaining if it is taken in context; whether you want to teach it for active use is beyond the scope of this book. For our purposes, if it can be understood, it is not a barrier to understanding, and to spend time teaching about it is pointless.

As we saw in Chapter 5, the same is true of new vocabulary. You may want to pre-teach a few key words, but others may be too unimportant to deserve attention, while others again can be used for practice in inferring meaning from context. A long list of key words is a warning that the text is too difficult.

If you use coursebook texts specifically intended to present new language, you cannot just ignore it. But the students have to learn to read as well; use supplementary texts for this if you can, but at least use the language-teaching texts for genuine reading tasks. This involves, among other things, not teaching all the new language beforehand; helping the students to use the context as a guide to interpreting some of the new language; and practising new items after reading, not before, in most cases.

Some problems are alleviated by dealing with the text in short sections as suggested earlier. The new language from a single section is more manageable than the new language from the whole text, so the preparatory work is split up into shorter, more digestible bits.

Finally, there are often opportunities for presenting key language items during your introduction to the text; this is more effective than presenting them in isolation.

Signpost questions

A signpost stands at a crossroads to show travellers the way. Its function is to direct them along the right road, making the journey quicker and saving them from getting lost. A ***signpost question (SPQ)*** has a similar function: its purpose is not to test but to guide the readers, directing their attention to the important points in the text, preventing them from going off along a false track.

Questions of this kind are particularly useful when the reading lesson is based (as I suggest it usually should be) mainly on silent reading. It is helpful to give the students a question or task (it does not have to be an actual question) *before* they read. This gives a specific reason for reading: they read more purposefully in order to find the answer or complete the task. Look at Text 1 in Appendix B (*Airships*): what name do the compilers of that text give to SPQs?

An obvious danger is that students will look only for the answer to the SPQ and not read the rest of the text carefully. To avoid this:

- Make sure students know there will be a lot more questions when they have finished reading. (Most of the work, of course, follows the reading.)
- Make sure the SPQ cannot be answered until the whole (or most) of the section has been read.
- Devise SPQs that require students to think about the meaning, not just locate information.

Devising signpost questions

Writing good SPQs requires some skill, which you can acquire by practice coupled with constructive criticism from colleagues. You may like to begin by criticizing somebody else's SPQs in Activity 9.3.

Activity 9.3 *Signpost questions*

Read Text 2, *A Son to be Proud of,* in Appendix A. Then decide which of the following would be the best SPQ for the whole text. If possible discuss your choice, and your reasons for rejecting the others, with your colleagues.

Possible SPQs for *A Son to be Proud of*

1 How old was Yusof when this story happened?
2 Why did Yusof run to the neighbour's house?
3 What did Leila tell Rahman?
4 Why was Rahman proud of his son?
5 Who put out the fire?
6 Why did Yusof run to the kitchen?

If you have tried the activity and checked the key, you will realize that the best SPQs relate either to the whole section (the whole text, in this case) or its final part, so that they cannot be answered until the whole section has been read and understood. Did you also keep in mind the function of the SPQ? – not to test but to help the reader to understand by directing attention to things that might otherwise be missed (particularly potential sources of misunderstanding) and by focusing on the main point.

You can of course ask more than one SPQ if you think this would be helpful, but the fewer the better, otherwise the signposting becomes less clear.

Using signpost questions

You can ask an easy SPQ on the whole text, as an initial top-down activity; and/or you can ask one for each section. Write the SPQ on the board or OHP. Ask the class to read the text silently and find the answer. After silent reading, perhaps followed by group discussion, check whether they have been able to do this. If a fair number have not, leave it open and explain that you will return to it later and that, as they read more closely, people should be looking for evidence to improve their answers. Turn to the other questions and tasks and return to the SPQ later, when the text is better understood. Avoid giving an answer yourself if you possibly can.

Guidance while reading is under way

How can you guide students while they are reading? To a great extent, the way you organize the class determines this; but you can vary the organization, and thus vary the way guidance is provided.

Three kinds of class organization

We will consider three broad modes of class organization.

The individual mode

In the ***individual mode***, each student works on his own for much of the time. Since the reading process is in essence private, this mode is particularly suitable for reading lessons. Every reader must understand the text for himself; hence it is often recommended that reading instruction should be made as individual as possible.

Carried to its logical conclusion, this entails providing a great variety of material to suit students with varying interests and proficiency levels, designed to be used independently of the teacher. Every student works on a different text and, in consultation with the teacher, is responsible for his own progress. Both keep records of the student's work, and the teacher monitors progress and gives support when necessary.

The advantage is that every student reads material that suits him and progresses at his own pace. This demands a plentiful supply of materials and meticulous organization; at its most sophisticated, this amounts to a ***self-access system***.

The teacher-centred class

At the opposite extreme is the familiar ***teacher-centred class***. In this mode, the class works with one text; the way it is tackled is controlled largely by the teacher, who decides the sequence of work, sets tasks, checks learning and tries to ensure that every student participates.

There are drawbacks to this approach: the whole class is obliged to work in roughly the same way and at roughly the same speed. But there are also advantages. The classroom interaction keeps the teacher continually aware of problems and weaknesses. It is usually cheaper to provide materials, and materials preparation and class management are easier than in the individualized mode. This is a significant advantage, for if class management is weak and the supply or design of materials inadequate, the individualized approach can be disastrous.

Groupwork

In the ***groupwork mode*** of organization, much of the guidance comes from fellow students. The effort to understand the text is made jointly – that is, individual efforts are pooled and discussed in the hope of arriving together at the best interpretation.

This suffers from some of the disadvantages of individualization (some people may not be working, some may waste time pursuing the wrong idea, etc) and of class-centred work (the pace and approach will not suit everyone), and has some of its own too – a student may get stuck in an uncongenial group, or the class may feel the lesson lacks a sense of direction.

These drawbacks can be dealt with, however, and there are important advantages. Motivation is generally high, provided the tasks are challenging and promote discussion. Individuals participate more actively, partly because it is less threatening than participating in front of the whole class and partly because it is more obvious that everyone's contribution counts. And the discussion helps students to see how to read thoughtfully.

Combining modes

These three modes can readily be combined during the sequence of a reading lesson, which might for example begin with individual reading, move on to groupwork and end with a teacher-centred feedback phase. This is ruled out only when a fully individualized programme is operating; but periods of individualized reading can of course be alternated with periods of group or teacher-centred work on a class text.

Guidance from the text: the individualized approach

If the student is expected to work on his own, all the guidance he needs must accompany the text in written form.

Self-access systems

A completely individualized system – a self-access system – needs a very wide range and a large number of texts, each with its own guidance material. These might be books but are more commonly shorter texts, often on stencilled sheets, perhaps mounted on card and laminated or kept in plastic envelopes, to give them a longer life. Commercially produced materials of this kind are available (eg the SRA Reading Laboratories), usually in the form of a large collection of reading cards (see p144).

Most reading card systems contain text and questions, with answers available (either separately or on the back of the card) so that the student can check his own progress. They can play a valuable part in the programme, because they are successful in motivating students to read. There is an obvious satisfaction in completing a card and getting another, in seeing the rising total of cards read, and your comprehension score improving steadily.

Presenting a text with supportive material

However, many students need more support than published reading cards tend to provide. It would be good to incorporate with the text some of the ways of supporting the reader that we refer to elsewhere, but this raises the problem of how to design supportive material. A text is a unit, not just a collection of fragments; also it is linear, that is, sequenced on the page. But the reading process is not linear; as we read, our minds dart ahead to anticipate what comes next, or return to previous sections to correct a misinterpretation, and so on. Moreover, although reading is ideally a unitary process, for many readers this ideal is only reached after a period of struggle with the difficult fragments that make up the whole text.

The question is: how do we present the text to a reader who will be studying it on his own? Do we print the tasks before it, after it or both? How do we indicate the most helpful ways of studying the text? Do we print a set of instructions which the student must follow in sequence, with the text printed separately? Or, if we want the student to focus on lines 1–4, for example, do we print just those lines together with questions or comments on them?

The ideal solution has yet to be found; if we were to give all the guidance and set all the tasks that might be needed, the text itself would be lost among them. For self-study, a sequenced set of instructions (incorporating tasks, questions and comments as well as instructions about what to do next) might be put on a separate sheet. The students would have to follow the sequence recommended on this sheet, rather than reading the text in their own way; there would thus be losses as well as gains.

Reading courses have tackled this problem in various ways. Examples appear in Appendix B. Some interrupt the text on the printed page by notes or questions. In some cases, these are placed in wide margins and printed in different type; in other cases, a different colour (not reproduced in this book) distinguishes the text from the study aids that accompany it.

It is important to recognize that many of the questions asked in these books are intended to provide 'scaffolding' similar to that which a good teacher gives her class. They draw attention to possible pitfalls, make the reader stop and think and, it is hoped, avoid them. A self-contained self-teaching text, which is what an individualized reading programme requires (since the teacher cannot give individual help to every student in the class) ideally offers not only answers to the questions, but also a brief explanation of why one is better than another. Testing questions, if any, follow the work on the text.

Texts prepared in this way can be put onto an OHP or distributed to the class (but see p179 on copyright). The class can then work independently of you, at any rate to begin with. But unless they can work on different texts to suit their different tastes and abilities, the effort of preparing the material is hardly worthwhile. If you are using what is basically a class text, it is more economical to use the next method.

Guidance from the teacher: the whole class approach

Some people criticize a teacher-centred approach, because it cannot cater for individual needs; but it has some decided advantages.

In the first place, it is possible to look at the text in much closer detail when working orally. (The page would get too cluttered if we wrote down all we might want to say.) This is only an advantage if there are a great many useful points to make or questions to ask; but this is usually the case with texts offering any degree of challenge.

Secondly, and more importantly, the questions you ask and the points you pursue in face-to-face interaction respond more sensitively to the students' needs than is possible if they have to be written down beforehand. If you have a good rapport with students, you will detect problems that need attention; you can probe to find out why a particular answer was given, prompt students who are hesitant, draw attention to clues that have been missed and, in short, thoroughly involve yourself with the readers' struggle for understanding. Your perception of their needs will dominate what you do.

A lesson of this kind is very much under the control of the teacher, with everyone working at the same rate and in the same way. You may prefer not to use this approach for every text, or every section of a text, but it provides valuable insights about the way students read, and the things they find difficult. Usually it comes best after the class has made a first attempt on the text silently. You can follow up the silent reading with some initial questioning and then, if the response justifies it, work through the text again in as much detail as you consider suitable.

Guidance from fellow students: the group approach

Working in groups makes it possible for students to help one another and, in successful groups, the interaction achieves far more than individuals can working on their own. Working together can be very motivating and a slight sense of competition between groups does no harm. (But stress on competition may lead groups to take short cuts to get results, instead of making sure that every member plays a full part.)

Organizing groups

Groups should not be large; if they have more than five members, it is too easy for people to opt out. Students who like to let others do the work can be grouped together; it may make them participate, you can give them extra attention and at any rate they will not be disturbing the others.

Each group should sit in a closed circle or square, not in a line or straggle; it is more difficult to leave people out if they are facing each other. A group table (or desks pushed together) is helpful but not essential.

Mixed ability or streamed groups?

In mixed groups, weaker students may benefit from the presence of stronger classmates, but may not participate confidently; and the stronger ones may be irritated by them. In streamed groups, weaker students working together may participate better and you can help them yourself, but some of the value of co-operative work may be lost.

Streamed groups can be assigned different tasks or different texts. This is worth doing if there is a wide ability range, but it makes class management complex and may rule out general follow-up work. Occasionally it is interesting to give each group the same text but a different task; the various aspects that are revealed, and the variety of responses, make for stimulating feedback.

The teacher's role in groupwork

While the groups are working, your job is mainly to be available for consultation. This does not mean solving problems for them, but rather showing them how to solve problems themselves. You will also want to listen to what is going on, without disturbing the work, in case matters crop up which ought to be dealt with in class later. If you assign different texts, you will have to spend time with each group because you will not be able to hold a report-back session with the whole class.

Planning group tasks

The teacher cannot be with more than one group at once; therefore the tasks must be explicit so that there is no doubt about what has to be done. Less explicit tasks such as *Discuss the text* are generally unsuccessful.

To be useful for groupwork, a task must specify exactly what is to be done, engage every member of the group and promote vigorous discussion. Some textbook questions or activities are suitable for groupwork, or you may have to supply extra tasks for this purpose. Suitable tasks are described elsewhere (eg p107–8, 118, 186–7, 200–1, 204, 208, 209). There are many other possibilities, some of which you can work out for yourself by doing Activity 9.4.

Activity 9.4 *Assessing tasks for groupwork*

Look at the questions and tasks set on the texts in Appendix B. Decide which of them would be suitable for groupwork. Can you modify the format of some of them to make them more suitable, while not changing the basic nature of the task? If so, write out the modified version in a form suitable for presenting to students.

Do this task with colleagues if possible, and if necessary use the key to promote discussion.

The way group activities are sequenced is important: early tasks may help students to do well on later ones. This may affect the design of the materials. For instance, if the tasks involve prediction, the students must see only part of the text, for you cannot expect them not to look ahead if they have the whole text. Look at the tasks you adapted for Activity 9.4: do any of them need special materials? For instance, if you want to use the cloze technique (see p208), a gapped text must be prepared; a jumbled text, or its paragraphs on separate pieces of paper, is needed for some kinds of task (eg p107). If you want to ensure all the work on the first section is completed before the second is tackled, you might want to distribute them separately; and so on.

There is no best way of structuring groupwork, but it does need care. One way is to spend a few minutes on introductory work with the whole class, and perhaps some individual skimming or scanning. Then you can get the groups to deal with the text section by section (as described earlier in this chapter), with a class report-back discussion after each section is completed. Timing may be unsuitable for some groups, but this is a problem in all lock-step work. You can end with work on the whole text, either in groups, individually or as a class. Many variations are possible.

Worksheets and answer sheets

A simple and effective way to control groupwork (especially useful with students who are not accustomed to working in groups) is a worksheet setting out the tasks in the order in which they are to be done, as in Appendix C Lesson 2, p257. Alternatively, several worksheets for a single text can be worked through in sequence. Groups work at their own speeds, but have to complete one worksheet satisfactorily before getting the next. This allows you to check progress and make sure the work is done properly. Moreover, completing one worksheet and collecting the next is motivating in itself.

Some of the tasks in Appendix B are suitable for use in a series of worksheets; have another look at the work you did for Activity 9.4 and consider the tasks with this in mind.

Preparing worksheets is time-consuming but they can be extremely effective. In any case, to make groupwork successful almost certainly means preparing special activities (additional to, or modifications of, those in the coursebook). It is easy to assemble all the activities on one worksheet; and the extra work involved in making a series of sequenced worksheets is minimal. This need not involve wasting paper, as they need not occupy a full page each; print several on a normal sheet of paper, which is then cut up.

For a large class where you cannot pay attention to every group, prepare answer sheets to match the worksheets. After completing the worksheet, the group collects the answer sheet; they are expected to check and discuss their own answers. The answer sheet can include some explanation of the reasons for accepting or rejecting answers, in the L1 if a target language explanation would be too difficult. Of course many group activities do not produce simple right and wrong answers; in this case, the only way to deal with them is a feedback session with the whole class.

Worksheets and answer sheets can be issued to each student, but it may be enough to prepare one for each group. An advantage is that this forces the group to work together, but it makes individual work difficult; take into account the nature of the tasks before deciding how to handle them. The sheets can be prepared for long-term use by mounting them on thin card and laminating them (ask colleagues in the library to teach you) or covering them with sealed plastic bags. Protected sheets will last several years, provided students are trained not to mark them. But try them out before going to all that trouble, so that you can change any that do not work well.

Guidance when reading has been completed

When the detailed work is over, global understanding must be returned to and the text as a whole evaluated and responded to.

Despite the global work you did before getting down to detail, there is always more to do afterwards. Now is the time to reconsider the hypotheses students made about the text in the early stages. Their opinions about the writer's aims, about the main message of the text and so on, can be substantiated and refined, or if necessary rejected and replaced.

Now is the time to put questions of ***evaluation*** and ***personal response*** (see Chapter 11, p188–9) and relate the text to the outside world. For instance, if it belongs to a particular field of study, now is the time to judge it in relation to the rest of the field. (Does it put forward accepted or controversial views? What research could be done to refute or substantiate them? What practical applications might result from it?)

If it is primarily argumentative, now is the time to evaluate the arguments, react to them personally and, for advanced students, assess how effectively they are presented. If it is a work of literature, now is the time to look at the effects the writer produces and consider why she has chosen to do it in this particular way. (How does she make us sympathize with this character but not that? Why has she adopted irony as a vehicle for her views? Suppose she had done this or that differently – what would be the result? etc.)

If it is taken from a book the class is reading, now is the time to consider the place of this passage in the development of the plot, theme, argument, etc, and to consider what may come next.

Each kind of text, and each individual text, requires different treatment. The work to be done at this stage may include some of the following:

- eliciting a personal response from the readers (agree/disagree, like/dislike, etc);
- linking the content with the readers' experience/knowledge;
- considering the significance of the text in the book from which it is taken;
- establishing the connection with other work in the same field;
- suggesting practical applications of theories or principles;
- working out the implications for research/policy/theory, etc, of the ideas or facts in the text;
- drawing comparisons/contrasts between facts, ideas, etc in this text and others;
- recognizing/discussing relationships of cause and effect;
- ascertaining chronological sequence (eg where a narrative shifts from one time to another or uses flashbacks);
- tracing the development of thought/argument;
- distinguishing fact from opinion;
- weighing evidence;
- recognizing bias;
- discussing/evaluating characters, incidents, ideas, arguments;
- speculating about what had happened before or would happen after the story; or about motives, reasons, feelings, if these are unexpressed.

Most of the work at this stage is best done orally, since discussion and exchange of views are of its essence, but it could well culminate in written work. Specific tasks can be undertaken in groups before whole class discussion. One which is worth considering is choosing a title; this can generate productive argument. At least initially, give four or five alternative titles rather than allowing a free choice; make sure that one is too broad, another too narrow, a third wrong in emphasis, and so on. This is an excellent way of summing up the accumulated understanding of the text.

Finally, it is at this point that most of the outcomes described in Chapter 12 can be introduced; you are asked to refer to that chapter for details.

Footnote: A possible sequence of teaching

To summarize the suggestions outlined in this chapter, they are tabulated below to show a possible sequence of teaching for an intensive reading lesson.

Remember: these are only suggestions. This is not a blueprint for a lesson. Any of the steps might be omitted or altered.

Step 1 Set overall purpose for reading this text.
Step 2 Introduce the text.
Step 3 Skimming/scanning or other top-down exercise on the whole text.
Step 4 Tackle the text section by section.

Procedure for each section:

a Deal with essential language points for section (if any).
b Assign SPQ for the section.
c Silent reading of the section by whole class.
d Check answer to SPQ and assign other questions for the section.

Class mode	Group mode
e Individuals reread text and do tasks/prepare answers to questions. **f** Class, with teacher's guidance, work through section orally, discussing questions/tasks and ensuring thorough understanding of all important elements. (If you must include reading aloud, it will come best at the end of this step.) **g** Return to SPQ if necessary and then assess the section as a whole; predict what will follow (unless it is the last section); relate it to what has gone before (unless it is the first); predict or discuss its function in, and contribution to, the whole text.	**e** Group reread, discuss tasks/questions and prepare answers. **f** Report-back session: answers of different groups compared and discussed by class. **g** As for **f** in class mode if necessary; or proceed to **h**. **h** As for **g** in class mode, but doing some of the work by means of further group assignments followed by class discussion of various group answers.

Step 5 After completing section-by-section study, assign tasks (group or individual) requiring response to the text as a whole, drawing together information obtained from the detailed study and including the contribution of each part to the total message.
Step 6 Groups or individuals attempt tasks.
Step 7 Report-back session and final discussion/evaluation.

Note: Depending on the text, these steps might be spread over several lesson periods and homework assignments.

Further reading

On general principles for teaching reading, see Further Reading for Chapter 3; also Anderson 1994. Nuttall 1985, Williams and Moran 1989, Moran and Williams 1993 review current thinking as it is embodied in materials for the teaching of reading.

On lesson design, see Lunzer et al 1984 (including lesson transcripts to show how texts can be exploited); Davies and Green 1984; Wray and Lewis 1992. None of these deals specifically with FL teaching, but many of their ideas are valid in any classroom.

On pre-reading activities see Wallace 1992; Hess 1991 is a collection of pre-reading tasks for use with many kinds of text. Brown 1990 argues the case for encouraging inference rather than providing information.

On group work, see eg Lunzer and Gardner 1979; Brumfit 1984; Bennett and Dunne 1994; for an alternative view, see Prabhu 1987, which also discusses the concept of 'mind-engaging' tasks.

On self-access and individualization see eg Sheerin 1989, 1991; Dickinson 1987; Waite 1994; Walker 1987.

On the design and production of worksheets, see Leach 1989; Wright and Haleem 1991.

Chapter 10
Selecting texts

Why teachers need to assess texts

EVEN if you have little control over the choice of textbooks, it helps to be aware of their strong points and limitations so that you can exploit them effectively, supplement them if necessary, and perhaps argue the case for their replacement.

Probably, too, you often have to look for material to fill a gap or to deal with a particular problem that you have not experienced before. Indeed, some classes have such specific needs that most of the material must be collected by the teacher.

So you are likely to find yourself having to evaluate texts for reading development. This chapter aims to help you to do this.

Criteria for evaluating texts for reading development

Three main criteria influence the choice of texts: suitability of content, exploitability, readability. And in considering your whole collection of texts, you also need to consider variety. Further issues are whether the texts should be authentic, simplified or specially written; and how they should be presented. We will examine each in turn.

Suitability of content

Far and away the most important criterion is that the text should interest the readers – preferably enthral and delight them.

Of course it is possible to develop reading skills on a text that bores you, but interesting content makes the learner's task far more rewarding. This is why publishers of EFL readers are increasingly offering well written gripping stories, presented to look like 'real' paperbacks, which attract students to read out of class. But enjoyable texts also make classwork more effective: hence modern coursebooks too attach importance to the quality of their texts and to the way they are presented.

Finding out what students like

Suggesting that you look for motivating material implies that you know what interests the students. Are you sure you do? It is worth carrying out an investigation, especially if you are planning to invest money (whether in class texts or extensive reading materials). There are several factors to bear in mind if you do decide to survey students' reading tastes.

First, be cautious about questionnaire responses. For instance, in some countries the classics (Shakespeare, Dickens and so on, in the case of English) retain a strong position. People may name such writers because they consider it the proper thing to do, even if they don't really enjoy them. Don't rely only on their stated preferences, even expressed anonymously.

One way to double-check is to find out what students actually read, bearing in mind that books read in the L1 may tell you more about reading tastes than those in the foreign language. For instance, find out which books are borrowed most often from the library: this is usually a reliable indicator of preferences. Keep an eye open for the sort of reading matter the students usually carry with them. If it does not include works of literary merit, there is no need to be surprised (let alone disappointed). But you might consider providing similar material in the target language: if the students want to read it, half the battle has been won. (A courageous tutor in a women's college had great success in promoting reading in English once she realized the appeal of Mills and Boon romances.) You can take care of literary merit later.

Finally, monitor the popularity of the materials you choose, and be prepared to change.

Selecting texts for classroom study

An enquiry of this kind particularly affects the choice of books for extensive reading, but has implications for classroom texts as well. You may not want to study in class the sort of material that has the most immediate appeal for your students; comics, romances and thrillers have all been used successfully by some teachers, but others prefer less controversial material for actual lessons. Nevertheless, you need texts that will interest most of the students and will not actually bore the others; and it is much easier to teach well if the texts interest *you*, too.

In addition to being interesting, some classroom texts at least should represent the kind of material students will need to handle after they leave the foreign language class. Sometimes these criteria conflict, but only you can decide how to balance them. It is often better to begin on material chosen chiefly for enjoyment, until reading skills improve. And even if you are training students specifically to read, for instance, university level medical texts, you may get better results if you use simpler and more motivating material to begin with. School textbooks often provide simple models of academic discourse; it is useful to have a collection of them (in the foreign language) on subjects suited to the class.

Exploitability

Exploitability – that is, facilitation of learning – is arguably the most important criterion after interest. When you exploit a text, you make use of it to develop the students' competence as readers. A text you cannot exploit is no use for teaching even if the students enjoy reading it. For what purposes should we exploit the text?

The purpose of the reading lesson

Do we teach reading in order to teach language? Of course we do, in one sense, for reading lessons are part of the language course. But I believe that students learn the language better by focusing on the meaning and purpose of the text (which involves learning how language works when it is in use). However, in a reading lesson we are not setting out to teach language; alternatively, if we are setting out to teach language, we are not giving a reading lesson.

Nor do we choose texts for intensive reading because we want the class to learn about history, biology, economics, and so on. We are not teachers of these subjects and any increase in the students' knowledge of the topic is an incidental bonus, not a primary aim.

So the focus in the reading lesson is neither language nor content, but the two together: how language is used for conveying content for a purpose. We want students to develop the ability to extract the content from the language that expresses it – to become effective independent readers.

An ideal reader would be able to extract the content from any text at all; but of course such a reader does not exist – he would need not only complete command of the language but also command of every area of knowledge. At the other extreme, we cannot be satisfied with a reader who can tackle only a single text. We have to push students as far as possible towards becoming 'ideal' readers for their own purposes, able to tackle any kind of text they are likely to encounter.

That is the target, even if we do not reach it. Every text he reads moves the student towards it: but that particular text is not the target, it is just a step in the right direction. You exploit the text effectively when you use it to develop interpretive strategies that can be applied to other texts.

Integrating reading skills

When choosing a text, therefore, you need to be clear how you can exploit it to help students to develop these interpretive strategies. Summarized in broad terms, the skills and strategies described in Part Two are:

1 Strategies involving flexibility of technique: variations in reading rate, skimming, scanning, study reading and so on. (Chapter 4)
2 Strategies of utilizing information that is not part of the linear text: reference apparatus, graphic conventions, figures (diagrams, etc). (Chapter 4)
3 Word attack skills: tackling unfamiliar lexical items by using morphology, inference from context, a dictionary, etc. (Chapter 5)
4 Text attack skills: interpreting the text as a whole, using all the clues available for both top-down and bottom-up strategies, including cohesion and rhetorical structure. (Chapters 6 and 7)

While we have dealt with these skills separately, and they can be practised separately up to a point, this is only an expedient to make discussion and teaching more focused. In reality, each depends on the others, as you can easily ascertain by thinking about the connections between any two of them. Thus it is important, when assessing texts for exploitability, to consider the possibilities not only for practising individual skills, but for outcomes and follow-up work requiring the integrated use of many skills together: the unitary skill of making sense of text. Sometimes, indeed, only a single integrated task may be needed: for instance, to draw a plan of a place may be a sufficient means of exploiting a descriptive text; to prepare a text diagram (described in Chapter 7) may adequately exploit a discursive one.

Simulating real-life purposes

Authentic texts (see below, p177, 178) can be motivating because they are proof that the language is used for real-life purposes by real people. But the motivation may not survive if the text is used only for academic exercises. In deciding how to exploit the text, and particularly in considering integrative tasks, a good question to start with is: What would the text be used for in the foreign language environment?

In the case of ***functional texts*** (those with a clear practical purpose), this is straightforward: a travel brochure could be used to plan a holiday, a consumer magazine might help you to choose a camera for a given purpose, a set of directions might guide you to a meeting place. Texts of this kind lend themselves to outcomes that integrate many skills: discussion leading to a group holiday plan or choice of camera (with reasons), a map showing how to get to the meeting place, and so on.

Other integrative tasks

Descriptive or discursive texts, and fiction, offer scope for integrative tasks of other kinds: considering whether you would rather have X or Y for a friend, how far you agree with the writer's arguments, and so on. A brilliantly simple example from *Headway Advanced* offers students a collection of newspaper reports of penal sentences received by criminals for a variety of crimes. Part of this material is shown in Figure 25; you will notice that the actual sentences are blacked out. They are given separately, in random order, and the first task is simply to allocate them correctly. Deciding which sentence fits which crime forces students to read thoughtfully, while a second task requires them to debate the issues raised. (Which crimes are worse? Are the sentences fair? and so on.) Chapter 7 (p121-123) gave further examples, and there are many others in Chapter 12.

Driver
[redacted]

A drink driver who killed a man while fleeing from police was [redacted] at Birmingham Crown Court. It was the second conviction involving drinking and driving in five months for Robert Smith, 30, who ran down Sidney Field.

How Erica put drug dealer behind bars

DRUG dealer Richard Nottingham has been [redacted] after he was trapped by a police operation code-named 'Erica'.

Throughout the summer weeks of last year crack drug squad officers from Herts mounted a secret surveillance operation on Nottingham's flat.

They logged down all the visitors before mounting a raid on the premises in Abbey View, Garston.

Nottingham, 35, and flatmate Neil Hornsby, 27, were both arrested after officers found unknown substances, syringes and needles.

It turned out the pair had been dealing in heroin.

Night intruder
[redacted]

A JILTED lover smashed his way into his ex-girlfriend's home and said, after grabbing her throat: 'I could kill you. No-one knows I am here,' a court heard on Monday.

Jobless Peter James, formerly of Bedwyn Walk, Aylesbury, appeared at Aylesbury Magistrates Court only three days before his 22nd birthday and admitted assault occasioning actual bodily harm, and criminal damage.

The court [redacted] James [redacted], and ordered him to pay £32 compensation for the window and £30 towards costs.

Figure 25 Integrative task using authentic texts
From Soars, J. and L. 1989 *Headway Advanced* (OUP)

Using longer texts

Inevitably, most texts for classroom use need to be short because of time constraints, and because intensive work on a long text can become tedious. But certain strategies – top-down skills such as prediction, reference skills such as using sub-headings to locate relevant sections, scanning and skimming – need some practice on longer texts.

Furthermore, short texts are frequently extracts: removing them from their context robs them of important elements of meaning. Choose at least some passages from longer works with which students are familiar (class readers, set texts for other subjects). Using an extract from a known context contributes many dimensions of study: it enables you to relate the passage to the wider text and to explore in detail the way the writer achieves effects that are already broadly familiar from the book as a whole. Provided you choose key passages (as suggested in Chapter 8 p147), this can be extremely rewarding.

The next two chapters discuss further the ways we can exploit texts and should help you to recognize texts with potential for exploitation.

Readability

The term ***readability*** is often used to refer to the combination of structural and lexical difficulty. This is what concerns us here; we set aside for the moment the important questions of conceptual difficulty and interest, though these strongly influence the ease with which a text can be read. Since the language of a text may be difficult for one student and easy for another, it is necessary to assess the right level for the students you teach; to do this, you must first assess the level of the students themselves.

Assessing the students' level

If you know the class, you already have a good idea of what vocabulary and structures they are familiar with. If you do not know the class well, you will have to find this out. You may be able to make use of vocabulary and structure lists supplied in the syllabus or textbooks used in earlier years; however, we all know that the presence of a word on a list does not guarantee that the students have learnt it, any more than its absence proves that they do not know it.

If the students have varied backgrounds, a period of trial and error is unavoidable. However, a series of graded cloze tests (see p215) can give you an idea of their level (or levels). The results can only be approximate, because the tests sample only a tiny percentage of what they know; but even limited information is better than none during the first few weeks with a new set of students.

A range of levels is likely in any one class; many teachers have to cope with classes where the gap between the strongest and weakest students is very wide. In an ideal world, every student would have material appropriate to his own needs. A library for extensive reading (Chapter 8) should certainly cater for the full range of levels. And classroom lessons can be valuably supplemented by self-access work at a variety of levels, as described in Chapter 9, p163.

However, most teachers work in circumstances where it is not possible to provide differentiated learning materials for regular classroom use. We shall assume that you have to compromise by choosing material that suits most of the class, and that you compensate for this by giving individual attention to students who are behind the others, or are capable of handling more difficult material.

How much new vocabulary?

Once you know the students' vocabulary level, you can count the new lexical items (words or phrases) in a text, including new uses of familiar words and new idiomatic combinations (such as phrasal verbs: see Chapter 5, p66). You then have to decide what proportion of new items is acceptable.

This partly depends on the purpose: if you only want students to get the gist of a text, they can skip unfamiliar words; on the other hand, for intensive reading – which is slow and careful anyway – it may be acceptable to have quite a lot of new words. The nature of the new items, and whether they are well spread out, is also relevant.

'A lot' is a relative term; 2 or 3 per cent is a lot in my view (it represents round about eighteen words on a page this size). Others suggest 5 per cent is acceptable, while Bright and McGregor (1970, p 80) argue that the ideal text for intensive work contains no new words at all, since students cannot respond fully to unfamiliar ones. Probably a compromise is best: some classroom texts can include only familiar words, so that the fullest possible response can be demanded, while others can include new words, so that students can develop the very necessary skills for dealing with them.

However, students will only read a great deal if they can do so with tolerable ease, so books for extensive reading should have a smaller proportion of new words – 1 per cent perhaps, that is about seven on a page this size.

You may be surprised that the recommended proportion of new words is so low; but to pursue vocabulary extension by choosing texts with a high proportion of new lexical items defeats the aims of the reading programme and is not an effective way of teaching vocabulary, either, because we learn words best when they occur in a well-understood context.

Structural difficulty

Readability also involves structural difficulty, which is harder to assess. New grammatical forms (tenses, structural words, etc) often cause no problems if the text is comprehensible in other respects. A more likely cause of structural difficulty, as we saw in Chapter 6, is sentence length and complexity.

Experienced teachers can usually assess whether a text is structurally about the right level without using formal methods. But it is also possible to work out its ***readability index***. This is a way of assessing a text by giving it a kind of score. To make use of it, you first need to work out the readability index of texts that you know are suitable for the students. This gives you a yardstick against which to measure the readability of texts you are considering using.

Calculating the readability index

There are many ways of measuring readability; these now include computer programs that will do the job for you if you type in samples from the text. For details of how to calculate readability indexes, see eg Harrison 1980, Chall 1984.

These measures are typically based on counts of average word length and sentence length. The assumption is that, if you pick a typical stretch of 100 words of text, the more syllables there are in it, the more difficult it will be. This is because more syllables = longer words, and longer words tend to be less familiar. Similarly, the fewer the sentences in the 100-word stretch, the more difficult, because fewer sentences = longer sentences, and thus more complex ones. To assess books, most methods suggest you choose three typical 100-word passages from near the beginning, middle and end, and average the counts from these. Sentence and word length are not the only factors influencing the ease with which a text can be read, but they provide a reasonably useful guide. The main drawback is that they are tedious to calculate.

If you decide to use a readability index, make sure the same system is used throughout the school. The index can be written into foreign language library books, to guide students. Also, teachers can work out the index of texts for use as supplementary material and file them accordingly, so that it is easy to find material at about the right level.

If the target language is a medium of instruction, a further advantage is that textbooks in other subjects can be checked for readability. Hence, teachers can avoid books which are more difficult than the level reached in the language class; or can at least bear in mind the likely problems. Any measure of readability takes time to get used to but you will be able to use it effectively once you have had practice in interpreting it. A readability index provides only a rough guide (because it cannot take account of a reader's knowledge and interest), but treated cautiously it can be useful.

Cloze as an indicator of readability

A readability index is useful because it enables you to compare new texts with familiar ones which you know are at the right level. An alternative measure is the ***cloze test***; it does not permit you to make comparisons, but it is often favoured because it needs little computation. Administrative considerations usually make it unsuitable for selecting classroom texts, but it is a useful adjunct to an extensive reading programme. (Each book needs its own test, as described in Chapter 13, p215.)

A text for classroom use should be such that a typical student could score about 45 per cent on a cloze extract; it would be challenging but not too difficult to read with support from the teacher. For independent reading, texts need to be easier; students should be advised to choose books on which they score at least 60 per cent.

A word of caution

Measures of readability are useful but not completely reliable. For one thing, the sample chosen may turn out not to be typical. For another, readability in the broad sense is not just a matter of language. It depends also on other factors, even quite superficial things such as the size of type or the presence of illustrations. Most important of all are the familiarity of the topic, the cultural background, the conceptual complexity of the content and the interest it has for the reader. A text that grips a reader will carry him along in spite of its difficulty.

In fact, the best way to judge readability is probably to rely on your own experience – especially if it can be pooled with the experience of colleagues – together with the opinions of the students. Be prepared to change an assessment that proves unsatisfactory. It will take time to form a reliable judgement, but if you start now to categorize materials on this basis (identifying each level by a number or colour, as suggested in Chapter 8), a year's use will reveal many of the anomalies to be corrected. After several years, provided you set up a good feedback system for students to record their views, you should have a reliable classification.

Variety

Reading courses can be made more interesting if a variety of texts is used over the year. This may be true even for classes with a fairly narrow and specific purpose for learning the language. Students often complain of boredom with an unrelieved diet of texts in a single field (eg physics) even when that is their professional interest. They may respond better to more varied material.

It can also be stimulating to use a variety of texts in a single lesson (eg Figures 25, 31, Appendix A Text 9). You cannot explore several texts as thoroughly as a single one, but for some activities (for example, making use of reference apparatus, prediction, skimming) thorough understanding is not necessary.

There is a contradictory consideration, however. Repeated exposure to the same vocabulary in different contexts ensures that many words are assimilated with little conscious effort. There is therefore some advantage in using texts all dealing with similar topics, because of the recycling of vocabulary to be expected. If the students are happy with this, it is worth trying; but the loss of stimulation may be too great a price to pay.

In a reading programme for general purposes, variety should be guaranteed, since one aim is to expose students to all the kinds of text they are likely to encounter after finishing the course. But it may also be worth including texts simply because they are entertaining or mind-engaging, and thus motivating. These are issues to discuss with colleagues, and if possible (ex-) students, when planning the programme.

Authenticity

Many teachers like to use ***authentic*** texts, ie texts written for use by the foreign language community, not for language learners. We have already suggested that these may be motivating, but there is another reason for preferring them. To pursue the crucial text attack skills (Chapters 6, 7), we need texts which exhibit the characteristics of true discourse: having something to say, being coherent and clearly organized. Composed (ie specially written) or simplified texts do not always have these qualities. The striving for simplicity may lead to vacuous texts (merely vehicles for language presentation, conveying little or no real message) or unnatural ones, lacking many of the features we expect to find in normal discourse. But writers are nowadays more aware of the pitfalls and many excellent recent materials show that it is possible to tell a story simply without distorting the natural use of language.

Simplification certainly carries risks. However, linguistically difficult texts are unlikely to be suitable for developing most reading skills, especially if they result in the use of translation, or any kind of substantial intervention from the teacher. There is another option: if an otherwise suitable text seems rather too difficult, you can exploit it by means of tasks which do not demand detailed understanding but make more use of top-down strategies (as discussed in Chapter 12, p192).

Nevertheless, the students must do detailed work as well. It may be necessary to simplify texts which are suitable in other respects, so that the students can do most of the work of making sense of them. Simplification for this purpose needs to be done with discretion. It involves removing barriers to understanding (difficult words, complex structures and so on), but if you are not careful, you may also remove its basic qualities as discourse; so it is important not to go too far.

If you make everything explicit, the students cannot develop their capacity to infer; so leave unsaid some at least of the things left unsaid in the original. Retain things that will challenge the students, so that you can ask interesting questions. Retain new words if the meaning can be inferred from the context. Do not insert discourse markers (*because*, *although*, etc) if the reader can work out the relationships between sentences without them.

In short, preserve whatever in the original will appeal to the students' intelligence, while removing elements which intelligence alone cannot deal with. Above all, retain as much as possible of the textual quality and discourse organization of the original.

However good a simplification is, something is always lost; this is why some teachers refuse to use simplified versions. Writing your own texts is another solution, but the results are often disappointing. Authentic material is the ideal, but if you cannot find enough at the right level, you will have to use simplified or specially written materials to begin with. Get these checked by several colleagues, because it is easy to make a text unconvincing. And above all, think carefully before choosing texts which are impossible for your class to handle independently.

Presentation

Looking authentic

The texts in modern reading coursebooks are often authentic, or at least devised to appear authentic. To enhance this, they are often presented in facsimile – for example, a news story is made to look like a piece cut out of a newspaper, or a set of rules is presented as a notice pinned to a board. Many texts are accompanied by figures (diagrams, photographs, etc) of the kind they would have had in the original context. Figure 25, and some texts in Appendix B, give an idea of the possibilities.

The intention of this 'authentic' presentation is to make the function of the text clearer by establishing a context in which it might appear. This is particularly helpful when the text is short (longer ones to some extent establish their own context). The idea is that readers understand the text better and are more interested if they can see how it would be used. A further advantage is that the text can be exploited by means of tasks which also reflect the purposes of real-life reading, as discussed below (p192).

Looking attractive

It goes without saying that an attractive-looking text is more likely to appeal to the reader. Appearance is only superficial but can be important in grabbing students' attention, especially for extensive reading. But it is worth fighting for the use of large clear type, a spacious layout, perhaps helpful sub-headings and the inclusion of illustrations, in classroom materials too.

Reproducing material for the classroom

You may not be able to present the texts as attractively as modern textbooks do, but at least you can look for authentic and interesting material by searching magazines in the target language (especially those intended for readers of the same age or interests as the students), newspapers, travel brochures, instruction leaflets, letters, and so on. If you can visit places where the target language is used, you will be able to collect a range of reading material used in everyday life, from tickets to application forms.

Much of this material can be retyped for distribution to the class, but even more can be done if you have access to a photocopier. This enables you to reproduce material in facsimile, and also makes it easy to assemble several short texts (some advertisements, for example, or several tickets for different journeys) on a single page, so that they can be compared.

Whatever means of reproduction you use, the texts need to be legible (and properly proof-read, if typed), and printed clearly and free from smudges. If you want students to care about reading them, they need to look as if you have cared about producing them. (I have seen some home-produced texts that nobody could be expected to care about.)

Copyright

Bear in mind the laws of copyright. Most countries protect the rights of the author and publisher by prohibiting the unsanctioned copying of text written or published by someone else, even for educational purposes. Permission should be sought from the publisher to reproduce material for use in class. In the UK, institutions can apply to the Copyright Licensing Agency (address in Appendix D) rather than approach publishers directly.

Footnote: Guidelines for choosing texts for classroom study

This checklist may be useful. Take a critical look at the texts you currently use for comprehension work: do they fulfil these criteria?

1 Will the text do one or more of these things?
  - **a** Tell the students things they don't already know.
  - **b** Introduce them to new and relevant ideas, make them think about things they haven't thought of before.
  - **c** Help them understand the way others feel or think (eg people with different backgrounds, problems or attitudes from their own).
  - **d** Make them want to read for themselves (to continue a story, find out more about a subject, and so on).

2 Does the text challenge the students' intelligence without making unreasonable demands on their knowledge of the language? (It is not necessary to express trivial thoughts just because you are restricted to simple language.)

3 Is the language natural, or has it been distorted by the desire to include numerous examples of a particular teaching item (eg a tense)?

4 Does the language reflect written or spoken usage? (The spoken language presented to beginners is often limited to describing the obvious – eg a picture; this may carry over into coursebook texts.)

5 If there are new lexical items, are they worth learning at this stage, and not too numerous? Can the meaning of some of them be worked out without the help of a dictionary? (See Chapter 5.) Can some be replaced by simpler words?

6 Is the text over-explicit? (If it says too much, there is no room for inference, an important reading skill that learners need to practise.)

7 Does the text lend itself to intensive study? That is, can you ask good questions (see Chapter 11) or devise other kinds of task (Chapter 12)?

Further reading

Johns and Davies 1983 is a classic discussion of the nature of text, text types and their use in teaching. For a range of criteria for choosing and exploiting texts see Nuttall 1985, Wallace 1992, Williams 1984, Silberstein 1994, Williams and Moran 1989, Davies 1995.

Widdowson is a major theorist in this field; see eg 1978, 1979, 1984. Brown 1989 discusses the notion of text (topic and task) difficulty.

Exploitability is not much discussed (but see Silberstein 1994, Hutchinson and Waters 1987); it is illustrated in the work of Lunzer et al 1984 Part 1B, Davies and Green 1984 and, of course, in all textbooks for the teaching of reading (for a selection, see bibliography entries prefixed T).

For a critique of readability formulas and of simplification, see Carrell 1987 (with exhaustive bibliography). Harrison 1980 is an excellent account of readability formulas, updated in Harrison 1986. See also Beard 1990 (on 'suitability'), Kintsch and Miller 1984, Chall 1984, Urquhart 1984. Bamford 1984 makes practical suggestions on grading books without using formulas.

On simplification and other forms of control see Davies and Widdowson 1974; Davies 1984; Widdowson 1979; Hedge 1985; Ulijn and Strother 1990; Simensen 1987, 1990; Tickoo 1993.

Breen 1985 and Bachman 1990 explore various types of authenticity; Williams 1983 discusses this and related issues.

On intuitive assessment of students entering a reading programme, see Bamford 1984; tests for this purpose are discussed in Harrison 1980 and in Chapter 13, where further reading on this topic will be found.

Clarke 1989 discusses the design and presentation of materials, particularly authenticity. Leach 1989 is an authoritative account of instructional text design in general. See also Hartley 1985, Ellis and Ellis 1987, Wright and Haleem 1991.

Chapter 11
Questioning

NOW THAT we have considered how to organize reading lessons (Chapter 9) and choose texts (Chapter 10), it is time to look in more detail at the activities to be used, and at ways of using them not to test understanding, but to bring it about. (We shall see in Chapter 13 that it is primarily the way activities are used that distinguishes teaching from testing.)

We shall consider two broad categories of classroom activity:

1 Types of question, and techniques for using them, that are primarily intended to assist learning.
2 Other techniques for helping students to develop their own strategies for making sense of text.

This chapter looks at the first of these. The second is considered in Chapter 12.

Can questions help readers?

The focus on what and how students learn is particularly problematic in the case of comprehension, given the invisibility of the comprehension process. Getting students to answer questions is one way for the teacher to get some access to what is going on in their minds. Wrong answers are often particularly illuminating, because they can suggest where the misunderstanding arises. And right answers may be right by accident, which is why we need to probe into the reasons for them.

So questions are helpful to the teacher; what about the student? First, let us consider the traditional approach: reading the text and then answering questions to check that you have understood. We want to improve on it, but we should be cautious of dismissing it outright. Has it anything to offer us? Probably you, like me, were trained by such means, and have had this experience: you read a difficult text; you cannot understand it; you struggle to answer the questions. Finally you read it again, and find that you understand it much better.

Between the first reading and the last, what happened? Is there a connection between answering questions and developing (not just demonstrating) understanding? If so, what kind of connection is it? Perhaps the clue is in the word *struggle*. The questions that help are those that make you work at the text. Well planned questions make you realize you do not understand, and focus attention on the difficult bits of the text.

Dealing with answers: the key role of the teacher

If the key word is *struggle*, then not just the type of questions, but the way they are used, is crucial. Even a challenging question is useless to most of the class if the teacher simply accepts the first correct answer and moves on; it can only help if every student tries hard to answer it. We have to make sure this happens, partly by the way we devise and handle questions, partly by showing the learners that reading tasks are opportunities for learning, not tests to be escaped if possible.

It is terribly easy for an inexperienced teacher to do things the wrong way: to accept an answer without even asking for the reasons why it is acceptable, let alone exploring other answers to see why they are not appropriate.

Yet in the reading class, the process by which the student arrived at an answer is critical. If he gives the right answer by accident, it is valueless. Or he may give an answer you dismiss, but which he could defend if given the opportunity; his interpretation may be valid even though it is different from yours. Every teacher of reading has to be prepared for this; it may not happen often, but we have to acknowledge it and even welcome it when it does.

That is why it is important to have a classroom climate that encourages people to say what they really think. Neither you nor the students must be afraid to be wrong. You must help them to see questions not as attempts to expose their ignorance, but as aids to successful exploration of the text. (This is difficult if you have to award marks for everything, so try to limit the mark-earning exercises.) Interesting questions explored in a supportive classroom atmosphere give you the opportunity to provide the 'scaffolding' discussed in Chapter 3.

One key factor is to make sure the students can look at the text when answering. The sort of questions we are interested in are not tests of memory, but the means of directing attention to the text. So students should refer to the text when they reply.

Your attitude to wrong answers is crucial. A perfect answer teaches little, but each imperfect answer is an opportunity for learning – not just for the answerer but for the whole class. It must be investigated to see why it was unacceptable, and how far. If it is partly acceptable, you can praise the student for what he has understood, and help him (and his classmates) to find clues that will lead to a completely satisfactory interpretation. This approach mirrors in the classroom the thoughtful searching that good readers undertake whenever they are not satisfied that they understand. It is probably the nearest you can get to 'teaching' anybody to read.

Exploring meaning through discussion

We can exemplify this thoughtful searching by looking at one way of using a resource which is very easy to use badly: multiple choice questions (MCQs). Used skilfully, they can be highly effective for training interpretive skills. Moreover, many teachers are obliged to use them. Hence a technique for using them effectively is important.

The procedure I will describe turns MCQs from shallow tests into the pointers needed for text exploration. Briefly, it is as follows:

a *Individually* the students read the text silently.

b *Individually* or *in groups/pairs*, students attempt the questions. Groupwork is preferred, because it forces students to defend their choice of option and produces instructive discussion.

c *As a class*, each group's choice of answer to each question in turn is recorded on the blackboard and, without disclosing which is the best, the teacher promotes discussion about the reasons for their choices. This often enables the students themselves to recognize their misinterpretations.

The approach can be used with any MCQs, but it is most successful when the distractors (ie the incorrect options) are constructed to take account of possible misinterpretations of the text. An ideal question setter, therefore, is sensitive to potential difficulties and capable of devising plausible options that students will choose if they misunderstand in the predicted way. This is not easy, and many MCQs in textbooks have not been constructed with this in mind; nevertheless, many produce worthwhile discussion if used in the suggested way.

Discussion is the key

Similar approaches can be used with questions of any kind, and with cloze exercises (as described on p208). The value lies not so much in the questions themselves, but in the way they are used. Even if there is no groupwork in the second stage, the third stage essentially includes discussion of alternative answers, and each is defended or criticized by the students themselves. The teacher does no more than keep the discussion on track and offer occasional prompts if the class misses an important clue. She also makes sure that everyone is involved, by directing suitable questions (ie ones they can probably answer) to students who are not contributing, and helping them (by probes and prompts) to respond.

This promotes the active struggle with the text, and the text talk, that we identified as a key to developing interpretive skills. Through discussion, the students learn the processes of critical thinking that good readers use. Groupwork is ideal, because in small groups (maximum five members), even the weaker students should be active and learning. The procedure works at almost any level, and discussion can be in the L1 if students cannot manage it in the FL. (For this purpose, quality of discussion overrides quantity of language practice.) And most classes enjoy it.

Your skill in using the questions is critical. The key ingredients are initial individual study and subsequent active participation in discussion.

The purpose of questioning

Poor questions defeat even the ablest teacher, so you may need to devise your own to supplement or even replace those in the textbook. How do you set about it?

First, let me stress again that the questions we are discussing here are not intended to test. Their purpose is to make students aware of the way language is used to convey meaning, and of the strategies readers can use to interpret texts. The questions themselves are not necessarily different from questions in tests, but their purpose and the way they are used is quite different.

It is useful to recall the aims of the reading class (discussed in Chapter 3 and the introduction to Part Three). Work on a text should always include time spent on some of these aims, even if later the text has to be used for language practice of other kinds.

1 The aim of a reading lesson is not primarily to investigate the language used in the text, nor to give practice in that language. However, it may be necessary to draw attention to a grammatical feature if it plays a part in the interpretation of the text. For example:

   a Emma lived here for ten years.
   b Emma has lived here for ten years.

   The verb tenses imply that in **a** Emma no longer lives here, while in **b** she probably still does. If the difference in meaning is not important, it is not worth mentioning. If it is, you could ask, for example, *Where does Emma live now?* and comment on the grammar only in connection with the response.

2 It is equally not our aim just to investigate the content. One sometimes finds questions that require general knowledge rather than an understanding of the text. These are only useful (if at all) for establishing the context for the students; they are not comprehension questions. Some straightforward content questions need to be asked at the start of work on a text, but paradoxically it is only when there is a chance the students will give wrong answers (based on a misreading of the text, not on ignorance) that the real work of developing understanding begins.

Having excluded pure language and pure content questions, we can identify the kinds of question that are relevant to our purpose. These are questions that show students how to interpret language in order to understand content.

Good questioning supports the approach outlined in earlier chapters. Some simple initial questions may result in scanning or skimming activities. Others may direct readers' attention to diagrams or other non-linear features that will help them to interpret the text. Some may promote the use of word attack skills (eg *Which meaning of this word is the one intended here?*). But the focus of most questions is the text attack skills, which lead to the ultimate goal, understanding the text as a whole.

This doesn't mean asking questions 'about', for example, cohesion. It means spotting a potential difficulty – involving cohesion, for instance – and asking questions which students will be able to answer if they have coped with the difficulty. If they cannot answer, that is the opportunity for 'scaffolding': helping the class to find the reasons for the problem, perhaps even giving some formal instruction about cohesion, or whatever has caused the difficulty.

The best questions make students aware of their difficulties. Recognizing that you do not understand, and then identifying the source of the problem, are essential reading skills. You cannot deal with a difficulty if you are not aware of it.

Questions which are worth asking contribute to this awareness. We will look more closely at four aspects of questions to see how they relate to the purpose just outlined:

1 **Forms of question:** their grammatical patterns
2 **Presentation of questions:** Spoken or written? Open-ended, multiple choice or true/false? What language for questions and responses?
3 **Types of question:** What are we to ask about?
4 **The questioner:** Teacher or student?

Forms of question

Questions can be classified according to their grammatical form, and it is sometimes suggested that each form in turn should be used in reading lessons, as each is progressively more difficult to handle. We will return to this suggestion shortly. However, it is often the grammatical form of the answer that makes a question difficult for students, as these examples show:

1 ***yes/no* questions**
Is a trout a fish? Yes (it is).
Did the man catch the trout? No (he didn't).

2 **Alternative questions**
Is a trout a fish or a bird? It's a fish.
Was the trout caught or did it escape? It escaped.

3 ***wh*-questions (who, what, which, when, where)**
What is a trout? It's a fish.
Where did the trout hide? Under a black stone.

4 ***how/why* questions**
How did the trout escape? It managed to hide under a black stone.
Why did the fisherman go away? He thought the trout had escaped.

Answers to *yes/no* questions are short, and the student need not compose a sentence unless he wishes (or is asked) to. At the other extreme, *how/why* questions often require full sentence answers which are quite different from the question in structure and content, and are thus quite challenging.

This classification is useful when you are focusing on graded language practice, but not for the teaching of reading. We need to keep the aims distinct. We choose reading questions not for their form, but to suit our reason for focusing on a particular aspect of the text. We are also not interested in the form of the student's reply, as long as it is intelligible. In reading classes, we can find a use for all the forms of question, but we shall from now on pay no further attention to this aspect of questioning.

Presentation of questions

Written or spoken?

Should you present questions in writing (eg in a book, on the blackboard, on a worksheet) or orally? There is something to be said for each.

Some kinds of question (notably multiple choice) are unsuitable for oral presentation, and written questions may provide the backbone of the lesson, if they cover all the important aspects of the text. But you cannot assume that all you need to do is get through the questions in the textbook. Sometimes they can be used after most of the work on the text has been completed, as a way of summing up; or they can be worked through one at a time, focusing on successive parts of the text. In either case, most of the work needs to be done orally.

There are two main reasons for this. First, for texts that you want to study intensively, the written questions are never enough. To write down all you need would be very off-putting: there would be so many. Secondly, many questions depend on the way the class responds; if they have difficulties you did not predict, you will want to prompt them (eg by further questions) to work out an answer, or probe to make sure a correct answer was not given for the wrong reason. Such questions cannot be written down in advance of the lesson.

Written questions do not necessarily have to be answered in writing. Oral responses are often enough. It is the work of analysing and discussing the text that matters – the process of arriving at the answer, as much as the answer itself. By this means the students learn how to set about the business of interpretation. They learn by sharing in the discussion and beginning to think analytically in the way you model for them and impel them to use themselves. This can be satisfactorily achieved only orally.

Open-ended, multiple choice or true/false?

There is no reason to exclude any of these types of question. ***Open-ended*** questions are those to which the student can give any response that he considers suitable; the examples on p185 are open-ended, but the term is applied particularly to the *wh-* and *how/why* forms, since they offer the greatest scope for the responder. In ***multiple choice questions*** (MCQs), the student has to choose from a set of possible responses. For example:

What happened to the trout?
a It was caught.
b It escaped down the stream.
c The fisherman had it for supper.
d It hid under a black stone.

True/false questions present a statement; the student has to decide if it is true or false according to the text. For example:

The trout was caught by the fisherman. **T/F**

Of these types, the T/F question is in some respects the most limited, but it can be useful and is not necessarily trivial. T/F questions can promote discussion, like MCQs (see p182–3); more choices make discussion more interesting, but T/F questions are preferable if there is only one likely misinterpretation of the text.

MCQs can be very effective, but they are the most difficult type to devise. The need for three or four options leads to some very implausible items (see examples on p191); but if they are not plausible, the number of genuine alternatives is reduced, so the choice is not really 'multiple' at all; in such cases, the T/F format is more satisfactory.

Open-ended questions may, as we saw, require very short answers, but typically they demand rather more; their disadvantages are thus:

1 **The answers cannot be assessed objectively.**
This is important for testing, but not when we are trying to teach people. As we have seen, a correct answer is not enough.
2 **They require students to produce responses in the target language.**
It is possible to understand target language texts without being able to express yourself adequately in that language. But if questions demand subtle or complicated answers, this is a problem; the student may understand both the text and the questions, but be unable to express the answers he would like to give. One solution is to accept answers in the L1 (as discussed in the next section).

However, open-ended questions have some important advantages:

1 **They are relatively easy to devise.**
Devising good questions always requires skill, but at least with open-ended ones you do not have to worry about supplying good distractors (as for MCQs) but can go to the point directly.
2 **They can be used for virtually any purpose.**
So can MCQs, but they are sometimes clumsy. If the point to be clarified by the question is straightforward, it may be uneconomical to use the MCQ format. If the point is very complex, the MCQ itself may have to be complex, so that understanding it is more difficult than understanding the text. In such cases, open-ended questions are preferred.

3 **They force the student to think things out for himself.**
Even the best MCQs have to include the correct answer as one of the options (unless you include 'None of the above'). This can be an advantage: it guides the students and yet, if the distractors are well chosen, it makes them think. But you may want advanced students to come to terms directly with the text, without an indication of your own view of the correct answer, even in company with less suitable choices. In this case, open-ended questions are the only possibility.

The language of responses

Inability to express themselves in the target language needlessly limits both the kind and the quality of the responses students give. It is quite possible that students who are permitted to use their L1 in responding will explore the text more accurately and thoroughly than those who are restricted to target language responses.

Whether this is acceptable depends on your local situation, but it is important not to dismiss the use of the mother tongue out of hand. Some students may never need to express themselves in the target language. Why should they not respond in the language that most clearly enables them to show that they understand, or to explain where their problems lie?

In many circumstances this would be unacceptable; and it is right to be cautious, lest there is a flood of L1 in the classroom. A good compromise is to accept L1 responses only when to insist on the target language would produce undue delay or result in poor quality answers.

The language of questions

It is not always possible to express the question you want to ask in straightforward language, especially if the text is itself difficult. People sometimes maintain that reading the questions is part of the reading task, but this is only partly valid. It is certainly *a* reading task, but *the* reading task is making sense of the text itself, and we could argue that anything that distracts from this is unhelpful.

The language used for questions (especially written ones, where your voice and, if necessary, extra explanation, are not available), should be as clear as you can make it. At the very least, it ought not to be more difficult than the language of the text itself. If you find this impossible, there are two other solutions to explore.

The first of these is to ask some questions in the L1. You should consider this only if the alternative is to ask questions you do not want to ask, simply because they are within the linguistic competence of the students. This is not a decision to take lightly, but it could certainly improve the quality of questions asked.

The second solution to the problem of difficult language in questions is to explore completely different approaches, which we discuss in the next chapter.

Types of question: what are we to ask about?

It is also possible to classify questions according to the skills they require from the reader; for the reading teacher, this is much more important than their grammatical form. The classification presented here is intended as a checklist; by checking your questions against it, you can find out whether you are omitting any important types of question, and thus failing to give practice in some important skills.

Type 1 Questions of literal comprehension

These are questions whose answers are directly and explicitly expressed in the text. They can often be answered in the words of the text (though most teachers would not wish this to happen).

Such questions are often a preliminary to serious work on a text, because more sophisticated exercises tend to depend on the students having first understood the plain sense. Literal questions on Appendix A Text 2 might include these:

1 When did Leila have an accident?
2 What was Yusof doing when the accident happened?
3 Why didn't Yusof help his mother?

Type 2 Questions involving reorganization or reinterpretation

Slightly more difficult than Type 1 are questions which require the student either to reinterpret literal information or to obtain it from various parts of the text and put it together in a new way, perhaps using elementary inferencing. Often both skills are needed; the distinction between them is not worth labouring.

Such questions make the student consider the text as a whole, rather than sentence by sentence; and/or make him process the information in the text for fuller understanding. Examples for Appendix A Text 2:

1 How old was Yusof? (Reinterpret *third birthday, the week before*)
2 How many children had Rahman? (Reorganize: 1 (*Yusof*) + 2 (*both the other children*) = 3)
3 Was Yusof playing in the kitchen? (Reinterpret *ran to the kitchen*)

Type 3 Questions of inference

These questions oblige the students to consider what is implied but not explicitly stated. Like Type 2, they may require the reader to put together pieces of information that are scattered throughout the text; the two types are not always distinct, but the inferences demanded in Type 3 are more sophisticated.

Type 3 questions are more difficult (intellectually rather than linguistically) than Types 1 or 2, because the reader has to understand the text well enough to work out its implications. Examples for Appendix A Text 2:

1 Which people were in Rahman's house when the accident happened?
2 Why was Rahman proud of his son?

Examples for Appendix A Text 3:

1 What differences would you find between trees in Dorset and trees near Birmingham?
2 What hypothesis is confirmed by Dr Kettlewell's experiment in Dorset?

Type 4 Questions of evaluation

Evaluative questions ask for a considered judgement about the text in terms of what the writer is trying to do and how far she has achieved it. The reader may be asked to judge, for example, the writer's honesty or bias (eg in newspaper reporting or advertisements), the force of her argument (eg quality of evidence), or the effectiveness of her narrative power (eg in a novel).

Such questions can often be tackled by fairly elementary students (using a largely top-down approach), but they can also demand advanced skills, since they ask the reader to analyse his response to the text and discover objective reasons to justify it, as well as measuring it against the presumed intention of the writer. Questions of literary appreciation are the most sophisticated representatives of this type.

Type 5 Questions of personal response

Of all the types, the answers to these depend least on the writer. The reader is not asked to assess the techniques by means of which the writer influences him (that is Type 4), but simply to record his reaction to the text. This might range from 'I'm convinced' or 'I'm not interested' to 'I'm moved' or 'I'm not prepared to accept the position the writer expects me to adopt.'

Nevertheless, such responses cannot ignore the textual evidence; they do not rely only on the reader, but involve him with the writer. So the response must at least be based on adequate understanding of the text and ideally students are able to explain why it makes them feel as they do. These questions thus overlap with Type 4.

The category includes questions such as 'What is your opinion of X's behaviour?' 'Would you like to live in Y?' 'How would you have felt if you were Z?' Personal response is naturally most often invoked by creative writing, but can be appropriate to other kinds of writing too, for example: 'What does the writer contribute to our understanding of this field?' 'Do you sympathize with the writer's arguments?' 'How far does your own experience agree with that described?'

Type 6 Questions concerned with how writers say what they mean

The types of question we have looked at so far all have as their main concern *what the writer says* (or, in the case of Type 5, how the reader reacts). Another type of question, much in use now, has as its main concern *how the writer says what she means*. This kind of question (even more than the others) is intended to give students strategies for handling texts in general, rather than simply helping them to understand one particular text. It is aimed at making students aware of word-attack and text-attack skills, ie making them conscious of what they do when they interpret text. As we have seen in previous chapters, these questions need not be particularly difficult to answer, but they are sometimes difficult to devise if the text is not reasonably authentic. Plenty of examples were offered in Chapters 6 and 7.

Categorizing questions in this way may be helpful for evaluating questions in textbooks, and for developing your own. Questions in older textbooks tend to be of Type 1, with perhaps a few Types 2 and 5. Of course literal comprehension and personal response are important, but it is Types 2, 3, 4 and 6 that ought to concern us, since it is these that force readers to think not just about what the writer has written, but how and why she has written it, thus equipping themselves to tackle further and more difficult texts.

The questioner

Traditionally, it is the teacher who asks the questions and the student who replies. (That is one reason why many students are not very good at forming questions.) But we have seen that readers have to learn to 'interrogate the text'. The teacher's questions can of course force them to do this, but they ought also to try doing it for themselves. As you know from your own experience, having to ask questions on a text is a very good way to ensure that you read it carefully!

It is not necessary to wait for the class to reach an advanced level; even elementary students are able to ask some kinds of questions, and if their intelligence is greater than their language proficiency, they may ask very challenging ones. (They might need your help in formulating them, or you could allow them to use the L1.)

You can give guidelines (eg asking for particular types of question, or questions to clarify a particular difficulty) and the activity can lead to groups or individuals putting their questions to one another, perhaps as a competition, and to evaluation of the questions by the other students.

Assessing questions

Here is a check list to use when you assess questions.

1 *Can the questions be answered without reading the text?*
The answer should be 'No'! It is surprising how often it turns out to be 'Yes', especially when MCQs are concerned. Have a look at the examples of unsatisfactory questions in Activity 11.1 below: why is it possible to answer them without having seen the text?

2 *Are there several questions on every part of the text?*
This is not a principle to be maintained at all costs, but it is unusual to find part of a text that is not worth any attention.

3 *Are there enough questions?*
We have seen that textbooks rarely offer anything like enough questions, but that many of the extra ones should be dealt with orally and geared to the difficulties that arise in class.

4 *Are the questions varied in type?*
Often we ask a lot of Type 1 questions first, followed by questions of Types 2 and 3, perhaps Types 4 and 6 and finally Type 5. But this sequence can be varied: for instance, you might start with Type 5 and then go back to the text to find out what has produced the response.

5 *Do some questions try to make students aware of the strategies a reader needs?*
This is to remind you to include some Type 6 questions even at elementary levels.

6 *Do the questions attempt to help students to understand?*
Or are they intended simply to test? This is to remind you that more of our time should be devoted to teaching than to testing; however, this is more a matter of lesson procedures than question design.

7 *Are the questions written in language that is more difficult than the text?*
We hope for the answer 'No'.

8 *Do the answers require language that is beyond the students' proficiency?*
Again, we hope for the answer 'No'.

Tailpiece: unsatisfactory questions

The examples in Activity 11.1 are closely based (believe it or not) on questions from actual textbooks. Working out the right answer without the text may help you to avoid similar mistakes.

Activity 11.1 *Unsatisfactory questions*

Study the following examples of questions and try to establish the correct answers – even though you do not have the texts to which they refer. In each case, try to decide what is wrong with the question.

1 Daniel's father considered him a model son, although
  a he was not old enough to be interested in girls.
  b he was a very fine footballer.
  c his disobedience was extremely worrying.
  d at his age many sons are very troublesome.

2 The murderer took the woman's corpse into the forest because
  a he did not want to hurt her any more.
  b he wanted her to be comfortable.
  c he did not want anyone to find her.
  d he needed her car.

3 Re-attaching severed limbs by microsurgery is
  a never attempted.
  b a very skilled task.
  c always successful.
  d simple.

4 People use mousetraps because
  a mice run about in the house.
  b mice are very old.
  c mice do a lot of damage.
  d mice like cheese.

5 World War II began in
  a 1945.
  b 1940.
  c 1914.
  d 1939.

6 The word *allege* in line 10 means
  a claim
  b agree
  c request
  d refuse

Further reading

Various types of question are distinguished, for instance, by Barrett (n.d.) (unpublished, but see eg Beard 1990). See also Davies and Widdowson 1974, Widdowson 1978, Williams 1984.

Munby 1968 demonstrates how to use questions to promote discussion.

Chapter 12 Other kinds of reading task

A more flexible approach

THE activities described in this chapter tend to seek a more global or holistic response than those in Chapter 11, requiring generally a more top-down approach. Because of this, they are often particularly enjoyable to do, and offer success to students who are discouraged by a more analytical bottom-up approach. Both approaches have their place.

Once you recognize that reading lessons can follow many patterns, and that different texts call for different treatments, all kinds of interesting possibilities open up. Some activities involve the spoken language; others the use of writing; some seek responses that do not require language at all. You can choose them to suit the text, and to suit your purpose.

Varying the level of the task

If you sometimes have to use texts that are too difficult for your students, you can at least devise tasks that allow them to use a top-down approach, in which intelligence and experience count for more than language proficiency. You cannot continually dodge the problems, but detailed analytical work is not always appropriate or necessary, and all students need the frequent motivation of enjoyment and success, instead of being always conscious of their linguistic inadequacy.

The general idea is that the more difficult the text, the easier you should make the tasks. The easy tasks can lead on to more difficult ones on the same text; but sometimes they are enough in themselves. For example, look at Appendix B Text 2, *Survival of the Fittest*. The step-by-step tasks are straightforward; they require students to grasp the gist of each section and follow the argument, but they are not demanding linguistically. Similarly, Figure 26 opposite offers a moderately difficult text, but the tasks ask students simply to match and sequence the paragraphs, which are presented in jumbled order. (There is only room for part of the text here.) Another difficult text is Appendix A Text 8, *The Mountain People*; instead of exploring its language, a discussion of the controversial moral issues raised (eg *How would you have behaved if you had been in the writer's position?*) might be more in keeping with the passionate feelings it arouses.

Matching the task with the text

A good rule of thumb, when deciding how to use a text, is to consider first the sort of things a target reader (ie the sort of person for whom the text was originally written) is likely to do with it. This often suggests activities you can use in class, especially if the text has clear practical applications. Much real-life reading does not demand a high degree of accuracy, so this approach can fit in with the suggestion about devising an easy task if the text is difficult.

Unit 9 Sissinghurst Castle

Sissinghurst Castle is an old house with a beautiful garden in Kent, England. The main buildings date from the sixteenth century, although parts of it are much older. It was bought and restored in the 1930s by Vita Sackville-West, the writer, and her husband, Harold Nicolson.

Extracting main ideas

Read the description of Sissinghurst and choose a suitable title for each paragraph from the list below. Use the map to help you.

a) The Library
b) The Rose Garden
c) The Tower Lawn
d) The Cottage Garden
e) The Tower
f) The Lime Walk
g) The White Garden
h) The Moat and the Orchard
i) The Tudor Buildings
j) The Herb Garden
k) The Moat Walk
l) The Tower Courtyard

Understanding text organisation

The paragraphs form a guided tour of Sissinghurst which is marked on the map. Use the map to put the paragraphs in the order shown by the guided tour.

A The tower with its two octagonal turrets was completed by Sir Richard Baker shortly before Queen Elizabeth I spent three nights at Sissinghurst in August 1573. The left-hand turret contains a spiral staircase of 78 steps, while the right-hand turret forms small octagonal rooms on each of the floors above.

B Leaving the Rondel by the south side, one comes to this delightful walk, also known as the Spring Garden. Although at other times of the year it is apt to be a little bare, in March, April and early May the two borders along each side of a flagged path, shaded by pleached limes and punctuated by garden pots from Tuscany, form a picture which reminded V. Sackville-West of the foreground of Botticelli's *Primavera*.

C This has been described as 'the most beautiful garden at Sissinghurst, and indeed of all England.' It lies at the foot of the Priest's House, and is divided by neat low hedges of box. A path leads past the entrance of the Priest's House to a wooden door in the wall, and so back to the entrance courtyard.

Paragraphs D–L from the original text have been omitted.

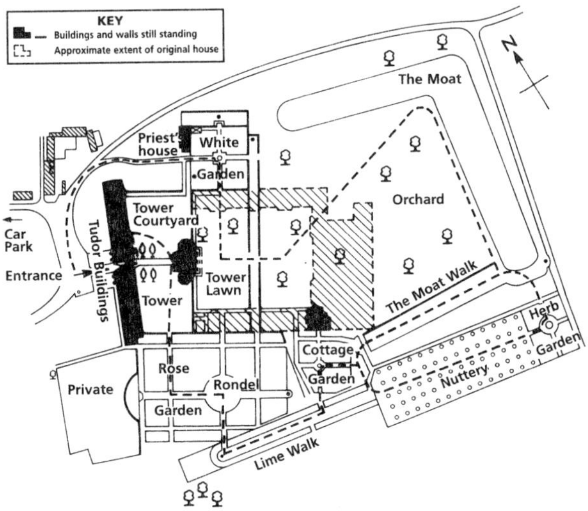

Figure 26 A simple task for a difficult text
From Greenall, S. and Swan, M. 1986 *Effective Reading* (CUP)

For instance, why would people read a guidebook to a town? Perhaps to plan how to spend some time there? So if you can supply some guidebook pages, a suitable task would be to produce a programme for a visit of a given duration. Similarly, a page of job advertisements and profiles of job seekers (*a woman of 45 with no educational qualifications who wants to work part time*, etc) could be used for a matching task, provoking discussion and perhaps leading on to writing a job application or roleplaying an interview. Try Activity 12.1 to see if you can use this approach.

Activity 12.1 *Agony aunt letters*

Why are 'agony aunt' letters like these popular with magazine readers? How could you use a collection (as many as you like) of such letters and responses in a reading lesson? Try to preserve the elements that make them popular.

My son bites!

My little boy (age 2) has developed an embarrassing habit. He is very sweet in most ways, but he has started biting people whenever he doesn't get his own way. The doctor says he will grow out of it, but what should we do until he does? Someone suggested we should bite him back but I am not so sure. Please help me, I am really at a loss.

This is a very common problem, so try not to worry so much. I don't advise biting your little boy – it would give him the idea that biting people is acceptable, even if it is not very pleasant. Instead, try to show how you feel by making him leave the room for a few minutes – young children hate not being where the action is!

Afraid of her own son

I am terribly worried about my mother. My brother, who lives with her, has become very violent. He drinks a lot and has alarming changes of mood. He has frequently hit her and she has had to call the police several times. Now she has come to live with my husband and me, because she is too afraid to return to her own home. We want her to take legal action, but she refuses because she thinks it would make things worse. What do you think we should do?

You must be firm with your mother – just as you want her to be with your brother. It is clear that he badly needs medical help and you are helping neither him nor your mother by not insisting on her taking action. Perhaps if you point out to her that he is a danger to himself in his present condition, she will realize her responsibility. Do talk to your doctor about the options open to you.

Tasks with outcomes requiring little or no language

Outcomes involving little speaking or writing can be encouraging to less proficient students, as they allow students to demonstrate comprehension without making unrealistic demands on their active control of the language.

Using figures

Among the easier and more motivating tasks, we can include here many of those that involve figures (we continue to use this cover term) – grids, flow charts, maps, graphs and so on. Figures often help by setting out information in ways that supplement and clarify the written text, and offer opportunities for highly motivating tasks.

Many tasks involving figures are ***transfer of information*** activities. Transfer of information works two ways. We can have visual information re-expressed in words (the basis for writing activities: see below, p205), or verbal information re-expressed by means of figures. Since we are concerned chiefly with interpretive strategies, we shall look mainly at activities asking the student to provide or complete or label figures on the basis of a text, or to study the relationship of text and figure and note correspondences, mismatches and so on.

In Chapter 4 we dealt with figures found in the original text; here we are also concerned with figures devised specifically to assist or check the reader's comprehension. Various aspects of the text can be represented visually. The list below includes some of those that are suited to diagrammatic treatment, but less promising aspects have also been handled; for instance Figure 27 deals with writer's attitude. Texts referred to are in Appendix B.

- chronological sequence (eg narrative; historical account): see Text 1 *Airships* ex 4; task in Lesson 1, *Shin-pyu* Appendix C, p254
- sequence of process (eg manufacturing coffee; repairing a puncture) see Text 4 *Danger from Fire* ex 2; Figure 28 (p196);
- cause and effect: see Figure 29 (p196);
- classification, definition and other semantic relationships: see Figure 30 (p197);
- comparison, contrast, advantages/disadvantages, etc: see Figures 31 and 32 (p197-8);

Task 1

This activity is designed to help you identify your own response to the way the article is written.

1 Work out your own response to the article by ringing the appropriate number on each of the scales below.

In *Don't talk, listen!* I consider that Dale Spender is:

calm	1	2	3	4	5	angry
serious	1	2	3	4	5	frivolous
logical	1	2	3	4	5	illogical
impersonal	1	2	3	4	5	personal
objective	1	2	3	4	5	subjective
fair	1	2	3	4	5	unfair

2 Work in a group (a mixed group, if possible). Compare your responses with those of the other members of your group.

Discuss any differences.

Figure 27 Diagram relating to reader's response and writer's attitude
From Tomlinson, B. and Ellis, R. 1988 *Reading Advanced* (OUP)

The wet process First the fresh fruit is pulped by a pulping machine[2]. Some pulp still clings to the coffee, however, and this residue is removed by fermentation in tanks. The few remaining traces of pulp are then removed by washing. The coffee seeds are then dried to a moisture content of about 12 per cent either by exposure to the sun or by hot-air driers. If dried in the sun, they must be turned by hand several times a day for even drying[3].

2 The coffee seeds are separated from the pulp by a pulping machine. ∴ *pulp* in this context means: the pulp from the seeds.

3 The beans must be turned so that parts of the bean are given the same exposure. ∴ *even* means:
a divisible by two
b flat
c equally balanced
d calm.

1 Complete the following diagram to show the different stages of the wet process.

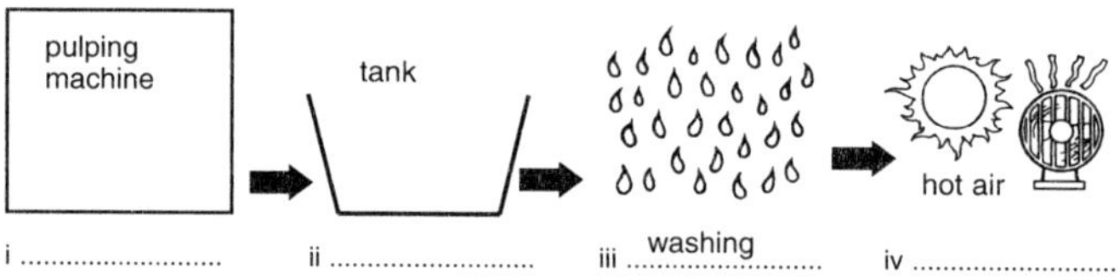

Figure 28 Diagram illustrating a process
From Moore, J. D. et al 1979 *Discovering Discourse* (OUP)

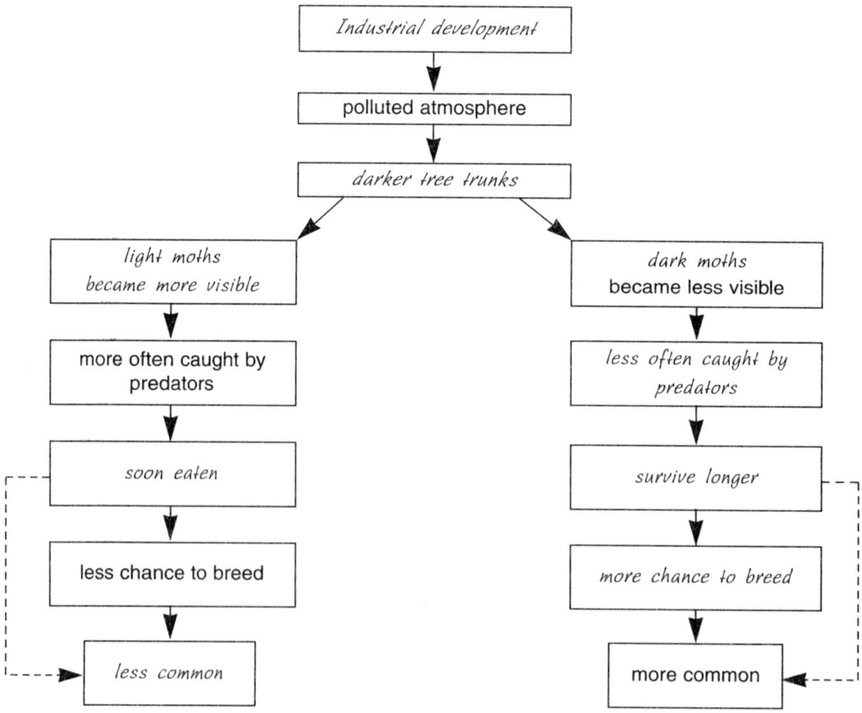

Figure 29 Why dark moths are more common in industrial areas: cause and effect diagram relating to Appendix A Text 2 *Survival of the Fittest*

EXERCISE F *Information transfer : definitions and descriptions*

The following diagram conveys the same information as the statement below it.

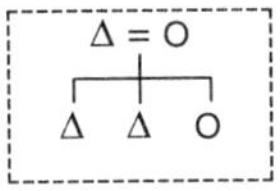

Δ male
O female
= sexual bond
-- residential boundary

(a) *Definition* A nuclear family is a group consisting of a man and a woman and their offspring sharing a common residence.

(b) *Description* This is a nuclear family consisting of a man and a woman, their two sons and one daughter.

1. Draw a diagram to correspond with the following definition and description:

(a) *Definition* A polygynous family is a group consisting of one man and more than one woman and their offspring sharing a common residence.

(b) *Description* This is a polygynous family consisting of one man and two women, two sons of the man and one woman and one son and two daughters of the second woman.

2. Write a definition and a description based on the following diagram:

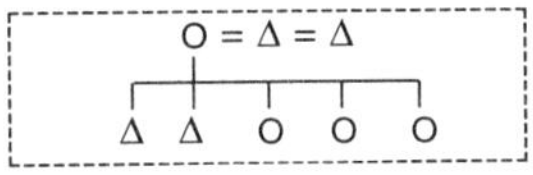

Figure 30 Diagram illustrating a definition
From Allen, J. P. B. and Widdowson, H. G. 1978 *English in Focus: English in Social Studies* (OUP)

4 Here are five other horoscopes for John's birthday.

A

TODAY'S BIRTHDAY

This will be a good year for you. Everything will go well. Friends will want to know you, romance flourishes, and you will make money. There could be a promotion at work.

B

LEO July 24 — August 23
If you left work unfinished yesterday – finish it now. Health good. Home and family life well-starred. Long distance travel is indicated. There could be trouble over money.

C

IF IT'S YOUR BIRTHDAY TODAY

The Sun, close to the planet Jupiter makes this a spectacular year for romance. A change at home does not make you happy. Take care of your health in the winter.

D

LEO July 23 to August 22

The influences of the stars are unpredictable, some are for you and some against you. Take advantage of a career offer at work, others think well of you at the moment. Do not try to force financial decisions. Be patient. Later in the week your friendly personality brings you luck.

E

It's your birthday today: You are independent, and have strong opinions about life and religion. This could cause trouble with your friends. Your health is better, but you are often depressed. You will be better working alone, as people do not understand you. You will be lucky with money, and if an offer to travel comes – take it!

COMPARE and CONTRAST the horoscopes, like this:

1 Use this chart to show which topics are referred to in each horoscope.
2 Choose one of the topics. Which horoscopes refer to this topic? Are the predictions about the topic the *same* or *different*?
3 Choose another topic. Which horoscopes refer to this topic? Are the predictions about the topic *good* news or *bad* news?
4 If these horoscopes were for *your* birthday, which one would you prefer to have?

TOPICS	HOROSCOPES				
	A	B	C	D	E
1 career/work	✓	✓		✓	✓
2 friends					
3 health					
4 home					
5 money					
6 personality					
7 romance					
8 travel					

Figure 31 Grid to show comparison and contrast
From Davies, E. and Whitney, N. 1981 *Strategies for Reading* (Heinemann)

Task 12

Identify some advantages and disadvantages of each alternative then complete the chart below:

Alternative	Advantages	Disadvantages
1	easy solution	2 ....
multi-user microcomputer/ supermicro	speed and power of minicomputer 3 .... 4	5 ....
minicomputer	speed and power 6	7 .... and ....
8	9 .... 10 .... 11	12 ....

Note There are several advantages to choose from for questions 9, 10 and 11.

Figure 32 Table to show advantages and disadvantages. (This task follows a text describing various forms of computer)
From Revell, R. and Sweeney, S. 1993 *In Print* (CUP)

Tasks involving figures are often integrative: many skills are needed to complete them, including making inferences and reorganizing information from different parts of the text. The pitfalls of traditional comprehension questions are avoided: the student cannot resort to responses which merely juggle the words of the text, but is forced to think hard about the meaning and consider the application of what he reads. Many of these tasks can also be considered as exercises in ***summarizing:*** they require the student to extract the main points of the text, or points relating to a particular topic. An interesting example requiring summary skills is Appendix B Text 4 *Danger from Fire* exercise 1.

Figures are excellent for checking that students understand the application of what they read. For instance, the tasks in Figure 15 (p122) can only be done if the rules of the game of ayo have been understood.

You have to decide how much information to present to the students and how much they are to supply. Advanced students can be challenged by tasks that draw attention to the structure of the text, involving constructing or labelling a text diagram (see Chapter 7, p109). Even beginners can be challenged by simple problem-solving tasks such as Figure 33.

1 Look at this picture

2 Read this

Six monkeys are sitting in a tree. They have hats on their heads.

Two hats are yellow. Two hats are red. One hat is blue and one hat is green.

The first monkey is fat. The second monkey is thin. They have the same colour hats.

The third monkey is black. His hat is not blue.

The fourth monkey has a green hat.

The fifth monkey has a red hat. He is small. The sixth monkey is big. The big monkey and the small monkey have different colour hats.

3 Can you colour the hats?

Figure 33 A simple problem-solving task

The students can be asked to *prepare* or *choose* a figure to match the text (see Activity 7.3, p104), to *arrange* (eg pictures to match a text), to *complete* or *correct* (eg a figure that is incomplete or does not match the text in all details), or to *label* (eg a graph in accordance with the text), as in Figure 34, p205, and so on.

One caution is in order: text and figure are often so closely related that neither is complete without the other, so that deletions may be impossible to restore. If you expect students to restore a text by collecting information from a figure, or to complete a figure with information from a text, check that what you are asking is possible, by getting colleagues to try out the task.

Other non-language activities

Also enjoyable, and often fairly easy, is the kind of task that requires students to follow instructions in the text. If the text explains how to operate a machine (eg a leaflet accompanying a cassette recorder), make a model (eg an extract from a book on origami), play a game, etc, the most effective outcome is to get the students to do as the text instructs. This is usually interesting in itself, as well as good practice in functional comprehension, though not always easy to arrange!

Tasks with outcomes involving spoken language

We are not dealing here with oral questioning (covered in Chapter 11), but with more creative and integrative activities requiring the students to use the spoken language. As well as being enjoyable, these can be designed to ensure that preparatory tasks involve thorough work on the text. They can also provide illuminating feedback for the teacher.

Drama, simulation and roleplay

Drama can be used to exploit suitable texts (primarily narratives) in ways that go far beyond the extemporizing of dialogue. For students learning to interpret text, the value is in the preparation, not the performance.

Understanding is deepened and made clearer when, for example, the student playing the role of X has to decide – with the help of the others – what X is doing at any given point, what expression he is likely to have on his face, how he will behave towards Y (is he hostile or merely suspicious?), why he says this rather than that.

To make these decisions, you have to read closely and explore X's character, his relationship with Y, what has happened to them in earlier parts of the story and so on. It is easy to base such work on a superficial reading, from which the students will learn very little, so for dramatization to be worthwhile, the preparation must involve frequent interruption (by you if necessary, ideally by other students) and reference to the text to support one interpretation rather than another. Conducted in this way, dramatization is enjoyable and leads to learning through discussion focused on the text, although – like many good methods – it is time-consuming.

While drama is most obviously appropriate for literary texts, its close relative ***roleplay*** can be used over a wider range of genres. It is particularly appropriate when you want to focus on points of view rather than characters. For example, an article about teenagers in conflict with their parents could be prepared for by asking students to act out relevant situations in the roles of a teenager and his parents, two parents with different attitudes, and so on. Cultural differences (how does the behaviour described compare with behaviour in our own society?) could be explored by using roles from different cultures, perhaps requiring students to do some research in order to present the views of people from elsewhere.

Any texts that involve analysis of people's actions or discussion of different points of view can be brought alive by means of an extended form of roleplay, ***simulation***, in which students represent perhaps the people involved in the actions described (eg meeting years later to discuss what happened), or protagonists of different viewpoints.

The nature of the simulation depends on the text: a text discussing various approaches to education might be explored through a simulated meeting of school teachers; alternative economic policies could be embodied in a group of advisers trying to agree development policy; a village meeting attended by farmers and agricultural extension workers could provide the means for discussing improved agricultural techniques; and so on.

It is of course not implied that any such meeting is described in the text; the idea is that having identified various points of view in the text, each student adopts the role of a person holding one of these, masters the argument presented in the text and prepares to defend it against others. You may decide to let students go beyond the text and produce their own additional points; if so, instructive comparisons can be drawn between the points made in the text and those made in the simulation.

Conventional acting ability is not needed for roleplay and simulation; it is helpful if students can identify with the point of view they have to present, but not strictly necessary. (Playing devil's advocate can be educative as well as amusing.)

It is important to understand that what we have in mind is not a display in which a few students are actors while the others are an audience. On the contrary, the strength of this approach is that everyone is actively involved in suggesting, discussing interpretations and so on. As soon as the class is familiar with the approach, groupwork can be used (with or without a presentation at the end). All groups work concurrently, each developing their understanding in their own way. This process is what counts, not a polished performance as an end product.

Debate and discussion

Much of what was said about roleplay applies also to ***debates*** based on the text; in fact, roleplay is often a form of debate made more lively by the viewpoints being embodied in human beings. However, debate generally uses the text simply as a spark to set discussion going, students being free to put forward their own opinions, while in roleplay they have to represent a view which they may not share.

Although the debate may not demand much reference to the text, it is one way of involving the students with the topic and exposing them to different points of view. In fact, some teachers find that roleplay or debate are useful for focusing students on the topic before reading the text, so that they bring ideas, understanding, sympathy and so on to their interpretation of it.

Informal class or group discussion is often more effective than a formal debate (with proposer, seconder and so on). You may like to use the ***buzz group*** technique: small groups discuss an issue for a given short time (five minutes or so; it depends on the issue). Each group then reports to the class and whole class discussion follows. Questions of evaluation and personal response (see p188–9) are suitable for this treatment. There should be a specific task (or tasks, for it can be valuable for each group to discuss a different aspect of the issue) in order to promote well focused discussion. The second stage is more effective if groups have to produce specific outcomes (eg a poster or OHP transparency to embody their views).

Reading aloud

My instinct here is simply to repeat 'Don't'. We noted (p32) that reading aloud round the class is too often used at the expense of silent reading for meaning. Nothing is easier for the teacher, or drearier for the students, and few commonly used activities have less value. Look at the faces of the students who are not actually reading aloud; their minds are miles away, and nine times out of ten they are not even hearing a text read well. Moreover, reading aloud is much slower than silent reading, so frequent exposure deters students from improving their silent reading speeds.

However, the fact that an activity is open to abuse does not mean that it is bad of itself. Does reading aloud have any value? If so, how should it be used?

First, there is no doubt that to hear a text well read – for example, by the teacher – is a tremendous aid to comprehension. The one who reads aloud has already interpreted the text, and her voice reflects her understanding. Occasional help of this kind is legitimate (with a difficult text, for instance), provided you recognize that you have done some of the work which the students must sooner or later learn to handle for themselves.

But what about reading aloud by the students? It seems to me that it could be justified for two purposes:

1 to round off work on a text;
2 to help inadequate readers to read in sense groups (which we saw in Chapter 4 is important).

We will deal with **1** first. Good reading aloud certainly shows some sort of understanding of the text. Yet paradoxically, people who read aloud fluently can often give only the sketchiest impression of what they have just read. Presumably, when we concentrate on pronunciation or expression, the mind lacks the capacity to process the meaning as well. Yet for most students, the important thing is not to give a polished performance of a text, but to understand it.

In fact, reading aloud by students is not of much practical use. It does not help the one who reads aloud to learn much about the meaning of the text. On the contrary, a good reading demonstrates what he has already learnt (so it is a kind of test). This is why I suggest that, if used at all, it should be the culmination of work on a text; an unsatisfactory attempt can be repeated after the meaning has been further discussed and alternatives explored. However, it is an advanced skill, reflecting oral ability as well as understanding; we should not underrate the demands it makes.

Turning to **2**, let us consider the 'read and look up' procedure described in West 1960. Intended for use with students whose reading is at an elementary level, it can promote some good reading habits, notably reading in *sense groups* (see p54–5). Briefly, this is the procedure:

1 Break up the text into manageable sense units. (The length depends on both reader and text: five to ten words is likely to be the most anyone can recall easily.) Normally this is done by the teacher in advance. When a reader is able to do it for himself, during rather than before reading aloud, this is a sign that he is developing the skill of reading in sense groups, which is the reason for using this technique. Students who need support should mark the sense groups in the text beforehand. For example:

   Mark looked out of the window./It was raining again/and the sky was dark./'Why does it always rain on Saturdays?' he thought./

2 Once the text is marked, the student who is to read aloud assimilates silently the words in the first sense group.

3 Then he looks up from the text and looks at the audience.

4 Now he speaks the words without referring to the text, addressing the listeners directly and making every effort to convey the meaning.

5 Then he repeats steps **2** to **4** with each subsequent sense group.

The benefit of this is that it makes the reader take in a chunk of text and retain it in his mind long enough to look up and speak it. Practising reading in sense groups, instead of word by word, provides the foundation for improving both speed and comprehension.

There is another advantage: the pressure to look up while speaking ensures that meaning takes precedence. Provided the student keeps the meaning of the text, it does not really matter if he departs slightly from the original words; indeed, this is a sign that he has interpreted the text and is not merely parroting.

In conclusion, if you want to use reading aloud by the students despite its many drawbacks, then:

- use it after the class has worked on interpretation of the text, not before;
- use the 'read and look up' technique;
- use it sparingly.

Listening with the text

Although a good oral reading can help students to understand the text, we have just noted that students will not become rapid fluent silent readers as long as they are tied to texts presented orally. So oral presentation must be treated cautiously. But it does have its uses.

For very slow readers

Some students read so slowly and hesitantly that a text read aloud well is actually too fast for them. However, following the text with their eyes while listening gradually improves both speed and comprehension; so this is a very useful technique for this limited purpose. The easiest way to organize it is to have texts read aloud and recorded on cassettes. You need some which are read very slowly, for the student to start on, as he will give up if the rate is too far ahead of his own. Try to prepare several sets at increasing speeds, enough to bring the student up to the normal reading aloud rate. There is plenty of commercial material available for use thereafter.

The student borrows both the text and the tape and listens as often as he likes while following the text with his eyes, if necessary using a card guide as described on p59. If you have a number of poor readers, they can listen as a group, while the rest of the class gets on with other work.

After considerable exposure to taped texts, the students' reading rate should improve to the point where they can continue to improve without this support. They can then be encouraged to increase their speed still further by some of the means suggested in Chapter 4.

To enhance enjoyment of literature

Listening with the text is also enjoyable in its own right and may kindle a love of reading. Good spoken presentations (especially of narratives, plays or poems) are available commercially and are popular with students.

Most publishers of graded readers (see Appendix D) issue cassette recordings of some of their titles, which are an excellent source of material. Alternatively, you and your colleagues can build up a library of cassettes read by the best speakers available locally. In fact, you should do this in any case, because you will need recordings of texts that are not available commercially, but which suit the needs of your students.

Many students now have access to cassette players at home, but some will be needed in the school too, for use whenever students have a spare moment. Using a headphone prevents disturbance, and some cassette players have facilities for group listening through headphones. Luckily, for listening to speech, fairly cheap machines give adequate reproduction.

Outcomes involving writing

Many students who need to read the foreign language do not need to be able to write it, so writing is often played down. This is a pity, because some of the most interesting ways of exploiting texts involve written outcomes. Reading and writing are so closely associated, as two sides of the same coin, that it is natural for work on either to support work on the other.

Reassembling and making use of information

A good means of ensuring that students get to grips with the text is a task requiring them to make use of what they have read. Many writing tasks fall into this category.

The task must not allow the students simply to quote chunks of the text, as this can be done without thorough understanding. Ideally it will involve using information derived from reading, in order to do something comparatively unrelated to the text itself. Here are some examples:

1 Plan a tourist brochure for a place described in the text.
2 Plan a documentary film to illuminate the points made in the text (with or without actual commentary/dialogue).
3 Write a memorandum from an appropriate official (health officer, forestry researcher, etc) proposing a course of action to tackle the problems outlined in the text.
4 Write a series of numbered rules/instructions for the (game/ procedure/process, etc) described in the text.
5 Read these alternative reports of an incident/event, etc and note the points on which they differ. Now write a report for the (factory supervisor/police/principal, etc) attempting to explain what actually happened and accounting for the different versions.
6 (*For a text explaining a classification system.) Supply a selection of relevant pictures/diagrams/descriptions – or the objects themselves.*) Study these (objects) and classify them according to the criteria explained in the text. Prepare a classified catalogue explaining the grounds for your decisions.
7 (*For a semi-scientific text*) Write five statements that are supported by the information given in the text./Write a hypothesis to explain the phenomena described in the text./Suggest an experiment that would test the hypothesis made in the text. Be prepared to justify your answers in discussion.
8 The story is told from (Jan's) point of view. Recount the incident as it must have appeared to (Lorna).
9 Would you prefer (Dorothea) or (Celia) as a sister? Why?

These are random examples to give some idea of the scope. The possibilities are very wide; every text has its own potential and must be exploited in its own way.

Many tasks of this kind can be effectively used for groupwork, especially those which give scope for discussion and co-operative effort. If the aim is primarily to explore the text, rather than to practise writing, a group product is perfectly acceptable; alternatively, individual writing can follow the group discussion.

Using figures

Diagrams and other figures offer excellent scope for written work of the 'transfer of information' type. We saw in Chapter 4 that figures can be used to support reading; the mirror image of this is to use them as a basis for writing. When the figure reflects the text, and vice versa, either may come first (Figure 30 on p197 demonstrates this). We can make use of these relationships in devising tasks.

A simple way of using a figure is to remove or gap the accompanying text or make the figure disagree with it, as in Figure 35 on p206. The task is then to recreate or correct the text, using the figure as a guide. This works well with the text diagrams described in Chapter 7, and with any figure which sufficiently mirrors the structure of an accompanying text.

Solvent sniffing

Young people today sometimes sniff solvents (for example, butane gas, glue, aerosol spray) in order to get intoxicated. The habit can be dangerous. This text (from a leaflet of advice for parents) explains how widespread it is in Britain.

Read the text and then show that you understand it by filling in the boxes in the key below, so that they match the correct section of the pie chart.

How many young people sniff?

Only about one in ten secondary school children try sniffing, and most of these will only experiment; they won't sniff for very long. But a few may become heavy and frequent solvent misusers. The number of youngsters sniffing varies from place to place and at different times. Some people say there is more sniffing in the summer, but perhaps it's just more obvious in the long summer evenings. Sniffing will vary from school to school, from youth club to youth club and from one residential children's home to another. It can be quite a craze in a neighbourhood for a while and then almost disappear.

Most young people will never try sniffing. And most of those who do will only try it once or a few times. A few youngsters may go on sniffing for a while – perhaps regularly with their friends. A very few will carry on, sometimes very heavily, for a number of years.

- ☐ **Only tried it**
- ☐ **Sniffed for a few weeks or months**
- ☐ **Long term users**
- ☐ **Never sniffed**

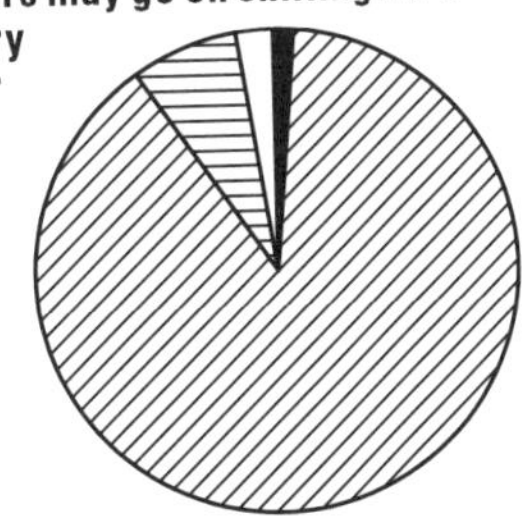

Figure 34 Labelling a pie chart to match a text
From *Solvents: a parent's guide* (Department of Health 1994)

Activity 1 **Understanding the meanings of word and sentence patterns**

Below is a description of a spaceship by somebody who said he had seen it - an eyewitness. With it there is a drawing of the spaceship. Read the eyewitness's account and write down the sections of it that do not correspond to the drawing. Then rewrite those sections so that they do correspond. Notice what changes in grammar and vocabulary you make in your corrections.

The spaceship was about two metres high. It was round at the bottom and pointed at the top. The craft was supported by three legs which were taller than the main body of the ship. I saw a small green man with two horns who had probably jumped from the ship as there was no ladder. I remember clearly a mysterious sign on the side of the craft. It showed a triangle surrounded by a circle. I am sure this is a message to people on Earth.

Figure 35 Correcting a text to match a picture
From Moore, J.D. et al 1979 *Reading and Thinking in English: Discovering Discourse* (OUP)

Another possibility is to study a text and figure and then present a second figure, similar in type, but relating to different content. For example, the students read a text about the production of coffee, and complete a process diagram (see Figure 28 on p196) to illustrate it. Then they are given a process diagram about the production of cocoa, and use it to write a description of cocoa production. Many variations are possible: for instance, a text describing a journey (plus map), or a house layout (plus plan), could be recreated with differences by basing the writing on a similar but not identical map, plan, etc.

Once you learn to view the figure as a kind of intermediary between the text that is read and the text that is written, you will find many other ways of using figures to provoke written work.

Summarizing and note-taking

It is a pity that summarizing has become unfashionable, because it is a very valuable exercise. It demands full understanding of the text, including the ability to distinguish between main points and examples, to perceive the relationships between the various parts of the argument, and so on.

It does, however, also require lucid and accurate expression. This may be too much to expect of your students, so I do not suggest they write a full summary to begin with. More guided approaches produce good results. For instance, you can supply a gapped summary (the omissions can be chosen to pinpoint possible misinterpretations) for the students to complete (eg Appendix B Text 2 *Survival of the Fittest* Activity C). Or an inaccurate one, for them to correct.

Functional summary

A ***functional summary*** is not the sort of task that instructs 'summarize the passage in 150 words', but a summary for a specified and plausible 'real life' purpose (like the report for the supervisor in topic 5 on p204).

A simple functional summary would not require students to write extended prose, but perhaps to list or make notes (eg producing a family tree and biographical notes on the members, after reading a story in which several generations feature; or an annotated list of the wildlife to be seen, after reading about a visit to a National Park).

If the students can express themselves reasonably well you can go on to more demanding tasks. To devise these, consider why someone might want a condensed version of the information in the text, or some of it. Many tasks involve selecting the relevant information as well as summarizing it; you need not ask for a summary of the whole text. Learning to assess relevance is a vital step towards becoming a selective reader.

Some samples of functional summary tasks:

1 (*Text discussing various issues – economic, social, political and so on – involved in constructing a new road in a rural area.*) Summarize for the director of the road works department the social factors he needs to consider before deciding the course of the road.
2 (*Text recounting an incident in a school, for which several students were to blame.*) The principal is to interview the students responsible. She needs to be briefed about the part played by each, and would like an opinion on how far each was to blame. Prepare the briefing notes for her.
3 (*Text discussing safety procedures in factories.*) The factory manager is proposing to display a simple list of DOs and DON'Ts, based on the various safety precautions discussed in the text. Draw this up for him.
4 (*Text in which X – eg a person, an incident – is both described and assessed.*) (Your boss) disagrees with the views expressed and plans to write a rebuttal; to help him/her prepare this, make two lists:
   a every fact stated about X, with its source when indicated;
   b every opinion expressed about X, with any reasons given.

Tasks like this also give practice in the sort of note-taking needed for study purposes. Making notes for an essay, on a topic that might reasonably follow from reading the text, is also excellent practice. It is not necessary to write the essay itself; the reading and thinking needed to assemble the notes is what counts. This is a particularly valuable way to study novels or plays; the discipline of focusing on a specific aspect or interpretation (eg *What evidence is there that Willy Loman was an unsatisfactory father? How far do you agree that Okonkwo's downfall was caused by his fear of seeming weak?*) leads to deepened insights and a clearer grasp of the work's structure.

Translation

Translation demands a literal understanding of the text, a sensitive response and a high level of competence in both languages. It is thus a supreme outcome of the interpretation of a text, but makes great demands on the translator's creativity and command of both languages. Many students do not need the skill of translating and it is often beyond their capacity, at least where the texts in question are beyond the level of business letters or reports.

Translation is undoubtedly an activity that forces students to get to grips with the text in the active way required for full comprehension. With the right kind of students – having the right level of linguistic ability, and having the need to master the art of translation – it is an activity worth doing for its own sake. Considered purely as an outcome of reading, however, because it is time-consuming and difficult to do satisfactorily, it is not particularly appropriate for general use.

Cloze procedure as a teaching device

While the cloze technique is familiar as a means of testing (see Chapter 13), its value for teaching is less well known.

A cloze exercise is easy to prepare. At its simplest, you just delete every *n*th word of the chosen text, and make sure that there is enough text (at least one sentence – more if the text is long) without deletions at the beginning to set the context. In this example (a much shorter text than a teacher would normally use), every seventh word is deleted:

> At last, the young hatch, chipping their way out of their shells with a small egg-tooth on the tip of the bill. Many of those that nest on ....1....... ground are covered with down when ....2....... emerge and this gives them excellent ....3....... . They run away from their nest ....4....... as soon as they are dry ....5....... search for food under their mother's ....6....... .
>
> From Attenborough, D. 1979 *Life on Earth* (Collins/BBC)

Deleting words more frequently – every fifth word, for instance – makes the task more difficult; less frequent deletions make it easier and are useful for introducing the activity for the first time.

In using multiple choice questions for teaching (see Chapter 11, p182), options are given which reflect predicted misunderstandings. In using cloze this is not necessary (though it can be done by supplying options for each gap); in other respects, the two techniques are similar. In cloze, the options are normally supplied by the students themselves in deciding what words would best fit each gap; the words thus reflect their actual misunderstandings.

Classroom procedure for teaching with cloze

After deciding what gaps to use, the cloze text is copied for individual use or prepared for use as a central visual (see p42). One way to begin is to let the class quickly read the undoctored text (skimming might be used), just to establish the context, topic and text structure. It need not involve any questions or other interpretive work. (This approach is used by some computerized cloze programs, which provide practice similar to that described below.)

If you choose to go straight to the gapped version, then everyone should first be given time to read right through it; it is not easy to suggest appropriate options until you have a general idea of the type of text, its topic and its structure. Start by asking for impressions about these.

After the class has established what kind of text it is, and discussed the context, you are ready to call for suggestions for the first gap. Write up the serious contenders on the board, and make a note of the others, because they are clues to the students' ability to process text and you may want to follow some of them up.

This is where the learning begins. Not merely the correct choices but the incorrect ones should be considered, the students themselves choosing the best. Reasons – particularly reasons for rejection – should be given. Some rejected words may be not so much incorrect as simply not what the writer chose; in this case, the reasons for her choice (and the effects of an alternative) may be explored with advanced students, especially if the text is a literary one. Some may be grammatically unsuitable, leading to covert or overt grammar teaching. Others – the most interesting for a teacher of reading comprehension – will be wrong because they do not fit in with the meaning of the text and thus illustrate the students' misunderstandings; these can then be explored and the students led to recognize what caused them.

Once the class has learned what to do under your guidance, this activity is ideal for groupwork (see p164).

Deletions for particular purposes

Choosing the right word necessitates reading ahead, as well as bearing in mind what has been read already; and it may involve using inference as well as understanding what is directly stated. To train these skills, deletion of words at regular intervals may not be the best procedure. For example, the passage above might be more useful if the deletions ran as follows:

> Many of those that nest on the ....1....... are covered with down when they ....2....... and this gives them excellent ....3....... . They run away from their ....4....... almost as soon as they are dry to ....5....... for food .... 6....... their mother's supervision.

Here, gap 1 is difficult to fill until you reach the words *run away*, which provide a clue. The other gaps are likely to be filled with choices that are not so much wrong as different from the writer's; they will provide material for discussion and, for advanced students, for work on register or style. Selective deletions can also be used to draw attention to specific features of text. For example, in this version the deletions are of cohesive devices such as reference words:

> Many of ....1....... that nest on ....2....... ground are covered with down when ....3....... emerge and ....4....... gives them excellent camouflage. ....5....... run away from ....6....... nest almost as soon as ....7....... are dry to search for food under ....8....... mother's supervision.

Jigsaw reading

Jigsaw reading is a technique that involves close attention to text, oral exchange of information (A needs information that B has, and vice versa: the ***information gap*** principle) and often a problem-solving element.

The activity requires several linked texts. These can be separate texts all dealing with linked situations, or parts of a single text: for instance, different parts of a story. The point of the activity is that unless you have information from all the texts, you cannot understand some key aspect of the situation or story, or perform some key task.

Jigsaw tasks are popular with students and can be used at all levels, as you can see from Figure 36 p210, which shows a very simple pairwork jigsaw with a problem-solving element. A more complex jigsaw task is used in Appendix C Lesson 2, p257: have a look at it now to get an idea of what is involved.

Here is one way of organizing a jigsaw activity. Divide the students into three groups, A, B, and C. Each group gets a different linked text with one or two tasks relating to it, and also one task (usually common to all the texts) that cannot be satisfactorily answered from any text alone. In a big class, to keep the groups small, you can have as many A, B and C groups as you like, as long as there are the same number of each type.

Unit 8 115 **A reading puzzle - half a story**

In the lift, but what floor?

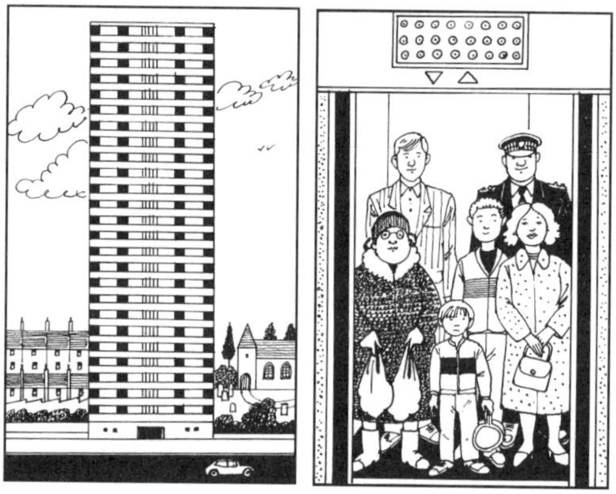

a Half the class together read Part A on page 99. The other half of the class read Part B on page 100. You can all take notes to help you, but you can t write more than 10 words.

If you are an A person, find a B person. Without looking at your books, tell each other your half of the story. A people start first.

What is the problem?

b Can you write down the answer to the problem? Do you want to ask your teacher some more questions? Your teacher can only answer with the words Yes or No .

Tell the class what you think is the best answer.

PART A

John lives with his family in a new block of flats two miles from the town centre. From his flat, they have a nice view of the town.

Every weekday, he leaves his flat at 8.05, and gets in the lift on the 24th floor. He presses the button for the ground floor. He gets out of the lift, says 'Good morning' to the man selling newspapers, goes to the bus stop and gets on a bus.

What floor do you think he lives on?
What floor does he get out of the lift on?

PART B

In the afternoon, John gets a bus about 4.15 and gets back to his block of flats at about 4.45. He usually stops off at the shop to buy some sweets or chocolate, and a newspaper.

He gets in the lift and he presses the button for the 14th floor. At the 14th floor, he gets out, and walks up the stairs to the 24th floor.

If there is someone else in the lift, he gets out at the 24th floor.

What floor do you think he lives on?
Why does he get out at the 14th floor if there is no-one else in the lift?

Figure 36 A simple jigsaw task
From Willis, J. and D. 1988 *Collins Cobuild English Course* Student's Book 1 (Collins ELT)

Each group read their own text (silently, if they are in the same room) and then discuss the questions. Then rearrange the class so that students are sitting in groups of three, with one A, one B and one C student in each. The task is now for each little group to exchange information orally, without looking at one another's texts, until they are able to work out the answer to the common task. They can come and report to you when they have done so. You need to have further activities for the ones who finish early – extensive reading, perhaps?

Texts that lend themselves to a problem-solving approach, and tasks that exploit this, are ideal. Some people do not include tasks for the first stage, but I find them useful for drawing students' attention to the facts in their own text which are going to be important when the exchange of information takes place. Usually students know that they need more information to answer the common question, but sometimes a surprise element is present (eg in Figure 36, they may not be clear about the problem until they exchange information).

Further reading

For general discussion of reading activities, see Davies 1995. On the concept of 'task' see Prabhu 1987; Nunan 1989; Candlin and Murphy 1987; Swales 1990. Johns and Davies 1983 analyses tasks to follow up reading. Matthews 1989 argues the importance of task sequence. Brown 1989 explores the nature of task difficulty.

Grellet 1981 remains the richest collection of activities to promote reading skills. Other collections of generalizable activities are Holme 1991, Maley and Duff 1989, Duff and Maley 1990, Maley 1994. Lunzer et al 1984 presents various task formats (DARTS: directed activities related to text) to produce text-focused discussion; see also Beard 1990; Davies 1995.

Other suggestions for classroom activities can be found in eg Williams 1984; Wallace 1992; Greenwood 1988 (not restricted to use with class readers); also Carter and Long 1991, Collie and Slater 1987 (not restricted to use with literary texts).

On drama, roleplay and simulation see eg Wessels 1987; Byron 1986; Eccles 1989. On discussion and debate see eg Ur 1981.

On the effectiveness of listening with tape see Pugh 1978, McMahon 1983.

On the relationship of reading and writing see eg Harris 1993, Zamel 1992, and coursebooks such as Johnson 1981, Cooper 1979. Edge 1983 describes a procedure to help students summarize text.

On the information gap principle see Rixon 1979, Prabhu 1987, Johnson and Morrow 1981. On jigsaw reading, see Geddes and Sturtridge 1982.

Chapter 13
The testing of reading

by J. Charles Alderson

Teaching or testing?

TEACHERS often feel that they do not know how to test reading. It might help them if they realized that the difference between testing and teaching is not as great as people believe, and that therefore answers to the question *How to test reading?* can be found in materials that deal with the teaching of reading. The difference is not so much the materials themselves as the way they are used and the purpose for which they are used.

Similarities between teaching and testing

The design of exercises or classroom activities does not in principle differ from the design of test items. Many textbooks contain exercises that resemble tests (eg cloze, multiple choice questions) and many tests contain 'authentic-looking' tasks more often associated with communicative textbooks. It is hard to think of a test method which could not be used successfully for teaching. It is equally difficult to imagine a teaching technique or an exercise which could not be turned into a test item with little or no adjustment. We shall illustrate this during the course of this chapter.

A common injunction is that teachers should test what they teach. This we certainly support in general, although we will later discuss how far it is feasible. But it can also be argued that teachers should teach what they test. If you feel that it is inappropriate to teach what you are testing, the value of what is being tested must be questioned. If you cannot teach towards a test in interesting, enjoyable ways, there are problems either with the test, or with the teacher and the way of teaching.

Differences between teaching and testing

When we urge teachers to teach rather than test, we have in mind particularly two major differences. First, students generally receive little or no support during tests, in contrast to what we expect during good teaching. Second, many tests are designed to discriminate, that is, to be difficult for some students, whereas teaching is intended to lead to successful learning for everyone. Two other important differences are that tests are only samples and that they often have consequences that teaching does not. We will discuss each of these distinctions in turn.

Tests are done without support

Students receive less support on tests than on exercises. If they get support during a test, this is typically considered to be 'cheating', whereas in class support is normal. When students find something difficult, the teacher's role is to make it simpler by means of 'scaffolding' (Chapter 3, p36).

In a test, on the other hand, students are expected to show how they can perform without outside assistance. That is, we suggest, the core meaning of 'test'. Collaboration is an important part of learning, but in a test, it results in a false picture of a student's ability, and is therefore usually discouraged. This often extends to the use of aids like dictionaries or grammar books, although it is now quite common to allow students to consult dictionaries in tests.

Moreover, in class a good teacher does not simply present a text, and expect students to understand it in a short period of time. She spends time repeating lesson points or activities for the benefit of those who are confused and gives all students enough time to absorb what is to be learnt. She probably also reviews, at some point, activities or points made earlier. In other words, much class time is spent in some form of repetition or review. A test must be somewhat more efficient or economical. Hence, some students may find they do not have enough time to complete all the required activities on a test. Thus a test may be completed under more pressure of time than a class activity, even though it is similar in design.

Because a student is not expected to receive support, the onus is on the test designer to be clear and explicit about what is required. Instructions must be simple; the tasks must be familiar to the student from having done similar tasks in class; the test items should be unambiguous; and it should be possible for a student who possesses the ability being tested to do the item. Such requirements are rarely made of exercises in textbooks: teachers can explain ambiguous instructions, or even omit materials which they find too difficult for their class. This may be why it is typically more difficult to write test items than exercises: they have to meet more stringent criteria of comprehensibility than most exercises simply because they have to stand alone.

Tests discriminate between students

Tests are often designed to be difficult for at least some students: they are intended to discriminate between those who have the ability, and those who do not. Although most tests start with a few easy items to encourage the weaker students, the items or tasks usually progress in difficulty so that even fairly good students will be challenged by later items and the weakest students will find many somewhat frustrating.

However, this is not a necessary condition for a test. It is perfectly rational to design tests on which most students will do well. Such tests, often called ***criterion-referenced*** or ***mastery*** tests, may simply be intended to show what students have learnt and what they can do, rather than to reveal weaknesses. Typically, ***progress*** or ***achievement*** tests designed by teachers would, we hope, be intended to be 'passed' by most students who have learnt what they were supposed to.

It is commonplace in education that 'success breeds success', and 'failure breeds failure'. Keeping such principles in mind, it seems eminently sensible to motivate students by designing tests which they stand a high chance of 'passing'. Failing tests which are purposely too difficult for many students is likely to discourage such students, and to lead them either to a low self-image, doubting their ability ever to learn the foreign language, or to reject the language as being too difficult.

Tests, in short, do not always need to discriminate very finely: much depends upon the purpose for which the test is given, and what will happen as a consequence of the results. It often makes pedagogic sense to make tests deliberately easy. Teachers who consider this somehow irresponsible should ask themselves why: what is the value in showing students what they cannot do, and what is the effect on those students?

Tests as samples

Inevitably less time can be devoted to 'testing' than to 'teaching'. We spend, or we certainly should spend, far less time testing than teaching – perhaps giving one two- or three-hour achievement test for a whole year's work. Clearly, therefore, a test can only relate to part of what is taught: it must sample. Ideally a good test will be a representative sample of what the teacher has done during class, but it is difficult to estimate the match between test and teaching when we are dealing with the assessment of skills (such as reading) rather than knowledge. For example, tests should not be based on the actual texts used in teaching. The texts should be similar to but different from those which have been used in class because we want to test what the students can do and not just what they remember. The problem is to decide whether a text used for a test adequately corresponds to the texts used during the teaching.

Tests have consequences

Tests often have consequences that teaching activities do not. Students can pass or fail tests; they should rarely be considered to pass or fail classroom activities. On many informal tests given by teachers, the individual results may not carry much weight, but their cumulative effect may be great – scores might be added up to arrive at a result for the term or the year. Such consequences are clearly very important, since they may determine future employment or other opportunities.

The important consequences of tests may lead to considerable pressure to perform well, to stress and anxiety, and to the danger of an atypical performance. The very fact that many tests are 'one-shot' affairs – a student is judged according to his performance on just one occasion – means that a test is a nerve-wracking experience for many. This is likely not to be the case when participating in ordinary classroom activities, where care is usually (although by no means always) taken to reduce stress.

Why test?

It is very important to consider the reason for testing: what purpose will be served by the test? If you cannot think of a reason for giving the test, then you should think very hard indeed about whether to give it! Similarly, if the only reason for giving the test is to force your students to work, you might think about other ways of motivating them.

Most teachers give tests in order to find out something about their students, preferably something they did not know already. Whilst we might be tempted to disbelieve a test that contradicts what we think about our students, a test that only confirms what we already know has little value.Teachers need to be prepared to be a little surprised by test results. Tests are given not only to confirm what you think you know, but to reveal things about students that you did not suspect. If we are not prepared to take seriously the results, even if they appear to contradict what we already know, then the test is probably not worth giving.

There are probably four main reasons why a teacher might give a reading test: ***placement*** into a reading class or programme; ***diagnosis*** of a student's reading needs or weaknesses; assessment of a student's ***progress*** over a given (usually fairly short) period of time; assessment of a student's ***achievement*** at the end of a course or year.

One other reason why reading tests might be given to students is to measure their ***proficiency*** in reading, but since such tests are usually designed by testing organizations or examination boards, rather than by teachers, we will deal with that sort of reading test only briefly.

Placement tests

Placement tests are designed to help a teacher decide where in a programme a student might best fit. In other words, they are intended to indicate the level of difficulty, or even the nature of course content, from which a student might best benefit.

Placement tests are designed to identify a student's level of reading ability or, alternatively, to identify the sorts of texts which a student will find readable. It clearly does not make sense to put a student into a class which is studying texts which are too difficult for him. Similarly, it does not make sense to put him into a programme which is teaching what he already knows.

If a reading course contains a number of texts graded in difficulty from easiest to most difficult, then a reasonable placement test takes samples of these (or similar texts), and sees how well students can read them. One simple way of doing this is to select short samples by, for example, taking the first 200 words from every tenth text in the programme. You can then create a number of *cloze tests* (see below, p222) on these samples, by deleting, say, every 7th word from them, and putting the resulting tests together into a booklet. Students are required to write the word they think is missing into the gap. Their responses are scored for the degree of understanding they show of the extracts. You expect to find that students' scores decrease as the difficulty of the sample text increases. A student is then placed into the programme at one or two levels lower than the level at which he ceased to show adequate understanding.

This rough and ready procedure is easy to develop and usually gives sufficient indication of a student's reading level for placement purposes. However, the value of such a test depends upon the texts in the programme being reliably graded into levels of difficulty – see Chapter 8. Since the consequences of misplacement are usually not serious, most teachers can probably live with such assumptions.

A variant of this procedure can be used in a class library, or an extensive reading programme (see Chapter 10, p176). You may feel that students would like to know whether a given book in the library is too difficult for them. A simple way to find out is to construct a cloze test from short passages from the book, and to stick that test in the back of the book. Students take the test, and then check their answers against a key on the reverse of the test. If they score above, say, 70 per cent, they should find that book within their reading ability. Again, the value of this procedure depends upon the representativeness of the passages on which the test was constructed.

Tests for diagnosis

The aim of a diagnostic test is to identify students' strengths and weaknesses. A diagnostic test needs to contain a number of questions in each relevant area, in order to give confidence that failure to respond correctly really does reflect a weakness, rather than some more random factor, like the difficulty of the passage, or a student's lack of attention to the wording of the question.

Typically, such tests are less concerned with the sort of text a student can read than with the skills that students have. Test questions are thus aimed at measuring such skills. When teachers write diagnostic tests, they may need to refer to lists or taxonomies of relevant skills. Commonly used lists include those in Munby (1978) and

Grellet (1981) and in this book. For more discussion of this, see the next section. The skills tested depend upon the level of the student: there is little point giving beginners diagnostic tests of their ability to evaluate an argument in expository text, when their major difficulties lie at the level of word attack skills (see Chapter 5). Thus, a diagnostic test is tailored to the students' known or expected problems.

Nevertheless, it is possible to glean useful diagnostic information from tests that are not fine-tuned or clearly focused. The use of cloze tests illustrates this point. Researchers often ask *What does the cloze test measure?* This is because different cloze tests seem to measure different abilities, or at least to provide different results from each other. However, it is still possible to derive useful diagnostic information from students' responses to cloze items. Consider this sample response:

> When Johnny got home with the shopping, ...bag...
> discovered that he had forgotten the butter.

Such a response suggests that the student has not paid attention to the punctuation and did not read on beyond the blank, to check what follows. Had he done so, he might have noticed that the next word, *discovered*, is a verb, which strongly suggests that what is needed is a noun or pronoun which can act as subject for this verb.

It could, of course, be the format of the test itself that has encouraged the student to respond to the item without reading the following text. However, it might be that the student has not learnt to suspend making a decision about meaning until later text has been understood. This is an important skill that intermediate level readers would benefit from applying. A teacher might check responses to other items to see whether a pattern of responses emerges.

This example also illustrates two important points about diagnostic tests. The first is that when we interpret the responses to items we have to make an intelligent guess at the reason why a student responded the way he did. Without corroborating information (for example, an interview with the student afterwards) we can only make guesses about why a student responded, and what that shows about his underlying ability. In other words, the diagnoses are unlikely to be 100 per cent accurate: they will be our best guesses, as experienced teachers.

The second point is that on diagnostic tests we are less likely to be interested in calculating a student's total score, and more interested in producing a ***profile***, that is, the pattern of a student's responses to similar sorts of items. By this means, we can identify where students' weaknesses lie.

Finally, lest you get the impression that diagnostic tests focus on weaknesses rather than strengths: this is not the case. Knowing that a student *has* the skill being tested is at least as important as knowing that he might *not* have it. However, we typically construct diagnostic tests to probe a student's ability in areas where we know, as experienced teachers, that some students do have weaknesses, which have important consequences for their reading. We are also more likely to test areas where we believe we can improve students' abilities: in other words, where a diagnosis might lead to remedial action.

Progress tests

Progess tests are intended to tell a teacher whether a student has, over a relatively short period of time, learnt what was intended. There are probably only a limited number of things that teachers can expect students to improve on in the short term: reading speed might gradually increase, and some skills, like the ability to guess unknown words from context, may be more quickly acquired than others.

A progress test will typically be relatively informal, short in length and time. On such tests, it is normal to expect, or to want, high scores. The teacher will be hoping that students can provide appropriate answers, and will not want to see many low scores. As high scores will motivate students, progress tests are useful ways of encouraging learning: success breeds success. If students tend to score low, she endeavours to ensure that adjustments in teaching allow them to catch up. If scores are high, she can be confident that the teaching is at the right level.

Two cautions are needed. First, be aware that you cannot use familiar texts to test progress in reading ability. If you use them, what you are testing is other things that have been learnt. Second, while you may be able to check progress in very specific skills (eg understanding a particular discourse marker), global reading ability takes a long time to develop, so it is not appropriate to try to measure it in a progress test. It is best measured at longer intervals by means of achievement tests, which we discuss next.

Achievement tests

In contrast with progress tests, achievement tests are more formal, and are typically given at set times of the school year. They may have important consequences for students (affecting whether they get promoted to the next class, for example): they are typically used to pass or fail students.

Achievement tests can be used ***formatively***: that is, the results may be used by teachers to slow down or speed up the pace of instruction, to change the textbook, to supplement materials with different activities, and so on. However, these changes may not benefit the students who took the test, but rather the new intake of students doing the course next term or next year.

Typically, however, achievement tests are used in a more ***summative*** fashion, that is, to deliver or to contribute to judgements on students and on courses. On the basis of achievement test results, students will be considered to have learnt or not to have learnt. Similarly, achievement tests may be used to evaluate courses.

Because of the importance of such judgements, achievement tests need to be longer, and more carefully constructed, than progress tests. Whereas a progress test might be the work of one teacher alone, and used only with her class, an achievement test might be written by all the teachers in a school or level, and is usually given to more than one class. To be valid, such a test needs to be based on the syllabus that each class is supposed to have covered. But perhaps some classes did not actually cover all of it. This presents problems for achievement test designers: should they include items that they know have not been covered by some, but should have been, or should they only cover content that is known to have been covered by all?

The answer to this question in part depends upon school policy and the reasons for not covering the material, as well as on the consequences of a student getting a low score. (The greater the consequences, the stronger the case for limiting the test to topics that everyone has covered. Otherwise students are penalised for factors beyond their control, like teacher competence or absence.)

However, in the case of reading achievement tests, the dilemma is less acute. Most reading courses and reading teachers aim to help students improve their reading ability rather than to cover specific texts. The teaching of reading involves the constant recycling of question types, task types and activities on different texts in order to help students develop relevant skills. In achievement tests of reading, therefore, teachers are *not* concerned to see how well a student can remember a text covered, but how well they can read texts similar to those covered in the course.

Thus, it is quite inappropriate in an achievement test to include texts that might have been seen by some or all students. Achievement tests should contain only unseen texts of similar type and difficulty to those in the course, and they should test the skills that have been taught. This is discussed in more detail later (p219).

Proficiency tests

Proficiency tests are not based upon any syllabus, but are designed to measure language ability more generally. They are often used to select candidates for higher education, or employment, and often test very broadly defined abilities. Teachers are not normally involved in designing proficiency tests for their own institutions, but they may find that externally designed tests are used to evaluate their teaching. This is only legitimate when the course objectives correspond to the objectives measured by the proficiency test – which is not always the case. You should ensure that the objectives of the proficiency test match your teaching or courses before you accept the results of such tests.

No purpose for testing

We suggested earlier that if teachers have no reason for testing, they should not give the test. But society has legitimate reasons for needing to assess students, so we would not be justified in refusing to give tests just because they may have a negative effect on students (where failure has important consequences, for example). However, when there is no compensating benefit to counterbalance the negative impact, tests are probably inappropriate.

This is arguably the case with extensive reading programmes, since their aim is to encourage students to read as much and as widely as possible, for sheer enjoyment. As we saw in Chapter 8, it is crucial that nothing impedes the readers' pleasure; being tested might well produce negative effects and reduce motivation. If it is thought important to measure student progress in extensive reading, a simple record for each student of the number of books read, and at which levels, is more appropriate.

The key point is that there are occasions when testing is appropriate and occasions when it is not. Those occasions vary from setting to setting, class to class. It is important to bear in mind the purpose for which one is deciding to give or not to give a test, and the likely impact on students of such a decision.

What to test?

Test content, teaching content

It should by now be apparent that the answer to the teacher who asks 'What should I put into my test of reading?' is 'It depends on why you are giving the test: what do you want to know?' In other words, test content is affected by test purpose, as we saw in the last section. In discussing what to test, we will assume that the prior question 'Why am I testing?' has been satisfactorily answered. At times, we will refer to how purpose affects content, but in the main we will now take an awareness of that relationship for granted.

Furthermore, it should by now be clear that what one *tests* is crucially affected by what one is *teaching*. Given that we see no essential difference in design between testing and teaching materials, any exercise intended to promote reading can be a potential candidate for a test item.

For example, take the prediction exercise illustrated in Chapter 7 (Task 3 on p120), or the jigsaw reading exercise in Chapter 12, p209. There is no reason why such exercises could not easily be adapted to form part of a test, provided that the students' responses can be rated as more or less adequate.

Similarly, any question that a teacher might ask in class, or that we might find in a textbook, could be used for testing purposes. For example, see the questions in Chapter 11, on Appendix A Texts 2 and 3 (p188).

It is normal to recommend that test writers should start with some statement of what is to be tested: in list form, or by categorizing skills, texts, tasks, and so on, into an inventory. Such a specification of test objectives looks rather similar to a specification of the objectives of teaching. For example, the objectives mentioned in the introduction to Part Three (pp125–6) could easily be included in such a specification. There is no reason in principle why a test specification would look any different from a syllabus specification.

Testing skills

It is normal practice to define the skills which one wishes to test, and then to attempt to write questions which involve such skills. An example might be *The ability to understand the literal meaning of sentences*. An item to test such an ability might be any of the Type 1 questions, p188. A further example could be *The ability to infer unstated meaning* and an example of such an item might be any of the Type 2 or 3 questions, p188.

Examples of exercises for training text attack skills that are usable as tests are Task **1** on p93 and Tasks **3** and **4** on p105.

Earlier chapters have given many examples of the sorts of skills one might wish to teach. It is important to be aware that if such skills are teachable, then they are probably testable. If, for example, the ability to understand anaphoric reference is being taught, it is probably testable. Similarly with word attack skills, and so on.

There are, however, three important qualifications to be made to this claim. One is that the less predictable the outcome of using a skill, the more difficult testing the skill is likely to be. The second is that we may not know what skill is involved in arriving at understanding. The third point is that it may matter less how one arrives at understanding, and more what understanding one reaches.

We will discuss each of these in turn.

Skills with unpredictable outcomes are hard to test

For example, one might wish to teach students to make predictions about what is coming next in a text, on the basis of text processed so far – be that headlines, accompanying illustrations, the first paragraph, a contents page, or whatever. The ability to make reasonable judgements about what is likely to appear next in text is important. However, in most cases we cannot fairly penalize a student for not predicting what the text actually says. Some answers may be more probable than others, and some can perhaps be ruled out, but the writer may choose to mislead or surprise the reader. It is thus difficult to judge the adequacy of a response. Such judgements might be made by using a rating scale of probability rather than a polar *right/wrong*, but it would be hard to administer and of dubious value.

It is also difficult to judge how far readers have the important ability to monitor their own ongoing comprehension as they read. A good reader identifies discrepancies between what he initially believed the text meant, and what subsequent reading shows that it means. This is most obvious, perhaps, in the case of ambiguity, or in the understanding of jokes. It is difficult to envisage a means of testing how well students are able to monitor their developing comprehension in this way.

We may not know what skill is involved in arriving at understanding

Readers can clearly arrive at the correct answer to comprehension questions or tasks by a variety of routes. Since these different routes may involve different skills, it becomes difficult to say that a single skill has been tested. A student's response will be affected by his knowledge of particular words, for example, and if he does not know the word, he will need to guess the meaning, whereas another student who knows the word will not need to use such skills.

But despite this problem, defining what one is trying to test, and then making a serious attempt to test it, is a useful discipline which is likely to lead to better test questions than if one made no attempt to think about the skills to be tested.

What matters is the global understanding, not the skill(s) used

How one arrives at a given understanding may be less important than the fact that one does actually understand. That is, we are less interested in the process by which a reader has arrived at an understanding than in the understanding itself. For many purposes it may simply be enough to determine whether or not a student has understood a text.

However, we have to be sensitive, in many settings, to the potential of ***negative washback***. If we do not test what we are trying to teach, there is a danger that students will not pay much attention to what is taught, or that teachers will cease to teach it. We certainly do not want our test to undermine what teachers are teaching. Thus there is a justification for trying to test skills, even though we cannot be certain that they are actually needed by all students in order to complete the test task successfully.

Testing top-down or bottom-up approaches?

It is difficult to envisage a reading test that would *require* students to adopt either a bottom-up or a top-down approach, since it may well be that either can result in a given understanding. Nevertheless, it might be useful for teachers to ask themselves, when looking at test questions they or their colleagues have devised: Is this a top-down/bottom-up question? Would top-down readers have a better chance of getting this item right?

Choice of texts

In testing reading, we are interested in knowing not only what skills a student has, but also, and arguably more importantly, what texts he can read.

Earlier we emphasized the importance of the purpose for which one is reading, and it has been suggested that the purpose is related to the type of text being read. We will delay discussion of how a test can affect or simulate reading purposes until the section on test method. We confine ourselves here to discussing the nature of texts, and the effect of text choice on measurement of understanding.

First, let us remind ourselves that for most purposes we should use in tests unseen texts that are similar to texts used in class. The interesting question is: how do we know when a text is similar? In general, the answer involves a judgement about a number of aspects: difficulty, topic and text type being the main features to consider.

We saw in Chapter 1 that text difficulty is a complex issue, but it is clearly very important in discussing what texts a student can understand. Indeed, some scales of reading ability define an individual's ability in terms of the sort of text he can understand.

Text difficulty has traditionally been measured by some form of readability index, as described in Chapter 10. Linguistic difficulty and even semi-linguistic variables like text organization, cohesion and coherence are reasonably well understood, and to some extent identifiable. Their effect on readability is also fairly predictable.

Perhaps less clear, certainly less predictable, but equally important is the difficulty caused by text topic. We saw in Chapter 1 the importance of a reader's schemata, or knowledge of the world, in text understanding. An individual's understanding is considerably affected by the text's content. Yet in reading tests we wish to measure how well a student can understand a given text, not what he knows about a topic. The dilemma is that, since knowledge of the world facilitates comprehension, there is a risk that the test is biased in favour of those students who have the most background knowledge. We ought either to ensure the same facilitation to all students, or to use texts on which nobody is likely to have prior knowledge.

The usual way out of this dilemma is to choose a number of texts for our reading tests, on a range of different subjects, where we trust that one student's advantage on one topic will be cancelled out by a lack of prior knowledge on another text.

Similarly for text type: different genres of text are doubtless variously familiar to and therefore easy for particular readers, especially adults who are familiar with a range of text types from their first language reading. We do not yet fully understand what it is about text type that creates difficulty for readers, but we can at least guard against bias by selecting a variety of different text types, at least in those test settings where no one type is expected to predominate.

One further variable to consider is text length. The length of a passage obviously affects how long it takes a student to read it and to answer the questions. Many teachers use short, paragraph-length texts for their tests. Yet we want to encourage our students to read selectively: reading to satisfy a given purpose, making judgements about relevance and irrelevance, main points and subsidiary detail, and so on. This argues for choosing at least some texts that are a page or more in length, to enable us to test these skills.

How to test?

Having selected our texts and decided what skills we wish to test, we now need to decide what method we will use to test comprehension of the texts, and the application of the skills.

No 'best method'

The first and most important thing to say is that there is No One Best Method for testing reading. No single test method can possibly be satisfactory for all the different purposes for which you might test, nor for all the skills and texts you want to assess. In this book, there has been much mention of the cloze procedure, perhaps giving the impression that the cloze is the answer. It is not. Cloze tests are very useful in many situations, partly because they are so easy to prepare, and partly because it is possible to discuss in class the responses that students give. As we have seen, it is even possible to make intelligent guesses about the processes students may go through when responding to cloze items. Nevertheless, the technique is not a panacea.

In practice, the only way to ensure that the teacher has written a good test item is to try it out on colleagues, friends, relatives, or even better, on similar students to those who will be taking the test eventually. It is very difficult to predict all responses to and interpretations of test questions, and therefore some form of pre-testing or trialling of the questions is desirable, indeed essential if the test has important consequences.

Discrete point vs. integrative methods

In a discrete-point approach, the teacher wants to test one thing at a time; in an integrative approach, on the other hand, the teacher wants a much more general idea of how well students read. In the latter case, this may be because the teacher recognizes that 'the whole is more than the sum of the parts'. It may also be simply because the teacher does not have the time, or even the skills, to test one thing at a time, or it may be that the test's purpose is such that she does not need to know what skills, or detailed understanding, a student has.

As we discuss later (p224), it may be that you believe that a discrete approach to reading is flawed, and that it makes more sense to take a more unitary approach, where no attempt is made to analyse reading into component parts. Instead, you may prefer a more global approach.

If you wish to take this more integrated approach, you will wish to find test methods of a more global nature. Some think that the cloze test is ideal for this because it is difficult to say what is being tested by the test as a whole.

The cloze test and gap-filling tests

The fact is that one cloze test can be very different from another cloze test based on the same text. The ***pseudo-random*** (every *n*th word) construction procedure guarantees that the test writer does not really know what is being tested: she simply hopes that if enough gaps are created, a variety of different skills and aspects of language use will be involved. Many cloze items are less sensitive to the constraints of discourse and more to the constraints of the immediately preceding context. Much depends upon which words are deleted, and since the words are deleted in a fixed order, the test constructor has minimal control over what is tested.

An alternative technique if you wish to know what you are testing is the gap-filling procedure. Sometimes this is known as the ***rational cloze technique***, but in order to emphasize the difference, we will use the term ***gap-filling procedure***. The procedure is almost as simple as the cloze procedure, but much more under the control of the teacher. The teacher decides which words to delete, but tries to leave at least five or six words between gaps (otherwise gaps are unduly difficult to restore).

Typically, when trying to test overall understanding of the text, a teacher deletes words which seem to carry the main ideas, or the cohesive devices that make connections across texts, including anaphoric references, discourse markers, and so on (as in the tasks on pp208–9). However, you then need to check, having deleted key words, that they are indeed restorable from the remaining context. It is very hard to put yourself into the shoes of somebody who does not know which word was deleted, and so it makes sense when constructing such tests to give the test to a few colleagues or students, to see whether they can indeed restore the missing words.

Multiple choice tests

Multiple choice questions (MCQs) are another common device for testing text comprehension. We discussed in Chapter 11 how to construct questions in order to achieve what needs to be achieved in teaching terms, and the same advice applies here. However, it is fair to add that MCQs are increasingly unpopular in the testing world. The problem with MCQs is that the presence of a number of distractors presents students with possibilities they may not otherwise have thought of. This may result in an untypical picture of their understanding. Indeed some researchers argue that the ability to answer MCQs is different from a reading ability. Some cultures do not use multiple choice questions at all, and students who are unfamiliar with them fare unusually badly on MCQ tests.

Short answer tests

An alternative to multiple choice is the short answer question: instead of presenting students with four choices, one of which is supposedly better than the other three, one simply asks them a question which requires a brief response, in a few words (not just *yes/no* or *true/false*). See, for example, Chapter 11, p188, types 2, 3 and occasionally 4.

The justification for this technique is that the teacher can interpret students' responses to see if they have really understood, whereas on MCQ items, students produce nothing, and certainly give no justification for the answer they have selected.

However, short answer questions are not easy to construct: it is essential to word the question in such a way that all possible answers are foreseeable. Otherwise the teacher will be left with a bewildering range of responses.

'Real-life' methods

The disadvantage of all the methods discussed so far is that they bear little or no relation to the text whose comprehension is being tested nor to the ways in which people read texts in normal life. Indeed, the purpose for which students read the text is simply to respond to the test question. Hence the way they read may not correspond with the way they normally read such texts, and the test may thus not reflect how they would understand similar texts in the real world.

We have seen how important reading purpose is in determining the outcome of reading. The challenge for the person constructing reading tests is how to vary the reader's purpose by creating test methods that might be more realistic than cloze tests and multiple choice techniques. Short answer questions come closer to the real world, in that one can imagine a discussion between readers that might use such questions, and one can even imagine readers asking themselves the sorts of questions found in short-answer tests. The problem is that readers do not usually answer somebody else's questions, as in a test. Instead, they ask themselves questions.
An increasingly common resolution of this problem is to start by asking oneself the

questions: What might a normal reader do with a text like this? What sort of self-generated questions might the reader try to answer?

To consider a simple example, imagine that you wish to test students' ability to understand the sort of magazine that gives details of radio and television programmes. Readers typically read such texts in order to find out what programmes are on at what time. Thus useful test questions might take the form 'What programme is on Channel X at 16.30?'

What distinguishes this sort of test question from the test methods discussed already is that there is an attempt to match *test task* to *text type* in an attempt to measure 'normal' comprehension. A further example of this is the exercise in Figure 15 on p122.

Information-transfer techniques

Another set of methods for testing students' understanding of texts is the use of information-transfer techniques, often associated with figures (as before, this term is used to cover all non-linear material such as charts, tables, illustrations). Examples were presented in Chapter 12, and such methods are easily used in reading tests. However, if you want students to restore information deleted from a figure, make sure that it is still possible to understand the verbal text without the deleted information.

Alternative integrated approaches

If you feel that discrete-point approaches are inappropriate, what alternatives are available, other than the cloze technique? In language testing generally, interest has recently been shown in a number of different techniques which may provide a more integrated picture of understanding.

The C-test

One such technique is a derivative of the cloze test, known as the C-test. In this technique, exemplified below, the second half of every second word is deleted and has to be restored by the reader.

> It is normal to leave the first sentence intact. Thereafter t..... second ha..... of ev..... second wo..... is del..... and t.... reader's ta..... is t..... restore t..... missing let..... .

The claim is that this technique is a more reliable and comprehensive measure of understanding than the cloze test. It has been suggested that the technique is less subject to variations in starting point for deletion and more sensitive to text difficulty. Many readers, however, find it even more irritating to complete than the cloze test, and it is hard to convince many teachers that this method actually measures understanding, rather than knowing how to take a C-test.

The cloze–elide test

A different alternative to the cloze technique, known in the 1960s as the 'intrusive word technique', but later relabelled the 'cloze–elide' technique, is a procedure whereby the test writer inserts words into text, instead of deleting them. The task of the reader is to delete each word that does not belong. Points are deducted for words wrongly deleted (that were indeed in the original text).

> An example of a this technique is this paragraph, where a number great of words have been always put into the text, and sometimes the job of the reader is try to

find them. It is claimed that by paying money attention to the overall meaning of the text, the reader person can remove the words that never do not belong.

The free-recall test

In free recall, students are asked simply to read a text, to put it to one side, and then to write down everything they can remember from the text. The comprehension score is the number of 'idea units' from the original text that are reproduced in the free recall.

For example, the previous paragraph contains the following idea units:

1 In free recall, students read a text.
2 Students put a text on one side.
3 Students write down all they can remember.
4 Comprehension score is the number of idea units reproduced.

One objection might be that this looks more like a test of memory than of understanding, but if the task follows immediately on the reading, this should not be too much of a problem.

The summary test

A more familiar variant of this, which requires students to organize their thoughts about the text, is the summary. Students read a text and then are asked to summarize the main ideas, either of the whole text or of a part. In order to do the task satisfactorily, students need to understand the main ideas of the text, to separate relevant from irrelevant ideas, and so on. The problem comes when marking the summaries: does the teacher, as in free recall, attempt to count the main ideas in the summary, or does she rate the quality of the summary holistically on some scale, say from 1 to 10? If the latter, the problem of subjectivity of marking needs to be addressed. Students may also suffer because they understand the text, but are unable to express their ideas adequately in the foreign language, especially within the time available for the task: summary writing tests writing skills as well as reading skills. This raises the question of whether first language responses (discussed in Chapter 11, p187) would not be more suitable in this form of test.

The gapped summary

An alternative which attempts to overcome both these objections is the gapped summary. Students read a text, and then read a summary, from which key words have been removed. Their task is to restore the missing words, which cannot be done without understanding the main ideas. Marking is relatively straightforward and the students' need to write is reduced to a minimum.

What is adequate understanding?

Perhaps the main problem faced by anybody who tries to test reading is not 'What method should I use?' nor even 'What should I test?' but rather 'What does it mean to say that somebody has understood this text?'

We have seen that the understanding of text varies according to one's knowledge of the world, and according to the purpose one has in reading. It also varies according to one's motivation, interest, knowledge of language, of text types, and so on. Different readers often arrive at different understandings of a text. This is particularly true for the meanings that readers create from text beyond the literal meaning of the words on the page. Implied meaning is one of these, sometimes referred to as 'reading between the lines'. Readers' own evaluations of the text, their appreciation and personal responses to the text, are another, sometimes called 'reading beyond the lines'. Such meanings are clearly important components of an understanding of a text, and therefore need to be included in tests of reading, if at all possible. Any test that confines itself to testing an understanding of the literal meaning risks serious deficiency.

These variable meanings are involved in the reading of non-literary texts, not just literary texts: even readers of scientific research articles disagree about what is being said. It is relatively commonplace in discussions of reading and interpretation to talk about 'the creative construction of meaning'. Insofar as meaning is not contained in text, but is created in the interaction between reader and writer through the medium of text, then the reader's contribution to the meaning created is crucial and, as we have seen, varies according to the nature and the state of the reader.

If this is true, then we are faced with the problem of deciding whose meaning is most accurate: this reader's or that one's? Is the writer's view the most authoritative? In other words, if there is disagreement about what a text 'means', ought we to ask the writer what she intended?

The fact is that for many texts, most competent readers agree on what is meant: there can be relatively little disagreement about the meaning in car repair manuals, or instructions on how to assemble furniture, or cooking recipes. How else can we explain that people are able to use such texts to repair cars, to assemble furniture, and to bake cakes? And this gives us the key to the notion of 'adequate understanding'. The definition of adequacy depends upon the text type, and the reader's purpose. Provided that a reader can satisfy his purpose in reading or using a given text, we conventionally say that that person has understood the text. Thus for many texts, we can test for adequacy of understanding by relating our test task to the text type, and thinking about readers' purposes, as we have suggested above.

In other cases, where texts are less use-oriented, we may need to appeal to the notion of consensus: if enough competent readers agree on the meaning of a given text, then we can say that somebody's understanding is competent to the extent that it matches theirs. Thus a useful technique for deciding what meaning to test in a text is to ask competent readers to say what that text means, either by writing a summary, or indeed even by answering questions about that text. In short, testing competent readers' understanding of a text is a way of arriving at the meaning to be tested when assessing the understanding of less competent readers.

Interpreting test results

Teachers understandably need to know what to make of the results of tests they have constructed or administered. In particular, they often need to know how to decide who has 'passed' the test and who has 'failed'. This is obviously a complex business, and we cannot do the topic justice here. However, there are two usefully different approaches to deciding how to interpret test results. One – called ***norm-referencing*** – simply involves putting students into rank-order based on their score on the test, and then comparing them with other students who have taken the test, at the same time, or previously. The good students are the ones who score higher than most others, and the weak ones are those who score worse.

The problem with this approach is, of course, that even those who score lower than other students may still read adequately. That is why the second approach – called ***criterion-referencing*** – has become popular. In this approach, it is necessary to decide what an adequate understanding of the text being tested is. This might involve asking readers who are known to be good to do the test, and noting the range of their scores. 'Good' students would be those who scored similarly. Typical good readers, against whom the students might be compared, are educated native speakers of the language, or students from previous classes who were known to be good readers.

One issue that often comes up in criterion-referenced testing is deciding when a reader who has not scored as high as the 'good' reader has nevertheless performed well enough to 'pass'. Sometimes the answer is deceptively simple: when he gets a given proportion of the questions correct. The proportion is often arbitrary, but it is typically a figure somewhere between 60 per cent and 80 per cent – it would be very unusual to decide that scores above 90 per cent were required to 'pass', and equally unusual to say that a score of 50 per cent or less was adequate.

Obviously, these decisions will vary according to the difficulty of the text, the nature of the tasks, and the purpose for which the test is being given. For example, if a test has to identify the best 10 per cent of readers in a class, simple norm-referencing and counting down from the top of the class will suffice. If the aim is to find readers who have severe difficulties, one would expect most readers to pass, and the pass mark might be set at, say, 30 per cent.

An alternative approach is to decide that a reader is 'good enough' on a reading test if he can understand the text sufficiently well to satisfy the purpose for which he is being asked to read it. Thus, if he can use information from the text to complete some real-life task adequately, that would constitute adequate reading. As discussed in the previous section, defining adequate understanding is difficult, but often necessary, and both norm-referencing and criterion-referencing provide some means of reaching difficult decisions.

Testing and evaluation

The results of tests can be used to assess how well your students can read. They can also tell you how successful your course has been, or how well you have taught the course. Depending upon your perspective, you can interpret test results as indicating students' strengths and weaknesses, the teacher's strengths and weaknesses, or the strengths and weaknesses of the course.

There are other ways of evaluating teachers and courses, which may be more appropriate than tests, depending on purpose or setting. However, the advantage of tests is that in order to construct them, the teacher is obliged to consider what her objectives were, how far she has covered the syllabus, and what aspects of the syllabus were most important. Since it is impossible to test everything from a course, the teacher must be selective in deciding what to test and this process of selection involves prioritising. The experience of devising tests is thus a good opportunity for the teacher to take a long hard look at what she is trying to teach, and what has been achieved.

Further reading

A basic introduction for teachers is provided by Hughes 1989. For more comprehensive information on the processes of constructing and validating language tests in general, see Alderson, Clapham and Wall 1995. For advice on writing test items for EFL see Heaton 1990, 1988. On the testing of reading, see also Weir 1990, 1993 and Cohen 1994. For classic arguments for using cloze tests see Oller 1980.

On recent research into reading, especially in a foreign language, see Alderson 1990, 1991; Anderson et al 1991, Childs 1988, and many articles in the journal *Reading in a Foreign Language*. On communicative tests of reading, see Alderson and Hughes 1981 and Bachman 1990 (especially his discussion of authenticity). Research in ESP testing is sparse, but see Alderson and Hughes 1981, Alderson and Urquhart 1985. On the assessment of literature see Brumfit 1991.

Chapter 14
The teacher as reader

THE BEST teachers of reading are also reading teachers, in the sense that they are teachers who read.

One of the easiest ways to improve your teaching is to read a lot yourself; with any luck, you will also enjoy the experience, painlessly improve your command of the target language and perhaps enhance your job prospects.

Readers are made by readers

Students follow the example of people they respect, and above all that of their teacher. If the teacher is seen to read with concentration, to enjoy reading and to make use of books, newspapers and so on, the students are more likely to take notice of her when she urges them to do the same.

It is important to demonstrate that you value reading, since we believe that reading is caught, not taught. Like an infectious disease (fortunately only in this respect), it cannot be caught from people who have not got it themselves.

Perhaps your students already read a great deal, at least in their L1, and do not need to catch reading from you; but some are likely to come from homes where little reading takes place. Some of them may not even recognize that reading is useful, let alone that it can be enjoyable. Others may not accept that this can be true of L2 reading.

Now you have these students with you for a year or so: not much in the context of a lifetime, but enough to set the habit of a lifetime if the opportunity is taken. For disadvantaged students, you may be the only reader they meet, the only person from whom they can 'catch' reading. This is why they must see that you are a reader, both in your L1 and (if it is different) in the target language.

How do you show that you value reading? You carry books around with you. You make sure that students see you reading – for pleasure as well as for professional reasons. You talk to them about what you are reading, and read out brief passages that might interest them. You take an interest in what they read, and can suggest books that would suit them. You treat books well, and make sure that students do the same, because you respect books for what they contain and because careful handling is considerate of other readers (underlining words and making notes in the margin is good study practice, but only if the book belongs to you); and because it makes economic sense: after all, books are expensive as well as valuable.

How much do you read?

This question may be no problem for many teachers, but a serious one for others. We will consider three possible answers:

1. I read a lot, both in the target language and (if it is different) the L1.
2. I read a lot in my L1 but not much in the target language.
3. I don't read much in any language.

If your answer is **1**, there is no problem for you. You just need to make sure that you communicate your love of reading to the students. This book has told you all it can and your own interest will make you a successful teacher of reading.

If you read very little in any language

If you don't read much in any language, start by asking yourself why. Perhaps you have never been lucky enough to catch reading from anyone; perhaps you live among people who consider it a waste of time; perhaps you have been discouraged by finding it difficult or tedious; perhaps you have never really considered the advantages you would have if you could read more effectively.

These are matters that only you can decide, but the fact that you are reading this means that reading has some interest for you. This can be developed to your own advantage, as well as to the advantage of your students.

First recognize that, if you want to, you can train yourself to read effectively. This means that you will read faster and hence read more than you do now, even if you do not spend more time reading. (This follows from the 'virtuous circle' displayed in Figure 17 p127.) You will, however, have to spend some time on the initial training.

If the prospect attracts you, make a plan, set yourself goals and offer yourself rewards. Start by improving your reading in the language that will be most use to you; this may be your L1. Read Chapter 4 again, or follow the suggestions in a book about reading efficiency. Once you have improved your L1 reading, you can go on to improve your target language reading in the ways suggested below.

If you don't read much in the target language

If you read a lot in your L1, your problem is not so serious. However, you will teach with more confidence and conviction if you can organize your time so that you do more FL reading than at present.

First of all, motivate yourself by choosing FL books that you enjoy and find easy to read. This is just as important for you as for your students, especially if you have no real need to read the FL. Many teachers read the FL mainly for their studies, and professional reading material is often difficult, so it is quite likely that you read too slowly. You can find out by testing your own speed as described in Chapter 4. If it is less than 350 wpm on straightforward material, you can improve it.

Reading the class library

A good way to start will kill two birds with the same stone. Read all the target language readers in the school or class library, starting with the easiest level and reading them as fast as you can. Gradually work upwards, reading all the books at each level before you go on to the next. Don't slow down your reading by stopping to look up new vocabulary or puzzling over difficulties. Use skimming for books that don't interest you.

This has the great benefit of familiarizing you with all the books available for your students, as well as giving you the right kind of practice. Jot down the author, title and level of the book, with two or three lines of comment, in a note book or card index you can maintain when new books arrive. You can refer to it when students want advice on what to read, or when you want to check how well they have read a book.

Improving your reading

Reading the graded readers is a good way to begin your programme. You can go on by using a reading efficiency handbook if you wish, but the most important thing is to increase the amount of reading.

For this purpose, choose short books that are easy enough to read quickly and that you will enjoy. Use simplified or abridged editions if you like. Perhaps you feel that teachers should not read light fiction or anything written in simplified language; but it isn't cheating to begin on books of this kind, it's common sense. The time to read long books, or those that deserve to be read with care, is after you have become a fluent reader; if you start with them, you will never reach that stage.

Read as you read the class library, fast and without much attention to detail. Skip difficulties. Try not to use a dictionary. In fact, use the strategies you will be helping your students to develop. The experience will be very useful to you in the classroom.

Try to do some target language reading every day and finish at least one book a week. This is quite realistic if you read in the way suggested. The key is to be honest with yourself about what you really enjoy, because that is the best way to motivate yourself to read. It is impossible to reach good speeds if the material is difficult or dull.

After only a few months, you should notice a very marked improvement in your reading efficiency. At that point you can begin to read more challenging material, go more deeply into topics that interest you, perhaps study for a further qualification. The point is that to get to this stage, a great deal of practice on easy interesting material is essential. Developing your own reading skill by this means will give your teaching the conviction that only comes from experience.

In addition, I hope that you will develop a love of reading that will not only help you to be an excellent reading teacher, but will give you a source of profit and pleasure that lasts throughout your life.

Further reading

Campbell 1989 and Wheldall and Entwhistle 1988 demonstrate the importance of the teacher as role model.

To improve your reading speed, try de Leeuw 1990 or (for EFL reading) Mosback 1976. Using a reading laboratory (see Appendix D) will improve both speed and other skills. Better still, get hold of Harri-Augstein et al 1982 (read the Epilogue first) or Montgomery et al 1992; both are stimulating and thorough programmes of personal reading development. Lunzer et al 1984 is also worth studying for its full discussion and analysis of texts.

You could also try some of the study skills courses in Chapter 4 Further Reading, and some of the reading courses prefixed T in the bibliography.

Appendix A
Texts

Text 1 Archaeopteryx

Almost all the characteristics that distinguish birds from other animals can be traced one way or another to the benefits brought by feathers. Indeed, the very possession of a feather is enough to define a creature as a bird.

When, in 1860, in Solnhofen in Bavaria, the delicate and unmistakable outline of a single isolated feather, seven centimetres long, was found impressed in a slab of limestone, it caused a sensation. It lay on the rock, as eloquent as a Red Indian sign, proclaiming that a bird had been there. Yet these limestones dated from the days of the dinosaurs, long before birds were thought to exist.

The sediments from which they are formed were deposited on the bottom of a shallow lagoon enclosed by a reef of sponges and lime-depositing algae. The water was tepid and poor in oxygen. Cut off from the open sea, there were few if any currents. Lime, partly from the disintegrating reef and partly produced by bacteria, was deposited as ooze on the bottom. Such conditions suited few animals. Those that did stray there and died, fell to the bottom and lay undisturbed in the still water as they were covered by the slowly accumulating ooze.

The Solnhofen limestones have been quarried for centuries because their fine even grain makes them excellent for building and ideal for use in lithographic printing. They are also immaculate blanks for nature to impress with the fine detail of the evidence of evolution. The stone, if it is thoroughly weathered, splits along the bedding planes so that a block can be opened into leaves, like a book. When you visit one of the quarries, it is almost impossible to resist the temptation to turn the pages of every boulder that you see, knowing that no one has ever looked at them before and that whatever they contain will not have been exposed to daylight for a hundred and forty million years. Most, of course, are blank, but every now and then, the quarrymen find fossils of a near-miraculous perfection – fish with every bone and shining scale in place, horseshoe crabs lying just where they died at the end of their last furrow through the silt, lobsters with even their finest antennae intact, small dinosaurs, ichthyosaurs and pterodactyls, lying with the bony scaffolds of their wings crumpled but unbroken and the shadow of their leathery flight membranes plain to see. But in 1860, that beautiful and enigmatic feather was the first indication that birds had been living in such company.

To what kind of bird had it belonged? Science, on the strength of the feather alone, called it Archaeopteryx, 'ancient bird'. A year later, in a quarry close by the first, searchers discovered an almost complete skeleton of a feathered creature the size of a pigeon. It lay sprawling on the rock, its wings outstretched, one long leg disarticulated, the other still connected with four clawed toes, and all around it, dramatically and indisputably, the clear impress of its feathers. It was certainly apt to call it an 'ancient bird' but it differed substantially from any known living bird. The long feathered tail that flared out behind it was supported by a bony extension of its spine; and it had claws, not only on its feet but on the three digits of its feathered forelimbs. It was almost as much a reptile as a bird and its discovery within two years of the publication of *The Origin of Species* was a providentially timed confirmation of Darwin's proposition that one group of animals developed into another by way of intermediate forms. Indeed, Huxley, Darwin's champion, had predicted that just such a creature must have existed, and had prophetically described its details. Even today, there is no more convincing example of such a link.

From Attenborough, D. 1979 *Life on Earth* (Collins/BBC)

Text 2 A Son to be Proud of

Last week, Rahman's wife Leila had an accident. Rahman's youngest child, Yusof, was at home when it happened. He was playing with his new toy car. Rahman had given it to him the week before, for his third birthday.

Suddenly Yusof heard his mother calling 'Help! Help!' He ran to the kitchen. His mother had burned herself with some hot cooking oil. She was crying with pain and the pan was on fire.

Rahman had gone to his office. Both the other children had gone to school. Yusof was too small to help his mother, and she was too frightened to speak sensibly to him. But he ran to the neighbour's house and asked her to come and help his mother. She soon put out the fire and took Yusof's mother to the clinic.

When Rahman came home, Leila told him what had happened. He was very proud of his son. 'When you are a man, you will be just like your father,' he said.

Text 3 Survival of the Fittest

On each tree there is a moth. They are both quite clearly visible. Any predator would see his prey very clearly. But suppose the light moth was sitting on the light tree and vice versa. A dark moth on a dark tree would be less visible and have a better chance of survival from the attacks of predators. This is known as camouflage. Some animals, like the chameleon, for instance, are able to change colour according to their background. This kind of change is not evolutionary change (though of course the chameleon has evolved this ability to make the change). However, a change in colour is evolutionary if the creature is able to reproduce itself so that its young also have the new colour.

The example of the moth is a real one and was investigated in England in the 1950s by a scientist called Dr Kettlewell. It is a very well-known example of evolutionary change.

The species of moth is the Peppered Moth. It was typically light brown in colour and settled on the trunks of trees which were a similar colour and camouflaged it. Then came a change in the environment. Industry began to grow up in parts of England with the result that smoke and other forms of pollution began to fill the atmosphere.

The pollution from the factories covered the bark on the tree trunks with soot and grime so the light brown Peppered Moths became very visible to their predators and were eaten. Then gradually they began to change colour. The darker ones were more likely to survive, so their colour gradually became darker. How did they become darker? This is one of the mysteries of science, but it has been called 'natural selection' since Charles Darwin published his famous book *The Origin of Species* in 1859. Natural selection does not make anything happen. You cannot force a moth to change colour, for instance, nor can a moth decide to change. The point is that every creature has a genetic structure consisting of genes and chromosomes. This structure can change naturally, by accident. Perhaps this change does not matter. Perhaps, on the other hand, it produces a 'deformed' individual which the others reject or even kill because it is different. These things happen all the time. But if the change (or 'mutation') happens to fit the new environment, then the new creature, instead of being rejected or killed by the others, will survive.

This is natural selection. A mutation (which is always possible) happens to suit a new environment, and the 'odd' creature survives because it is better fitted. Then it reproduces and a new type of creature evolves. Meanwhile the others have become unsuited to the changed environment. They must either change their behaviour or become extinct.

Dr Kettlewell wanted to discover whether the dark Peppered Moths were in fact a new type of Peppered Moth which had adapted to its environment. In the first experiment, he released light and dark moths into the woods near Birmingham (a large industrial city in England). In the second he released his moths into the woods in a country district called Dorset in the south of England. Finally, he placed examples of each kind of moth on trees of the opposite colour and watched what happened.

Here are the results from his experiment in Birmingham.

	light	dark
Number of moths released	201	601
Number of moths recaptured	34	205
Percentage of moths recaptured	16%	34.1%

Dr Kettlewell's technique was to release moths which were specially marked, then recapture as many as possible after a time.

Later, to find additional support for his hypothesis, Dr Kettlewell repeated the same experiment in Dorset. The result proved he was right:

	light	dark
Number of moths released	496	473
Number of moths recaptured	63	30
Percentage of moths recaptured	12.5%	6.3%

Finally, he placed an equal number of moths of each colour on trees and watched what happened. He quickly discovered that several species of birds searched the tree trunk for moths and other insects and that these birds more readily found the one that contrasted with its background than the one that blended with the bark:

	Moths eaten by birds	
	light	dark
Unpolluted woods	26	164
Polluted woods	43	15

From Ricklefs, R. E. 1973 *Ecology* (Nelson) in The Language Centre, University of Malaya 1980 *Skills for Learning: Reading for Academic Study* (University of Malaya Press/Nelson)

Text 4 Notices

Bay View Community College
Registration Directory

ALL GENERAL ENQUIRIES	Room 102
Hotel Management	103
Business Management	104
Science Courses (day)	106
Science Courses (night)	107
ALL NEW STUDENTS	110
Sociology	203
History	207
French	237
German	264
Spanish	276
OTHER FOREIGN LANGUAGES	281
English	290
Vocational Education	292
English as a Second Language (ESL)	310
Accounting	296
Drama	294
Art	311
Music	357
Physical Education	381
ALL OTHER COURSES	390

NOTICE TO ESL STUDENTS

Please sign up at the appropriate table

COURSE	TABLE
Part-time course in English conversation	A
Full-time course in general English	B
Part-time course in general English	C
Part-time course in spoken English	D
Full-time course in written English	E
Full-time course in technical English	F
Part-time course in technical English	G

From Davies, E., Whitney, N., Pike-Baky, M. and Blass, L. 1990 *Task Reading* (CUP)

Text 5 Airships

In the age of supersonic airliners it is difficult to realize that at the beginning of the twentieth century no one had ever flown in an aeroplane. However, people were flying in balloons and airships. The airship was based on the principle of the semi-rigid structure. In 1900 Ferdinand von Zeppelin fitted a petrol engine to a rigid balloon. This craft was the first really successful steerable airship. In 1919 an airship first carried passengers across the Atlantic, and in 1929 one travelled round the world. During this time the design of airships was constantly being improved and up to 1937 they carried thousands of passengers on regular transatlantic services for millions of miles.

However, airships had many defects. They were very large and could not fly well in bad weather. Above all, they suffered many accidents because of the inflammability of the hydrogen used to inflate them. In 1937 the Hindenburg airship exploded in New Jersey and 35 out of 100 passengers were killed.

Today airships cannot compete with jet aircraft. However, they have been greatly improved. They can be filled with helium, and advances in meteorology make it possible to choose calm routes. They can remain static in the air and are being used in the American navy for observation of icebergs in the Arctic. It is possible that they will be used for other purposes in the future.

From Moore, J.D. et al 1979 *Reading and Thinking in English: Exploring Functions* (OUP)

Text 6 Shin-pyu

SHIN-PYU: BECOMING A DIGNIFIED HUMAN BEING

The most important moment in the life of a young Burmese boy is that of his *shin-pyu*, his initiation as a novice in the order of monks.

Until a Buddhist has gone through the *shin-pyu* ceremony, he is regarded as no better than an animal. To become "human," he must for a time withdraw from secular life, following the example set forth by the Buddha when he left his family to seek enlightenment, and later by the Buddha's own young son, Rahula.

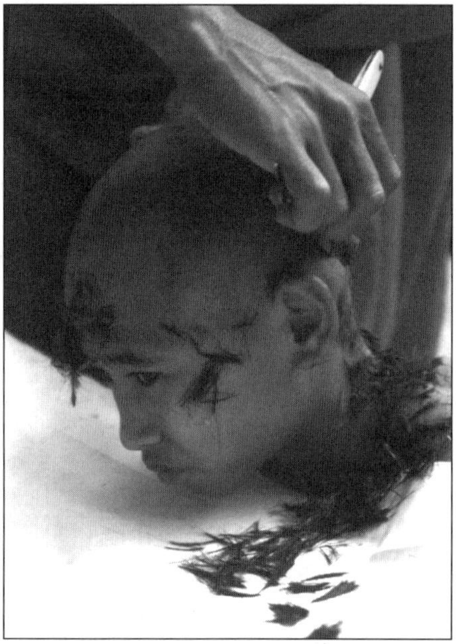

Unlike his illustrious predecessors, the novice monk probably will carry his alms bowl only a short time – maybe a few weeks or less, perhaps as long as several months – then return to his normal lifestyle. But his time spent as a monk, studying Buddhist scriptures and strictly following the code of discipline, makes him a dignified human being.

Some time between his ninth and twelfth birthdays, a boy is deemed ready to don the saffron-colored robes of the Sangha and become a "son of the Buddha." If his parents are very pious, they may arrange to have the *shin-pyu* staged on the full moon day of *Waso* (June/July), the beginning of the Buddhist Lent, so that the novice can remain in the monastery throughout the entire rainy season, until Lent ends with the Festival of Light in October.

Once the ceremony has been arranged, the boy's sisters announce it to the whole village or neighborhood. Everyone is invited, and contributions are collected for a festival which will dig deep into the savings of the boy's parents.

Traditionally, a *shin-pyu* is a time of extravagance. The boy is dressed in princely garments of silk, wears a gold headdress, and has a white horse. Musicians are hired to entertain guests. These objects are meant to symbolize the worldly goods that the novice monk must renounce in accepting the rules of the Sangha. Not all families can afford this, however, and many *shin-pyus* are more modest.

The night before a *shin-pyu* is a busy one. A feast is prepared for all the monks whose company the young boy will join, and they are elaborately fed early on the morning of the ceremony. Next, all men invited to the festivities are fed, and finally women can eat.

Later in the morning, the novitiate monk's head is shaved in preparation for his initiation. The boy's mother and eldest sister hold a white cloth to receive the falling hair, and later bury it near a pagoda. This head-shaving is a solemn moment; when completed, the boy already looks like a "son of the Buddha."

In the weeks before the ceremony, the lad has been familiarized with the language and behavior befitting a monk. He has learned how to address a superior; how to walk with decorum, keeping his eyes fixed on a point six feet in front of him; and how to respond to the questions put to him at the novitiation ceremony. He has also learned the Pali language words he must use in asking to be admitted to the Sangha.

His instruction serves him well when the time for the ceremony arrives. His request to enter the monkhood is approved, and he prostrates himself three times. Then he is robed. Now he is ready to walk the path of perfection first trodden by the Buddha. If he is steadfast enough, he might even reach nirvana.

At the moment that the *sayadaw* – the abbot who has presided over the ceremony – hangs the novitiate's *thabeit* (alms bowl) over his shoulder, innocent childhood is behind the boy. He has now been accepted as a monk.

During the time he spends in the monastery, the boy's parents must address him in honorific terms. He will call them "lay sister" and "lay brother," the same names he calls others who are not in the monkhood.

A boy's *shin-pyu* begins with head-shaving in front of his anxious mother (left); but little more than an hour after the ceremony begins, he is independent, a full-fledged novice in the Sangha (right):

From Klein, W. 1981 *Insight Guide to Burma* (APA Productions HK Ltd)

Text 7 Danger from Fire

In the bedroom

1 Don't smoke in bed – it causes about 1,000 fires a year, many with fatal results.
2 Don't overload your electrical points: the ideal is 'one appliance, one socket'.
3 Don't use an electric underblanket over you or an overblanket under you. An underblanket, unless of the low-voltage type, MUST be switched off before you get into bed.
4 Never let furnishings or clothing get close to a lighted fire. Make sure that there is a suitable guard for the room heater.
5 Keep aerosol-type containers away from heat and NEVER burn or puncture them.
6 Don't dim a table lamp by covering it: buy a low-wattage bulb.
7 Pyjamas and nightdresses, especially for children and elderly people, should be made from flame-resistant material.

If cut off by fire

8 Close the door of the room and any fanlight or other opening and block up any cracks with bedding etc.
9 Go to the window and try to attract attention.
10 If the room fills with smoke, lean out of the window unless prevented by smoke and flame coming from a room below or nearby. If you cannot lean out of the window, lie close to the floor where the air is clearer until you hear the fire brigade.
11 If you have to escape before the fire brigade arrives, make a rope by knotting together sheets or similar materials and tie it to a bed or other heavy piece of furniture.
12 If you cannot make a rope and the situation becomes intolerable, drop cushions or bedding from the window to break your fall, get through the window feet first, lower yourself to the full extent of your arms and drop.
13 If possible drop from a position above soft earth. If above the first floor, drop only as a last resort.

(Prepared for the Home Office and the Scottish Home and Health Department by the Central Office of Information 1975)

Text 8 The Mountain People

Partly through her madness, and partly because she was nearly dead anyway, her reactions became slower and slower. When she managed to find food – fruit peels, skins, bits of bone, half-eaten berries, whatever – she held it in her hand and looked at it with wonder and delight, savoring its taste before she ate it. Her playmates caught on quickly, and used to watch her wandering around, and even put tidbits in her way, and watched her simply drawn little face wrinkle in a smile as she looked at the food and savored it while it was yet in her hand. Then as she raised her hand to her mouth they set on her with cries of excitement, fun and laughter, beat her savagely over the head and left her. But that is not how she died. I took to feeding her, which is probably the cruellest thing I could have done, a gross selfishness on my part to try and salve and save, indeed, my own rapidly disappearing conscience. I had to protect her, physically, as I fed her. But the others would beat her anyway, and Adupa cried, not because of the pain in her body, but because of the pain she felt at that great, vast empty wasteland where love should have been.

It was *that* that killed her. She demanded that her parents love her. She kept going back to their compound, almost next to Atum's and the closest to my own. Finally they took her in, and Adupa was happy and stopped crying. She stopped crying forever, because her parents went away and closed the *asak* tight behind them, so tight that weak little Adupa could never have moved it if she had tried. But I doubt that she even thought of trying. She waited for them to come back with the food they promised her. When they came back she was still waiting for them. It was a week or ten days later, and her body was already almost too far gone to bury. In an Ik village who would notice the smell? And if she had cried, who would have noticed that? Her parents took what was left of her and threw it out, as one does the riper garbage, a good distance away. They even pulled some stones over it to stop the vultures and hyenas from scattering bits and pieces of their daughter in Atum's field; that would have been offensive, for they were good neighbors and shared the same *odok*.

From Turnbull, C. 1984 *The Mountain People* (Triad/Paladin)

Text 9 Good Neighbours

Is there one down your way?

They're the unsung heroes of every community, never expecting any reward for their work. This week BBC Radio launches a campaign to applaud them - with your help. The celebrities here have made their nominations – and now it's your turn.

DURING WHAT is characteristically the gloomiest and coldest time of year, many people need an extra amount of assistance. This week Radio 2, BBC Local Radio and BBC Radio in Scotland, Wales and Northern Ireland begin a celebration of care and concern in the community by launching a national campaign to find good neighbours. You are asked to nominate anyone you feel is giving time, energy, skills and commitment to others without asking for any rewards. Fill in the special Good Neighbours form on these pages or write to your BBC Local Radio station with your nominations. Include a brief résumé of the reasons for your choice.

Between 8 February and 4 March, local, regional and national programmes will be bringing you the stories of many of those chosen and Radio 2 will be spotlighting two good neighbours each day. Everyone featured will have an opportunity to share in special local activities, and representatives from each part of the UK will be invited to a large party in London in the middle of March. Celebrities, too, have been asked to take part: some of them along with their own good neighbours, talk to *Radio Times*.

Claire Rayner

'I WAS looking for someone who showed concern not just for people he knew but people he didn't know and those who might need help in the future,' says Claire Rayner. 'Tony Whitehead knew back in 1983 that AIDS was going to be a problem and asked some friends to a meeting in his sitting room. That was the start of the Terrence Higgins Trust. Being a good neighbour is enabling others to be so as well.'

Tony Whitehead, president of the trust, says he made his commitment after 'recognising that AIDS was hitting me and mine and believing that I and my colleagues really did have a lot to give the community. Volunteer response has been overwhelming for some time, but now our volunteers more fully represent a cross-section of society.'

Diane O'Brien is one example. 'I felt the AIDS issue was important and that more middle-aged, straight people should get involved,' she says. 'Being better informed helps to challenge people's prejudices about the gay community and AIDS. I'm a counsellor for the help line and face-to-face service. But I'm just one of a thousand doing different work - we're all bits of a big jigsaw puzzle.'

Gloria Hunniford

'I USED to live beside Lucy Brown - she was only 13 when I met her,' says Gloria Hunniford. 'She always struck me as one of the good people in life. When other kids were out enjoying themselves she always seemed to be going off to help handicapped people. It's refreshing to see someone that young fully understanding that there are people less privileged. Now, at 17, she is organising activities, holidays and outings: one ingenious idea she had was to buy a tandem bike so that blind or handicapped people could enjoy the sensation of being out. Lucy's not a dull, worthy sort – she just gets on with it and is a very lively, fun person.'

Lucy Brown explains the tandem: 'It came about because we wanted to take blind children on picnics. It is also used by a lot of mentally handicapped people. They enjoy it because it gives a feeling of freedom, coordination and being partly responsible for where the bike goes. My biggest involvement is with the mentally handicapped. It gives you a lovely warm feeling when they respond and welcome you. Once you recognise them more as your friends than as mentally handicapped you're past the frightening stage.'

Derek Nimmo

'I'M INVOLVED with the Save the Children Fund,' says actor Derek Nimmo. 'Last year Bashir Uddin Ahmed offered the fund the whole of one year's profit from his restaurant, the Dhaka Dynasty in Olney, Buckinghamshire. It will amount to about £65,000. He came to this country from Pakistan in 1969 and because he and his family have prospered he felt he wanted to give something back. What I like particularly about Mr Ahmed is that here is someone from outside this country who has come here and shown such concern for other people.'

Bashir Uddin Ahmed says: 'The last time I went to India and Bangladesh I saw how bad things were, especially how children were suffering. After I came back I thought a lot about it and saw a documentary a year ago about Princess Anne and the Save the Children Fund. I decided to support it with a year's profit. Last June I met Princess Anne at a special tea for the Save the Children Fund and we talked about her visit to Bangladesh. She was very pleased with our plan.'

KATIE GRIFFITHS

Who are the good neigbours in your area?

I would like to nominate ....

Address ....

....

Telephone number .... **Postcode** ....

He/She is a GOOD NEIGHBOUR because ....

....

....

....

....

....

....

....

My name is ....

Address ....

....

Telephone number .... **Postcode** ....

Send this form to arrive by Friday 26 February 1988 to
GOOD NEIGHBOURS, BBC Radio, Broadcasting House, London W1A 4WW

Text 10 The Secret Diary of Adrian Mole, Aged 13¾

Thursday March 12th

Woke up this morning to find my face covered in huge red spots. My mother said they were caused by nerves but I am still convinced that my diet is inadequate. We have been eating a lot of boil-in-the-bag stuff lately. Perhaps I am allergic to plastic. My mother rang Dr Gray's receptionist to make an appointment, but the earliest he can see me is next Monday! For all he knows I could have lassa fever and be spreading it all around the district! I told my mother to say that I was an emergency case but she said I was 'over-reacting as usual'. She said a few spots didn't mean I was dying. I couldn't believe it when she said she was going to work as usual. Surely her child should come before her job?

I rang my grandma and she came round in a taxi and took me to her house and put me to bed. I am there now. It is very clean and peaceful. I am wearing my dead grandad's pyjamas. I have just had a bowl of barley and beef soup. It is my first proper nourishment for weeks.

I expect there will be a row when my mother comes home and finds that I have gone. But frankly, my dear diary, I don't give a damn.

Friday March 13th

MOON'S FIRST QUARTER

The emergency doctor came to my grandma's last night at 11:30 pm. He diagnosed that I am suffering from *acne vulgaris*. He said it was so common that it is regarded as a normal state of adolescence. He thought it was highly unlikely that I have got lassa fever because I have not been to Africa this year. He told grandma to take the disinfected sheets off the doors and windows. Grandma said she would like a second opinion. That was when the doctor lost his temper. He shouted in a very loud voice, 'The lad has only got a few teenage spots, for Christ's sake!'

Grandma said she would complain to the Medical Council but the doctor just laughed and went downstairs and slammed the door. My father came round before he went to work and brought my Social Studies homework and the dog. He said that if I was not out of bed when he got home at lunchtime he would thrash me to within an inch of my life.

He took my grandma into the kitchen and had a loud talk with her. I heard him saying, 'Things are very bad between me and Pauline, and all we are arguing over now is who *doesn't* get custody of Adrian'. Surely my father made a mistake. He must have meant who *did* get custody of me.

So the worst has happened, my skin has gone to pot and my parents are splitting up.

From Townsend, S. 1982 *The Secret Diary of Adrian Mole, Aged 13¾* (Methuen)

Appendix B

Extracts from reading courses

Text 1 Airships

Part 4 Development

Study this part in the same way as Part 4 of Unit 3.

Introduction
Airships were equipped with a balloon filled with gas.
They were developed during the ninteenth century.
In the first part of the twentieth century, they carried passengers across the Atlantic Ocean.
They had many accidents.
They have been replaced by aeroplanes.
They are not now being used for passenger transport.

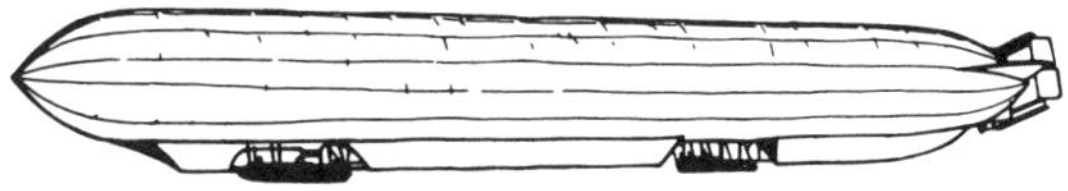

Purpose question

Which of these statements is the opinion of the writer?

a Airships are of no use today.
b Airships should replace jet aircraft.
c There is a possibility of using airships in the future.
d Airships have not been used since 1947.

THE HISTORY OF THE AIRSHIP

Supersonic airliners are very common today ∴ we forget that there were no aeroplanes in 1900.

***steerable* = can be steered**

***to improve* = make better**

In an age of supersonic airliners it is difficult to realize that at the beginning of the twentieth century no one had ever flown in an aeroplane. However, people were flying in balloons and airships.[1] The airship was based on the principle of the semi-rigid structure. In 1900 Ferdinand von Zeppelin fitted a petrol engine to a rigid balloon. This craft was the first really successful steerable airship. In 1919 an airship first carried passengers across the Atlantic, and in 1929 one travelled round the world.[2] During this time the design of airships was constantly being improved[3] and up to 1937 they carried thousands of passengers on regular transatlantic services for millions of miles.

[1] When were people flying in airships and balloons?

[2] Did airships carry passengers across the Atlantic before 1919?

[3] When was the design being improved?

1 What was the achievement of von Zepplin?
2 What were airships used for?

THIS PARAGRAPH LISTS SOME DISADVANTAGES OF AIRSHIPS

***above all* introduces the most important point**

However, airships had many defects. They were very large and could not fly well in bad weather. Above all, they suffered many accidents[4] because of the inflammability of the hydrogen used to inflate them.[5] In 1937 the Hindenburg airship exploded in New Jersey and 35 of 100 passengers were killed.

[4] What was their main defect?

[5] What caused the accidents?

3 Why did they not continue to be the main form of air transport?

THIS PARAGRAPH IS ABOUT AIRSHIPS TODAY.

Sentence 1 means that airships are not able to do what jet aircraft can do.

***static* = not moving**

Today airships cannot compete with jet aircraft. However, they have been greatly improved. They can be filled with helium,[6] and advances in meteorology make it possible to choose calm routes. They can remain static in the air and are being used by the American navy for observation of icebergs in the Arctic.[7] It is possible that they will be used for other purposes in the future.

[6] Helium can be used instead of ....

[7] Why are they appropriate for this purpose?

4 Use information from the whole passage to complete this table. The table summarizes the development of the airship.

Date	Event
	The first successful airship was built.
1919	
1919 – 1937	Designs were being improved.
1937	
1937	
	Airships in use for observation of icebergs.

5 Now use information from the whole passage to complete this table. The table shows how airships have been improved.

Defects of airships in the past	Modern improvements
size	
	can be inflated with helium

From Moore, J. D. et al 1979 *Reading and Thinking in English: Exploring Functions* (OUP)

Text 2 The Survival of the Fittest

In this second lesson on evolution you will be able to deepen your understanding of how animals adapt for survival. You will also get an opportunity to practise the skill of prediction and to relate a linear text to tables and a map.

Activity A Δ

What are your views on natural selection?

Answer these questions

1. Can you think of any creatures which are in danger of dying out?
2. Can you suggest any reasons why they are in danger?
3. Can you think of a way in which many creatures are adapted so that they can avoid being seen by their predators?

Activity B ❍●●●●

Read how creatures adapt to survive (1)

This is a step-by-step activity. At each step in the text you are given a choice of ideas or a question. The text describes the process by which some creatures survive and others die out.

Read each step and say what can logically follow, or answer the question. Tick the correct answers.

Step 1 On each tree there is a moth. They are both quite clearly visible. Any predator would see his prey very clearly. But suppose the light moth was sitting on the light tree and vice versa.

(a) It would not make any difference.
(b) The moth might survive.

Step 2 A dark moth on a dark tree would be less visible and have a better chance of survival from the attacks of predators. This is known as camouflage. Some animals, like the chameleon, for instance, are able to change colour according to their background. This kind of change is not evolutionary change (though of course the chameleon has evolved the ability to make this change). However, a change in colour is evolutionary if the new creature is able to reproduce itself so that its young also have the new colour.

The example of the moth is a real one and was investigated in England in the 1950's by a scientist called Dr. Kettlewell. It is a very well-known example of evolutionary change.

The species of moth is the Peppered Moth. It was typically light brown in colour and settled on the trunks of trees which were a similar colour and camouflaged it. Then came a change in the environment. Industry began to grow up in parts of England with the result that smoke and other forms of pollution began to fill the atmosphere. So:

(a) the moths turned black.
(b) the trees turned black.

Step 3 The pollution from the factories covered the bark on the tree trunks with soot and grime so the light brown Peppered Moths became very visible to their predators and were eaten. Then, gradually they began to change colour.

(a) They became lighter.
(b) They became darker.

Step 4 The darker ones were more likely to survive, so their colour gradually became darker. How did they become darker? This is one of the mysteries of science, but it has been called 'natural selection' since Charles Darwin published his famous book *The Origin of Species* in 1859. Natural selection does not make anything happen. You cannot force a moth to change colour, for instance, nor can a moth decide to change. The point is that every creature has a genetic structure consisting of genes and chromosomes. This structure can change naturally, by accident. Perhaps this change does not matter. Perhaps, on the other hand, it produces a 'deformed' individual which the others reject or even kill because it is different. These things happen all the time. But if the change (or 'mutation') happens to fit the new environment, then the new creature, instead of being rejected or killed by the others will

(a) die
(b) survive

Step 5 This is natural selection. A mutation (which is always possible) happens to suit a new environment, and the "odd" creature survives because it is better fitted. Then it reproduces and a new type of creature evolves. Meanwhile the others have become unsuited to the changed environment. They must either change their behaviour, or

(a) become extinct.
(b) change the environment.

Step 6 Dr. Kettlewell wanted to discover whether the dark Peppered Moths were in fact a new type of Peppered Moth which had adapted to its environment. In the first experiment, he released light and dark moths into the woods near Birmingham (a large industrial city in England). In the second he released his moths into the woods in a country district called Dorset in the south of England. Finally, he placed examples of each kind of moth on trees of the opposite colour and watched what happened.

Below is a list of hypotheses (things that can be predicted if your theory is right). Which of the hypotheses would support Dr. Kettlewell's theory that a new type of darker moth had evolved in industrial areas? More than one hypothesis may be necessary.

(a) More dark moths would survive in Birmingham than light ones.
(b) More dark moths would be eaten by birds in Dorset than light ones.
(c) The number of dark moths that survived in Dorset would be equal to the number of light moths that survived in Birmingham.
(d) All the dark moths in Birmingham would survive.
(e) The number of light moths surviving in Dorset would be equal to the number of dark moths surviving in Birmingham.

Here are the results from his experiment in Birmingham:

	light	dark
Number of moths released	201	601
Number of moths recaptured	34	205
Percentage of moths recaptured	16%	34.1%

Dr Kettlewell's technique was to release moths which were specially marked, then recapture as many as possible after a time.

Which of the following statements could Dr. Kettlewell make on the basis of the results? Notice that he released more dark ones than light ones.

(a) Six times as many dark moths seem to have survived.
(b) Just over twice as many dark moths seem to have survived.
(c) I have proved my hypothesis beyond doubt.
(d) The evidence supports my hypothesis.

Activity C ○●●

Complete a summary of what you have read

Here is a text with blanks. It summarizes the main points in the text you have read. A choice of words for each blank is given in the margin.

Complete the text by filling in the blanks with the correct words from the margin.

1. light / dark 2. rural / industrial 3. environment / individual 4. decrease / increase 5. light / dark	Dr.Kettlewell's observations clearly demonstrate that natural selection was responsible for the replacement of (1) .... forms of the Peppered Moth by dark forms in (2) .... regions. The theory of natural selection enables us to predict genetic changes in a population from our knowledge of changes in the (3) .... If pollution were controlled in industrial areas, and if this allowed forests to revert to their natural unpolluted state, we would predict that the frequency of the light form of the Peppered Moth would gradually begin to (4) .... In fact, smoke control programmes have been introduced in industrial regions in Britain since 1952, and the frequency of the (5) .... form of the Peppered Moth has shown a highly significant increase.

Activity D ○●●●● Read how creatures adapt to survive (2)

This is a step-by step activity. In it you are given a continuation of the report on Dr. Kettlewell's experiments. At each step in the text there is a question and a choice of answers.

Read each step carefully and then tick the correct answer to the question.

Step 8 Later, to find additional support for his hypotheses, Dr. Kettlewell repeated the same experiment in Dorset. The results proved he was right.

Which of these two tables shows the correct results from Dorset?

	light	dark
(a) Number of moths released	496	473
Number of moths recaptured	30	62
Percentage of moths recaptured	6.3%	12.5%

	light	dark
(b) Number of moths released	496	473
Number of moths recaptured	62	30
Percentage of moths recaptured	12.5%	6.3%

Step 9 Finally, he placed an equal number of moths of each colour on trees and watched what happened. He quickly discovered that several species of birds searched the tree trunks for moths and other insects and that these birds more readily found the one that contrasted with its background than the one that blended with the bark.

Which of these tables expresses the results?

		Moths eaten by birds	
		light	dark
(a)	Unpolluted woods	164	26
	Polluted woods	15	43
(b)	Unpolluted woods	26	164
	Polluted woods	43	15

Step 10 Here is a map of the British Isles showing where dark (melanistic) and light (typical) moths were found in the early 1950's.

There is no space here to reproduce the map presented in the original, which shows the frequency of melanistic populations of the Peppered Moth in various localities in Britain.

Do the results support Dr. Kettlewell's theory?
(a) Yes
(b) No

From University of Malaya Language Centre 1973 *Skills for Learning: Reading for Academic Study* (University of Malaya Press/Nelson)

Text 3 Notices

Reading for Information

5 NOTICES

1 Reading

When Machiko got to Bay View Community College, she found a lot of people there. She wondered what to do and where to go. At first, she stood with some other students in front of a bulletin board. On the bulletin board was a registration **directory**. She was going to ask the young man standing next to her for help, but he spoke to her first.

Bay View Community College Registration Directory

INFORMATION	Room	102
Hotel Management		103
Business Management		104
Science Courses (day)		106
Science Courses (night)		107
ALL NEW STUDENTS		110
Sociology		203
History		207
French		237
German		264
Spanish		276
OTHER FOREIGN LANGUAGES		281
English		290
Vocational Education		292
English as a Second Language (ESL)		310
Accounting		296
Drama		294
Art		311
Music		357
Physical Education		381
ALL OTHER COURSES		390

ROBERTO: Excuse me. Can you help me, please? I'm a new student and I want English classes.

MACHIKO: So do I.

ROBERTO: Oh! Are you a foreign student, too?

MACHIKO: Yes. I'm Japanese, You're Spanish, aren't you?

ROBERTO: No. I'm Brazilian, and I speak Portuguese.

MACHIKO: Well, I think we both go to Information in Room 102.

ROBERTO: But what about room 110, New Students? We are both new first-year students.

MACHIKO: Yes, you're right...No, wait a minute. Let's look at the whole list first....

ROBERTO: What about room 290, English? Do you think that's right?

MACHIKO: No, look, farther down, near the bottom...English as a Second Language.

ROBERTO: That's it!

MACHIKO: OK. Let's go to room 310. By the way, my name is Machiko Morita.

ROBERTO: I'm Roberto. Roberto Costa.

MACHIKO: Nice to meet you, Roberto.

ROBERTO: Nice to meet you too.

2 Practice

A Check the **two** correct facts about Roberto and Machiko.
They are

.... old students

.... new students

.... English students

.... foreign language students

.... English as a Second Language students

B Complete this sentence about Roberto and Machiko. Use these words:

English
Language
as
both
they

.... are .... students of .... a

Second ....

C Both Roberto and Machiko made a mistake. They both read slowly down the list of subjects and rooms in the registration directory instead of quickly reading the whole directory first.

What was the first word at which Machiko stopped reading?

What was the first word at which Roberto stopped reading?

D Roberto and Machiko are students of English as a Second Language. They register in Room 310. Where do these students register?

Maria, a second-year accounting student

David, a student in his third year of Spanish studies

Ann, a student doing a second-year biology course in the evening

Carol, a second-year history student

Paul, a student from another college looking for his sister

Michael, a music student in his first year at the college

Laura, a bank manager interested in physical education

Yoko, a photography student

Barbara, a drama student in her second year

John, a new student of Russian

E The room where ESL students register is on the third floor. Which floor are these rooms on?

business management
information
music
Chinese
daytime science courses
history
art
German
vocational education courses
hotel management

F Roberto wants a *full-time* course in *business* English.
Machiko wants a *part-time* course in *general* English.
The relevant words for Roberto are *full-time* and *business*.
The relevant words for Machiko are *part-time* and *general*.

In Room 310, they were given this **notice**.

Which table does Roberto want?

Which table does Machiko want?

NOTICE TO ESL STUDENTS

Please sign up at the appropriate table.

COURSE	TABLE
Part-time course in English conversation	A
Full-time course in general English	B
Part-time course in general English	C
Part-time course in spoken English	D
Full-time course in written English	E
Full-time course in business English	F
Part-time course in business English	G

From Davies, E., Whitney, N., Pike-Baky, M. and Blass, L. 1990 *Task Reading* (CUP)

Text 4 Danger from fire

Part I Instructions: How to do things

Unit 1 Danger from fire

This is part of a booklet distributed by local fire brigades in Great Britain.
Read the text *slowly*. Pause as often as you like. It will be easier to answer the questions if you imagine you have to make a summary of the text.
Read the text *twice*. The second time, take as much time as you need, and try to see how the different parts of the text fit together.
Then do the exercises. Do not worry if you cannot answer all the questions without referring to the text. This is normal: The exercises are to teach you, not test you.

In the bedroom

1. Don't smoke in bed - it causes about 1,000 fires a year, many with fatal results.
2. Don't overload you electrical points: the ideal is 'one appliance, one socket'.
3. Don't use an electric underblanket over you or an overblanket under you. An underblanket, unless of the low-voltage type, MUST be switched off before you get into bed.
4. Never let furnishings or clothing get close to a lighted fire. Make sure that there is a suitable guard for the room heater.
5. Keep aerosol-type containers away from heat and NEVER burn or puncture them.
6. Don't dim a table lamp by covering it: buy a low-wattage bulb.
7. Pyjamas and nightdresses, especially for children and elderly people, should be made from flame-resistant material.

If cut off by fire

8. Close the door of the room and any fanlight or other opening and block up any cracks with bedding etc.
9. Go to the window and try to attract attention.
10. If the room fills with smoke, lean out of the window unless prevented by smoke and flame coming from a room below or nearby. If you cannot lean out of the window, lie close to the floor where the air is clearer until you hear the fire brigade.
11. If you have to escape before the fire brigade arrives, make a rope by knotting together sheets or similar materials and tie it to a bed or other heavy piece of furniture.
12. If you cannot make a rope and the situation becomes intolerable, drop cushions or bedding from the window to break you fall, get through the window feet first, lower yourself to the full extent of your arms and drop.
13. If possible drop from a position above soft earth. If above the first floor, drop only as a last resort.

(Prepared for the Home Office and the Scottish Home and Health Department by the Central Office of Information 1975.)

fanlight: a window over a door.
appliance: something that uses electricity in the home (heater, washing machine, etc.)
aerosol-type containers: these have gas in them to help spray out liquid or foam.

Summary skills 1

Here is a picture of a dangerous bedroom. Each of the lines shows one of the dangers in the numbered instructions. Match the lines with their numbers.

Summary skills 2

Complete this chart with information from 'If cut off by fire'.

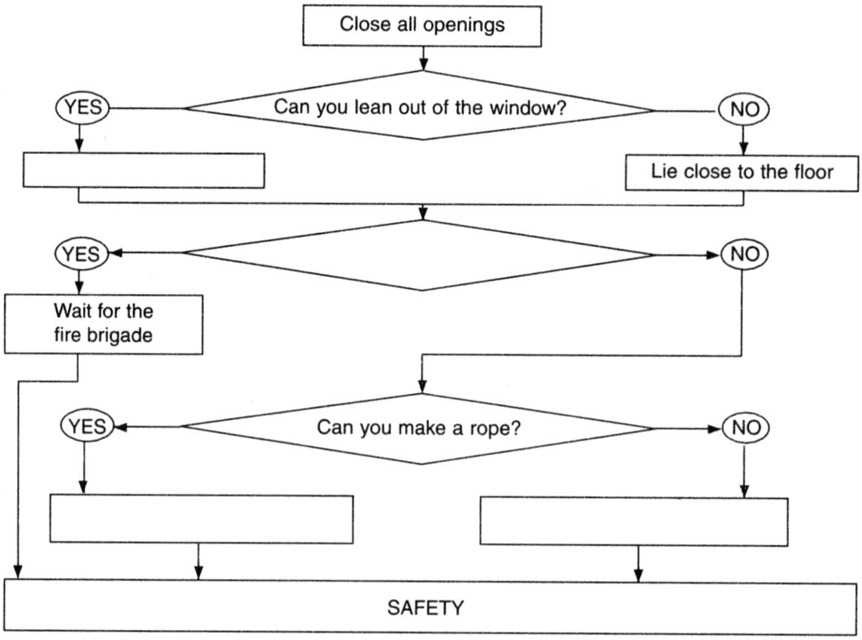

From Walter, C. 1982 *Authentic Reading* (CUP)

Appendix C
Lesson plans

THE FOUR lesson plans in this appendix are not 'models'. They are intended to give some idea of the wide range of possibilities and to counteract any suggestion that the sequence of teaching outlined at the end of Chapter 9 is intended as a 'model'.

Abbreviations used

BB blackboard **S/SS** student(s) **Q/QQ** question(s) **SPQ** signpost question
OHP overhead projector **OHT** OHP transparency **§/§§** paragraph(s)

Square brackets [ ] signal comments to you, not part of original plan.

Lesson 1 Shin-pyu: becoming a dignified human being

Refer to Appendix A Text 6

Class: University SS, upper-intermediate/advanced, sitting in groups of 4/5.
Materials: Text *Shin-pyu*, with a section (§§ 5–9) removed.
Missing section cut into separate §§ (1 set in an envelope for each group).
OHT of §§ 5–9, cut up into separate §§.
Time line worksheet (see p254).
Copy of worksheet on OHT.
Copy of main picture from text on OHT.

Time: 1¼ hours

Step 1 Write title on OHP bit by bit and get predictions. Let SS improve predictions as more words are added.

shin-pyu Any ideas? What part of the world? What kind of text?
becoming Any more ideas? (Who/what? How? Why?)
a dignified A dignified what? Whose definition of *dignified*? More ideas about topic (→cultural values)
human being As opposed to what? What kind of text do you expect?

Show the picture [novice monks]. Readjust predictions. Elicit clues. [Age/dress/objects/people/background] [NB Don't confirm predictions!] Elicit vocabulary: *novice, monk/monkhood/monastery, Buddhist, alms bowl, robe.* What questions is the text likely to answer?

About 5 minutes.

[Steps 2–6 to be done briskly – only about 10 minutes in all.]

Step 2 Distribute text (face down) to every S. Then ask SS to SKIM §1: What Q does this § answer? [What is *shin-pyu*?] What other QQ are answered? [Where? Who?]

Step 3 SCAN: Find the § that tells you WHEN the ceremony occurs (§4). Now SKIM that § and find 2 different answers (**1** When boy is aged 9–12. **2** Preferably full moon day of *Waso* – June/July.)

WORK SHEET

Complete the timetable below, so that it shows the correct sequence of activities and events relating to the shin-pyu ceremony. The left-hand column records what the boy does or what happens to him. The right-hand column records what is done by other people.

	THE BOY	OTHER PEOPLE
DAY A	THE BOY'S PARENTS DECIDE THAT THE SHIN-PYU CEREMONY WILL TAKE PLACE ON THE FULL MOON DAY OF WASO	
Several weeks	Learns language and behaviour befitting a monk. (How to address superior, walk with decorum keeping eyes fixed on point 6ft. in front, respond to questions at novitiation. Learns Pali words asking admittance to Sangha.)	The boy's sisters announce it to the whole village. Guests are invited. Contributions are collected. Clothes and white horse are obtained. Musicians are hired. A feast is prepared.
DAY B	FULL MOON DAY OF WASO : THE SHIN-PYU CEREMONY	
Early morning	Dressed in silk garments and gold head-dress. Rides white horse.	The monks are elaborately fed. Male guests are fed. The women eat.
Later morning	Head is shaved.	Mother and eldest sister catch hair in white cloth (later buried near pagoda).
Time of ceremony	Asks to enter monkhood. Prostrates himself 3 times. Is robed in saffron robe. He is accepted as a monk.	His request is approved. Sayadaw hangs alms bowl over boy's shoulder.
Several weeks or months	Carries alms bowl. Stays in monastery. Studies Buddhist scriptures. Follows strict code of discipline. Calls all lay people (including parents) 'lay sister', 'lay brother'.	Parents address boy in honorific terms.
DAY C	FESTIVAL OF LIGHT	
	Leaves Sangha.	

Time line worksheet for Lesson 1 *Shin-pyu*
(The worksheet shown here has been completed by a student.)

Step 4 SKIM: What question does §2 answer [Why? – reason for *shin-pyu*]

Step 5 READ §§ 2,3: Find out what being a novice monk involves. [Important to understand this but don't take more than 5 mins] INFER: Does the text tell us how long the Buddha and his son spent in their search for enlightenment? ['unlike his illustrious predecessors' + 'only a short time'—➤ a long time]

Step 6 Look again at §4. INFER: What is the meaning of *Sangha*? [Look also at caption, bottom right: order/community of monks]

Step 7 Further look at the two pictures in text: what is happening? How much more do they tell us about the ceremony, and about what is involved in being a novice monk?

Step 8 Skim the last 3 §§ and PREDICT: what will be in the missing §§?

Maximum for steps 7, 8: 5 minutes

Step 9 Distribute envelope [containing §§ 5–9 cut separately] and time line worksheet to each group. Explain there are two tasks:
1 Read to find out more about ceremony and complete worksheet.
2 Agree correct sequence for §§. [They are not in chronological order]

30 minutes

[Group members make their own arrangements for sharing/exchanging the §§ and co-operating on worksheet – they are accustomed to groupwork.]

Step 10 Feedback on group tasks. Groups help complete worksheet on OHP. Discuss correct sequence of §§ 5–9, using OHP and pointing out clues (coherence of thought, cohesion). [OHTs of separate §§ can be moved around on OHP to show effect of different sequences.]

30 minutes

Step 11 Discuss responses to the text: what's the most important moment in the life of a young boy in our society? How does it compare with that of the Burmese boy? (Bring out significance of alms bowl.)

Writing assignment [done out of class] Respond to the text in any way you like (poetry, story, discussion, imaginary report, letter to the boy ...).

Lesson 2 Good Neighbours

Refer to Appendix A Text 9

Class: Secondary school, 15–16 years, intermediate.
Materials: For each student:
Jigsaw activity task sheet (see p257)
Copy of introductory text *Good Neighbours*
ONE of the other 3 texts (*Claire Rayner/Gloria Hunniford/Derek Nimmo*) [equal numbers of each to be distributed]
2 copies of grid sheet
Nomination form (see Appendix A Text 9)
[See below for grid sheet, task sheet]

Time: 1½ hours (double period)

Step 1 Ask students for definitions of what they would consider a 'good neighbour'. Put key phrases on BB headed by title *CRITERIA* (ensure *criteria* is understood). Explain: we are going to take part in a competition to find the best neighbours in our locality (originally in UK).

About 10 minutes

Step 2 Distribute the materials to students, taking care to distribute as nearly as possible equal numbers of the three 'celebrity' texts (*Claire Rayner* etc). SS silently complete tasks 1 and 2 on Jigsaw Activity Task Sheet.

About 10 minutes

Step 3 Ask SS to form groups of 3–5 with others having same 'celebrity'. Then check that task 3 is clear. Groups do task 3 [completion of grid].

10–15 minutes

Step 4 After 10 minutes, call attention and ensure everyone understands how to do task 4. Urge class to start task 4. [Exchanging information on grids, orally, with members of other groups.] Monitor to make sure it is working.

10–15 minutes

Step 5 After 10 minutes, call attention and get people to return to groups to do tasks 5, 6 and 7. Go round groups to ensure everyone understands and enough time is given to individual work (task 6). [If discipline is good, you can allow groups that finish early to go on to tasks 8 and 9, while the others complete task 7.]

About 30 minutes

Step 6 Call attention and conduct whole class FEEDBACK session by getting each group to describe their nominee and defend the choice and the criteria used. Finally, all vote to choose a class nominee (from group nominees). [Go on to tasks 8 and 9 if time allows.]

About 30 minutes

[Possible follow-up work: roleplay radio interview with nominees; write letter to nominee, explaining why chosen; visit/interview (real) nominee(s) who are prepared to co-operate, and report back to class; debate or write article for eg school magazine on present-day views of good-neighbourliness.]

GOOD NEIGHBOURS GRID SHEET

Names	Proposer			
	Nominee			
Personal details of nominee				
Who does he/she help?				
How has he/she helped them?				
What first made him/her interested in them?				
Why does he/she feel he/she wants to help them?				
What criteria led the proposer to nominate him/her?				

Grid sheet for Lesson 2 *Good Neighbours* much reduced

JIGSAW ACTIVITY: GOOD NEIGHBOURS

There are quite a lot of tasks in this activity. Try to complete each one in sequence, as other groups will be involved from time to time. Approximate timing is given: try not to exceed it.

1 Individually, read the introductory text *Good Neighbours* and find out:
   a Why is the BBC holding the campaign now?
   b What is the purpose of the campaign?
   c What will happen to the nominations?
   d Who is going to the party? (3 mins)

2 Individually, read the text describing the person nominated by a celebrity (Gloria Hunniford, Derek Nimmo, Claire Rayner). (5 mins)

YOUR TEACHER WILL ASK YOU TO GET INTO GROUPS BEFORE STARTING TASK 3.

3 Now jointly complete the grid with information about your celebrity's nominee. Agree as a group what to put in each box. Everyone in the group should end up with an identical grid. (12 mins)

4 Split up and find someone from another group who has information about the good neighbour chosen by a different celebrity. Exchange information ORALLY: don't read each other's texts or grids. Complete your own grid. Repeat for the third celebrity. (10 mins)

5 Return to your group. Compare information and discuss the three nominees; try to agree as a group which one you would prefer as your own neighbour, and why. While discussing, take note of the CRITERIA the group uses to reach its decision, and list them. (10 mins)

6 Individually, use these criteria (and others if you wish) to choose someone you know whom you would like to nominate. Complete the nomination form with details of your nominee. (10 mins)

7 Compare notes and as a group agree which of the group members' nominees you prefer. Complete the second grid. Add any additional criteria to your list. (10 mins)

8 Split up and exchange details ORALLY with members of two other groups about each group's preferred nominees. Complete the grid with the information you collect. (10 mins)

9 Return to your own group and compare notes. Discuss the various nominees and be ready to debate the issue: which of these good neighbours would the entire class choose to nominate, and why?

Task sheet for Lesson 2 *Good Neighbours*

Lesson 3 The Secret Diary of Adrian Mole, aged 13¾

Refer to Appendix A Text 10

Class: Adults, intermediate (general evening class), sitting in pairs.
Materials: Text – without title – cut up into 4 sections: A §1; B §§2 and 3; C §4; D §§5 and 6. Copies of each section for each student.

Step 1 Distribute section A text. Explain: we are going to read someone's diary. Read this first part and look for clues about what sort of person the diarist is and how he/she feels about things. Then in pairs share your ideas and agree on a description of the diarist.

Step 2 Plenary discussion: pairs report and class agrees description of diarist. Insist on supporting evidence for all statements and take opportunity to check understanding of *boil-in-the-bag stuff, for all he knows, over-reacting*. Note main characteristics of diarist on BB.
Ask: How do you think the diarist will react to the situation? What might he/she do?

Step 3 Distribute section B. Ask SS to read it and refine their views of the diarist, and form views about the character of grandma. Discuss with partner as before.

Step 4 Plenary discussion: improve description of diarist. [Note *put me to bed* implies he/she is young; *wearing ... grandad's pyjamas* suggests it is a boy.] Discuss impressions of grandma and compare with impressions of mother.
Ask: How is the diarist feeling when he signs off? How will mother react when she gets home? What will grandma do?

Step 5 Distribute section C. Ask SS to read and answer this SPQ: *Why did the doctor lose his temper?* [Ensure *lose one's temper* understood]

Step 6 Discuss section C, first taking answers to the SPQ. [He has been called out late at night, supposedly for an emergency, but finds only a boy with acne and a grandma who believes the boy to be seriously ill with an exotic infection, and who will not accept his diagnosis.] Then make sure the rest of the text has been understood by asking further QQ:

1 What is *acne vulgaris*? [Translation acceptable for technical term]
2 Where is lassa fever endemic? [Africa – implied by text]
3 How do you know grandma was taking risk of infection seriously? [She had covered windows and door with disinfected bedsheets]
4 What is the doctor's attitude to grandma? What is grandma's attitude to the doctor? What is your view of events? [Ensure *second opinion, lad* are understood]

Step 7 Distribute section D. Ask SS to read and find answers to SPQs:

1 How far does the boy's father sympathize with him?
2 Who is Pauline?

Step 8 Discuss section D, first taking answers to SPQs. [**1**: Not at all. He threatens to beat him and does not want custody of him. **2**: The boy's mother (evidence is in arguments about custody, and Adrian's reference to parents splitting up).]

Ensure understanding of: *thrash (me) to within an inch of (my) life; things are very bad between us; get custody of; go to pot; split up*. [The last two can be inferred once the others are known.]

Step 9 Roleplay: Grandma has complained about the doctor and has accused Adrian's mother and father of cruelty. The Social Services are to hold an enquiry into what happened, to see who is really at fault and try to achieve conciliation. Each person involved has to give evidence and justify their behaviour. Form 5 groups. Each group prepares the case for one character [Adrian, mother, father, grandma, doctor], and chooses a S who will roleplay the character at the enquiry.

Step 10 Appoint a chairman of enquiry [or take the role yourself] and a panel of enquiry [whole class, if it is not large]. Call the 5 witnesses and let each make their case and be questioned by the panel. Attempt to reach conciliation through discussion. Chairman sums up (may apportion blame or let panel vote on it).

Follow-up: Write the entry for these two days in the diary written by grandma, mother or father; and/or write the next day's diary entry by Adrian.

Lesson 4 The Mountain People

Refer to Appendix A Text 8

Class: Adults (teachers of English on a refresher course): advanced.
Material: Copy of text for each student.
Time: 1 hour.

Step 1 Introduce the text: 'We're going to read a description of events that may strike you as inexplicable. As you read, look for clues in the text that may help to explain what is happening. Start by skimming through the text to find out as much as you can about the person called 'she' in the first sentence. You have 3 minutes.'

Step 2 Collect information about the girl (her name, age, etc) but do not expect much after a quick skim. Record brief facts on BB. Accept all views that are not challenged by other students. [Name – Adupa – only towards end of §. Age: clues are *playmates, little face*. Other elements: *mad* (mentally retarded?), *half-starved* (look at examples of 'food'), capable of happiness (*wonder, delight, smile, savored*), naive/innocent/ unsuspecting/ affectionate.]
Any evidence about where the events are taking place? [No – unless the name, and perhaps the shortage of food, suggest the Third World to some readers.]
If the students seem to have misunderstood, explain that you think some of the responses may turn out to need revision, but do not give your own view yet.

Step 3 Ask SS to give their impression so far on the type of book – genre – from which this text comes. An academic study? A novel? Or what? Why do they think so? [Leave the answer open.]

Step 4 SS read §1 silently and underline any parts that puzzle them.

Step 5 In groups, compare notes about what they find puzzling and list the questions §1 raises in the reader's mind.

Step 6 Plenary discussion of §1. Compare lists of questions. In discussion, bring out *nearly dead anyway*, and any significant points not yet mentioned.

If not mentioned by SS, raise QQ: What had happened to Adupa? Why did a child have to find her own food? Why was there nobody to love her? What sort of activity would you expect to cause fun and laughter in children? Why did the children treat her so cruelly? Why did the writer want to feed Adupa? Why does he call it 'cruel' and 'gross selfishness' to do so? Why did the writer have to protect Adupa as he fed her? [*The others would beat her anyway:* but why?] Why the need to *salve and save* his

conscience and why is this *rapidly disappearing*? [No real evidence, but SS might speculate. In fact, in the book, it is clear that he is beginning to dislike the Ik people rather violently and feels bad about it.]
If necessary, return to list of facts about Adupa and get SS to correct it.

Step 7 Ask SS to read the second § down to the words ... *the food they promised her*, noting their own response to the account, and identifying the reasons for it.

Step 8 Plenary discussion of why this account is shocking [which is the likely response]. (Or why not, if SS have other views.) In discussion, bring out: child doesn't normally need to *demand that her parents love her* – and why should it kill her? If she *kept going back to their compound*, where was she living? [Check understanding of *compound*: here = home] Why were the parents reluctant (indicated by *finally*) to take her in? *She stopped crying forever*: sounds as if she will be 'happy ever after' – but what happens next? What is an *asak*? Does it matter that you don't know'? [No – it is clear that it is some kind of barrier to prevent her getting out. It is actually the entrance through a stockade into a dwelling, which can be closed up with thorn bushes.] How do we feel towards Adupa? (Sympathy? Pity? Note *weak little A*.) How do we feel towards her parents? (Betrayal? Unnatural behaviour?)

Step 9 Ask SS to read to end, trying to find out what the Ik people's moral values seem to be, how the writer succeeds in conveying the Ik view of events, and what social conditions might have led the Ik to think like this.

Step 10 In discussion, bring out:
- sinister meaning of *When they came back she was still waiting for them.*
- view of Ik village given by writer.

Cumulative effect of these descriptions: *what was left of her; threw it out; as one does the riper garbage; a good distance away; bits and pieces of their daughter*. [Language for referring to things, not people.]

Force of *they even pulled some stones over it* [Why *even*? Isn't that what you would expect parents to do to protect the corpse?] Why did they make this special effort? [Not out of affection, but because good neighbourliness required it.]

Does it matter that you don't know the meaning of *odok*? What does it signify here? [Fairly clear it represents community solidarity, common values. Actually gateway in outer stockade, shared by several dwellings.]

Step 11 Return to the questions raised earlier. It should now be possible for SS to suggest Africa as the location (clues are *compound, vultures, hyenas*). Explain (if SS do not offer the suggestion) that this is from an anthropologist's account of field work in central Africa – so not fiction. Can SS offer suggestions about the extraordinary value system described? [The Ik had been deprived of their traditional way of life, resettled on poor land and were so near starvation that survival was the only moral imperative. They could not afford the luxury of helping the weak. Other values (such as good neighbourliness) remained only if they did not threaten survival. It would be remarkable if SS were able to predict any of this, but it's worth trying.]

Step 12 If time, discuss the morality of the writer's attempts to feed Adupa: what moral values should an outsider adopt in the circumstances in which he found himself?

Appendix D
Useful addresses

British publishers of supplementary readers

Cambridge University Press, ELT Marketing, The Edinburgh Building, Shaftesbury Road, Cambridge CB2 2RU, UK. Tel: (01223) 325846/7 Fax: (01223) 325984

Macmillan Heinemann ELT, Macmillan Oxford, Between Towns Road, Oxford OX4 3PP, UK. Tel: (01865) 405700 Fax: (01865) 405701

Longman ELT, Longman Group (UK) Ltd, Longman House, Burnt Mill, Harlow, Essex CM20 2JE, UK. Tel: (01279) 426721 Fax: (01279) 431059

Oxford University Press, English Language Teaching Promotions Department, Walton Street, Oxford OX2 6DP, UK. Tel: (01865) 56767 Fax: (01865) 267633
Journal: *ELT Journal*

Penguin English, Penguin Books Ltd, 27 Wrights Lane, London W8 5TZ, UK. Tel: (0171) 416 3000 Fax: (0171) 416 3060

Phoenix ELT (formerly Prentice Hall), Campus 400, Maylands Avenue, Hemel Hempstead, Herts, HP2 7EZ, UK. Tel: (01442) 881900 Fax: (01442) 252544

Publishers of reading laboratories, workshops and other materials

Science Research Associates Ltd, Newtown Road, Henley-on-Thames, Oxfordshire RG9 1EW, UK. Tel: (01491) 410111 Fax: (01491) 410824

Ward Lock Educational Co Ltd, 1 Christopher Road, East Grinstead, Sussex RH19 3BT, UK. Tel: (01342) 318980 Fax: (01342) 410980

Associations and publishers of journals

Blackwell Publishers, 108 Cowley Road, Oxford OX4 1JF, UK. *Journal of Research in Reading*

British Association for Applied Linguistics (BAAL), Frankfurt Lodge, Clevedon Hall, Victoria Road, Clevedon, Avon BS21 7SJ, UK.
Journal: *Applied Linguistics*. Occasional publications

International Association of Teachers of English as a Foreign Language (IATEFL), 3 Kingsdown Chambers, Kingsdown Park, Whitstable, Kent CT5 2DJ, UK.

International Education Centre, College of St Mark and St John, Derriford Road, Plymouth PL6 8BH, UK.
Journal: *Reading in a Foreign Language*

International Reading Association (IRA), 800 Barksdale Road, PO Box 8139, Newark, Delaware 19714-8139, USA.
Journals: *Journal of Reading, The Reading Teacher, Reading Research Quarterly*

Library Association, 7 Ridgmount Street, London WC1E 7AE, UK.
Journal: *The Library Association Record*. Other publications

Reading and Language Information Centre, University of Reading, Bulmershe Court, Earley, Reading RG6 1HY, UK.
Information clearing house and associated publications

School Library Association, Liden Library, Barrington Close, Liden, Swindon, Wiltshire SN3 6HF, UK.
Journal: *The School Librarian*. Other publications

Teachers of English to Speakers of Other Languages (TESOL), Central Office, Suite 300, 1600 Cameron Street, Alexandria, Virginia 223144-2751, USA.
Journal: *TESOL Quarterly*. Other publications

United Kingdom Reading Association (UKRA), c/o Warrington Road C P School, Naylor Road, Widnes, Cheshire WA8 0BP, UK.
Journal: *Reading*. Other publications

The Edinburgh Project on Extensive Reading (EPER)

EPER, Institute for Applied Language Studies, University of Edinburgh, 21 Hill Place, Edinburgh EH8 9DP, UK.

Carries out research in extensive reading and provides an information service, with database of details (level, type of content, sensitive issues etc) of over 2000 individual titles to assist selection. Provides management of EFL extensive reading projects throughout the world, and also training, including materials writing. Produces and publishes materials, including placement tests, activity cards for use with library readers, teaching guides for class readers and packs of reading cards for EFL students needing very easy material.

Book supply

You are recommended to use book suppliers in your own locality whenever possible. In case of difficulty, contact your local British Council office for advice on mail order suppliers, or write to the publisher.

Copyright permissions

To obtain permission to copy copyright material, readers overseas should write to the publisher. Those in the UK should contact: Copyright Licensing Agency Ltd, 90 Tottenham Court Road, London W1P 9HE.

Key to the activities

Activity 2.2

- **a** Instead of repeating nouns, pronouns are used, eg *James Brown's → his*; *the present → it*.
- **b** *The* is used instead of *a* or *some* for subsequent mention of something already referred to, eg *some perfume → the present*.
- **c** Redundant words are omitted, eg the subject of *forgot* is not expressed.
- **d** Connectives (column one) show how parts of the text are related and may give a clue to their value, eg *however* signals some reversal of expectation.
- **e** Lexical choice: the text now makes clear that Mrs Brown is James's wife (not eg his mother). And we have an example of ***elegant variation*** (see Chapter 6 p91): by using *present* to refer to the perfume, the writer avoids repetition.

Activity 2.5

Text 3 *Survival of the Fittest*: **Definition/description of process S1**: reintroduces the term *natural selection* to sum up the description in the previous paragraph. **S2, 3, 4, 5**: explicate meaning of term by describing process. **S2**: outlines situation. **S3**: result of situation. **S4**: another result of situation. **S5**: final outcome.

Text 6 *Shin-pyu*: **Generalization and elaboration S1**: generalization. **S2**: examples of extravagance. **S3**: another example. **S4**: explains and justifies the expenses just described. **S5**: modifies generalization by counter-statement.

Text 8 *The Mountain People*: **Assertion and explanation S1**: assertion of cause and effect. **S2:** explains/extends meaning of *that* in S1. **S3**: narrates events giving evidence for S2. **S4**: as S3. **S5**: narrates events giving evidence for S1. **S6**: comment, partly explaining view asserted in S1. **S7**: narration; explains reason for comment in S6. **S8**: narration. **S9**: narration; explicates S1. **S10**: comment (disguised as rhetorical question) explaining why event was possible. **S11**: as S10. **S12**: narration. **S13**: narration, with explanation of act described.

Text 9 *Good Neighbours*: **Description/opinion S1**: establishes authority of speaker. **S2**: comment, opinion. **S3**: description to support S2. **S4**: further comment; refers back to S3, expands S2. **S5**: further description supporting S4. **S6**: further comment expanding S2, S4.

Text 10: *Adrian Mole*: **Narrative report**. The sentences are in chronological sequence.

Activity 5.1

The original text is as follows:

> The question of speed reading is considered in detail elsewhere (Pugh 1978) and it is not the principal issue in the present paper. The history of eye-movement research in general, and with reference to reading in particular, is fairly readily available, as are technical details of various apparatus; therefore a brief outline and guide to sources is all that is offered here. What is not so easily available is a review of the findings of eye-movement studies as they relate to reading of the type undertaken in LSP. Nor is there full appreciation of the possibilities, resulting from developments in eye-movement monitoring apparatus and from enhanced interest in text structure by linguists and cognitive psychologists, for naturalistic studies of visual behaviour related to text structure.
> (Pugh and Ulijn 1984)

The paragraph implies that the following topics will be covered in the paper: **b**, **c**, **d**. It explicitly excludes **a** and (more or less) **e**.

ACTIVITY 6.1

1 See S1 (= Sentence 1) and S2: this paragraph deals with one feature of the writers' approach; so the next paragraph can be expected to deal with the second. It will be extremely surprising if you spotted this (nobody else has).

2 A possible summary is:
The approach in this book should appeal to teachers because it will equip them to handle any authentic speech they want to use. Most previous books supply invented examples to illustrate the intonation systems they put forward; the systems are no use for analysing genuine speech, because they are not fully generalizable, and because in trying to be simple, they end up being wrong. It is reasonable to begin by teaching about the cases where there is a one-to-one correspondence between intonation pattern and grammatical structure; but a good system must also be able to handle data where this is not the case.

3 This is intended to make you realize that vocabulary is not the only source of difficulties: if you know most of the words, but still find the text difficult, the reason must lie elsewhere, for example in the grammatical structure. Remember the purpose of this whole activity is to demonstrate the importance of grammatical understanding in text comprehension.

4 If you were able to formulate some ideas, and some questions that you suspect the text is addressing, you have done well. This will help you to do subsequent parts of the activity.

5 Rereading in order to clarify half-formed ideas, and find answers to questions you think the text is tackling, should make your reading more purposeful and therefore more successful. If it did not, can you establish why? If it did, were you able to clarify the ideas and refine the questions after further reading? And will it help to repeat the operation?

6 I offer here an analysis of S3 as an example of the approach. It looks complex because it is complex. That is the whole point: everyone with whom I have used this text considers it very difficult. But students are frequently faced with equally difficult writing in their studies.
Refer to Sentence 3 and the procedure outlined on pp82–6.

a *Identify cohesive elements*
by contrast: what is contrasted with what? The topic of this sentence contrasts with the point of S2, that this intonation system equips the teacher to deal with any spoken material. (This should give us some idea of what this sentence will be saying: ie that not all intonation systems do this.)
they, them: it is fairly easy to see that these words refer to *(existing partial) descriptions*.
There are other cohesive elements, but perhaps none that strike the reader at this point.

b *Remove coordinating conjunctions*
We have several examples of *and*, in each case linking noun groups. In order to discern the bare structure of the sentence, we can simplify these groups:
existing partial descriptions (and X)
inevitably engender disappointment (and Y)
when they are applied ...
In this sentence, the word *while* is operating in much the same way as the word *and* or *moreover*; it is not a time conjunction. We can remove it and make two sentences, A and B:
A Existing partial descriptions ...
inevitably engender disappointment ...
when they are applied to material ...
B Moreover, speech produced
spontaneously ... presents problems
The skeleton of this sentence is thus: **By contrast, A and moreover B** (ie both these points contrast with S2 as noted above).

c Simplify noun groups by removing post-modifiers
the highly specific values [they tend to ascribe to intonation features]
material [other than the set of items the manual writers invent to exemplify them]
the set of items [the manual writers invent to exemplify them] (We really should simplify *the set* first, but this seems needless)
speech [produced spontaneously and in real time]
problems [for which earlier systematic work has provided no preparation]
The simplified sentence would read something like this:
By contrast, existing partial descriptions and the highly specific values ... inevitably engender disappointment ... when they are applied to material .... Moreover, speech ... almost always presents problems ....

Of course this does not make complete sense as it stands, but the reader can now see the skeletal structure and fill out the gaps systematically, one at a time.

d *Sort out nominalizations*
There are none in this sentence.

e *Identify the verbs and find the subject/object, etc of each*
The finite verbs are: *tend, engender, are applied, invent, presents, has provided.*
Using the *Who or what is or does what?* technique enables us to see:
What tends to do what? They (= partial descriptions) tend to ascribe highly specific values
What engenders what? Partial descriptions engender disappointment
What are applied to what? They (= partial descriptions) are applied to material (of a particular kind)
Who/what invent what? The manual writers invent the set of items to exemplify them (= partial descriptions)
Who/what presents what? Speech (of a certain kind) almost always presents problems (of a certain kind)
Who/what has provided what? Earlier systematic work has provided no preparation (for problems)

f *Identify prepositional, participial and infinitive phrases and find out where they fit into the structure*
to ascribe: **As** tend to ascribe **Bs** to **Cs** ... (As = existing partial descriptions, Bs = highly specific values, Cs = intonation features)
to intonation features: the **Bs** that **As** tend to ascribe to intonation features ...
to material: when **As** are applied to **D** (D = material)
other than the set of items: **D** other than **E** (E = the set of items (which) the manual writers invent)
to exemplify them: **E** to exemplify **As** (the partial descriptions)
produced spontaneously and in real time: $\mathbf{F^1}$ presents problems (F^1 = speech (which is) produced spontaneously)
in real time: $\mathbf{F^2}$ presents problems (F^2 = speech [which is] produced in real time)
for which earlier systematic work has provided no preparation: problems for which **G** has provided no preparation. (G = earlier systematic work)

This gives us a simplified sentence something like this:
By contrast, As and Bs inevitably engender disappointment when they are applied to D other than E. Moreover, F almost always presents problems for which G has provided no preparation.

Even after such exhaustive analysis, some elements remain to be 'pinned down' (see p92), for instance:
existing partial descriptions: Descriptions of what? (Intonation.) In what way are they partial? (They do not describe the whole system.)
the highly specific values (these descriptions) ascribe to intonation features: What sort of values? (Perhaps they mean values such as interrogation (eg a rising intonation signals a question), or contrast)
engender disappointment and frustration: In whom? (Presumably in the teacher who is trying to use them.) Why? (Presumably because the system will not work except with the invented examples that were used to illustrate it.)
material other than ....: What is meant here by material? (Samples of spoken English)
the manual writers: What is the meaning of manual here? (A textbook; it doesn't mean 'people who write by hand'.)
(produced) in real time: What is unreal time? (This is a term derived from computer technology; it means approximately "(speech produced) at the moment that you hear it, not pre-recorded, not rehearsed".)
earlier systematic work: earlier than what? (Before the moment when we want to describe spontaneous speech? Earlier in the course?) What sort of work? (The work of describing and practising the use of a system for interpreting intonation.)

We have come to the end of our analysis of sentence 3; complex as it is, it is only about a third of the entire text.

Activity 6.3

a *Man is seen in perspective as just another piece in this grand jigsaw, and his activities* ***are seen*** *in terms of the effects ...* etc
b *Our experience suggests ... if our transcriptions are to be followed and* ***if*** *the main lines of exposition* ***which*** *they are used to illustrate* ***are to be*** *grasped.*

Activity 7.3

In my opinion, diagram C fits the paragraph best. This interpretation takes the text to mean that the large size of the airships was the reason why they could not fly well in bad weather. You might argue that the text can be taken to mean that these are two separate defects (diagram A); but this seems less likely, as there is no obvious reason why size alone should be considered a defect.

Activity 7.5

The labels are here arranged in the correct order, and a fifth expansion is supplied:

CONTEXT Asserting the importance of feathers in distinguishing birds from other animals
KEY EVENT Sensational discovery of fossilized feather
EXPLANATION 1 Geological processes underlying event
EXPLANATION 2 Characteristics of limestone, effects of this and examples
SUBSEQUENT EVENT Description and assessment of significance

Activity 7.7

1 Conclusive evidence: *beak* in paragraph 1 sentence 2. Supporting evidence: *peck* (paragraph 2): rarely used except of birds; *brood* and *nest* (paragraph 3), though both can be used for other kinds of creature.

2 The second sentence is not difficult linguistically, but a student might well be baffled by the situation described: why should the tit encounter nuts dangling from strings? This is part of a familiar schema to anyone who has lived in countries where people put out food (including suspending peanuts threaded on string) to attract birds. There is nothing in the text to enable the reader to bridge the gap; either he is familiar with the concept, or he will be unable to make complete sense of the sentence. Inference is of little help without at least some background knowledge.

3 The plain sense of the milk-stealing account, and the point the writer makes about the ingenious naughtiness of tits, are clear; so the main message of the text can be understood. But a detailed schema relating to the distribution of milk in Britain is presupposed. Common sense allows us to infer that in Britain, milk is supplied in bottles. Since common sense also tells us that the birds cannot remove the glass, we may be able to infer that *tops* are closures (= caps) which can be removed. But why should 300 bottles be left at a school? To solve this, inferencing is needed: milk is nutritious; perhaps milk is supplied to nourish school children; presumably it is supplied in bottles. But even then, why should they be outside the school? It requires quite an inferential leap to arrive at the idea of milk delivered daily and left outside the school to be distributed.

4 In this case, the inferences depend on general schemata – including schemata relating to the way texts are constructed – rather than specialized schemata about British life. First, the writer makes a general statement about the value of tits to the gardener. A practised reader will expect the next sentence to substantiate this. Even if he does not know that caterpillars are destructive to plants, he should be able to infer this, or something similar, because he is already looking for evidence that tits are helpful in the garden. The sequence of reasoning would be something like this:

1 Gardeners grow plants and want to preserve them.
2 Caterpillars destroy plants.
3 Therefore caterpillars are enemies to gardeners.
4 Tits feed their young on caterpillars in great quantities.
5 Therefore tits destroy caterpillars in great quantities.
6 Therefore tits are good friends to gardeners.
7 Therefore it is wise to encourage tits to nest in the garden.
8 Nest-boxes are intended to encourage tits to nest.
9 Therefore wise gardeners put up nest-boxes.

Activity 9.3

1 The answer is important but comes too early in the text.
2 Better, but again comes rather early.
3 Too easy to answer by direct quotation from the text.
4 The best choice; cannot be answered without understanding the whole text.
5 Not really important enough.
6 Too early in the text and not important enough.

Activity 9.4

B1 AIRSHIPS
Purpose question: suitable for discussion. (See Chapter 11 p182 on the use of multiple choice questions for discussion.)
Marginal questions and questions 1, 2, 3: not very suitable, though members might complete them individually and compare answers.
Questions 4, 5: suitable for groupwork; one member can act as clerk, completing the table as agreed by the whole group.

B2 SURVIVAL OF THE FITTEST
Activity A: fairly suitable, though a bit imprecise; more specific instructions (eg *List five creatures* ...) might produce more fruitful discussion.

Activities B, D: very suitable; the group can discuss and agree on their choice of (a) or (b) in each case.
Activity C: quite suitable, as the choices for filling the gaps depend on understanding the arguments and thus give scope for discussion.

B3 NOTICES
1 Reading: Not really suitable for groupwork, as the reading needs to be individual.
2 Practices A, B: quite suitable for group decision, though not likely to provoke much discussion (rather easy).
Practices C, D, E, F: quite suitable, as they involve problem solving; best to let individuals try first, then compare answers and agree group answers.

B4 DANGER FROM FIRE
Reading: This is essentially individual as presented in the book (and that's perfectly acceptable). It would be possible to make it more suitable for groupwork; for example, you could:

- **a** Split the text into two: (1) *In the bedroom* and (2) *If cut off by fire.*
- **b** Distribute (1) as a doctored text, eg by omitting one line from each of the numbered points and supplying the omitted lines separately. The group then has to agree where each line fits.
- **c** Then move on to *Summary Skills 1*, which is fine for groupwork.
- **d** Then repeat the process with (2) and *Summary Skills 2*, which is quite suitable for groupwork as it stands, being likely to provoke discussion.

Activity 11.1

1. The word *although* shows that what follows must contradict the notion of 'a model son'; so **b** does not make sense. Nor does **a** seem to fit – it is neither a reason for thinking him perfect, nor the opposite. **c** is plausible at first sight; but would the father consider him perfect if he were extremely worried by his behaviour? In the end, **d** is the only serious candidate.
2. Common sense dismisses **a** and **b** (you cannot hurt a dead woman or make her comfortable). **d** does not seem relevant – why should he take the body into the forest in order to take the car? Only the obvious answer, **c**, is plausible.
3. Again, common sense and world knowledge dismiss all except **b**, the obvious answer.
4. **a** and **d** are true, but not really reasons for killing mice. **b** is nonsense (what can it possibly mean?). We are left with **c**, again the obvious answer.
5. Even if the correct answer **d** can be inferred from the text, many readers will know it already, so the question is not reliably checking text comprehension.
6. This tests vocabulary knowledge, not comprehension; if you know that **a** is correct, you can answer without reading the text. (It is not a matter of a word having several meanings, of which only one suits the context.)

Activity 12.1

One reason 'agony aunt' letters are popular is that readers like to argue about the advice offered. A good task is to present several rather similar problems and jumble the answers. The task is to decide which matches which problem, perhaps following up by students writing problem letters or offering advice themselves.

Select bibliography

Textbooks for the teaching of reading are indicated by the prefix T.

Titles preceded by an asterisk * are particularly recommended.

Abbreviations

AL	**Applied Linguistics**
CUP	**Cambridge University Press**
ELTJ	**English Language Teaching Journal**
JRR	**Journal of Research in Reading**
OUP	**Oxford University Press**
RFL	**Reading in a Foreign Language**
RRQ	**Reading Research Quarterly**
TESOL Q	**TESOL Quarterly**

Alderson, J. C. 1990, 1991 'Testing reading comprehension skills'. Part One *RFL* 6/2, Part Two *RFL* 7/1

Alderson, J. C., Clapham, C. M., Wall, D. M. 1995 *Language test construction and evaluation*. Cambridge: CUP

Alderson, J. C. and Hughes, A. (eds) 1981 *Issues in language testing (ELT Documents 111)*. London: The British Council

* **Alderson, J. C. and Urquhart, A. H.** 1984 *Reading in a foreign language*. Harlow: Longman

Alderson, J. C. and Urquhart, A. H. 1985 'The effect of students' academic discipline on their performance on ESP reading tests'. *Language Testing* 2/2

Anderson, N. J. 1994 'Developing active readers: a pedagogical framework for the second language reading class'. *System* 22/2: 177–94

Anderson, N. J., Bachman, L., Perkins, K., Cohen, A. 1991 'An exploratory study into the construct validity of a reading comprehension test: triangulation of data sources'. *Language Testing:* 8/1

Aslanian, Y. 1985 'Investigating the reading problems of ESL students: an alternative'. *ELTJ* 39/1: 20-7

Bachman, L. 1990 *Fundamental considerations in language testing*. Oxford: OUP

* **Bamford, J.** 1984 'Extensive reading by means of graded readers'. *RFL* 2/2 218–60

Banton-Smith, N. 1972 'Speed reading: benefits and dangers' reprinted in Melnik, A. and Merritt, J. *The reading curriculum*. London: University of London Press/The Open University 246–65

T **Barham, M., Parry, A.** 1989 *Penguin elementary reading skills*. London: Penguin English

T **Barr, P., Clegg, J., Wallace, C.** 1981 *Advanced reading skills*. Harlow: Longman

Barrett, T. C. n.d. 'Taxonomy of the cognitive and affective dimensions of reading comprehension'. In Clymer, T. 'What is 'reading'?: some current concepts' reprinted in Melnik, A. and Merritt, J. 1972 *Reading today and tomorrow*. London: University of London Press/The Open University 48–66

* **Beard, R.** 1990 (2nd ed) *Developing reading 3–13*. London: Hodder and Stoughton

Bennett, N. and Dunne, E. 1994 'Managing groupwork'. Chapter 22 of Moon, B. and Mayes, A. S. *Teaching and learning in the secondary school*. London: Routledge/The Open University

Blakemore, D. 1992 *Understanding utterances.* Oxford: Basil Blackwell

Block, E. L. 1986 'The comprehension strategies of second language readers'. *TESOL Q* 20/3: 463–94

Block, E. L. 1992 'See how they read: comprehension monitoring of L1 and L2 readers' TESOL Q 26/2: 319–43

Bloor, M. 1985 'Some approaches to the design of reading courses in English as a foreign language'. *RFL* 3/1: 341–361

Breen, M.P. 1985 'Authenticity in the language classroom'. *AL* 6/1: 60–70

Bright, J. A. and McGregor, G. P. 1970 *Teaching English as a second language.* London: Longman

Brown, G. 1989 'Making sense: the interaction of linguistic expression and contextual information'. *AL* 10/1: 97–108

Brown, G. 1990 'Cultural values: the interpretation of discourse'. *ELTJ* 44/1: 11–17

Brown, G., Malmkjaer, K., Pollitt, A., Williams, J. (eds) 1994 *Language and understanding* Oxford:OUP

Brown, G. and Yule, G. 1983 *Discourse analysis.* Cambridge: CUP

Brumfit, C. J. 1984 *Communicative methodology in language teaching: the roles of fluency and accuracy.* Cambridge: CUP

Brumfit, C. J. (ed) 1991 *Assessment in literature teaching* (Developments in ELT series). Hemel Hempstead: Prentice Hall International

Brusch, W. 1991 'The role of reading in FL acquisition'. *ELTJ* 45/2: 156–63

Byron, K. 1986 *Drama in the English classroom.* London: Methuen

Cairney, T. 1990 *Teaching reading comprehension.* Milton Keynes: Open University Press

Cairney, T. 1992 'Mountain or molehill: the genre debate viewed from "Down Under" '. *Reading* 26/1: 23–9

Campbell, R. 1989 'The teacher as a role model during sustained silent reading'. *Reading* 23/3: 179–83

Candlin, C. N. and Murphy, D. F. (eds) 1987 *Language learning tasks* (Lancaster Papers in English Language Education vol 7). London: Prentice Hall International/Lancaster University

Carrell, P. L. 1984 'The effects of rhetorical organization on ESL readers'. *TESOL Q* 18/3: 441–69

Carrell, P. L. 1985 'Facilitating ESL reading by teaching text structure'. *TESOL Q* 19/4: 727–52

Carrell, P. L. 1987 'Readability in ESL'. *RFL* 4/1: 21–40

Carrell, P. L. 1991 'Second language reading: reading ability or language proficiency?' *AL* 12/2: 159–79

* **Carrell, P. L., Devine, J., Eskey, D. E.** 1988 *Interactive approaches to second language reading.* Cambridge: CUP

Carter, R. A. 1987a 'Vocabulary and second/foreign language teaching' (State of the art article). *Language Teaching* 20/1: 3–16

Carter, R. A. 1987b *Vocabulary: applied linguistic perspectives.* London: Allen and Unwin

Carter, R. A. and Long, M. N. 1991 *Teaching literature.* Harlow: Longman

Carter, R. A. and McCarthy, M. (eds) 1988 *Vocabulary and language teaching.* Harlow: Longman

Casanave, C. P. 1988 'Comprehension monitoring in ESL reading: a neglected essential'. *TESOL Q* 22/2: 283-302

Chall, J. S. 1984 'Readability and prose comprehension: continuities and discontinuities'. In Flood (ed) 233–46

Chambers, A. 1991 *The reading environment.* Stroud, Glos: Thimble Press

Childs, J. 1988 'Issues in reading proficiency assessment: a framework for discussion' in Lowe, P. and Stansfield, C. W. (eds) *Second language proficiency assessment*. Englewood Cliffs NJ: Prentice Hall Regents

Clarke, D. F. 1989 'Communicative theory and its influence on materials production' (State of the art article). *Language Teaching* 22/2: 73–86

Cohen, A. 1994 (2nd ed) *Assessing language ability in the classroom*. Boston: Heinle and Heinle

Collie, J. and Slater, S. 1987 *Literature in the language classroom: a resource book of ideas and activities*. Cambridge: CUP

Collins Cobuild 1993 *English Guide 2: Word Formation*. London: HarperCollins

* **Cook, G.** 1989 *Discourse*. Oxford: OUP

T **Cooper, J.** 1979 *Think and link*. London: Nelson

Coulthard, M. 1985 2nd ed *An introduction to discourse analysis*. Harlow: Longman

Crystal, D. 1988 *Rediscover grammar*. Harlow: Longman

Davies, A. 1984 'Simple, simplified and simplification: what is authentic?'. In Alderson and Urquhart 181–198

Davies, A. and Widdowson, H. G. 1974 'Reading and writing'. Chapter 6 of Allan, J. P. B. and Corder, S. P. (eds) *Techniques in Applied Linguistics* (Vol 3 of the Edinburgh Course in Applied Linguistics). Oxford: OUP

T **Davies, E. and Whitney, N.** 1979–83 3 vols: *Reasons for reading*; *Strategies for reading*; *Study skills for reading* (Reading Comprehension Course). Oxford: Heinemann Educational Books

T **Davies, E., Whitney, N., Pike-Baky, M., Blass, L.** 1990 *Task reading*. New York: CUP

* **Davies, F.** 1995 *Introducing reading*. London: Penguin English

Davies, F. and Green, T. 1984 *Reading for learning in the sciences*. Edinburgh: Oliver and Boyd for the Schools Council

Davis, C. 1995 'Extensive reading: an expensive extravagance?' *ELTJ* 49/4: 329-36

De Leeuw, E. M. 1990 new ed *Read better, read faster*. Harmondsworth: Penguin

Department of Education and Science 1989 *Reading policy and practice at ages 5–14* (HMI report). London: Her Majesty's Stationery Office

Dickinson, L. 1987 *Self-instruction in language learning*. Cambridge: CUP

Duff, A. and Maley, A. 1990 *Literature* (Resource Books for Teachers). Oxford: OUP

Eccles, D. 1989 *English through drama*. London: Hutchinson Education

Edge, J. 1983 'Reading to take notes and to summarise: a classroom procedure'. *RFL* 1/2: 93-98

Elley, W. 1991 'Acquiring literacy in a second language: the effect of book-based programmes'. *Language Learning* 41/3: 375–411

Elley, W. B. and Mangubhai, F. 1983 'The impact of reading on second language learning'. *RRQ* 19/1: 53–67

Ellis, G. and McCrae, J. 1991 *The extensive reading handbook for secondary schools*. Harmondsworth: Penguin

Ellis, G. and Sinclair, B. 1989 *Learning to learn English: a course in learner training*. Cambridge: CUP

T **Ellis, M. and P.** 1984 4 vols: *At first sight*; *Shades of meaning*; *Between the lines*; *Take it as read* (Nelson Skills Programme: the skill of reading). London: Nelson

Ellis, M. and P. 1987 'Learning by design: some design criteria for EFL coursebooks'. In Sheldon, L. (ed) *ELT textbooks and materials: problems in evaluation and development* (ELT Documents 126). London: Modern English Publications/The British Council 90–8

Fairbairn, G. J. and Winch, C. 1991 *Reading, writing and reasoning: a guide for students*. Society for Research into Higher Education/Open University Press

Fairclough, N. (ed) 1992 *Critical language awareness.* Harlow: Longman
Flood, J. (ed) 1984 *Understanding reading comprehension.* Newark, Del: International Reading Association
T **Foll, D.** 1990 *Contrasts: developing text awareness.* Harlow: Longman
Fox, G. and Kirkby, D. (eds) 1987 *Learning real English with Collins Cobuild English Language Dictionary.* London: Collins ELT
Fry, E. 1963 *Teaching faster reading.* Cambridge: CUP
Gairns, R. and Redman, S. 1986 *Working with words.* Cambridge: CUP
T **Geddes, M. and Sturtridge, G.** 1982 *Reading links.* London: Heinemann Educational Books
Gillham, B. (ed) 1986 *The language of school subjects.* London: Heinemann Educational Books
Glendinning, E. and Holmström, B. 1992 *Study reading.* Cambridge: CUP
Goodman, K. S. 1967 'Reading: a psycholinguistic guessing game'. *Journal of the Reading Specialist* 6
T **Greenall, S. and Pye, D.** 1991/2 4 vols: *Reading 1, 2, 3, 4* (Skills for Fluency). Cambridge: CUP
T **Greenall, S. and Swan, M.** 1986 *Effective Reading.* Cambridge: CUP
Greenwood, J. 1988 *Class readers.* Oxford: OUP
* **Grellet, F.** 1981 *Developing reading skills.* Cambridge: CUP
Hafiz, F. M. and Tudor, I. 1989 'Extensive reading and the development of language skills'. *ELTJ* 43/1: 4–13
Hafiz, F. M. and Tudor, I. 1990 'Graded readers as an input medium in L2 learning'. *System* 18/1: 31–42
Halliday, M. A. K. 1985 *An introduction to functional grammar.* London: Edward Arnold
* **Halliday, M. A. K. and Hasan, R.** 1976 *Cohesion in English.* London: Longman
Halliday, M. A. K. and Hasan, R. 1989 *Language, context and text: aspects of language in a social-semiotic perspective.* Oxford: OUP
Hardisty, D. and Windeatt, S. 1989 *CALL* (Resource Books for Teachers). Oxford: OUP
Harmer, J. and Rossner, R. 1991 *More than words* vols 1, 2. Harlow: Longman
* **Harri-Augstein, S., Smith, M., Thomas, L.** 1982 *Reading to learn* London: Methuen
Harris, J. 1993 *Introducing writing.* London: Penguin English
* **Harrison, C.** 1980 *Readability in the classroom.* Cambridge: CUP
Harrison, C. 1986 'New directions in text research and readability'. In Cashdan, A. (ed) *Literacy: teaching and learning language skills.* Oxford: Blackwell
Harrison, C. and Coles, M. 1992 *The reading for real handbook.* London: Routledge
Hartley, J. 1985 2nd ed *Designing instructional text.* London: Kogan Page
Hayhoe, M. and Parker, S. 1990 *Reading and response.* Milton Keynes: The Open University
Heaton, J. B. 1988 (2nd ed) *Writing English language tests.* Harlow: Longman
Heaton, J. B. 1990 *Classroom testing.* Harlow: Longman
* **Hedge, T.** 1985 *Using readers in language teaching.* London: Macmillan
Henshaw, A. 1991 '"Are you a good reader now?" Secondary school remedial readers' perceptions of their reading ability'. *Reading* 25/2: 17–25
Hess, N. 1991 *Headstarts.* Harlow: Longman
Hill, D. R. 1992 *The EPER guide to organizing programmes of extensive reading.* Edinburgh: Edinburgh Project on Extensive Reading, Institute for Applied Language Studies, University of Edinburgh
Hill, D. R. and Reid Thomas, H. 1988a, b 'Survey review of graded readers' Part 1 *ELTJ* 42/1: 44–52; Part 2. *ELTJ* 42/2: 124–36

Hill, D. R. and Reid-Thomas, H. 1989 'Survey review: seven series of graded readers'. *ELTJ* 43/3: 221–31
Hill, J. 1986 *Using literature in language teaching*. London: Macmillan
Hoey, M. 1991 *Patterns of lexis in text*. Oxford: OUP
Holdaway, D. 1979 *The foundations of literacy*. Sydney: Ashton Scholastic
Holme, R. 1991 *Talking texts*. Harlow: Longman
Holmes, J. 1987 'Using non-English texts in EAP'. *The ESPecialist* no. 17: 95–105
Hughes, A. 1989 *Testing for language teachers*. Cambridge: CUP
Hulstijn, J. H. and Matter, J. F. (eds) 1991 *Reading in two languages*. Amsterdam: AILA/Free University Press
Hutchinson, T. and Waters, A. 1987 *English for specific purposes: a learning-centred approach*. Cambridge: CUP
* **Johns, T. and Davies, F.** 1983 'Text as a vehicle for information: the classroom use of written texts in teaching reading in a foreign language'. *RFL* 1/1: 1–19
Johnson, K. 1981 *Communicate in writing*. Harlow: Longman
Johnson, K. and Morrow, K. 1981 *Communication in the classroom*. Harlow: Longman
Johnson, K. and Porter, D. 1983 *Perspectives in communicative language teaching*. London: Academic Press
Jones, C. and Fortescue, S. 1987 *Using computers in the language classroom*. Harlow: Longman
Jonz, J. 1989 'Textual sequence and second language comprehension'. *Language Learning* 39/1: 207–49
Kern, R. G. 1989 'Second language reading strategy instruction: its effects on comprehension and word inference ability'. *Modern Language Journal* 73/2: 135–49
Kimmel, S. and MacGinitie, W. H. 1984 'Identifying children who use a perseverative text-processing strategy'. *RRQ* 19/2: 162–72
Kintsch, W. and Miller, J. R. 1984 'Readability: a view from cognitive psychology'. In Flood 220–32
Krashen, S. 1985 *The Input Hypothesis*. London: Longman
Krashen, S. 1989 'We acquire vocabulary and spelling by reading: additional evidence for the Input Hypothesis'. *Modern Language Journal* 73/4: 440–64
Krashen, S. 1993 *The power of reading: insights from research*. Englewood Co: Libraries Unlimited
Leach, R. 1989 2nd ed *Making using and adapting materials*. Cambridge: National Extension College
Leech, G. N. 1983 *Principles of pragmatics*. Harlow: Longman
Leech, G. N. and Svartvik, J. 1994 (new ed) *A communicative grammar of English*. Harlow: Longman
Levinson, S. C. 1983 *Pragmatics*. Cambridge: CUP
Littlefair, A. 1991 *Reading all types of writing: importance of genre and register for reading development*. Milton Keynes: Open University Press
* **Lunzer, E. and Gardner, K.** 1979 *The effective use of reading*. London: Heinemann Educational Books/The Schools Council
* **Lunzer, E., Gardner, K., Davies, F., Greene, T.** 1984 *Learning from the written word*. Edinburgh: Oliver and Boyd/The Schools Council
McAlpin, J. 1988 *Longman dictionary skills handbook*. Harlow: Longman
* **McCarthy, M. J.** 1990 *Vocabulary*. Oxford: OUP
* **McCarthy, M. J.** 1991 *Discourse analysis for language teachers*. Cambridge: CUP
McCarthy, M. J. and O'Dell, F. 1994 *English vocabulary in use*. Cambridge: CUP
T **McGovern, D., Matthews, M., Mackay, S. E.** 1994 *Reading* (English for Academic Study Series). Hemel Hempstead: Prentice Hall

Mackay, D., Thompson, B., Schaub, P. 1979 3rd ed illustd *Breakthrough to literacy teacher's manual*. Harlow: Longman/The Schools Council

McMahon, M. L. 1983 'Development of reading-while-listening skills in the primary grades'. *RRQ* 19/1: 38–52

Maley, A. 1994 *Short and Sweet 1*. London: Penguin English

Maley, A. and Duff, A. 1989 *The inward ear: poetry in the language classroom*. Cambridge: CUP

Mallett, M. 1992 *Making facts matter*. London: Paul Chapman

Marland, M. 1977 *Language across the curriculum*. London: Heinemann Educational Books

Marland, M. and Hill, S. 1981 *Departmental management*. London: Heinemann Educational Books

Martin, T. 1989 *The strugglers*. Milton Keynes: Open University Press

Matthews, M. 1989 'Woods and trees: the correction of myopia in L2 reading'. *RFL* 6/1: 357–61

Meek, M. 1983 *Achieving literacy*. London: Routledge and Kegan Paul

* **Montgomery, M., Durant, A., Fabb, N., Furniss, T., Mills, S.** 1992 *Ways of reading*. London: Routledge

T **Moore, J. D. et al** 1979–80 4 vols: *Concepts in use*; *Exploring functions*; *Discovering discourse*; *Discourse in Action* (Reading and thinking in English). Oxford: OUP

Moore, P. J. 1988 'Reciprocal teaching and reading comprehension: a review'. *JRR* 11/1: 3–14

Morgan, J. and Rinvolucri, M. 1986 *Vocabulary* (Resource Books for Teachers). Oxford: OUP

Moran, C. and Williams, E. 1993 'Survey review: recent materials for the teaching of reading at intermediate level and above'. *ELTJ* 47/1: 64–84

Mosback, G. and V. 1976 *Practical faster reading*. Cambridge: CUP

Munby, J. 1968 *Read and think*. Harlow: Longman

Munby, J. 1978 *Communicative syllabus design*. Cambridge: CUP

Nation, I. S. P. 1979 'The curse of the comprehension question'. in Khoo, R. (ed) *Guidelines for teaching reading skills* (RELC Journal Supplement no 2). Singapore: SEAMEO Regional Language Centre 85–103

Nation, I. S. P. 1990 *Teaching and learning vocabulary*. New York: Newbury House

Nation, P. and Carter, R. (eds) 1989 *Vocabulary acquisition* (AILA Review no 6). Amsterdam: AILA/Free University Press

Nelson, P. 1984 'Towards a more communicative reading course: motivating students who are not "reading addicts"'. *RFL* 2/1: 188–96

Northedge, A. 1990 *The good study guide*. Milton Keynes: Open University Press

Nunan, D. 1989 *Designing tasks for the communicative classroom*. Cambridge: CUP

Nunan, D. 1993 *Introducing discourse analysis*. London: Penguin English

Nuttall, C. E. 1985 'Survey review: recent materials for the teaching of reading'. *ELTJ* 39/3: 198–207

* **Oakhill, J. and Garnham, A.** 1988 *Becoming a skilled reader*. Oxford: Blackwell

Oller, J. W. (Jnr) 1980 *Language tests at school*. Harlow: Longman

Owen, C. 1989 *Collins Cobuild essential English dictionary workbook*. London: Collins ELT

Prabhu, N. S. 1987 *Second language pedagogy*. Oxford: OUP

Pressley, M., Ghatala, E. S., Wolosyn, V., Pirie, J. 1990 'Sometimes adults miss the main ideas and do not realize it: confidence in response to short-answer and multiple choice comprehension questions'. *RRQ* 25/3: 232–49

Pressley, M., Johnson, C. J., Symons, S., McGoldrick, J. A., Kurita, J. A. 1989 'Strategies that improve children's memory and comprehension of text'. *The Elementary School Journal* 90/1 3:–32
Pugh, A. K. 1978 *Silent reading*. London: Heinemann Educational Books
Pugh, A. K. and Ulijn, J. M. (eds) 1984 *Reading for professional purposes*. London: Heinemann Educational Books
Pumfrey, P. D. 1991 *Improving children's reading in the junior school: challenges and responses*. London: Cassell Education
* **Quirk, R., Greenbaum, S., Leech, G., Svartvik, J.** 1985 *A comprehensive grammar of the English language*. Harlow: Longman
Rayner, K. and Pollatsek, A. 1989 *The psychology of reading*. Englewood Cliffs NJ: Prentice Hall International
Reid-Thomas, H. C. and Hill, D. R. 1993 'Survey review: seventeen series of graded readers'. *ELTJ* 47/3: 250–67
T **Revell, R. and Sweeney, S.** 1993 *In print: reading business English*. Cambridge: CUP
Richards, J. C. 1990 *The language teaching matrix*. Cambridge: CUP
Rigg, P. 1990 'Using the language experience approach with ESL adults'. In Bell, J. (ed) *ESL literacy: TESL Talk* 20/1 Theme Issue
Rixon, S. 1979 'The "information gap" and the "opinion gap" – ensuring that communication games are communicative'. *ELTJ* 33/2: 104–6
Robb, T. N. and Susser, B. 1989 'Extensive reading vs. skills building in an EFL context'. *RFL* 5/2: 239–51
Robinson, F. P. 1964 new ed *Effective study*. New York: Harper and Row
Roller, C. M. 1990 'Commentary: the interaction of knowledge and structure variables in the processing of expository prose'. *RRQ* 25/1: 79–89
Rönnqvist, L. and Sell, R. D. 1994 'Teenage books for teenagers: reflections on literature in language education'. *ELTJ* 48/2: 125–32
Rowntree, D. 1982 (2nd ed) *Educational technology in curriculum development*. London: Harper and Row
Rowntree, D. 1985 *Developing courses for students*. London: Harper and Row
Sheerin, S. 1991 'Self-access' (State of the art article). *Language Teaching* 24/3: 143–57
Sheerin, S.1989 *Self-access*. Oxford: OUP
Silberstein, S. 1994 *Techniques and resources in teaching reading*. New York: OUP
Simensen, A. M. 1987 'Adapted readers: how are they adapted?' *RFL* 4/1: 41–57
Simensen, A. M. 1990 'Adapted texts: a discussion of some aspects of reference'. *RFL* 6/2: 399–411
Sinclair, J. M. (ed) 1990 *Collins Cobuild English grammar*. London: HarperCollins
Smith, F. 1983 *Essays into literacy*. New York: Holt Rinehart and Winston
* **Smith, F.** 1985 new ed *Reading*. Cambridge: CUP
Smith, M. and G. 1990 *A study skills handbook*. Melbourne: OUP
Spires, H. 1990 'Metacognition and reading: implications for instruction'. *Reading* 24/3: 151–6
Stubbs, M. 1983 *Discourse analysis*. Oxford: Blackwell
Swales, J. M. 1990 *Genre analysis*. Cambridge: CUP
Tickoo, M. L. 1993 *Simplification: theory and application* (Anthology Series 31). Singapore: SEAMEO Regional Language Centre
Tomlinson, B. 1991 'Survey review: vocabulary practice books'. *ELTJ* 45/2: 169–73
T **Tomlinson, B. and Ellis, R.** 1987 *Reading Upper Intermediate*; 1988 *Reading Advanced* (Oxford Supplementary Skills). Oxford: OUP
Tudor, I. and Hafiz, F. 1989 'Extensive reading as a means of input to L2 learning'. *JRR* 12/2: 164–78

Ulijn, J. and Strother, J. B. 1990 'Simplification on reading EST texts in L1 and L2'. *JRR* 13/1: 38–54

T **University of Malaya Language Centre** 1979–83 5 vols: *Foundation*; *Development*; *Progression*; *Application*; *Reading Projects Science*. (Skills for learning). London: Nelson/University of Malaya Press

Ur, P. 1981 *Discussions that work*. Cambridge: CUP

Urquhart, A. H. 1984 'The effect of rhetorical ordering on readability'. In Alderson and Urquhart 160–80

Vygotsky, L. S. 1978 *Mind in society: the development of higher psychological processes* (ed. Cole, M., John-Steiner, V., Scribner, S., Souberman, E.). Cambridge MA: Harvard University Press

Waite, S. 1994 'Low-resourced self-access with EAP in the developing world: the great enabler?' *ELTJ* 48/3: 233–42

Walker, C. 1987 'Individualizing reading'. *ELTJ* 41/1 46–50

Walker, R., Rattanavich, S., Oller, J. W. Jnr 1992 *Teaching all the children to read* (Rethinking Reading series). Milton Keynes: Open University Press

Wallace, C. 1986 *Learning to read in a multicultural society*. Oxford: Pergamon

Wallace, C. 1992 *Reading*. Oxford: OUP

T **Walter, C.** 1982 *Authentic reading*. Cambridge: CUP

Waterland, L. 1988 *Read with me*. Stroud, Glos: Thimble Press

Weaver, C. 1988 *Reading process and practice*. Portsmouth US: Heinemann Educational Books

Weir, C. J. 1990 *Communicative language testing* Englewood Cliffs NJ: Prentice Hall International

Weir, C. J. 1993 *Understanding and developing language tests*. Englewood Cliffs NJ: Prentice Hall International

Wessels, C. 1987 *Drama* (Resource Books for Teachers) Oxford: OUP

West, M. 1960 *Teaching English in difficult circumstances*. London: Longman

Wheldall, K. and Entwhistle, J. 1988 'Back in the USSR: the effect of teacher modelling of silent reading on pupils' reading behaviour in the primary school classroom'. *Educational Psychology* 8: 51–66

Widdowson, H. G. 1978 *Teaching language as communication*. Oxford: OUP

Widdowson, H. G. 1979 *Explorations in applied linguistics*. Oxford: OUP

Widdowson, H. G. 1984 *Explorations in applied linguistics 2*. Oxford: OUP

Widdowson, H. G. 1990 *Aspects of language teaching*. Oxford: OUP

Williams, E. 1983 'Communicative reading'. In Johnson and Porter 171–88

* **Williams, E.** 1984 *Reading in the language classroom*. London: Macmillan

Williams, E. and Moran, C. 1989 'Reading in a foreign language at intermediate and advanced levels with particular reference to English' (State of the art article). *Language Teaching* 22/4: 217–28

Williams, K. 1989 *Study skills*. London: Macmillan

Williams, R. 1986 'Top ten principles for teaching reading'. *ELTJ* 40/1: 42–5

Winter, E. O. 1982 *Towards a contextual grammar of English*. London: Allen and Unwin

Wodinsky, M. and Nation, P. 1988 'Learning from graded readers'. *RFL* 5/1: 155–61

Wood, D. 1988 *How children think and learn*. Oxford: Blackwell

Wray, D. 1994 *Literacy and awareness*. London: Hodder and Stoughton/UKRA

Wray, D. and Lewis, M. 1992 'Primary children's use of information books'. *Reading* 26/3: 19–24

Wright, A. and Haleem, S. 1991 *Visuals for the language classroom*. Harlow: Longman

Zamel, V. 1992 'Writing one's way into reading'. *TESOL Q* 26/3: 463–85

Subject index